Applause for Robert J. Mrazek's

# A Dawn Like THUNDER

## THE TRUE STORY OF TORPEDO SQUADRON EIGHT

"A remarkably vivid tale of valor, fate, and young men dying young. Robert Mrazek's epic story, reconstructed with breathtaking research and recounted with a novelist's keen eye for detail, is a worthy monument to Torpedo Squadron Eight."
—Rick Atkinson, author of *The Day of Battle* and *An Army at Dawn*

"The most highly decorated Navy Flyboys of World War II flew through hell and suffered the highest combat losses. Strap yourself in as Robert Mrazek takes you on a heroic flight into history."
—James Bradley, author of *Flyboys* and *Flags of Our Fathers*

"Fast-paced and yet personal, Mrazek's narrative carries the reader to Midway quickly. But it does not stop there, as so many other accounts have. . . . In his first foray into history, Mrazek avoids hagiography and tells the story of Torpedo Eight and the war in the Pacific as it was, not as some might wish it had been. . . . With *A Dawn Like Thunder* Mrazek earns the title of historian, one that this reviewer does not apply lightly."
—Robert Bateman, *Washington Post*

"A must-read for any World War II buff. . . . The hard-to-put-down book is told informally, as if Mrazek were one of the pilots telling stories about his squadron-mates. . . . Mrazek fully captures the tension leading up to the first attack on the Japanese fleet at Midway. . . . *A Dawn Like Thunder* is gripping like few history books are, with the immediacy of Mrazek's prose and descriptions making you feel like you're part of the action."   —Dave Roy, Curledup.com

"A compelling account."   —Jack Torry, *Columbus Dispatch*

"Bob Mrazek has found fresh material about the two pivotal Pacific battles of 1942 and written a marvelous book. His research and obvious affection for his heroes are indeed extraordinary. *A Dawn Like Thunder* is a spectacular achievement and a vital addition to any Pacific War library."   —Hon. Charles Wilson of *Charlie Wilson's War*

"Fast-paced, emotional, and surprising. . . . This meticulously researched book reads like a thrilling war novel. . . . Mrazek reveals through impressive documentation of military records and survivor accounts the blunders that cost the lives of 45 of the 48 Torpedo Eight members in the Battle of Midway. . . . This heart-wrenching book doesn't just bring home the realities of war. It takes readers into the swamp or the noisy cockpit. It gives readers the ability to feel the fear, the pride, the frustrations, and the joy of the men as they try to help America win any advantage in a war they hope will end the need for any others."   —Amy Donaldson, *Deseret News*

"Mrazek brilliantly captures the bravery of Squadron Eight. . . . His clipped narrative offers fascinating vignettes of the aviators' prewar lives. . . . His gripping account of the group's bombing activities is rich in detail and tactical analysis. A special treat is Mrazek's winsome epilogue, which details the postwar achievements of the surviving squadron officers and men. A well-written and meticulously researched account of one of America's most distinguished World War II aerial groups."

   —John Carver Edwards, *Library Journal*

"Mrazek's work is extensively researched, but the research doesn't overwhelm a comfortable narrative. . . . His work fills a significant gap in the World War II bookshelf and fills it well. This definitive work is a fitting tribute to the men of Torpedo 8."

—Russ Smith, *Fredericksburg Free Lance-Star*

"Satisfying. . . . Mrazek provides gripping details that do not tarnish the squadron's heroism but reveal spectacular incompetence among higher commanders. . . . Events undoubtedly happened more or less as Mrazek describes, and his massive original research has produced a richly detailed story that never flags. . . . An admirable addition to the histories of air battles that turned the tide against the Japanese."

—*Kirkus Review*

"Robert Mrazek brings the daredevil pilots of Torpedo Squadron Eight to life in a narrative so vivid and heartbreaking that their courage reaches across the decades, leaving us moved by their incredible sacrifice and heroism."

—Thurston Clarke, author of *The Last Campaign* and *Pearl Harbor Ghosts*

"Robert Mrazek has, with a raw, unsparing telling, given grace and life to so many who died so young, so everyday, so gallantly. Wonderfully uplifting."

—Frank Deford, author of *The Entitled* and *The Old Ball Game*

# A Dawn Like Thunder

# A Dawn Like
# THUNDER

## THE TRUE STORY OF
## TORPEDO SQUADRON EIGHT

# Robert J. Mrazek

BACK BAY BOOKS
LITTLE, BROWN AND COMPANY
NEW YORK    BOSTON    LONDON

Back Bay Books / Little, Brown and Company
Hachette Book Group
237 Park Avenue, New York, NY 10017
www.hachettebookgroup.com

Originally published in hardcover by Little, Brown and Company, December 2008
First Back Bay paperback edition, November 2009

Back Bay Books is an imprint of Little, Brown and Company.
The Back Bay Books name and logo are trademarks of Hachette Book Group, Inc.

Library of Congress Cataloging-in-Publication Data
Mrazek, Robert J.
   A dawn like thunder : the true story of Torpedo Squadron Eight / Robert J.
Mrazek. —1st ed.
     p.     cm.
   Includes bibliographical references and index.
   ISBN 978-0-316-02139-5 (hc) / 978-0-316-05653-3 (pb)
   1. United States. Navy. Torpedo Squadron 8.   2. World War, 1939–1945—Aerial
operations, American.   3. World War, 1939–1945—Naval operations,
American.   4. World War, 1939–1945—Regimental histories—United
States.   5. World War, 1939–1945—Campaigns—Pacific Ocean.   I. Title.
   D790.3788th.M73   2008
   940.54'5973—dc22                                               2008028556

10  9  8  7  6  5  4  3  2  1
RRD-IN
Book design by Fearn Cutler de Vicq
Maps by Julie Krick
Printed in the United States of America

*For my son,*

1st Lieutenant James Nicholas Mrazek, U.S. Army,
1st Battalion, 501st Parachute Infantry Regiment,
Forward Operating Base-ISKAN, Iskandariah, Iraq
(2006–2007)

They did their share.

"An' the dawn comes up like thunder..."
Rudyard Kipling

"Many men who never received mention
gave everything they had — they're still out there."
Gregory Boyington (USMC)

"Below the sea of clouds lies eternity."
Antoine de Saint-Exupéry

# Contents

ENSIGN WILLIAM ROBINSON EVANS JR., AGE 23
PILOT, TORPEDO SQUADRON EIGHT
NORFOLK, VIRGINIA

*December 7, 1941*

*My dear family,*

*What a day — the incredulousness of it all still gives each new announcement of the Pearl Harbor attack the unreality of a fairy tale. How can they have been so mad? Though I suppose we have all known it would come sometime, there was always that inner small voice whispering — no, we are too big, too rich, too powerful, this war is for some poor fools somewhere else. It will never touch us here. And then this noon that world fell apart.*

*Today has been feverish, not with the excitement of emotional crowds cheering and bands playing, but with the quiet conviction and determination of serious men settling down to the business of war. Everywhere little groups of officers listening to the radio, men hurrying in from liberty, quickly changing clothes, and reporting to battle stations. Scarcely an officer seemed to know why we were at war and it seemed to me there is a certain sadness for that reason. If the reports I've heard today are true, the Japanese have performed the impossible, have carried out one of the most daring and successful raids in all history. They knew the setup perfectly — got there on the one fatal day — Sunday — officers and men away for the weekend or recovering from Saturday night. The whole thing was brilliant. People will not realize, I fear, for some time how serious this matter is, the indifference of labor and capital to our danger is* an infectious virus and the public has come to think contemptuously of Japan. And that I fear is a fatal mistake. Today has given evidence of that. This war will be more difficult than any war this country has ever fought.

Tonight I put away all my civilian clothes. I fear the moths will find them good fare in the years to come. There is such a finality to wearing a uniform all the time. It is the one thing I fear — the loss of my individualism in a world of uniforms. But kings and puppets alike are being moved now by the master — destiny.

It is growing late and tomorrow will undoubtedly be a busy day. Once more the whole world is afire — in the period approaching Christmas it seems bitterly ironic to mouth again the timeworn phrases concerning peace on earth — goodwill to men, with so many millions hard at work figuring out ways to reduce other millions to slavery or death. I find it hard to see the inherent difference between man and the rest of the animal kingdom. Faith lost — all is lost. Let us hope tonight that people, all people throughout this great country, have the faith to once again sacrifice for the things we hold essential to life and happiness. Let us defend these principles to the last ounce of blood — but then above all retain reason enough to have "charity for all and malice toward none." If the world ever goes through this again — mankind is doomed. This time it has to be a better world.

All my love,
Bill

# Introduction

Following its devastating attack on Pearl Harbor, the Japanese Empire embarked on one of the most stunning military campaigns in world history, conquering the American-held Philippines, the mighty British fortress of Singapore, Java, Malaya, the oil-rich Dutch East Indies, Sumatra, Hong Kong, Guam, and Wake Island. In the process, they virtually annihilated the Far Eastern fleets of Great Britain, the United States, Australia, and the Netherlands.

In less than six months, the Japanese killed or captured more than five hundred thousand Allied soldiers, and came to control the destiny of one hundred fifty million new subjects. They had conquered an empire that it took the Western colonial powers almost four centuries to acquire.

Along the Pacific coast of the United States, panic-stricken Americans feared an imminent invasion. In February 1942, President Roosevelt ordered 112,000 Japanese-Americans to be rounded up and sent to detention camps. It was a time of apprehension and alarm. For most Americans, the outcome of the war was in genuine doubt.

In early May 1942, American code breakers deduced from intercepted radio messages that the Japanese Imperial Navy was planning to eliminate the U.S. presence in the Central Pacific by drawing American forces into a final and decisive battle. Their target was Midway Atoll, consisting of two islands and an airfield lying twelve hundred miles west of Hawaii. Gambling that his code breakers were right, Admiral Chester Nimitz, the commander-in-chief of the U.S. Pacific Fleet, committed his available forces to setting up an ambush.

Midway has been called the most important naval battle ever fought between two great powers. The Japanese thought it would be a walkover, or in the words of one senior Japanese officer, "as easy as twisting a baby's arm." After everything their navy had accomplished up to that point, there was little reason to doubt his words.

The Japanese Empire was at the pinnacle of its glory. Having destroyed the last vestiges of European colonial power in the western Pacific, their confidence in their commanders, warships, combat aircraft, and each other was boundless. Many had come to believe that they were racially superior to the "mongrelized" and "decadent" Americans.

Against the five Japanese battleships, eight aircraft carriers, fourteen cruisers, fifty-five destroyers, and dozens of auxiliary ships now heading toward Midway, Admiral Nimitz had a combined force of three carriers, eight cruisers, and thirteen destroyers. Twenty-four ships against one hundred sixty-two.

Only two of his carriers, the *Hornet* and the *Enterprise,* were prepared for battle. His third carrier, the USS *Yorktown,* had absorbed a five-hundred-pound bomb hit in the Battle of the Coral Sea. Informed that the ship would require at least a month to be made seaworthy, Nimitz gave his repair division seventy-two hours to accomplish the task.

In spite of these fearful odds, on June 4, 1942, the Americans chose to confront the Imperial Navy at Midway. In assessing the battle's importance, former defense secretary James Schlesinger wrote that "it was far more than the turning of the tide in the Pacific War. In a strategic sense, it was a turning point in world history."

Just two months later, the second pivotal battle of the Pacific War was fought on the island of Guadalcanal. Guadalcanal was the land-based strategic equivalent of Midway, a savage and bloody campaign that determined the outcome of Japanese aspirations to secure control of its vast new Pacific empire.

Unlike Midway, the battle took place in malarial swamps and sweltering jungle, as well as in the skies above them. It is doubtful that a more harrowing succession of weeks ever took place in the history of warfare. Guadalcanal was the first of many Pacific campaigns in which the Japanese fought to virtually the last man. The challenge was compounded for the Americans by the fact that they were cut off from support, and existing in part on supplies left behind by the Japanese. "For those who fought there," wrote Admiral Samuel Eliot Morison, "Guadalcanal was not just a name. . . . It was an emotion."

The Americans went into both of these crucial battles with vastly inferior forces. If the Japanese had won at Midway, they would have been free to advance eastward, taking the Hawaiian Islands and threatening the West Coast of the United States. President Roosevelt would have been forced to abandon his strategy of fighting Germany first. History might well have turned out quite differently.

The story of these two pivotal battles has been written many times and far too well for me to replicate them once again. This book is not about the battles. It is about one small group of men who fought in both of them.

*A Dawn Like Thunder* tells the story of one naval air squadron, a group of young Americans from every part of the country who began the war flying outmoded aircraft that launched unreliable torpedoes against enemy warships.

Through a combination of courage, sacrifice, luck, and timing, it was the fate of these men to help change the course of history. More than sixty years later, the record of their contribution has faded into the past, and the last handful of survivors provide the only living link to their deeds in the first critical months of the Second World War.

This book was not written to mythologize war. In the twenty-first century, that would be a sacrilege. All but a few of the men depicted in the book were fighting to help win what they hoped would be a lasting peace, and then to come home and enjoy the rest of their lives.

The novelist Stephen Crane was once asked why he wrote *The Red Badge of Courage*. "I wanted to be there," he said. That is the goal of this book, to again bring alive on the page these extraordinary young men, who they were and what they did, for a modern generation of readers.

This is their story.

# THE SENTINELS

Smiley

His first glimpse of the Hawaiian Islands was just a distant smudge on the sun-splashed sea, but it was enough for him to feel a shiver of excitement. Like many of the Navy pilots crossing the Pacific on the military transport *Chaumont,* twenty-four-year-old Ensign Corwin F. Morgan of Tampa, Florida, savored the prospect of high adventure awaiting him aboard the aircraft carrier USS *Hornet.*

They called him Smiley.

With his rugged, square-jawed face, he didn't look like a Smiley, and he didn't smile more than any other pilot in Torpedo Squadron Eight. Morgan had earned his enduring nickname at a poker game back in Norfolk, Virginia, after joining the torpedo squadron shortly before the Japanese attacked Pearl Harbor.

Rain had washed out the afternoon's training flights, and a group of pilots had started playing poker. The game went on most of the night. Morgan was an inspired gambler, and had won more than two hundred dollars when someone started dealing blackjack and he encountered a run of terrible cards, losing hand after hand. The sudden twist of luck struck him as absurd, and he couldn't stop grinning as he gave back half of what he had won.

"I can't believe you, Morgan," said James Hill Cook, the boyish-looking Southerner with the deep drawl from Grand Cane, Louisiana. "You smile when you win and you smile when you lose. From now on, I'm calling you Smiley."

The name stuck.

Smiley Morgan had grown up in Richmond, Missouri, the self-proclaimed mushroom capital of the world. His father was the local veterinarian. One summer afternoon the boy had been dozing near a swimming hole at his grandfather's farm when he happened to gaze up and notice a flight of barnstormers doing loops and barrel rolls over the county fairgrounds a couple miles away. Like a youth answering a religious calling, he had tramped through cornfields and pastures until he finally reached the fairgrounds, where he stood mesmerized next to his first airplane.

At the University of Florida in Gainesville, he proved to be an exceptional athlete, and a not-so-motivated student. Before he dropped out of college, he joined the Civilian Pilot Training Program and earned his flying license. Deciding to join the Navy, he was accepted for flight training. After he won his wings in Pensacola, Florida, Morgan was assigned to Torpedo Squadron Eight in Norfolk, Virginia.

When he arrived at East Field in Norfolk, he was told to report to the squadron's commanding officer. Lieutenant Commander John Waldron had just returned from a training flight, and was still wearing his flight suit. He kept Morgan standing at attention in his office while he quickly signed a batch of papers. Looking down at Waldron as he worked, Smiley thought he looked old enough to be his father, and then some.

"Ensign," said Waldron without looking up, "I am going to give you your first duty in this squadron. Go over to the blackboard and print your name."

Smiley wrote, "Corwin F. Morgan."

Standing up, Waldron repeated it aloud and came over to shake his hand. His fierce-looking face looked gaunt. The imprint of flying goggles was etched on his cheeks.

There was a lot for him to learn about flying a torpedo plane, he said, and he would have to work hard to master it all. They started every morning before dawn, and worked until well after dark.

"Welcome to the outfit," he concluded.

That was one of the few times Smiley ever talked to the Skipper alone. Nine days later, the Japanese attacked Pearl Harbor. From then on, Waldron ran the squadron like there was no tomorrow, seven days a week without letup. Smiley had never worked harder in his life. As the months passed, he began to feel a deep sense of pride at having mastered flying in every kind of weather and at all hours of the day and night.

Now he was on his way to war.

There had been little for the pilots to do aboard the *Chaumont* as it crossed the Pacific. During the day, they sunbathed on deck, ate their meals in the wardroom, exercised, studied torpedo attack problems, and read the dog-eared books and old magazines in the small wardroom library.

After dark, the ship was always blacked out in case a Japanese submarine lurked in their path. Morgan spent most of the night hours on the fantail with his friend Ensign John Taurman, a big, easygoing pilot from Cincinnati, Ohio. The two of them would sit against a stanchion, gazing backward as the ship's wake cut a crystal path behind them in the roiling sea, wondering what would await them when they finally arrived at Pearl Harbor.

Torpedo Squadron Eight had been temporarily split in half back in Norfolk. In early March 1942, Lieutenant Commander Waldron and most of the senior pilots had gone to sea aboard the carrier *Hornet,* sailing for the West Coast via the Panama Canal, after which the carrier headed out to the Pacific to engage the Japanese. Waldron's squadron was equipped with the Navy's outmoded torpedo plane, the Douglas TBD Devastator.

The second half of the squadron had stayed behind in Norfolk to receive delivery of the Navy's brand-new torpedo attack plane, the Grumman TBF Avenger. After the new planes had been flight-tested, Smiley and the rest of the pilots had flown them across the United States. In San Francisco, the crews and their aircraft had been put aboard fast transport ships. Their goal was to catch up to the *Hornet* before the next big battle against the Japanese.

The sea was almost flat calm as the *Chaumont* finally turned for the final leg of the passage between Molokai and Oahu, the islands lush and inviting beneath green mountains under the midday sun.

All of the pilots crowded the deck railing to get their first look at Pearl Harbor. Like the others, the twenty-four-year-old Morgan had seen the newspaper and magazine photographs of the devastation caused by the Japanese attack less than six months earlier. He thought he was prepared for what they would see. He was wrong.

After passing through the submarine nets protecting the entrance to the harbor, the *Chaumont* steamed slowly past Battleship Row. Lying upside down at one mooring, the capsized *Oklahoma* was dull brown in the sunlight. More than two football fields long, its rust-covered hull rose above the oily surface like a humpback whale. Next in line lay the battleship *West Virginia*, which had sunk at its mooring after taking six torpedoes and two armor-piercing bombs.

Farther down the anchorage, a small utility vessel was tethered next to the shattered wreck of the *Arizona*, its work party of salvage divers trying to start a gas engine suction pump.

What remained of the *Arizona*'s superstructure above the waterline was nothing more than a rusting mass of battered metal. The officers' boisterous shouting suddenly ceased, and they sailed slowly past it in awestruck silence. If there was any lingering doubt about what they were fighting for, it ended there.

When the breeze dropped, Morgan smelled the reek of crude oil mixed with the fetid water seeping out of the ships. Along with the stench of the oil, he could smell something else.

"Hundreds of guys never made it out of the ships," said one of the officers at the deck railing. "They're all still down there."

Beyond the ships, the cluttered shoreline was fouled by almost a foot of sludge. A slew of dead birds were snared in the coils of barbed wire that had been strung along the beach in the days after the attack.

Suddenly, another shout went up and Morgan turned in time to see a gigantic aircraft carrier towering high above one of the Pearl Harbor dry docks. At ten stories, the ship's island almost blocked out the landscape. Hundreds of workers were swarming over her, the flash of their torches arcing brightly across the water. Along with the welders and steamfitters, Morgan could see electricians crawling past fire-blistered hatches and torn bulkheads, and dragging heavy electrical cables behind them. It reminded him of the scene in *Gulliver's Travels* in which the Lilliputians frantically tied down the giant with heavy hawsers.

"It's the *Yorktown*," someone shouted as the *Chaumont* nosed into its pier at Ford Island and came to a stop.

The *Yorktown* was one of the three American carriers left in the Central Pacific after the Japanese had sunk the *Lexington* a month earlier. But where were the *Hornet* and the *Enterprise*? Morgan wondered as he anxiously scanned the rest of the anchorage. The other two carriers weren't in sight.

Across the dock, antiaircraft batteries were dug in behind mounds of sandbags. Armed military policemen carrying gas masks were manning a roadblock at the gatepost to Luke Airfield, which occupied most of Ford Island.

Carrying their overseas bags, the seventeen pilots of Torpedo Squadron Eight disembarked from the ship. Lieutenant Harold "Swede" Larsen, the strapping blond Annapolis graduate temporarily in command, was waiting for them near the foot of the gangway with Lieutenant Langdon Fieberling, the second-highest-ranking officer in their detachment. The pilots gathered in a loose circle.

Larsen told Fieberling to take them over to the Bachelor Officers' Quarters and wait for him there, while he went to find out where Lieutenant Commander Waldron and the rest of the squadron were.

They set off on foot across Ford Island carrying their bags. As they passed the transport ship *Hammondsport,* a crane was already extracting one of their new, bluish gray Grumman Avengers from the ship's hold. The torpedo plane rose slowly into the air above them, its retractable wings folded back along the fuselage like a dozing mallard's.

At the gatepost to Luke Field, Lieutenant Fieberling had to produce his Navy identity card before they were allowed through. When they came to the first hangar at the edge of the airfield, Morgan saw that it had been reduced to a steel skeleton by Japanese bombs. A bulldozer was scraping together a massive pile of charred timber, concrete rubble, and airplane parts.

They found the Bachelor Officers' Quarters at the end of the runway near the northern tip of the island, its once manicured lawn scarred by newly dug slit trenches. Inside the crowded lobby, the officers dropped their overseas bags and immediately headed toward the bar.

The manager stepped forward to tell Fieberling that the new facility was full. There were men already sleeping in the corridors, he said apologetically. The detachment was welcome to eat its meals there, but that was all the BOQ could provide.

"Where can we find a temporary billet?" asked Fieberling. The manager said that they might still have room over at the old BOQ, which was down near the shoreline along Battleship Row.

Morgan remembered the smell from the sunken battleships as the men plodded over to the older facility in a long, ragged line. Through the trees that ringed the grounds around the building, he could see the tangled wreck of the sunken *Arizona* that they had passed on their way into the *Chaumont*'s anchorage.

At the lobby desk, the manager informed them that there was no room for them there either. Fieberling, who was leading-man handsome, flashed a confident grin and asked for the manager's name, telling him that his squadron's orders to lodge there had come directly from Admiral Nimitz, and he would need to advise the commander-in-chief why his order had been disobeyed. It was a bald-faced lie, but the manager nervously disappeared into his office. A minute later he came back out smiling at Fieberling as if he had just won the lottery.

"I've arranged to set up cots for all of your men in the lanai," he said.

The men moved their bags out to the BOQ's screened porch and sat down to wait for Swede Larsen. When he finally arrived, his face was tense. He sought out Fieberling and the other senior officers.

The *Hornet* had left port yesterday with the *Enterprise*, he told them bitterly. No one was saying where they went, but it sounded like the carriers were going into action. They had gotten there just one day too late.

Swede said that he had been ordered to get their planes checked out as quickly as possible in case of another Japanese attack on Hawaii. The city was under martial law, and a curfew and blackout were in place after sundown. Swede said he was heading over to Luke Field to make sure the squadron's mechanics would have the planes ready to be flight-tested in the morning.

Langdon Fieberling called the pilots together and gave them the news. To a chorus of groans, he told them that because of the island-wide curfew they were restricted to the base. There would be no excursions to the nightspots in Honolulu. He then softened the blow by giving them the rest of the day off to explore Ford Island.

Sitting on his newly unfolded cot in the screened lanai, Smiley Morgan watched Ensign Vic Lewis unpack his overseas bag. At twenty-two, Vic was the youngest pilot in the squadron. It looked to Morgan like he had brought a library with him, including hardbound books on military history and ornithology. The prim, open-faced Lewis grinned at him and said he thought they would probably have a lot of time to read when they weren't flying.

Smiley nodded encouragingly, but his own ambitions were decidedly different. When they weren't flying, he wasn't planning to do any reading. As soon as the curfew was lifted, he was going to head straight for the Royal Hawaiian Hotel to hopefully meet a beautiful Hawaiian girl.

Across the porch, the tall, lanky John Taurman tossed his bag down on another cot. Morgan asked him if he wanted to explore the island with him, and Taurman agreed. Together, they headed across the lawn and down to the edge of the anchorage.

Two cage masts that had once adorned the stricken battleships lay piled in a heap near the shoreline. Smiley and Taurman started walking south along the cluttered shoreline. Farther down the anchorage, they came to a long gangplank that led over to the deck of the battleship *West Virginia*. The deck and superstructure were coated with a film of oily scum, as if the ship had recently been refloated. At Smiley's urging, he and Taurman decided to go aboard.

When they crossed the still-sloping deck plates to observe the extent of the damage, Morgan saw that the ship had been hit by a number of armor-piercing bombs. One of them had wrecked the port casemates, causing a big section of the deck to collapse.

Behind a massive gun turret, he and Taurman encountered a team of salvage divers taking a break from their work. The divers confirmed that the ship had been raised about a week earlier, and was to be towed over to a dry-dock facility.

One of them said that while he was searching an air pocket in a watertight compartment deep inside the ship, he had found a 1941 pinup calendar. One of the sailors trapped inside the compartment had marked off the days after December 7 while he waited for rescue. The last date he had scratched off before he died was December 23, more than two weeks after the *West Virginia* was sunk.

Morgan and Taurman decided they needed a drink, and walked back to the bar in the new BOQ at the end of the runway. As they were drinking a cold beer, Smiley heard a booming laugh and his friend Ensign Bob Ries lumbered up to join them. Smiley hadn't seen him since they had gotten into trouble together in San Francisco.

Ries was a relentless skirt-chaser, and with his apple cheeks and reddish-blond hair, he occasionally scored. He and Morgan had been having dinner at the Bal Tabarin restaurant with Taurman and a few of the other pilots when Ries spied the legs on the hatcheck girl. An hour later, he had persuaded her to go barhopping with him.

Smiley was invited to go along, and they had stayed out until four in the morning before the three of them ended up at the girl's apartment. By the time Smiley woke up on the couch in her living room, they were already two hours late for Swede Larsen's final squadron meeting.

When they reported in, an angry Larsen restricted them to the ship until it left port the following day. He thought of an additional punishment the next morning, ordering Ries to vacate the stateroom he was sharing with Morgan aboard the *Chaumont,* and make the Pacific crossing on the *Hammondsport,* the older transport that had once ferried Key West passenger trains. It was carrying the squadron's planes and enlisted men.

Now Ries was glad to be back with Morgan and the other officers.

It was almost midnight when Smiley returned to the darkened porch facing the anchorage. Through an open window above him, he could hear Artie Shaw's "Begin the Beguine" playing on a portable phonograph. It had been his favorite song before the war.

The lanai was already filled with sleeping men when he stripped off his rumpled uniform and dropped onto his cot. Lying there in the darkness, he could smell Pearl Harbor, even if he could no longer see it. An hour later, he was still wide awake.

Rolling over, he stared out into the night. From the far side of the trees fringing the shoreline, he could hear the slow, steady rhythm of the gas-engined suction pump he had seen earlier that afternoon on the buoy tender anchored by the *Arizona*. He wondered what they could still be pumping out at this hour.

Someone had managed to acquire a bottle of whiskey, and a few of the pilots were silently passing it back and forth between swigs. The lit embers of their cigarettes glowed like fireflies across the room, but the smoke didn't mask the sepulchral smell from Battleship Row.

Morgan couldn't rid his mind of the horrible vision of the hundreds of men still entombed just a stone's throw from where he was lying. He forced himself to think of home, and the last Florida Gators football game he had gone to see in Gainesville with his girlfriend, Caroline. It didn't work. As the hours dragged slowly past, his earlier excitement at the prospect of high adventure aboard the *Hornet* was replaced by somber thoughts on the grim reality of death.

He never slept. The pump ran all night.

The Skipper

Each of the first days at sea dawned like a South Seas travel poster. Cotton clouds dappled a bluebird sky. The air temperature was almost balmy and cool breezes drifted across the flight deck as the massive carrier plowed through long sea swells at a speed of twenty-two knots.

Now the skies had grayed and it was colder. Gathered in loose formation in the lee of the carrier's island superstructure, the eighteen pilots of Torpedo Squadron Eight were going through their regular calisthenics program under the watchful gaze of their commanding officer.

They all knew where they were going by now, and what they were up against. Soon after the *Hornet* had left Pearl Harbor, the captain had read a statement over the loudspeaker to the entire crew.

"The enemy is approaching for an attempt to seize the island of Midway," he had announced. "We are going to prevent them from taking Midway if possible. Be ready and keep on the alert."

As the impending battle approached, John Waldron took every opportunity to observe the men of his squadron as they went through their daily routines, including the morning exercise regimen. He would stand off to the side with his feet spread, his leathery skin browned by the sun, gazing at them like a fierce bird of prey protecting its young.

Torpedo Eight was the only squadron aboard ship that did daily physical exercise. Every day, pilots from the other squadrons would stand across the flight deck with amused looks on their faces as Waldron's men went through their routine of push-ups and jumping jacks. Often, the others would shout sarcastic comments before disappearing below, laughing.

Waldron was used to people making fun of both him and his methods. Back in his Annapolis days, some of the midshipmen had mocked him as the class "Redskin" and a "seagoing cowpuncher." There was a derisive edge to many of their jibes, as if he were some kind of hayseed with no social graces who had to be tolerated by the scions of the generations-old Navy families. It only made his ambition to succeed in the Navy burn more intensely.

At forty-two, he was almost twenty years older than most of the men he now commanded. Tall and rugged, he had the face and bearing of an Oglala Sioux warrior. In fact, he was descended from two of them on his mother's side.

Born in Fort Pierre, South Dakota, he had grown up on an Indian reservation where his father sold vegetables to the local tribe in exchange for dried fish. He had never seen an ocean until his appointment to Annapolis in 1920.

Now, twenty-two years later, he was considered to be one of the exceptional air squadron commanders in the Navy. His peers expected him to move up quickly now that America was in a shooting war.

Aboard the *Hornet*, Waldron's thirty-one-year-old executive officer, Lieutenant James C. "Jimmy" Owens, would assign one of the junior ensigns to lead the calisthenics each morning. Serious and efficient, Owens was so frugal he saved the tinfoil from his empty cigarette packs, carefully folding each square before storing it in his uniform blouse. He was the perfect subordinate to carry out the daily cascade of the Skipper's orders and requests.

A former quarterback at the University of Southern California, Jimmy Owens had been in the Navy long enough to serve under plenty of tough, uncompromising officers. But none of them had been anything like the Skipper. The old man was like a force of nature, an incredibly hard driver at everything he did, and when he got the bit in his teeth, there was no stopping him.

A few months after the squadron had been formed back in 1941, they had been doing practice carrier landings in their old worn-out

Brewster SBN training planes off Norfolk, and a new pilot had been killed trying to land one. That was when the Skipper had stormed up to Washington and told them he wouldn't allow his boys to go up in those planes anymore. Jimmy Owens was amazed when new replacement planes began arriving a week later.

Most of the pilots in the outfit had been fresh from flight training when they joined the squadron. They had come from every part of the country: Oregon, Texas, Iowa, Massachusetts, California, Missouri, New York, Virginia, and Indiana. A few had grown up wealthy in cities like San Francisco and New York. Others had been Depression-poor and came from hardscrabble towns with horse-drawn buggies for transportation and no running water or electricity.

Nearly all of them had attended college. A few had gone to the military academies like Annapolis and the Virginia Military Institute, some to elite universities such as Yale and Berkeley, many to football powerhouses like Alabama and Texas A&M, and others to tiny schools like Reedly Junior College and Duluth State.

Now they were all John Waldron's boys, proud to be reflections of the old man's unique leadership style. In private, they would grouse about his endless training demands, but they wouldn't brook criticism of him from an outsider, and the squadron was as tight-knit as a big Irish family.

Surveying them across the flight deck, Waldron knew that they had come to trust him with their lives. To a man, they would follow him anywhere. It was a trust he didn't take lightly, and he didn't want to ever let them down.

One inescapable fact deeply troubled him. The torpedo planes his men flew were terribly outmoded. Some of his pilots derisively referred to them as "flying coffins," and by 1942, they weren't far wrong.

American naval doctrine decreed that each American carrier should have four air squadrons: a fighter squadron, two dive-bombing squadrons, and a torpedo plane squadron. The dive-bombers and torpedo planes were the enemy ship killers, the principal reason for the carriers' existence.

In 1942, there were two ways to sink enemy ships: to dive-bomb them or to put torpedoes in them. The bombers attacked from high altitude, diving on an enemy ship before releasing their payload. The torpedo planes went in at low altitude just above the wave tops to launch their torpedoes. The role of the carriers' fighters was to provide protection for the bombers and torpedo planes against the enemy fighters trying to shoot them down.

Two of the three aircraft types in the American carrier arsenal had recently been upgraded. The fighter squadrons were now equipped with Grumman Wildcats, the Navy's tough new pursuit plane. A new generation of dive-bombers had also been added. The Douglas Dauntless dive-bomber was capable of flying at two hundred fifty miles an hour, and was equally rugged.

The old Douglas Devastator torpedo planes were being phased out. They flew at little more than a hundred miles an hour. The speed of the enemy's vaunted new fighter, the Mitsubishi Zero, was reportedly three hundred.

The Devastator's armament was grossly inadequate in an aerial gun battle. Against the twenty-millimeter cannons of the Japanese Zero, the Devastator had just two Colt/Browning thirty-caliber machine guns. One was operated by the pilot in the nose, and the second one fired by the rear gunner. Popguns, the men called them.

Well aware of the Devastator's shortcomings, Waldron had ridden his new pilots hard from the start, ordering them to fly four hours in the morning and four more in the afternoon in order to master formation flying and torpedo-launching tactics.

He made them fly constant "bounce" drills at all hours of the day and night in order to simulate landing on an aircraft carrier. Meanwhile, he had tirelessly railed to the Navy about the squadron's inadequate equipment, their underpowered aircraft, and the failure to supply him with practice torpedoes.

Thanks to his constant hectoring, Waldron's squadron was the first one chosen to be equipped with the Navy's brand-new torpedo plane, the Grumman Avenger, manufactured in Bethpage, New York.

With its fourteen-cylinder, air-cooled radial engine, the Avenger was almost as fast as a Wildcat fighter and had steel armor plating to protect the crew, along with self-sealing fuel tanks that virtually swallowed bullets, and a swiveling turret for the fifty-caliber machine gun located in the center of the fuselage. It carried a crew of three, including the pilot, who could fire a machine gun from the nose, the turret gunner in the center, and a radioman who could fire a third machine gun from underneath the plane's tail section.

When the *Hornet* departed for the Pacific back in March, the first batch of Avengers was just coming off the Grumman assembly line. Until the new planes arrived out in the Pacific, Waldron's pilots would have to fly the Devastators.

Back in February, the *Hornet* had been chosen to launch the first air attack on Tokyo. In San Francisco, sixteen B-25 Army Air Force bombers were lowered by crane onto the *Hornet*'s flight deck. The daring raid was strictly an Army show, led by Lieutenant Colonel James Doolittle. Before the raid, no one was sure that a fully loaded B-25 bomber could be launched successfully off an aircraft carrier, but Doolittle had trained his crews to do just that. After dropping their bombs in Japan, his bombers would attempt to fly on to China, where they would land at air bases in Allied hands.

And they had done their job. On April 18, 1942, the sixteen B-25s had taken off from the *Hornet* in the face of gale-force winds and had hit their targets. After the planes were launched from the *Hornet*, the carrier turned around and headed back to Pearl Harbor.

In early May, the first major Pacific naval battle took place between American and Japanese forces in the Coral Sea, southwest of the Solomon Islands. The *Hornet* did not participate in the action, which led to a Japanese tactical victory. The American carrier *Lexington* was sunk along with two other ships, while the Japanese lost the light carrier *Shoho*.

Waldron was desperate to receive his new Avengers before the next major battle took place. When the planes arrived at Pearl Harbor aboard the transport ship, he was planning to work his senior pilots around the clock to qualify them. If there wasn't time for it, the younger pilots who had trained on them back at Norfolk would fly in combat. Either way, Waldron planned to lead them.

But they hadn't come in time.

Signaling that calisthenics were over, Owens sent the pilots off on a full lap around the perimeter of the huge flight deck, and the Skipper headed down to the officers' wardroom for his daily powwow over coffee with Commander Ed Creehan.

Ed Creehan was the stocky, heavy-jawed engineer officer on the

*Hornet*, and a close pal of Waldron's from their Annapolis days. He was also a member of the inner circle of the *Hornet*'s captain, Marc "Pete" Mitscher, and he often picked up the latest scuttlebutt before anyone else. Waldron could share a confidence with him and know that the information wouldn't travel further.

Waldron joined Creehan in the carrier's low-ceilinged wardroom, where the ship's officers ate their meals and gathered for meetings and briefings. It ran the entire breadth of the ship, with parallel rows of white linen–covered tables laid with flatware bearing the *Hornet* crest.

With the Midway battle just a few days away, the *Hornet*'s officers were excited about the chance to put a serious dent in the Japanese fleet and make up for the loss of the *Lexington* a month earlier. The *Hornet* had not arrived in time to participate in the Coral Sea battle. Midway would be her first test.

That morning, the *Hornet* air group leaders would receive their first intelligence briefing from Lieutenant Steve Jurika, the senior intelligence officer aboard the *Hornet*. He would provide the latest information on the Japanese intentions at Midway, as well as Admiral Nimitz's proposed strategy for blocking them. After that, the *Hornet*'s air group commander, Stanhope Cotton Ring, would outline his own plans for attacking the Japanese carriers.

Up on deck, the morning's gunnery practice was inaugurated with the concussive blast of the ship's five-inch guns. The noise reverberated through the ship like successive hammer blows. A few minutes later, the cannon salvos were followed by the stuttering racket of antiaircraft machine gun fire.

Their coffee break over, Ed Creehan left to resume his engineering duties, and Waldron joined the group assembling for the briefing by Jurika and the intelligence staff. Like John Waldron, the other three air squadron commanders were career naval officers and Annapolis men. They were Lieutenant Commander Samuel "Pat" Mitchell, who led the *Hornet*'s fighter squadron, and Lieutenant Commanders Walter Rodee and Robert "Ruff" Johnson, who led the two dive-bombing squadrons.

The *Hornet*'s air group commander, Stanhope Cotton Ring, had graduated from Annapolis one year ahead of Waldron in 1923. The two men came from different worlds. They were very different men.

Unlike the hard-charging Waldron, who had spent his boyhood years on Indian reservations in South Dakota and Saskatchewan, Canada, the reserved and courtly Ring had been raised in Quincy, Massachusetts, the son of a Navy commodore.

At six feet two inches, the handsome Ring liked to relax by playing a pear-shaped mandolin, and was an expert at bridge. At Annapolis, he had been a magnet for attractive debutantes. When it came to the ladies, he was considered a "snake" by his fellow midshipmen.

In those days, the homely Waldron had to scrap for female companionship, once spraining both ankles when climbing over the wall after a nocturnal encounter. Later, he was docked twenty-five demerits for being discovered behind Bancroft Hall with two local girls.

Observing Ring aboard the *Hornet*, Lieutenant Steve Jurika thought he would have made a superb Foreign Service officer, and, in fact, Ring had served overseas as an assistant naval attaché. After returning from his embassy posting in London, he began carrying a British swagger stick. Three years later, he was still carrying it tucked under his arm. It had made him an object of ridicule among some of the younger pilots in the group, who thought it was a riding crop.

When the *Hornet* had returned to Pearl Harbor after arriving too late for the Coral Sea battle, its air group had flown ashore on May 26 to their base at Ewa Field. Along with the pilots of the carrier *Enterprise*, they were looking forward to a two-day liberty. While the *Enterprise* pilots headed to the Royal Hawaiian Hotel for two days on Waikiki Beach, however, Commander Ring had kept his entire air group at Ewa Field on full alert. It led to what one pilot called a near mutiny.

Cool and aloof, Ring had no sense of humor to help him establish rapport with the pilots serving under him, and he didn't seem to care. The *Hornet*'s captain, Pete Mitscher, was due to be promoted to rear admiral any day now. The scuttlebutt was that Ring would soon be leaving as air group commander for a job on his staff.

It couldn't be too soon for the *Hornet*'s fliers. Few, if any, of the air group's pilots had confidence in Stanhope Ring's leadership or flying ability. He had made a number of serious mistakes on previous flights, including one embarrassing crash landing. While on a group training mission in the Gulf of Mexico, it had been necessary for him to turn over command to junior officer Gus Widhelm after he got lost while trying to lead the air group back to the ship.

At one point, Lieutenant George Ellenberg, one of the *Hornet*'s seasoned dive-bomber pilots, joined with several other fliers to seriously discuss the idea of shooting Ring down before his incompetence cost men their lives.

For better or worse, Ring would soon be leading them into battle.

At Steve Jurika's intelligence briefing, the participants also included Captain Mitscher and the members of the *Hornet*'s air staff, including Commander Apollo Soucek, the air officer, and Lieutenant Commander John Foster, the operations officer.

Jurika told them that the Japanese fleet was expected to reach striking distance of Midway on the following Wednesday or Thursday. He then gave them a detailed and comprehensive breakdown of the ships in the Japanese armada, focusing on the aircraft carriers, which were the key to the Japanese hopes for success.

He didn't tell them how the intelligence staff got all of this information, and no one asked, although it was widely suspected that analysts back at Pearl Harbor must have broken the Japanese code.

Midway was located more than twelve hundred miles northwest of Hawaii in the Central Pacific. It was a fortified U.S. territory, and its islands held two important airfields. By invading the islands, the Japanese hoped to lure the American carriers out from Pearl Harbor, where the massive Japanese striking force could destroy them. The Japanese Empire could then invade Hawaii, or simply consolidate its other gains in the Western Pacific.

Admiral Nimitz's plan to defeat the Japanese invasion fleet was simple: ambush the Japanese carriers in the striking force while their air groups were off attacking Midway Atoll.

Once the Japanese carriers were sunk, the enemy pilots returning from Midway would be forced to ditch in the ocean. Without air cover, the rest of the Japanese fleet would be ripe for the plucking by the American dive-bombers and torpedo planes.

Lieutenant Jurika went on to brief them about some of the air combat tactics employed by the Japanese carriers. The Battle of the Coral Sea had been fought less than a month earlier, and it had provided many useful lessons.

Although the Yorktown's and Lexington's After Action Reports had not yet been officially circulated, Waldron and the other squadron commanders knew that the air groups on the Yorktown and the Lexington had divided their fighter strength in the course of the two-day battle. Half of the fighters had flown cover for the slow-moving torpedo planes, and the other half had protected the carrier's dive-bombers from attacks by the Japanese Zeroes.

On May 8, Lieutenant Commander Joe Taylor had led the Yorktown's torpedo squadron in the battle. As the Yorktown's air group approached the Japanese fleet, four of its Grumman F4F Wildcat fighters had stayed low with Taylor's slow-moving Devastators as they launched their torpedoes at one of the Japanese carriers. The remaining two Wildcats had flown cover for the Yorktown's dive-bombers at a much higher altitude.

A swarm of Japanese Zeroes had come down to attack the Devastators, but were driven off long enough for Joe Taylor and his men to launch nine torpedoes at the carrier, claiming three hits. All of his torpedo planes had returned safely to the Yorktown.

The Lexington's air group had functioned in precisely the same way. The planes in the fighter escort were split up between the dive-bombers and the torpedo planes, keeping the Zeroes busy long enough for the Devastators of Jimmy Brett's torpedo squadron to make a successful run.

In the two days of attacks, Brett had claimed five torpedo hits, and all but one of his Devastators made it safely back to their ship. Unfortunately, three of the four fighters covering them had been shot down. The dive-bombing squadrons had taken serious losses, too.

Toward the end of his briefing, Jurika stressed to the squadron commanders that it would be a big mistake to underestimate the skill and courage of the Japanese pilots. The Zero was one hell of a fine aircraft, he told them. It would not be a cakewalk. The Japanese were really good.

After Jurika finished, Stanhope Ring informed the squadron commanders that he was planning to approach the upcoming battle differently than the air groups at the Coral Sea. He said that he was going to keep the *Hornet*'s fighters together as one unit. There would only be ten of them available, and they would stay up to protect the dive-bombers, which would fly at around eighteen thousand feet.

Ring thought the Zeroes would concentrate their attacks up there, leaving Waldron's squadron of Devastators to go in relatively untouched at around five hundred feet above the ocean surface. The key, he said, was for the whole group to attack with tactical cohesion in a single high-low formation. He would personally lead the air group in a dive-bomber.

John Waldron had flown enough missions since 1927 to know that things didn't always go as planned. What if they got separated by heavy cloud cover or some other circumstance on the way to the enemy? His squadron would be separated from the others by almost four miles of altitude. He immediately spoke up, urging that the *Hornet* air group employ the same tactics that were used at the Coral Sea. When the meeting broke up, there was no final resolution of the question.

Although Waldron was confident that his torpedo squadron could make hits on the Japanese carriers, he was deeply upset about this change in tactics. If nothing else, the briefing had convinced him that fighter protection would be one of the keys to a successful attack by his slow-moving planes, and success was all he was after.

He wasn't about to give up fighter protection so easily. Pat Mitchell, who commanded the *Hornet*'s fighter squadron, agreed with him. So did Lieutenant Stan Ruehlow, Mitchell's flight officer.

After the briefing, Waldron returned to his pilots in Ready Room Four. Like the other squadron ready rooms, it was located close to the flight deck so the fliers could reach their aircraft quickly when there was an order to man their planes.

About twenty by forty feet square, it was where they met for briefings, drills, and instruction in everything from torpedo plane tactics to enemy ship recognition. A Teletype machine with a big screen on top of it sat at the front of the room, its keys ready to automatically print out information about enemy sightings and the latest weather information.

The steel-walled room was big enough for each pilot to have his own cushioned chair with a reclining back and a small storage locker beneath the seat to stow personal gear. The right armrest had a retractable writing desk for the pilots to take notes on. As they waited for a mission, the fliers could read, sleep, or eat a quick meal.

Even though it was Sunday, the pilots had spent most of the morning on a torpedo attack exercise. "If you know how to lead a target from any direction at every possible speed, you're almost certain to get hits," Waldron had drummed into them over and over.

A few of the pilots looked up to him like a stern father. He had tried to put the stamp of his determination on every one of them. When he thought they were getting complacent back in Norfolk, he would stage an "enemy attack" exercise, a drill in which the squadron had to arm its planes and take off as if Japanese planes were about to attack. It required them to pitch in together, pilots and crews alike, to launch the planes while he stood by measuring their response time on his watch like a racehorse trainer.

Waldron had toughened them in every way he knew to make them ready for whatever emergency might arise. Working with the plane crews, he had made sure that every aircraft was equipped with canteens, pocket compasses, emergency supplies, and other survival equipment in case they were shot down in the ocean.

"Someday, one of you might be all alone out there when something goes wrong, and at least you'll know what to do," he had told them.

Just before they left Pearl Harbor, he had cajoled the Navy materiel office into giving them twin thirty-caliber machine gun mounts that up to then had been allotted solely to the dive-bomber squadrons. The new mounts were installed on every Devastator.

He was well aware that some of the men had come to resent the amount of work he made them do, at least compared to the other air squadrons assigned to the *Hornet*. One of the ensign pilots privately referred to him as "the old goat."

But they were good. They had done everything he had asked of them. It had paid off, all of the hundreds of hours of formation flying, the bounce drills, the carrier takeoff and landing drills, the fighter evasion techniques, the antiaircraft fire avoidance tactics, the hours of bombing practice, the lessons in navigation, the fitness training, survival drills, and more torpedo firing tactics. Always more torpedo tactics.

Together, they had come to the end of a long road. The training was over. They would be going into action in a few days. Now he would let them rest up, like a finely tuned football team before the Rose Bowl.

When the attack exercise was finished, the Skipper asked for their attention. They would soon be intercepting a large force of Japanese, he told them, and Torpedo Eight would be part of a coordinated attack with the rest of the *Hornet*'s air group. He didn't mention that there would be no fighter protection for the Devastators.

Without the protection of at least a few fighters, though, he knew his Devastators could be sitting ducks no matter how well he had trained these men. If only Swede Larsen had gotten there in time with the new Grumman Avengers.

Swede

To many of the junior officers who found themselves temporarily serving under him, Harold H. "Swede" Larsen, was a bullheaded young martinet with the charming leadership style of Captain William Bligh of the HMS *Bounty*. The enlisted men who served under him hadn't read about Captain Bligh, but a lot of them thought Swede was a prick. One man had already thought about shooting him.

He knew what the men thought of him, and he didn't care. Waldron had left him in command of the detachment when the *Hornet* went to sea. In Swede's vision of how to run a combat unit, he was the hammer. The men who served under him were the nails.

For Swede, toughness and domination weren't a recent character development. His peers at Annapolis had noted the domineering side of his personality in his *Lucky Bag* yearbook citation. In an institution where young men were taught that privileges had to be earned, he was already used to getting his own way, once arranging a weekend pass down to Washington thanks to his uncle, Karl Stefan, who was a U.S. congressman.

Bravado was at the heart of his personality. It had only gotten worse after Waldron departed for the Pacific with the rest of the squadron, leaving Swede in command at Norfolk to train the younger pilots on the new Grumman Avengers.

Waldron had driven them hard, but the men sensed that each grueling exercise in the training regimen might one day save their lives. And they knew that Waldron drove himself just as hard as the officers and enlisted men he commanded. That wasn't the case with Swede. They quickly got the sense that he genuinely enjoyed being a bastard.

No one doubted his guts or personal courage. In an aircraft, he took chances that sometimes bordered on reckless. But, unlike Waldron's, a lot of his methods seemed to have no purpose but to make their lives more miserable. He would often keep his pilots in the air until just after the mess hall had closed, forcing them to miss dinner. After the first few times, they knew it was intentional.

Swede liked to rule by fear and public humiliation. Whenever he decided to upbraid one of the men, he invariably did it in front of the rest of them. It had led to simmering resentment, particularly among the enlisted sailors. After landing from a training flight a few months earlier, Larsen had climbed down from the cockpit and stormed over to the ground crewman who had been responsible for preparing the plane.

"Goddamnit . . . you tried to kill me!" he screamed in the enlisted man's face.

"I don't know what you're talking about, sir," came back Aviation Machinist's Mate Bill Tunstall.

"You never filled my gas tanks, goddamnit," he shouted. "I almost ran out of gas out there."

"That's not true, sir," protested Tunstall.

"You're a liar," shouted Larsen.

Stepping back, Tunstall hollered over to Chief Petty Officer Ed Hawkins, who was in charge of the flights that morning. When Hawkins came up, Tunstall asked him to tell Swede what he had been doing just before takeoff.

"You were topping off the fuel tanks," said Chief Hawkins, who, like Tunstall, was from Massachusetts and spoke with a clipped New England accent. "I was right heah."

Larsen glared at them as if they were both in on the conspiracy to murder him.

"I'll remember this," he had shouted before stalking off.

Swede was an enthusiastic hater. He particularly loathed Negroes and Jews. Above all, he hated the Japanese, and what he hungered for more than anything was a chance to go up against them in combat. He had already vowed to one officer that he would come home from the Pacific with the Medal of Honor.

Now he was stuck at Pearl Harbor after arriving just twenty-four hours too late to join the *Hornet* as it headed into harm's way. The thought of missing the battle was enough to send him into a seething rage.

Over the weekend, the squadron's new Avengers were put through a set of rigorous engine, instrument, and hydraulic checks. Then the pilots began flight-testing each plane until it was pronounced ready, after which Larsen would activate it to combat status.

At around midday on Sunday, May 31, Larsen headed over to the admin building to find out if there had been an update in their orders. Later that afternoon, Fieberling was working on the week's duty roster with several of the officers when Larsen returned with electrifying news. He had been told to prepare six Avengers for a flight to Midway Atoll to augment the air garrison there. The planes would need to be equipped with belly fuel tanks in order to make it.

The prospect of impending action apparently hadn't made Swede any happier than when he had left. They quickly learned why. Admiral Leigh Noyes, who had issued the order, wouldn't let Swede lead the mission.

As second-in-command, Fieberling would be taking the detachment. Swede told him to ask for volunteers for the other five planes. He would then make the final decision and the list would be posted at the office in Carrier Air Support Unit Five.

Word spread quickly about the upcoming flight. None of the pilots had any idea what the mission involved or what they would be expected to do once they got to Midway. Some of them didn't even know where it was, but they all decided to volunteer, particularly after they heard that Fieberling would be leading the mission instead of Swede.

Smiley Morgan was among the first. "I'll pass along your request," Fieberling told him.

Some of the pilots went directly to Swede. Ensign Gene Hanson, a second-generation Swede from Cedar Rapids, Iowa, sought him out to volunteer. Larsen told him he couldn't go. "I need you here," he said.

Meanwhile, the squadron's mechanics and ordnancemen had begun to prepare the six aircraft for the long flight. As the first Avenger was towed into the enormous hangar, another group of men went to track down the auxiliary fuel tanks that were to be attached inside the planes' bomb bays.

The pilots hung around the squadron office until they saw a yeoman pinning the typewritten list of who was going on the bulletin board near the door. Approaching it, Smiley Morgan felt the same sense of apprehension he'd experienced as a student when his exam grades had been posted at the University of Florida. He only had to glance at the list for a few seconds to see that his name wasn't there. It read:

**Lt. Langdon K. Fieberling, Commanding**
**Ensign O. J. Gaynier**
**Ensign A. K. Earnest**
**Ensign V. A. Lewis**
**Ensign C. E. Brannon**
**AMM1c D. D. Woodside**

Morgan felt a deep surge of disappointment. He could certainly understand why Ozzie Gaynier had been chosen. He was the senior ensign in the squadron after Waldron's group left on the *Hornet*. But why Swede had chosen the rest of them, he had no idea.

Albert Kyle "Bert" Earnest, of Richmond, Virginia, felt a jolt of excitement when he learned he was going. It meant he was finally going to get away from Swede. And he was glad that Charlie Brannon was going, too. The singles tennis champion at the University of Alabama, Charlie had been Bert's roommate back in Norfolk, and Bert had served as the best man at his recent wedding.

The pilots who wouldn't be going began to slowly drift away. Langdon Fieberling sought out Smiley Morgan as he was heading out of the hangar, and pulled him aside.

Smiley was the navigation officer, and Fieberling wanted him to pick up all the charts he could find that would help them plan the flight. Perhaps seeing the lingering disappointment on Smiley's face,

Fieberling told him not to worry, that they would all have plenty of chances in this war.

CASU-5 suddenly came alive with furious activity. While mechanics swarmed under the bomb bays of the six Avengers, Fieberling brought the chosen pilots together for a preliminary briefing.

Machinist's Mate Bill Magee, who was helping fit a belly tank into one of the nearby planes, thought the pilots looked amazingly relaxed as they sat in a semicircle around Fieberling. As the sun touched the edge of the open hangar bay, he watched Charlie Brannon take off his uniform shirt so that his back could absorb the last rays.

As night fell, the doors to the hangar were shut tight due to the strict blackout. Under the harsh glare of the hangar's shop lights, the six Avengers looked gigantic. With a wingspan of fifty-four feet, each one was almost as big as a bomber.

While mechanics worked to attach the auxiliary fuel tanks, the pilots and crews headed over to the old BOQ to gather their footlockers and personal gear. On his way back to the hangar with the navigational charts, Smiley heard a bugler blowing taps at one of the military installations near Ford Island. Knowing that he wasn't flying with the others, he felt even more melancholy at the mournful sound.

Inside the hangar, the frenetic activity continued. Surrounded by the noise of clanging metal, Ozzie Gaynier couldn't stop thinking about his wife, Rete. She would be celebrating her twenty-third birthday in two days. Restricted to the base, Ozzie hadn't been able to buy anything to send her. Sitting amid the clutter of machinery and personal gear, he sat down to write her a letter.

As preparations were completed on each plane, it was towed out of the hangar to the compass rose at the end of the runway. At the compass rose, it was jacked up and slowly swung around in a full circle to make sure the compasses were running true. With a thirteen-hundred-mile flight in the offing, this was one of the most important steps in the process.

Back in CASU-5, Smiley was helping the pilots stow their gear aboard the planes when Darrel Woodside, the only enlisted pilot in the flight, walked over to him. Darrel had grown up in Clearfield, Iowa, population one hundred seventy.

"I just wanted to explain about the ten dollars I owe you," he said.

When they had been flying the Avengers across the United States, bad weather had forced their flight down in North Carolina and they had ridden out the storm there. Several of the pilots, including Darrel, had run out of money, and he had borrowed ten dollars from Morgan.

"Don't worry about it," Smiley told him. "It's no big deal. Forget it."

Woodside shook his head and said that if anything happened to him, he had made arrangements with Red Doggett to cover it after the next payday. Doggett was another enlisted pilot in the squadron. He owed money to Darrel from when they were back in Norfolk.

"You'll get back," said Morgan, embarrassed.

"Sure," said Woodside. "But just in case."

They shook hands.

The Squire

All that day, it had been damp and chilly with a dingy gray sky above them and ghostly patches of fog that would suddenly envelop the ship before releasing it a few minutes later. Due to the bad weather, patrol flights had been canceled, and gunnery practice had been called off.

Aboard the *Hornet*, Steve Jurika was conducting another intelligence briefing, this one to all of the pilots in the air group, and the low-ceilinged wardroom was packed with men.

As he had briefed the squadron commanders earlier in the day, Jurika told them they would soon be confronting a huge Japanese striking force, with carriers, battleships, and dozens of other screening vessels. A separate enemy invasion force was also on its way, he told them, with more carriers and battleships and transports loaded with Japanese soldiers.

The *Hornet* wasn't alone. In addition to the *Yorktown* and the *Enterprise,* the carrier *Saratoga* was on its way from the West Coast to hopefully join the battle. In addition to the aircraft carriers, Midway Atoll was garrisoned with a group of Marine fighters and dive-bombers, along with a squadron of B-17s.

The next piece of news stunned the pilots of Torpedo Eight. Jurika announced that a detachment of new Grumman Avenger torpedo planes had arrived at Pearl Harbor, and some of them were being flown out to join the air garrison at Midway.

It had to be Swede Larsen's detachment of planes from Torpedo Eight.

Twenty-three-year-old William Robinson Evans Jr. sat among the pilots of Torpedo Eight in the smoke-filled wardroom with his usual studied air of nonchalance. In truth, he was often far away from them, living in his imagination, visualizing another line in a new poem or essay, seeing the words come alive through his writer's eyes.

The man his squadron mates called "the Squire" didn't think of himself as all that different from the others, but he was. Born into a Quaker family in Indianapolis, Indiana, on August 11, 1918, he was the youngest of the squadron pilots aboard the *Hornet*.

He was certainly the only one in the squadron, maybe in the whole *Hornet* air group, who had decided to become a Navy flier after reading a book. In 1940, he had been finishing his senior year at Wesleyan University in Connecticut when a friend lent him *Wind, Sand, and Stars* by Antoine de Saint-Exupéry. It recounted the French pilot's real-life adventures flying mail all over the world for Aéropostale in the 1930s.

To Bill Evans it was far more than an adventure story filled with accounts of near fatal crashes in the Andes and the Sahara Desert. It represented a soaring of the human spirit, for intertwined with these tales of danger and breathless beauty was Saint-Exupéry's almost mystical attitude toward the sea and sky, and his internal voyage of self-discovery to find his destiny.

"I, delivered, shall read my course in the stars," Saint-Exupéry had written.

It was the book that changed Bill Evans's life. For inextricably tied to his creative and intellectual gifts was a similar thirst for adventure. More than anything, Saint-Exupéry's book appealed to his restless soul.

In spite of his Quaker upbringing, Bill Evans was a pure romantic.

From conscientious Eagle Scout, he had matured into a young man who enjoyed close-hauling a sailboat in fierce storms and racing a well-engineered car. One of his annual thrills was attending the Indianapolis 500 race that took place a few miles from his home.

Behind Evans's calm facade and whimsical charm was an inner

intensity that drove him to explore the limits of his mind and body. He brought the same spirit to every challenge, whether it was skiing and sailing, or studying biology and poetry.

His roommate at Wesleyan, Charles Gillispie, believed that in some inexplicable way Evans was on a higher plane than the rest of the students, possessing a fine-grained visionary quality that set him apart. If this was true, he wasn't haughty or egotistical about it.

To Gillispie, Evans did not appear unusually patriotic either, although one incident suggested that he held deep convictions on the subject. It was after England had entered the war, and they were talking one night in their dorm room about Gillispie's friend Neil, who was a Scottish exchange student at Union College.

"How can he remain a student here while his country is at war?" Bill asked quietly.

After reading *Wind, Sand, and Stars*, Bill Evans's new goal became flying. Upon his graduation with honors from Wesleyan, he was accepted as a naval aviation cadet and underwent flight training in Jacksonville, Florida.

Flying high-speed aircraft turned out to be more exciting than any physical challenge he had ever undertaken. "There are few arts in this world more closely akin to communion with the gods than flying upwards to the morning sun," he wrote to a friend while at Jacksonville.

The pilots in Torpedo Eight knew Evans was different as soon as he joined the squadron in September 1941. At first, they weren't sure what to make of him. With his crew-cut hair and boyish face, he looked more like the product of an expensive New England prep school than a red-blooded pilot in the United States Navy.

Off duty, he often wore a tweed smoking jacket and two-toned saddleback shoes. When the others would head into Norfolk to try to pick up nurses, Evans usually stayed behind with his head stuck in a novel or a book of poetry.

The other pilots didn't need to romanticize flying. For them, it was something to be experienced, the sheer thrill of it, down to the core. Bill Evans felt that, too, but like Saint-Exupéry, his attachment to the sky was almost mystical, a spiritual thing.

The rest of the squadron soon learned that while he might have had the soul of a poet, Evans could fly as well as any man in the squadron. And like most of the others, he was a natural athlete, although his favorite sports were skiing and tennis rather than football and boxing.

As their training continued, he showed other strengths. In the seemingly endless classes Waldron conducted on technical flying issues, Evans's impromptu answers to his complicated questions usually came out like well-researched essays.

Waldron wasn't easily impressed, but Bill Evans impressed him, which was why he decided to make him the squadron's intelligence officer. Later on, Waldron would turn to him to settle any argument the men got into involving politics or history.

"Our Yale man will know the answer to that one," he would gently jibe him, well aware that Evans had gone to Wesleyan.

The other pilots finally came to the conclusion that Evans wasn't putting on airs. Hell, they decided, he probably didn't even know he was different. It was just the way he was. In a joshing mood, one of them had called him the Squire, and the name stuck. After that, he was accepted.

Aboard the *Hornet,* Evans spent a good part of his off-duty time writing in his personal journal. It wasn't a diary. He wrote on whatever was at hand, from the backs of envelopes and old stationery to colored index cards. He wrote poetry, letters, and his impressions of what took place around him. One sketch dealt with the death of a *Hornet* sailor and the funeral ceremony that took place on the hangar deck.

*Four destroyers, two heavy cruisers, and an aircraft carrier flew their ensigns at half-mast in tribute to one reserve apprentice seaman, symbolizing as effectively as anything I have yet seen, the tangible evidence that this nation holds the life of even its lowliest as worthy of tribute as the mighty. Where else in this world can such be so? Words speak poorly in trying to catch the mood of that last far journey across the horizon; even in our thoughts we cannot bridge the chasm which separates the mystery of life from the mystery to which we go. It is fitting that men and officers stand quietly in the sun, stand quietly while taps are*

*sounded, stand quietly as the smallest of boxes returns the unex-*
*plainable to the unexplainable. How fitting that man and his*
*creations take cognizance of these things in which they are so lit-*
*tle. Tomorrow or the next day it will be done again and then*
*again as from the beginning of time, as we return mystery to*
*mystery, and the wisdom of the sea accepts them all.*

When Waldron released the pilots from duty, one of the things
Evans enjoyed most was taking solitary walks around the ship, especially after dark. The *Hornet* was three football fields long and, belowdecks, he felt like he was plugged into the galvanic current of
some huge alien life force, the internal organic components of which
were never at rest. He wrote about his observations of the two-
thousand-member crew in their various jobs, with red-, green-, or
yellow-colored lamps in each passageway signifying the different
workstations.

He was struck by the obvious disparity between the lives of the
men he served with up in "officers' country," and the enlisted men
who were serving belowdecks. Exploring deep inside the ship, he
would watch teams of men with iron bars chipping endless coats of
paint off the rusting bulkheads. Down closer to the propeller screws,
he could feel the steel plates vibrating beneath his shoes as he walked
through massive sleeping compartments where the bunks were
stacked five high from the deck to the ceiling.

The smell of coffee usually drew him to the enlisted men's mess,
which never stopped dispensing food and drink to the men coming
on and off watch. While he and the other pilots tucked into a breakfast of steak and shirred eggs on monogrammed china in the officers' wardroom, the enlisted men ate their own fare of dry cereal
with watery powdered milk, or navy beans in ketchup sauce, on steel
trays.

He always finished his walks on the windswept flight deck. Standing there in the darkness, he could imagine the Japanese war fleet
coming inexorably toward them as it closed on Midway, narrowing
the distance with each passing hour.

Like his hero Saint-Exupéry, who had joined the French air force
to fight the German Luftwaffe, Bill Evans understood what was at

stake if the Allies lost the war. He had recently written to a professor from his Wesleyan days, summing up his thoughts.

*The Fates have been kind to me. In a war where any semblance of pleasure is, to say the least, bad taste, I find many things that would please you. When you hear others saying harsh things about American youth, know how wrong they all are.*

*So many times now that it has become commonplace, I've seen incidents that make me know that we are not soft or bitter; perhaps stupid at first, but never weak. The boys who brought nothing but contempt and indifference in college — who showed an apparent lack of responsibility — carry now the load with a pride no Spartan ever bettered.*

*Many of my friends are now dead. To a man, each died with a nonchalance that they would have denied was courage. They simply called it lack of fear, and forgot the triumph. If anything great or good is born of this war, it should not be valued in the colonies we may win or in the pages historians will attempt to write, but rather in the youth of our country, who never trained for war, rather almost never believed in war, but who have, from some hidden source, brought forth a gallantry which is homespun it is so real.*

*I say these things because I know you liked and understood boys, because I wanted you to know that they have not let you down. That out here, between a spaceless sea and sky, American youth has found itself and given itself so that at home the spark may catch, burst into flame and burn high. If the country takes these sacrifices with indifference it will be the cruelest ingratitude the world has ever known. . . .*

*My luck can't hold out much longer, but the flame goes on and on — that is important. Please give my best wishes to all of the family, and may all you do find favor in God's grace.*

*Bill*

Old Langdon

MONDAY, 1 JUNE 1942
LUKE FIELD
FORD ISLAND, PEARL HARBOR
CARRIER AIR SUPPORT UNIT (CASU-5)

Although he was only thirty-two years old, "Old Langdon" was the name many of the younger pilots used in referring to him, as in, "Man, there goes Old Langdon." It was said with a mixture of envy and admiration, both for Fieberling's leadership style and for the sophisticated way he led his personal life. Langdon Kellogg Fieberling was a polished ladies' man.

The other lieutenants called him "Count" or "Fieb." To Lieutenant DeWitt "Pete" Peterkin, he was just Lang. A 1937 graduate of Yale, Pete Peterkin was one of the ground officers responsible for supervising the dozens of enlisted men who maintained and repaired the squadron's aircraft. He had become Fieberling's closest friend in Torpedo Eight.

Already going gray at the temples of his thick brown hair, Fieberling drove a bright green, highly polished Lincoln Zephyr convertible. When he was off duty, there would usually be a good-looking young woman riding alongside him in the passenger seat. Tall and slender, he dressed impeccably in tailored gabardine uniforms.

More important to the men who served under him was the fact that his good-natured personality was almost the exact opposite of Swede Larsen's. There was no bravado in him at all. In the face of tough situations, he always seemed calm and self-contained.

Although a full lieutenant, he projected an attitude that no job in the Navy was beneath him. If he decided that a hangar needed to be swept, he might start doing it himself, only to find himself surrounded by pilots and enlisted men anxious to help him finish the job. Usually, he would only have to suggest that something needed to be done for one of his men to eagerly undertake the task.

Fieberling took his own share of abuse from Larsen, but always remained cool and seemingly unperturbed in the face of it. Without ever undermining Larsen's authority, he quietly urged the pilots to simply do their jobs until the whole squadron reconnected again under Commander Waldron on the *Hornet*.

On the Sunday night before their long flight to Midway Atoll, he worked alongside the others to prepare the planes in CASU-5. He had an ability to remember names and numbers, and used the gift as they went over the checklists to make sure that all the crews and aircraft were equipped with everything they needed.

At about midnight, he went around to each of the departing crews, urging the pilots and gunners to catch a few hours of sleep. Due to their nervous excitement, it came hard for all of them.

At 0600 on the first of June, he brought the five other pilots together in the small squadron office at the back of CASU-5. Lieutenant Jack Barnum, the flight officer, Smiley Morgan, the navigation officer, and Pete Peterkin, the engineer officer, joined them there.

None of the pilots in the squadron had any experience flying great distances over water, and Swede Larsen had arranged for two Navy pilots who flew long-range PBY patrol bombers to accompany the detachment on the flight. Patrol pilots received far more rigorous training in navigation, and they were going to serve as the navigators for the trip.

Aside from Ozzie Gaynier, who was twenty-seven, the pilots ranged in age from twenty-two to twenty-five. Vic Lewis was the youngest by just one day behind Charlie Brannon. Fieberling surveyed their solemn faces, keeping his eyes, voice, and manner calm and reassuring.

They would be making a pretty long hop across the Pacific, he told them. Someone had said it might be the longest formation flight ever attempted using single-engine aircraft. The distance was more than twelve hundred nautical miles, and the flight would take most of the day. They would be flying over open ocean all the way.

The other pilots were well aware of what the result would be if a crew had to ditch in the middle of the Pacific. With a battle approaching, the chance of a recovery ship being sent for them was practically nil.

Fieberling himself would lead the first element, with Bert Earnest on his left wing and Charlie Brannon on his right. Ozzie Gaynier would lead the second element, in right echelon behind Brannon, with Vic Lewis and Darrel Woodside on his wings. The two PBY pilots would fly in the flight leaders' planes.

There was to be radio silence all the way. No one knew how far their radios carried, and it was essential that the Japanese not be made aware of reinforcements being sent to garrison Midway. All communication would be made with hand signals.

If Fieberling knew anything about their future missions once they reached Midway, he didn't tell them. He asked if there were any questions. There weren't. Standing up, he wished them all good luck and said it was time to man their planes.

As the others grabbed their gear and headed out of the hangar, Fieberling motioned Pete Peterkin to remain behind. When they were alone, he grinned and said, "I'd like to ask you a favor, Pete."

"Anything," said Peterkin.

"If something happens to me out there, I was hoping you could visit Laura in San Francisco."

He left the rest of it unsaid. Peterkin knew exactly what he meant. On the morning the *Chaumont* had left San Francisco for Pearl Harbor, Fieberling had been standing at the railing between Smiley Morgan and Pete Peterkin as the ship passed Alcatraz Island and headed across the bay to the open sea.

Looking toward the Oakland Hills, Smiley could see the unusual bell tower at the University of California at Berkeley. He suddenly remembered that Lieutenant Fieberling had gone there.

"It will probably be a long time before I see her again," Fieberling had said wistfully.

Morgan thought he was referring to his college alma mater, but Pete Peterkin knew he was talking about Laura Cassidy, the girl Fieberling had just asked to marry him. Lang had told him the whole story the night before.

Fieberling said that he had always had a wild streak in him. After growing up in his parents' home on Wesley Avenue in Oakland Hills, he had met Laura in a class at Oakland High School. They dated until he left to attend Berkeley, and had continued going out together when Laura followed him there. It was clear to him that she wanted to get married, but he wasn't ready.

A star of the University of California rugby team, he had joined the Phi Delta Theta fraternity. Then he discovered fast girls and convertibles. Quitting college when his grades suffered, he had traveled around the country for two years working jobs at expensive resorts before eventually joining the Navy as an aviation cadet, earning his wings in 1937.

For the next five years he had lived for the moment, playing the field and sweeping it clean. Shortly before the squadron was set to fly to San Francisco, he had been amazed to learn through a mutual friend that Laura hadn't seriously dated anyone since he had left, and was apparently still waiting for him in the hope he would one day come back to her.

While flying across the country in his Avenger, Fieberling came to a horrible awakening. It was the stark awareness that he had wasted five years in casual love affairs, while passing up the real happiness he could have shared with the one woman who truly loved him. In the darkness of his cockpit, he realized that he loved her, too.

As soon as the squadron arrived in San Francisco, he borrowed a car at the Alameda Naval Air Station and drove straight to her home. Later that night, he proposed to her and she tearfully accepted him. They had three days together before the *Chaumont* departed. He had never been happier, he told Peterkin. His only regret was having let her down all of those years.

As they emerged from CASU-5, light was just beginning to seep over the roofs of the buildings on the eastern edge of Ford Island. In the coolness of dawn, the six blue-gray Avengers were lined up on one of the aprons next to the runway. The undersides of the wings and fuselages had been painted white. The planes were warmed up and ready to go.

A large group of men had assembled near the runway to watch the takeoff. The crowd included most of the squadron's mechanics, ordnancemen, and other ground personnel, who had worked all night to prepare the planes. The pilots who hadn't been chosen came, too.

Swede Larsen arrived in a jeep as the six flight crews were ready to board their planes. He was holding a stack of brightly colored decals that he had planned to cement to the fuselages of the planes.

Each decal showed a large closed fist. Underneath it in large block letters was the word "ATTACK." Now there wasn't time to mount them. Instead, Swede handed one to each pilot and shook his hand.

There's going to be a big battle out there, he told them. He wanted each man to remember the motto of the squadron when they got there. Thrusting his right arm forward, he raised his closed fist high into the air.

"ATTACK!" he shouted. "ATTACK . . . ATTACK!"

Bert Earnest and Charlie Brannon were standing nearby, barely managing to suppress their grins. Brannon was always a practical joker. Aside from Dorothy, his wife of two months, and flying, he didn't take anything seriously.

He had found a kindred spirit in Bert Earnest.

When Larsen's back was turned, the two of them silently brandished the salute that Larsen had just demonstrated. After raising their fists aloft, they simultaneously extended their middle fingers into the air.

The crews boarded the planes. At a signal from Fieberling, the pilots turned over the already warmed-up engines. He led them out onto the runway, and they took off in single file.

Smiley Morgan watched the planes as they slowly climbed into the sky over Ford Island and headed west toward the horizon. As he said a prayer for them, the growling pitch of the seventeen-hundred-horsepower Wright Cyclone engines slowly faded into the distance.

Tex

MONDAY, 1 JUNE 1942
NORTHEAST OF MIDWAY ATOLL
USS *HORNET*

The Skipper stood up from his cushioned chair in the front row of Ready Room Four and turned to face the seventeen other pilots in his squadron. His eyes were deadly serious, and his words conveyed the magnitude of what they were up against.

"They'll get here Wednesday or Thursday morning," he said. "I figure the odds to be about two and a half to one against us."

Tex Gay had listened to Lieutenant Jurika's briefing on Sunday when the intelligence officer had described the carriers, battleships, cruisers, and destroyers that were part of the huge Japanese striking force. Tex didn't like the sound of the odds then, either. And he didn't like the feeling they gave him in the pit of his stomach.

"Based on all the current dope," Waldron said, "we'll probably be making our first attack against the Jap fleet early in the morning. When we're finished, we'll all return to the carrier, refuel, and make a second attack later in the morning."

The Skipper told them that he was trying to persuade the air group commander to let him make another attack after dark. His idea was that the Japanese would be punch-drunk and reeling from the daylight assaults, and the squadron could get in close for more hits in the darkness.

"Get as much sack time as you can," he said, before adding, "and you might want to tidy up your personal affairs and write a letter home just in case some of us don't get back."

Not for the first time since the *Hornet* had sailed, Tex Gay had to silently wrestle with a truly repugnant thought. He wondered if he would turn yellow when the moment of truth arrived and he was face-to-face with the Japanese fighter planes.

The pressure of imminent battle was weighing heavily on him, and it was something he had to work hard to control. He wondered if the others were feeling it, too. From what he could see, the banter among them continued unabated, as if they didn't have a care in the world. One of the pilots, Whitey Moore, seemed to sleep right through it all.

Tex knew the strain had definitely gotten to some of them. Just hours before the *Hornet* had left Pearl Harbor for Midway, Eddie Fayle, a Torpedo Eight pilot from New Jersey who had grown up in France and was, of course, nicknamed "Frenchy," had gone out by himself into a pineapple field near their barracks. He came back with a deep wound in his right leg.

Frenchy's story was that he had been looking for a ripe pineapple and had accidentally fallen off a lava rock, driving the knife into his leg. Ensign Bill Evans had been the duty officer that day, and was a man who chose his words carefully. In the Torpedo Eight official log he wrote, "27 May 1942. Ens. Fayle received at his own hand a knife wound in his right leg. . . ."

Tex thought it was an accident. Frenchy did a lot of stupid things but he was no coward. Either way, Frenchy had to be left behind in the hospital when the *Hornet* departed the next morning.

*You might want to tidy up your personal affairs and write a letter home just in case some of us don't get back.*

It had never struck Tex Gay that he wouldn't get back. It might happen to one of the others, but not to him. He would get through. The lessons he had learned in life were to do your best in the face of whatever challenge came your way. He wasn't one to dwell on things over which he had no control.

He had been born in Waco, Texas, on March 8, 1917. His mother's people had arrived there by covered wagon. In the 1920s, his father built a good business in the Texas oil fields handling the legal end of leasing development sites to the independent drillers called "wildcatters." When his father's job forced them to move to Dallas, George had started his education at a private school. He was a typical young

Texan in almost every sense but one. Although it was unusual for Texas boys to take swimming lessons, his mother had insisted he learn how. He never found out why.

Tex experienced a life-changing event one summer when the family was attending the Texas State Fair. One of the oil companies had arranged to take people up on twenty-minute sightseeing flights in a Ford Tri-Motor airplane. He asked his parents to take him but they refused.

His grandmother was standing off to the side, and when she saw the boy's disappointment, she said, "Come on, son . . . I came here in a covered wagon and I'm not afraid of that thing."

Once in the air, the two of them had a ball. Soaring over the fairground was by far the most exhilarating thing George had ever done. As soon as they were back on the ground, he wanted to go back up again, but a long waiting line stretched across the field.

From then on, he wanted to fly a plane himself.

After the stock market crashed, the family faced hard times. The oil fields were shut down and his father was thrown out of work along with thousands of others. The boy helped the family make ends meet by working at a local drugstore for ten cents an hour. He started a paper route, eventually taking over four of them.

It wasn't enough, and the family had to split up. George's sister stayed with their parents, and he went to live with an aunt and uncle until his father found work again. Eventually, Tex saved enough money to attend the mechanical engineering school at Texas A & M, where he started in 1936. Hoping to fly airplanes, he joined the Reserve Officers' Training Corps.

He was forced to quit school three years later when his money ran out. By then, the war clouds over Europe were gathering again. Although his father was convinced that America would soon be in another war, he wanted his son to finish college. Tex made the case that he wanted to be a flier.

He took the physical for the Army Air Corps, but failed it. The Army doctor said he had an irregular heartbeat and wasn't suitable pilot material. However, a friend told him that the Navy was also looking for pilots. Surprisingly, he had no problem passing the Navy's physical exam and went on to earn his wings at Opa-Locka,

Florida. A month before Pearl Harbor, he was assigned to Torpedo Eight.

When Waldron wasn't running the squadron through their daily gauntlet of bounce drills and torpedo attack exercises, Tex had dated a lot of girls, mostly nurses. He was a roving and enthusiastic bachelor and enjoyed going out almost every night he was off duty. Some nights, he never had to go out at all. The girls came to the pilots.

After December 7, dashing Navy pilots became almost irresistible to the opposite sex. The opportunities were dazzling. By then, he was billeted in the new brick Bachelor Officers' Quarters at Breezy Point on the Norfolk Naval Base. Security was lax. On Sunday mornings, there would usually be several women at the breakfast table or in one of the shower rooms.

Now the fun was over. After thinking over the Skipper's words about tidying up his personal affairs, he decided that it would probably be bad luck to write a last letter home. Besides, if anything happened to him, his parents would be able to read the diary he had started just before the *Hornet* left for the Pacific.

None of his fellow pilots knew he was keeping one. Most of them wouldn't have believed it. Squire Evans sure, but not Tex Gay. Unlike the Squire, he had never done any serious writing in college. Or reading for that matter.

One day back in February, he had found an unused daily journal in a secondhand shop and suddenly felt compelled to begin writing a diary. Since the blank journal was from 1940, he had to change all the dates to correspond to 1942. Soon he was scribbling down his thoughts and impressions at the end of each day. He called it his log, just like the one the Navy provided for him to record all of his hours in the air.

With strict censorship of correspondence enforced after the *Hornet* left for the Pacific, the diary enabled him to write things the Navy never would have allowed him to send home in a letter. He decided to put his most candid thoughts in it, including his assessments of the Skipper, his fellow pilots, and many of the things they experienced together as the *Hornet* made its way out to the Pacific.

In April, he recorded his excitement at discovering that the ship was carrying sixteen Mitchell B-25 bombers, along with a full squadron of Army Air Force pilots and crews to fly them. He quickly realized he might soon be witnessing an important moment in history.

*Had a big powwow in the wardroom. Colonel Jimmy Doolittle read telegrams of good wishes from General Arnold, Admiral King, and President Roosevelt. Then he told us the target — TOKYO — Boy, oh Boy!!! . . . Things begin to make sense. Landing fields in China are already prepared, plans and dates set. . . . We even have subs lying in Japanese harbors giving us daily reports, and that calls for GUTS!!*

*April 18: Just east of Tokyo. We stood on the catwalks, the antiaircraft batteries, hanging from every spot to watch the planes prepare for takeoff. . . . The 2nd one stalled and almost settled in but they all made it.*

With tears running down his face, Tex watched as each bomber headed west toward Japan. For the first time, America was striking back. Soon, it would be their turn, and he hoped he was prepared.

As the days had passed, he wrote of his fervent hope that the squadron's obsolete Devastators would soon be replaced with the new Grumman TBF Avengers. He had even begun to construct a model of the TBF from a drawing he had found in the pilot's handbook.

The squadron's failure to receive them led to an angry entry in his diary.

*Sometimes I wonder what I am doing way out here. What really bugs me is being here with such poor equipment to work with while at home, a bunch of "supposed to be" Americans are kicking about a 40-hour work week. If we had TBFs, I don't know of a place in the world I would rather be than here with a chance to do our part.*

He continued to record any hint or rumor that suggested the Avengers might still be coming.

*The TBFs were in Dago [San Diego] not long ago. Hope we get them soon.*

And later in May:

*Still . . . don't have the TBFs. Wonder if we will ever get them.*

Now, as the *Hornet* drew ever closer to its rendezvous with the Japanese striking force off Midway, Tex knew they never would. Instead, they would have to fly the slow-moving Devastators and hope for the best.

In all of his months of training he had never actually launched a torpedo. In fact, he had never carried one in a plane. He had never even seen it done. They had been told that the Navy didn't have any to spare. Now, just like most of the others in the squadron, he would be carrying and launching one for the first time. In combat.

Sitting in the ready room, Tex remembered all the times the Skipper had ordered them to fly low across the Virginia panhandle, barely clearing hedgerows and scaring the hell out of herds of grazing Herefords, pretending that a tree line was a Japanese carrier, flat-hatting in so low on the bays and inlets that the long TBD propellers would sometimes slash the surface of the water.

Every day, some farmer or fisherman would call in to complain, but Waldron always ignored them. Going in low was exactly what his boys would have to do, just as low as their guts would allow them to. That's what it all came down to, thought Tex.

Guts.

He silently prayed he would have his share when the time came.

Bert and Harry

T he rubber tire streaks on the concrete runway swept past the Avenger's windscreen as the big plane rapidly picked up speed. Airborne, Bert Earnest glanced down to the right and glimpsed the shattered hulk of the *Arizona*. Off to his left, the *Utah* lay in its shallow grave on the north side of Ford Island.

As the flight of Avengers banked to the west, the thought suddenly struck him that he had never actually flown out of sight of land before. He wasn't really bothered by the notion. The thought of flying more than twelve hundred miles across the Pacific didn't concern him at all. It was a simple fact, like the powerful and reassuring roar of the radial engine in front of him.

He had less than ninety hours of flying time in the Avenger, and a solid portion of that had been logged flying across the country, but he knew the plane was good. He had no qualms about taking it into combat if that was what they were facing at Midway. She was the finest ship he had ever flown.

He moved smoothly into position off Fieberling's left wing. Charlie Brannon came up on the right. The flight leveled off at fifteen hundred feet, and Fieberling headed west on a compass heading of 270 degrees true. The rising brilliance of the morning sun transformed the dark gray sea ahead of them into a soft aqua green.

Bert's eyes swept the gauges on the instrument panel. Everything read normally. Inside the closed cockpit, the smells were all pleasingly familiar, from the hint of high-octane gas in the air to the pungent smell of hot metal. The plane was in perfect trim. He turned to look over at Charlie Brannon. The joker was grinning back at him. He gave him the thumbs-up.

He had no idea what was waiting for them out there, but after all the months of hard training he was finally on his way. He settled his behind onto the parachute pack, and leaned back against the molded backrest.

It seemed almost a lifetime ago that he had reported for duty to the squadron, but it had only been five months. After finishing flight school at Pensacola, his orders were to report to Norfolk, Virginia, on December 10, 1941.

He had decided to stop home in Richmond first, and was sitting with his date in the dining room of the Country Club of Virginia on Sunday, December 7, when someone called out from the men's bar that the Japanese had attacked Pearl Harbor.

After immediately driving the girl home, he rushed to the Navy department building in Richmond, telling the officer on duty that although he wasn't scheduled to report to his squadron for three more days, he was ready to pitch in if there was something they needed him to do right away.

The officer had grinned and said, "Ensign Earnest, it's my fervent hope that the Navy can survive without you for three more days."

He had trained under Waldron and Swede Larsen for almost six months. It was the most rigorous set of challenges he had ever undertaken, and he had survived them all. His fitness reports attested to the fact that he was one of the most naturally gifted pilots in the squadron, if not the *Hornet*'s air group. Even flying this brand-new airplane, he felt prepared for whatever might come.

The Avenger was almost flying itself now. His eyes found the twenty-four-hour clock on the instrument panel. They were already two hours out of Pearl Harbor. The adrenaline rush he had felt at the takeoff was slowly wearing off. That was when he realized that he had forgotten to bring the thermos he had filled with coffee just before the pilots' meeting in CASU-5. He wondered what the rest of the squadron was doing back at Pearl. They were probably being run ragged by Swede. He was glad to be on his way.

Soon, his thoughts wandered back home to Richmond, where

Bert was born on April Fool's Day, 1917. He had grown up on Kensington Avenue near the Old Soldiers' Home on the Boulevard. As a boy, he remembered, he often watched the last surviving Confederate soldiers as they dozed on the porch or rocked their chairs in the afternoon sun.

Although he had no great interest in his own rebel ancestry, his mother made sure he joined the Sons of Confederate Veterans. In high school, he developed a far more serious interest in jazz, and was one of a handful of white boys in the audience when Cab Calloway came to perform in Richmond. It was one of his most vivid memories.

In the late 1920s, the state capital was still a sleepy Southern town. Life moved slowly there, especially in the summer heat. Richmond society still rode to the hounds in pursuit of the fox. His father, James Earnest, was the chairman of the Country Club of Virginia. He kept a stable of horses and led many of the fox hunts.

Bert was in the same class at school as the son of Governor Byrd. He was an early reader, and partial to Tom Mix stories. A very good student, he skipped two grades before following his brother Jim to the Virginia Military Institute.

Sitting in the cockpit, he found himself wondering where his brother rats were at that very moment. His best friends from VMI were in the 17th Field Artillery. Flying was definitely more fun than lobbing artillery shells, he thought.

VMI had been great, all except the midnight curfew on Saturday night, after which their weekend dates would sometimes get stolen by the Washington and Lee boys who lived a mile down the road. He remembered one of his roommate's dates waving from the veranda of one of the W & L fraternity houses in a bathrobe as the VMI cadets marched by on their way to Sunday chapel services.

Not for the first time, he wondered why he had been one of the six pilots selected to go on the flight. Swede hadn't said a word to him about it. Was it because he was a good pilot or because Swede thought he was expendable? Hell, they were all good pilots. Every one of them had gone through the pressure of elimination training before joining the squadron.

Maybe he had been chosen because he had flown with Swede up

to the Quonset torpedo range in Rhode Island, and was one of the few men who had actually launched a torpedo. But Smiley Morgan had flown up there with them, too, and he hadn't been picked.

He thought about the two young crewmen flying with him in the plane. They were just kids, seventeen or eighteen. He didn't know either one of them very well. J. D. Manning, the eighteen-year-old who had been assigned as his turret gunner, was lean and strong. Harry Ferrier, the radioman-tail gunner from Springfield, Massachusetts, looked no more than fifteen. Bert might have flown with him back in Norfolk, but he couldn't remember for sure. Pilots rarely flew with the same crews more than once on practice missions.

The way the plane was configured, there was no way for him to visually check on the crew. But if there had been a problem, one of them would have spoken up on the plane's intercom.

He was feeling drowsy once more and unlatched the cockpit canopy, sliding it back far enough to feel a constant gust of cool air on his face. After using the piss tube to relieve himself, he took several sips of water from the canteen the plane captain had stowed near his feet. He hadn't thought to bring any food with him, and he found he was hungry.

When his eyes ranged over the instrument console again, they were drawn to the name he had scrawled in pencil next to one of the gauges. He had written it there in large crude letters just before they took off from Ford Island.

JERRY.

Jerry Jenkins. After meeting her at a party in Richmond, he thought he was probably in love with her. She was smart and beautiful, a combination he found incredibly attractive. Jerry was a very classy girl, a student at Smith College up in Massachusetts. She had promised to wait for him until he returned from the Pacific. When he did, he figured he would probably ask her to marry him. The thought that he might possibly be killed in the war never entered his mind.

He came from a military family. During the First World War, his father had enlisted in the Richmond Light Blues. One of his uncles had been a Navy aviator. His uncle Herb had served in the U.S. Cavalry. Coming back from France, Herb had decided to make the Army his career. He was now a brigade commander serving under a general named George Patton.

✪ ✪ ✪

BERT HAD WANTED to be a flier from the time he was ten years old. He remembered the rush of exhilaration he felt right after hearing the news on the radio that Charles Lindbergh had made it solo across the Atlantic. A few months before that, his father had taken him to see one of Lindbergh's famous daredevil rivals, Clarence Chamberlin, at the Richmond Airfield.

As the flight of Avengers continued on their compass heading, he wondered where Lieutenant Commander Waldron and the rest of Torpedo Eight was. The last scuttlebutt he had heard before leaving Ford Island was that the *Hornet* was probably guarding the northwest approaches to Pearl Harbor in case of another Japanese sneak attack. It was only through a twist of fate that he wasn't already with them.

Back in March, he had been told that he was one of the pilots who would be going with Commander Waldron when the *Hornet* left Norfolk. He had borrowed a footlocker and packed all of his personal gear in it for the long passage. It was already stowed aboard the carrier when at the last minute he was told that Hal Ellison, a married pilot from Buffalo, New York, was going in his place. He wasn't told why. At the time, he had felt only bitter disappointment. As the days passed, he got over it, especially after meeting Jerry Jenkins. But he had never found out the reason for the change.

The flight of Avengers passed through a low cloud bank and rain began spattering the windshield. He kept his speed steady until they broke out of the cloud cover a minute later. He checked the clock again. They were better than halfway there.

✪ ✪ ✪

FROM HIS CRAMPED position in the tail of Bert's plane, seventeen-year-old radioman-gunner Harry Ferrier had an unobstructed view through the rear gun port of the three planes following them.

Ensign Gaynier led the second element, with Darrel Woodside on his left and Vic Lewis to the right. Through the little porthole on the side of the fuselage, Harry could see Ensign Brannon's plane, too, although he was almost completely blind to everything unfolding ahead of them. Aside from monitoring the radio, the teenager had nothing to do for the entire flight. No one had broken radio silence.

They had flown across hundreds of miles of the Pacific, but Harry hadn't seen a single ship, airplane, or any other sign of human civilization. As hour after hour passed, it seemed as if they were the ancient mariners, the first men to explore this remote corner of the world.

The plane was a honey, the best one he had flown in since joining the Navy. Back at Pearl Harbor, one of the mechanics had told him it was the first Avenger to ever roll off the assembly line at the Grumman factory up on Long Island.

Since quitting high school to join the Navy, Harry had become a smoker, and he indulged his new habit while periodically checking his equipment to make sure it was functioning properly.

Occasionally, he looked up the passageway of the fuselage to where Jay Manning was sitting in his turret gun harness, facing forward. Unlike Harry, Jay had the best seat in the plane. He could see what was going on in every direction.

About eight hours into the flight, the throaty roar of the engine suddenly changed pitch, and he saw the three planes behind him shift into a single formation. That's when he knew they had arrived somewhere and were about to land. Harry craned his head around to the side porthole and gazed downward.

Staring into the glare of the afternoon sun, it was difficult to see anything on the surface of the dazzling sea. Then the tiny hump of a sandy beach suddenly materialized below him. It was Midway Atoll.

As they came in to land, Harry's eyes took in the landscape beyond the beach. It was flat and sandy, and there were no trees. The island was small, completely dwarfed by the vast expanse of deep blue ocean, but what he saw below the plane sent a thrill through him.

Wingtip to wingtip, the hardpan aprons along the two intersecting runways were crowded with combat planes. There were so many of them down there it seemed they would barely have room to land. In the moments before the plane touched down, Harry saw a huge B-17 Flying Fortress, a warplane he had only seen in photographs.

Taxiing off the runway, Bert came to a stop on one of the crushed coral parking aprons near the runway. The moist salty air was tinged with the reek of aviation gas as Harry climbed out of the tail compartment.

He was quickly surrounded by a crowd of naval officers, Marines, ordnancemen, mechanics, and other ground personnel. None of them had ever seen an Avenger before. One of the men joked that it looked like a pregnant Grumman Wildcat. Most were suitably impressed. Lieutenant Fieberling asked that the belly fuel tanks be removed from the planes as quickly as possible, and replaced with torpedoes.

As the ground personnel swarmed around the planes, the Avengers' air crews were left to fend for themselves. It didn't take more than ten minutes for Harry to learn why they had been sent out there.

The Japanese were coming. A big invasion force, with carriers and battleships, transports and shock troops, and a horde of attack planes. A few weeks earlier, Admiral Nimitz himself had come out to Midway to look things over. After that, everything had started to pop. This was it. Midway was where they would make a stand.

This astonishing news didn't frighten Harry. He knew his job, and he knew that their new Avengers were really good. He felt sure they would hold their own when the time came.

In the meantime, Harry was bombarded with questions about the latest scuttlebutt back at Pearl Harbor. The simple answer had to be repeated over and over. He had no idea what was going on.

Someone told him to take his personal gear over to a string of tents pitched near the perimeter of the airfield. It looked like a hobo jungle, with sagging canvas and crude lean-tos.

He and the other enlisted crewmen from the six Avengers were assigned two six-man tents. They moved their gear inside before heading off to explore the island. The first thing Harry wanted to see was one of those big new B-17s. They were the biggest planes in the Army Air Forces, with fifty-caliber machine guns sticking out all over the place. In addition to the Fortresses, there were four other Army planes, Martin B-26 Marauders that were supposed to be fast. Bigger than the Avengers, they carried a crew of seven, including three machine gunners. The ordnance men had jury-rigged each Marauder to carry a torpedo instead of bombs.

The B-26 crews seemed a little doubtful about their planes' ability to successfully launch a torpedo. They had arrived a few weeks earlier at Pearl Harbor with six planes, and the aircraft had turned out to be balky even without carrying a torpedo. Two of them had crashed while landing at Ford Island.

Aside from the planes, the first thing Harry noticed on the island was the horde of big, oddly shaped birds called gooneys. There were hundreds of them, comically trudging around the island on their oversized triangular feet, seemingly oblivious to their human visitors. The birds were so trusting that they rarely got out of the way of either men or machines. When they were being chased, the gooneys would always try to run in the direction of the wind, just as a carrier would turn into the wind before launching its planes. Using their sizable wing spread, the birds would catch the upwind breeze and rise slowly into the air before coasting down to a stop twenty yards away to resume their search for food.

Harry spent the rest of the afternoon walking around the island, which was alive in a whirlwind of activity. In addition to the 6th Marine Defense Battalion, a company of Carlson's Marine Raiders had arrived a few days earlier, and they were digging in to meet the expected Japanese attack.

Those men seemed to be everywhere, bare-chested and dangerous-looking, wearing bandoliers across their shoulders, digging slit trenches near the shoreline, and setting up defensive positions. One group near the shoreline was filling empty whiskey bottles with gasoline to make Molotov cocktails.

They had strung barbed wire everywhere along the beach, and most of the shore area had been laced with land mines. Machine gun nests were being set up to provide intersecting fields of fire at every point that Japanese assault troops might come ashore.

Standing next to the bronzed Marine Raiders, Harry Ferrier was well aware that he didn't cut quite so menacing a figure. In fact, he looked like a boy surrounded by grown men. As in truth, he was. He might well have been the youngest enlisted sailor or Marine on the whole island, for the date that appeared on his birth certificate and Navy enlistment papers had been doctored.

Harry's father had emigrated from Scotland, and had died when

Harry was thirteen. His insurance policy had lapsed and Harry was sent to live with a family friend. When his mother married again, he was allowed to return home. The new husband turned out to be an alcoholic. Divorcing him, she married again. The third husband was both a drunk and abusive.

Harry told his mother he wanted to join the Navy. At fifteen, he was still two years too young, even with her approval. Using a friend's typewriter, he changed the last number in his birth certificate and went down to the recruiting office to sign up. At his physical, the doctor told him he had hammertoes. Three days after his sixteenth birthday, the Navy took him anyway.

Just a hundred twenty pounds, he sometimes had to endure the nickname "Runt." Harry Ferrier might have been pint-size, but he was smart and worked hard. After recruit training, he had been assigned to radio school in Jacksonville, Florida, where he was a standout in his class and able to key more than twenty words per minute in Morse code. Assigned to Torpedo Squadron Eight, he had again been promoted to the rank of radioman third class. Now he was about to go to war.

After exploring the island, Harry joined Jay Manning back in their tent. Both of them were excited, and the two teenagers began to discuss what they could do to help defeat the Japanese invasion force.

Harry was the one who came up with the idea, and Jay agreed it was good. Heading over to their Avenger, they took several needed measurements before assembling what they needed. Using strips of masking tape, they made what hopefully looked like a set of individual machine gun ports along the front edges of both wings. After taping them into position, they painted big black circles in the center of each one.

The idea was that the Japanese fighter pilots would be so scared when they got close enough to see the full array of machine guns that they would take off. Standing back to admire their work, they agreed that it wouldn't stop the Japanese striking force, but one never knew. It just might save their lives.

Grant and Whitey

The typed message had come down to Ready Room Four from the bridge along with the Plan of the Day, which itemized the mundane daily routines and chores aboard ship, such as: "0800—VB-8 Squadron air bedding on forecastle."

The words of this typed message were neither routine nor mundane. They were electrifying. In the smoke-fogged room, Ensign Grant Teats listened to the message as it was read aloud by the Skipper.

> *AN ATTACK FOR THE PURPOSE OF CAPTURING MIDWAY ISLAND EXPECTED. THE ATTACKING FORCE MAY BE COMPOSED OF ALL COMBAT TYPES INCLUDING FOUR OR FIVE CARRIERS PLUS TRANSPORTS AND TRAIN VESSELS. IF PRESENCE OF TASK FORCES 16 AND 17 REMAINS UNKNOWN TO ENEMY WE SHOULD BE ABLE TO MAKE SURPRISE FLANK ATTACKS ON ENEMY CARRIERS FROM POSITIONS NORTHEAST OF MIDWAY. FURTHER OPERATIONS WILL BE BASED ON RESULT OF THESE ATTACKS DAMAGE INFLICTED BY MIDWAY FORCES AND INFORMATION ENEMY MOVEMENT. THE SUCCESSFUL CONCLUSION OF THE OPERATIONS NOW COMMENCING WILL BE OF GREAT VALUE TO OUR COUNTRY.*

Navy patrol planes were already searching the skies northwest of Midway in hopes of an early sighting of the Japanese striking force. The Japanese had scout planes, too, the Skipper told them, and there was always the chance they might find the American carriers first. Things could break loose at any time.

On the previous night, wild rumors had begun to course through the ship, passing from mouth to ear like a primitive telegraph system. The Japanese attack at Midway was just a diversion, according to one. The real invasion force had already slipped around Hawaii and was heading for San Francisco.

Most of the rumors were ludicrous, but one thing was sure. They would be in combat soon. Ensign Grant Teats knew he should be focused on his first mission against the Japanese striking force, but it was hard.

The reason it had become hard was a young woman named Diana. Grant had become unofficially engaged to her on the night before the *Hornet* had left Norfolk back in March.

The first letter Diana had written to him was cheerful and upbeat.

*Grant dear,*

*It's a beautiful spring day here — trees are beginning to bud and flowers and shrubs blooming — just too pretty to stay indoors. Mother and Dad came for a visit on Sunday. I told them everything and Mother said to tell you that if you are half as good as I say, you are the one. . . . No matter where you are or what you are doing, I love you Grant and pray for you every night. . . . Hurry home and love always,*

*Diana*

Now, as he sat in the squadron's ready room holding the letters he had received since, Grant looked like a heavyweight prizefighter who had just gone fifteen rounds with Joe Louis. He was still trying to decipher them, as if they were in some long-extinct language.

Whitey Moore, his roommate and closest friend, was the one

man in the squadron who knew why. In a way, Whitey felt responsible for everything that had happened. It was his girlfriend Betty Watkins who had arranged the blind date for Grant and Diana about a month before the *Hornet* sailed for the Pacific

Diana was twenty-two years old and from North Carolina. Like Betty, she was a student nurse at Norfolk Naval Hospital, and she had recently broken up with her boyfriend after a long-term relationship.

Grant liked her immediately. To start with, she was pretty, with long blond hair and a trim figure. But he had dated a lot of pretty girls before, and rarely asked them out a second time. Somehow, Diana seemed different. Part of it was her lilting Southern accent.

More important, she said she was an outdoors girl, telling him she had grown up as a tomboy, fishing and hunting with her father in the woods of North Carolina. She also had a way of making him laugh, which took his mind off the war.

He, Diana, Whitey, and Betty had had a great time that first night. Whitey was an incredible jitterbugger, the kind of fluid and acrobatic dancer who could twirl a small girl like Betty over his shoulder and pull her through his legs just like they did in the newsreels. At parties, other couples would often stop dancing just to watch them fly.

Grant wasn't an exceptional dancer, but he enjoyed it, and so did Diana. She quickly learned that Grant was different from the Navy fliers who seemed always on the make when it came to a pretty nurse. A raw-boned six-footer, he towered over Whitey, but his circus strongman physique belied a gentle nature and an unassuming personality. At first, it was hard for Diana to get him to talk about himself. It wasn't that he was shy. He just didn't feel he needed to prove himself in the company of others.

When the evening was over, he asked her out again for the following night and she accepted. From then on, they were together whenever their work schedules allowed it. Diana didn't wait for him to ask her to marry him. She proposed just two weeks after they met. She was honest in telling him about another young man she had fallen in love with before him, but said it had felt nothing like this.

He tried to explain why it wasn't the most prudent thing to do.

After all, they had known one another less than a month. He also told her the risks that went with marrying a Navy combat flier, and how he had watched five flight cadets die in accidents at Pensacola. He didn't mention that his mother frowned on wartime marriages, and had cautioned him about what to do if the situation arose. Any girl worth having would be willing to wait for him, she had written. "Grant, you must be sensible in these times."

But Grant had discovered there was nothing sensible about love.

Growing up in the forested magnificence of Sheridan, Oregon, he'd been taught by his parents to always do the right and honorable thing. Everything he had accomplished, from his exploits on the football field to the track records he set under Coach Doc Swan at Oregon State University, reflected a serious young man who worked hard to make his family proud of him. His love for his parents and his sister Charlotte was central to his life.

During the Depression, the Teats family had fallen on difficult times. It hadn't always been so. One of his great uncles was Commodore William Bainbridge, who had commanded Old Ironsides. Another ancestor had founded the town of Sheridan in 1866. When Grant was growing up there, his father had been a highly respected high school principal.

After retirement, Bert Teats had gone through a succession of jobs, eventually setting up a small insurance business at home. Grant's mother, Jennie Teats, helped make ends meet by opening a small café next to the Yamhill River. In high school, Grant would eat his supper there after coming back from football practice and before doing his homework. In the summers, he worked at the plywood mill or in one of the lumber camps.

It came as a shock to his parents when he first told them he wanted to fly. At the time, he had been a sophomore at Oregon State. A friend of his had joined the college flying program at an airfield near Corvallis, and Grant had become keen to try it himself. After finishing college, he went right into the Navy.

During his months of flight training, Grant wrote more than a hundred letters home, long optimistic ones full of vivid descriptions of snap rolls, spins, loops, and whip stalls. They made his parents feel they were right there with him in the cockpit as he learned to meet each new challenge. Writing paper was often scarce, and some of the letters were written on sheets of scrap, every inch filled with his narrow, cramped writing.

In many of them, he would include a money order to help them make ends meet. If he couldn't, he would apologize for not sending anything. A portion of the $62.50 he earned each month went straight home, as did most of his monthly poker winnings, which often exceeded his paycheck.

In addition to being a star athlete, Grant was good at games. At the age of twelve, he filled in at a bridge tournament attended by his parents. At the end of the evening, he had the highest score. He was even better at poker, playing conservatively but also having an instinctive sense of when to bluff. Over the months he served with Torpedo Eight, he was usually the biggest winner in the squadron.

Beneath the forbidding brow, he also had a dry sense of humor. One of the challenges the pilots faced aboard ship was sheer boredom. As they sat in the ready room one afternoon, he got up from his chair and walked to the front of the room. Turning to face the others, he said, "It has come to my attention that no one here is familiar with the process of making plywood. Let me enlighten you." He then began a lecture on the subject, speaking extemporaneously on the whole process from cutting down a tree to the final product. It was both illuminating and funny, and the rest of the pilots loved it.

Although gentle in nature, Grant sometimes had to work at controlling his temper. Officers who thought it might be amusing to intentionally mispronounce his last name as "Tits" never did it a second time.

When Swede Larsen singled him out for one of his public tirades back at Norfolk, Grant had almost lost control and decked him. Afterward, he wrote home to say that it had helped him to mentally picture Swede as the hind end of a horse.

On their last night in Norfolk, Grant and Whitey took the girls aboard the *Hornet* for a candlelight dinner in the wardroom. They wore their best uniforms, and the girls were on cloud nine.

When the *Hornet* arrived in San Francisco, Grant received the next batch of letters from Diana. The words almost sent him into a tailspin. She was supposed to finish her nursing training and wait for his return. Her thinking had obviously changed.

*Dearest Grant,*

*First of all, I might as well tell you I hate this hospital and everything that goes with it. I'll go crazy if I have to live through much more. We were so happy together those few weeks and to have it end with me here and you there. . . . Do you understand what I'm trying to tell you, Grant? Now that I'm living through these dark days, I must admit I am a coward and can't make it alone. What do you want me to do? I'll never finish nurse's training. I just can't.*

*Love, Diana*

How could he possibly be with her now? He was on his way to fight the Japanese. They were in the middle of a world war. He wrote back that it was just as hard for him, as well as the other fliers in the squadron who were married, engaged, or in love. They had to go on with their work and do their best. He said things were bound to get better when she no longer had to work nights. He received her reply when the *Hornet* arrived at Pearl Harbor.

*Dearest Grant,*

*I have a confession to make. Last night I went to the "O" Club with Bill Valentine. And I got plastered. A toast to the boys at sea, to the boys on shore, to our engagement, to Brownie's marriage, and oh so many others. And was I sick . . . Bill's opinion of me isn't much I'm sure. But that doesn't worry me. What do you think? Grant, it never would have happened if you had been there, I know. Scotch and water. I'll never touch it again until you return. I promise.*

Whitey told him not to put too much stock in the incident. Betty had written to him about it, too, and said that Diana hadn't done anything wrong. All of the wives and girlfriends were just going nuts with worry.

Anxious about Diana's emotional well-being, Grant fell back on his principal weakness, food. Already the biggest pilot aboard ship, he had put on ten pounds since they had left Norfolk, and the Skipper started ragging him that he wouldn't be able to fit in the cockpit. He didn't care.

He was able to write on May 28, the morning they left Pearl Harbor for Midway, assuring her that everything would be fine when he got back. He also took a minute to write a quick note to his parents in pencil. He wasn't sure where they were headed, and wrote, "Someplace . . . Somewhere. I'll do the best I can. Love, G."

One of Diana's letters came in the next mailbag the *Hornet* received.

*Grant darling:*

*I was thrown from my bike on my head and almost killed myself . . . and when I finally did come back to life my face was ruined I thought. The right side had lacerations upon lacerations and my right eye was closed. . . . I came out of the hospital yesterday afternoon. I don't feel like living. I want to see you so badly I just can't live much longer without you. No I can't. . . . But don't worry about me now Grant, 'cause I'll pull through some way. Do you still love me? Grant, if you have changed your mind, well I'll just end it all. It wouldn't be hard to do. . . . Be sweet darling, don't stop loving me.*

*All my love, Diana*

Grant wasn't the only pilot struggling with anxiety. With each successive clanging of the ship's bells to toll the passing hours, the nervous strain on the men grew into something almost physical. They dealt with it in different ways. Sitting in the cushioned seat next to Grant Teats, Whitey Moore dealt with it by sleeping.

His capacity for sleep had led Bill Evans to label him "the somnambulist" after a character in Saint-Exupéry's *Wind, Sand, and Stars*. It had also led to a wager among the other members of the squadron as to just how deep Whitey's slumber really was.

They had waited to test the issue until Grant Teats was gone. No one wanted to take a chance that the big man would react negatively to the wager they had made, even though he and Whitey were always ribbing each other. Whitey would loudly threaten to whip Grant if he didn't stop ragging him, but it was said in good humor.

When Teats left, the pilots gathered around Whitey's chair at the back of the ready room. As usual, he had a contented smile on his cherubic face, as if he was dreaming about a date he was on with Lana Turner.

Tex Gay was ready with a charcoal stick. Reaching around the back of the cushioned backrest, he drew a thick black mustache across Moore's upper lip. Whitey never moved. A few seconds later, Gay added a goatee. Whitey kept breathing with calm regularity.

That was when the Skipper arrived. Seeing the pilots clustered around Moore, he walked over to find out what was happening. Realizing what they had done, he began chewing them out as a bunch of idiots.

Whitey and Grant. They were definitely an odd couple. Mutt and Jeff. The biggest man in the squadron and the smallest. Grant had a beard like sandpaper. Whitey had blond hair the texture of goose down. Grant hated regimentation and chafed at the often petty rules that dictated their lives. Whitey could always roll with the punches.

Since the time they had begun rooming together at Norfolk, the two men had grown exceptionally close. For one thing, Grant was able to confide to Whitey his concerns about Diana. Whitey had had his own star-crossed relationship in the past.

The two men shared something else. They were both homesick. For Grant, it was a yearning for the ancient forests in Oregon, whose breathtaking beauty had a powerful hold on him. For Whitey, it was the mountains of West Virginia.

He loved to reminisce about his hometown of Bluefield, located a half mile up in the Appalachians. He missed its clear cold winter mornings. He missed steam engine 1203 as it thundered past on the Norfolk Southern main line under a full head of steam. He missed the hot dogs Gus Theodorou made for him down at the Dough Boy on Bluefield Avenue.

And he missed Catherine.

Bluefield was a railroad town, the place where the Norfolk Southern Railroad had built one of the largest roundhouses in the country. Three shifts a day serviced the gigantic coal-fired steam engines, each one with a five-man nomadic crew that rode them around the country.

The railroad workers needed a temporary place to live, and for many of them it was the YMCA, where Whitey's father, Lloyd E. Moore, was the manager. Kindhearted and gregarious, he spent the Depression years easing the hardships of railroad families. Growing up, Whitey was strongly influenced by his father's attitudes and values.

No one ever accused Whitey of having movie-star looks, but he was the most popular boy in his 1935 graduating class at Beaver High School, primarily because he always seemed to make things fun for the kids around him. He was only five foot six, and the girls thought he was cute as a button. They enjoyed mothering him and he seemed to enjoy it, too.

Physical and mental challenges came easy for him. Just about everything did except falling in love. That turned out to be the hardest thing he ever tried. On a break between classes during his second year at Bluefield Junior College, he had heard voices in the college theater and strolled inside. That's when he first saw her. Catherine Dunn was rehearsing for a school play. As if hypnotized, he walked down to the edge of the stage and stared up at her. He came to the next rehearsal, too. When he asked her for a date, she accepted.

Along with curly chestnut hair and a wholesome smile, Catherine was smart. Her father cherished the classics, and Shakespeare's plays were read aloud by the family after dinner. In some ways, she seemed too good to be true. Early on, she told Whitey she had never kissed a boy. He did his best to win her heart, taking her to hear the big bands that came to the Colonial Theater in Bluefield. One Saturday afternoon, he drove her to see a piece of land he was hoping to buy someday. The pastures were separated by rows of ancient stone fences, and looked out on magnificent mountain views.

When Whitey left Bluefield to attend West Virginia University, she would come up to Morgantown for football weekends and to attend his Kappa Alpha fraternity parties. The girls stayed together at a rooming house, and the boys would come to pick them up bearing gardenias.

After his graduation from WVU, Whitey joined the Navy. Returning on leave after flight training at Pensacola, he proudly showed Catherine his new gold wings. On the morning he left to go back, he asked her to wait for him, and she agreed.

When the Japanese attacked Pearl Harbor, all of their male friends enlisted in the service. And several months later, Catherine began dating an older man who was an executive at the local bank. The banker was in his thirties, and too old to be drafted. When he asked her to marry him, she said yes and wrote to tell Whitey the news.

Whitey knew he wasn't the first man to receive a Dear John letter, and he wouldn't be the last. At Norfolk, he met Betty Watkins, one of the nurses at the hospital. Betty was just over five feet tall and weighed a hundred pounds. He felt like Gary Cooper standing next to her. There were nightly parties at the Breezy Point BOQ, and as the liquor began to flow, it was a standing joke for one of the pilots to say, "Just give those two the cork. That's all they need to get tight."

He thought he was falling in love with her, and wrote home to tell his parents so. He was older now, and with the war on, there wasn't time for a storybook romance. When he and Grant shipped out, Betty said she would wait for him, too.

Ozzie and Rete

O swald "Ozzie" Gaynier had figured out the odds.

He knew the Midway garrison faced an uphill battle against the Japanese invasion force coming at them. Ozzie and the other Avenger pilots had been briefed by Langdon Fieberling after Fieberling's meeting with the Marine air group commander, Colonel Ira Kimes.

Secrecy was paramount to the success of Nimitz's ambush plan, and the forces on Midway were not informed that three American carriers would soon be rendezvousing only a few hundred miles to the northeast.

As far as Kimes knew, the combined Army-Navy-Marine air group at Midway, along with the 6th Marine Defense Battalion, was all that stood in the way of the Japanese fleet. Kimes said he believed that the American carriers were all back protecting the approaches to Pearl Harbor.

"We're alone," Fieberling told his pilots afterward. "The Japanese want these airfields. The planes we have on this island are everything we've got to stop them. Nothing else is coming."

Ozzie had already taken a careful look at the other aircraft in the garrison. Like the Avengers, some of the planes were really impressive, as good as anything the Army and Navy had in their arsenals. But aside from the Flying Fortresses, the four Marauders, and a handful of Wildcat fighters and Dauntless dive-bombers, the rest of the combat planes looked like they came from the boneyard.

Most of the fighters at Midway were Brewster Buffaloes. Six months earlier, the British had sent their Buffaloes up against the Japanese Zeroes over Singapore and Burma, and they had been slaughtered like their Great Plains namesakes.

Most of the dive-bombers were obsolete Vought Vindicators, with canvas fabric skins so decrepit that their fuselages were wrapped with four-inch-wide hospital adhesive tape to keep the peeling fabric in place. The Marine pilots who would be flying them were fresh from flight school, totally green. None of them had even seen a Vindicator before.

Ozzie had calculated their chances with the same calm logic he brought to every aspect of his life. Like the other pilots, he had seen a copy of the general order prepared for the defense of Midway's two islands by Lieutenant Colonel Harold D. Shannon, who commanded the Marine battalion that would attempt to repel the Japanese invasion.

> *Information available indicates that the Japanese plan an all-out attack on Midway with a view to its capture. This attack may start any hour now. . . . Our job is to hold Midway.*

If the Japanese planned to take the two islands, it meant they were bringing a substantial force of shock troops, presumably enough men to overwhelm the two thousand defenders dug in around him.

> *Our aviation forces have been strongly reinforced. As long as we keep our aircraft flying, they can work on hostile carriers, transports, and other surface craft.*

*Other surface craft.* That meant Japanese battleships and heavy cruisers, enough of them to protect their aircraft carriers, and enough to bombard the island's defenses to rubble if they won control of the air.

> *After the Japs figure that our Air Force is out and that defensive installations have been sufficiently weakened, they will*

*attempt a landing. This time they are coming to us and we have
the opportunity of a lifetime to reflect glory on our Corps. . . .*

*An opportunity of a lifetime.* That was one way of putting it. Some
of the words in Shannon's order sounded like those of Colonel William Travis at the Alamo. Or Custer at the Little Big Horn.

Ozzie Gaynier had grown up in Monroe, Michigan, the boyhood
home of General George Armstrong Custer. He passed Custer's
statue every day on his way to school. The trumpeting of glorious
deeds didn't go a long way with him.

The words were obviously meant to inspire the men, but Ozzie
hadn't found too many defenders at Midway who were out for glory.
The men he met went about their jobs with quiet determination and
an awareness that the Japanese had to be stopped.

To have a chance, the Midway air garrison would have to intercept the Japanese force before it got to Midway, take them by surprise, and inflict enough damage to make them turn back. If the
enemy carriers and battleships got through, there would be no way
to save the island, even with a couple thousand salty Marines defending it. Molotov cocktails and machine guns wouldn't stop a
carpet bombardment by battleships.

In most places, the island's water table was only three feet beneath the surface of the sand. There was no way to dig deep bunkers. After the Japanese battleships finished shelling the island with
fourteen-inch guns, there wouldn't be a lot of men left.

At the same time, Gaynier and the others knew they had to fight
with whatever weapons were available. And the battle had to be
really important if Admiral Nimitz had come out here himself to
look things over.

PBY patrol craft had been dispatched to the north and west in
hopes of spotting the Japanese advance ships as quickly as possible.
Toward dawn, the pilots would warm up their aircraft and wait in
the cockpits in case the Japanese arrived early.

At least it wasn't cold. Ozzie Gaynier had always hated the cold.

Back in Norfolk, Torpedo Eight had trained through one of the
harshest winters in local memory. At night they would do landing
practice drills with the cockpit canopies wide open. The constant

blast of frigid air had been brutal as he sat in the middle seat behind a succession of new pilots, flying around Monogram Field in the darkness, sometimes no more than fifty feet over the trees. Frozen to the bone, he knew that the green pilot in front of him was one small miscalculation from killing them both.

Growing up in Michigan, Ozzie had come to hate the winter. His father, Ezra Gaynier, was descended from French Canadians and seemed oblivious to it. The only part of Michigan winters Ozzie enjoyed was Christmas. There were eight children in the family, and Ozzie was the second oldest. Each year they would search the nearby woods for the perfect tree and decorate every room in the three-story house with fresh evergreen boughs.

The year before he started high school, he had bought a Santa costume with a large molded Santa mask. On Christmas Eve, he waited until bedtime to set up ladders against the two sides of the house where the kids slept in the second- and third-floor bedrooms. While the little ones were still awake in their beds, he surprised them by throwing open their window and tossing their bag of gifts inside. While they were still screaming with excitement, he ran around to the other side of the house and did the same thing for the others.

Though he finished high school, he hadn't taken to higher education. He lasted just one day as a freshman at Michigan State before going home again. Something about it didn't feel right.

After working for a year, he went back the next fall to try again. This time, he lasted three days, forfeiting the entire fall semester tuition of fifteen dollars. By then, he was twenty years old and bored with small-town life. The wanderlust was in him, and he left Monroe in the empty boxcar of a westbound freight train. For six months, he crisscrossed the West, working odd jobs and occasionally living in hobo jungles.

Remembering that one of his cousins had married a lumber baron in central Oregon, Ozzie hitchhiked up there and asked for a job. After several months of cutting down trees, he decided that an education might be more enjoyable after all.

He started at Michigan State again, and this time it took. An English major, he also became an intercollegiate track star, eventually breaking all of the Michigan records as a pole vaulter.

And then he met Rete.

There was definitely such a thing as love at first sight. He was living proof of it. With perfect symmetry, the tall, willowy blonde felt exactly the same way about him. Rete thought Ozzie seemed larger than life, as if he had already seen it all in his twenty-four years.

Rete had just started her sophomore year at college. The first dance that fall was at the Phi Delta house, and Ozzie asked her to dance. He had just won the college middleweight boxing championship, and looked like a man among boys. He walked her home from the party.

From that night on, she didn't date anyone else. A few weeks later, he told her he loved her, and took her home to Monroe to meet his family.

In his final year of school Ozzie decided to become a Navy pilot. By then, the war in Europe was raging, and he believed America would be drawn in soon. Accepted for flight training, he left for Pensacola in the summer of 1941. Rete had just started her junior year when Ozzie called her from Florida and said, "I want you here with me."

He told her that Navy regulations prohibited him from marrying her for two years, but they would get married as soon as it was legal to do so. In the meantime, he missed her too much to wait.

For Rete, it was an easy decision, although her sister Florence, who had been helping Rete with tuition bills, hit the roof. She angrily demanded that Rete finish her schooling before anything else.

"I'm going," said Rete.

Ozzie found her a studio apartment over a garage in Pensacola, but it was rare they were in it together. Training pilots were given few privileges. She saw him two nights out of every fourteen. Her days were spent working in the local dime store to help pay their bills.

When Ozzie won his wings, they were secretly married in front of a Miami justice of the peace. Rete couldn't afford a wedding dress. He wore his Navy blues, and she wore a navy-colored dress and matching hat.

On training missions, he would often fly over their little apartment house. Rete knew it was him because they had arranged a signal in which he would gun the engine three times in low pitch as he came over. She would come running out into the yard and wave up at him.

By the time Ozzie joined Torpedo Eight, the Navy had relaxed its ban on marriage, and Rete joined the small band of pilots' wives at Norfolk. Commander Waldron's wife, Adelaide, put her at ease from the start. Adelaide had a great sense of humor, and had seen just about everything. She was there for Rete with wise advice.

When Ozzie and the other pilots were ordered to fly the new Avengers to San Francisco, the wives followed, driving together to catch up to them before they left for the Pacific aboard the USS *Chaumont*.

On their last night together, Ozzie took Rete to Fisherman's Wharf, where they shared a candlelight dinner. When he left their hotel the next morning, she gave him one last hug, only breaking down after he was gone. A few hours later, there was a knock at the door of her room. When she opened it, Ozzie was standing there with a huge grin on his face.

"We're not sailing today," he said. "We've got one more night."

When the time came for their final parting, it was even harder than the previous one. With a reassuring smile, he said to her, "Don't worry, darling. I'll come back."

Now, at Midway, all he could do was wait. There was no way to predict the future, but if he had to cash in his chips, he honestly felt that he had enjoyed a good life.

Today was Rete's birthday. June 2. She was twenty-three years old.

Freddy

Although he had been part of the squadron for less than a week, Fred Mears was still lobbying the Skipper to let him fly with the others when they sprang the ambush on the Japanese fleet.

After arriving at Pearl Harbor in early May, he had been assigned to the torpedo squadron on the carrier USS *Lexington*. While he was enjoying a week of liberty in his suite at the Royal Hawaiian Hotel, a rumor began to spread that the "Lady Lex" had been torpedoed and sunk in the Coral Sea. It was true.

On May 27, a typewritten note arrived at the hotel ordering Fred to report immediately to Kaneohe Bay Naval Air Station. Putting on his uniform, he flagged a taxi and headed over to the duty office. At Kaneohe he was told to report to Commander John Waldron at Torpedo Squadron Eight, temporarily based at Ewa Field.

Through the grapevine, Fred had heard that a big battle was brewing in the Central Pacific. This might just be his ticket to the party. He hustled over to Ewa, only to be kept waiting along with other pilots who were hoping to join the squadron.

When he got in to see Waldron, the craggy old officer was brusquely polite. The truth was that Waldron didn't want him. Although Mears had flown plenty of hours in a Devastator, he had never actually landed one on a carrier. With the *Hornet*'s departure just hours away, Waldron told Mears there was no time for him to become carrier-qualified.

Fred promised Waldron that he would spend every waking hour aboard ship learning what he needed to know. The Skipper finally relented, signing his transfer papers.

True to his word, Mears had put his Yale-educated mind to work absorbing the tactical lessons in Waldron's "bible," spending hour after hour getting up to speed on things that had been drilled into most of the others over the course of six months.

To Mears, the pilots in Torpedo Eight were like a big boisterous family. It was also clear they did not yet view him as part of it. Occasionally, the Skipper would take a few minutes to test him on one of his tactical exercises. Fixed with Waldron's intimidating stare, Mears usually gave the right answer.

With twelve hours to go before the expected arrival of the enemy fleet, Fred was still waiting for Waldron to decide whether he could fly. Even though he had never landed on a carrier, he was sure he could do it. When it came to flying, he was convinced he could do anything.

At twenty-six, Fred Mears had faithfully pursued two passions in his young life. The first was flying combat aircraft, the faster and more maneuverable the better. He loved taking an airplane right to the edge. Danger was his ultimate high.

His second passion was women, and he could afford to indulge them both. Fred wasn't just any fly jockey. Frederick Mears III was born on Christmas Day 1915, to an influential society family in Seattle, Washington. "Old money," as the social arbiters used to say. His sisters called him Freddy.

Fred's father, Colonel Frederick Mears, was a brilliant engineering officer who had been chosen to oversee the construction of the Alaska Railroad across hundreds of miles of tundra and wilderness. He had created the city of Anchorage, Alaska.

His uncle was Lieutenant General Jonathan Wainwright, who had commanded all the American forces in the Philippines after President Roosevelt ordered General Douglas MacArthur to leave Corregidor. Less than a month earlier, Wainwright had been forced to surrender those forces, and had gone into Japanese captivity.

Fred had enjoyed a privileged childhood, growing up in an imposing home next to Lake Washington. His upbringing was focused on godliness, service, and intellectual attainment. When he went east to study at Yale, he was exposed to less righteous behavior.

Perhaps in reaction to the chaste piety enforced at home, Fred discovered that he adored the opposite sex. His passion had nothing to do with courting a life partner. He was entranced with the species. He loved their complexity, their perfumed scents, and their myriad moods. Along with his academic pursuits, he became a student of women. It became his metaphorical major at Yale.

"Anyone who doesn't appreciate the varied pleasures a woman adds to a man's existence," he wrote in his diary, "hasn't been without one very long or else is a damn fool." Fred conducted his alternative "studies" with debutantes in Seattle, feather dancers in Tijuana, Mexico, and lovely movie extras desperate for Hollywood stardom.

As the war drew closer, the love of flying supplanted his passion for women. He drove every plane as fast as possible, even the ones that weren't designed for speed. Although he exhibited the unrestrained temperament of a fighter pilot, the Navy put him into the slow-crawling Douglas Devastator. His response was to try to make the torpedo plane act like a fighter.

All in all, he loved the flier's life, discovering that he bonded just as easily with his fellow pilots as he had with his female friends. He enjoyed the camaraderie, the endless discussions of flying tactics, and their nights on the prowl together.

"It's going to be awfully drunk out the next few days," he wrote after receiving one weekend pass.

Sitting in a nightclub after the Pearl Harbor attack, he and three of his closest pals, all Navy pilots, had torn a dollar bill into four parts — one for each man. Each vowed to keep his piece as a lucky talisman. Now, less than six months later, two of the three others were already dead.

Fred was still waiting for Waldron's decision on whether he would fly, when the Skipper strode into the crowded ready room. He was carrying a stack of mimeographed pages. The banter suddenly ceased when Waldron began to pass out the sheets to the men sitting at the front of each row. Silently, they all read the single page.

*Just a word to let you know how I feel. We are all ready. We have had a very short time to train, and we have worked under the most severe difficulties. But we have truly done the best humanly possible. I actually believe that under these conditions, we are the best in the world. My greatest hope is that we encounter a favorable tactical situation, but if we don't and worst comes to worst, I want each of us to do his utmost to destroy our enemies. If there is only one plane left to make the final run-in, I want that man to go in and get a hit. May God be with us all. Good luck, happy landings, and give 'em hell.*

"Don't worry . . . we'll be back, Skipper," said Bill "Abbie" Abercrombie. "I'm leaving for Kansas City in the morning."

Abercrombie hated flying the slow-moving Devastators, but he had a knack for relieving tension with his irrepressible sense of humor. Once when they were lost on a training flight, he had radioed, "Any idea how far we are from Kansas City?" Kansas City was his hometown and his lodestar.

As the pilots got up to leave the ready room, Waldron walked over to Fred Mears.

"You're not going on the first strike," said the Skipper. Trying to soften the blow, he added, "Maybe the third or fourth mission."

Fred understood. Only if they took a few losses and were really desperate would he have a chance to see action. Maybe the Skipper was right. It was clear there would be plenty more battles to come.

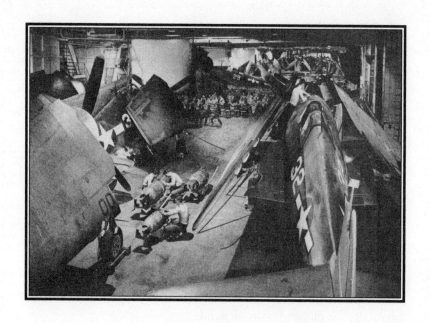

# Eventide

Most of Waldron's men were asleep in their berths, or at least making the effort. After a spirited poker game in Grant Teats's room, Abbie Abercrombie and Grant had ended up the big winners, as usual. Jimmy Owens had taken it on the chin. Whitey and the other players just enjoyed the ride. The bantering didn't seem any different than in the past, although when the game broke up, the players all shook hands.

In his stateroom, John Waldron removed a page of stationery from the drawer of his desk and began writing a letter to his wife, Adelaide. Most of the pilots hadn't taken his advice about writing home. Few, if any, thought they were marked for death.

At the age of forty-two, Waldron knew mortality was all too real. Death could come at any moment in the air, and he had narrowly escaped it at least six times since winning his wings back in 1927. Adelaide understood.

He had met Adelaide Wentworth at a Navy dance in Pensacola, her hometown. He immediately began courting her. They were married in 1929, the year the stock market crashed. His Navy career eventually took them all over the country. Along the way, they raised two daughters, Nancy and Anne.

Adelaide had provided a shield of unconditional love and support through the many lean years. She was the ideal Navy wife, uncomplaining about his long absences, and always ready to help the wives of his younger officers by employing a combination of humor and sympathy to support them during the same tough times she had experienced. Waldron knew she would understand everything he was about to write to her.

> *Dear Adelaide,*
>
> *There is not a bit of news that I can tell you now except that I am well. I have yours and the children's pictures here with me all the time and I think of you all most of the time.*
>
> *I believe that we will be in battle very soon. I wish we were there today. But, as we are up to the very eve of serious business, I wish to record to you that I am feeling fine. My own morale is excellent and from my continued observation of the squadron, their morale is excellent also. You may rest assured that I will go in with the expectation of coming back in good shape. If I do not come back, well, you and the little girls can know that this squadron struck for the highest objective in Naval warfare — to sink the enemy. . . .*
>
> *I love you and the children very dearly and I long to be with you. But, I could not be happy ashore at this time. My place is here with the fight. I could not be happy otherwise. I know you wish me luck and I believe I will have it.*
>
> *You know, Adelaide, in this business of the torpedo attack, I acknowledge we must have a break. I believe that I have the experience and enough Sioux in me to profit by and recognize the break when it comes, and it will come.*
>
> *I dislike having the censors read a letter from me such as this, however, at this time I felt I must record the thoughts listed in the foregoing.*
>
> *God bless you, dear. You are a wonderful wife and mother. Kiss and love the little girls for me and be of good cheer.*
>
> *Love to all from Daddy and Johnny*

*I acknowledge we must have a break.* He had been fighting for one most of that day. For the last three days. It was fighter protection. That would be the biggest break they could possibly have, and he wasn't through trying to get it.

Earlier that day, the pilot of a PBY patrol plane had radioed that he had spotted elements of a Japanese naval task force about seven hundred miles west of Midway. That report was quickly followed by a coded dispatch from Admiral Nimitz in Pearl Harbor that indicated he already knew it wasn't the Japanese striking force.

> *FROM CINCPAC URGENT X THAT IS NOT THE EN-EMY STRIKING FORCE X THAT IS THE LANDING FORCE X THE STRIKING FORCE WILL HIT FROM THE NORTH-WEST AT DAYLIGHT TOMORROW X*

By then, it was clear to Waldron that the intelligence people had broken the Japanese code. Later in the day, there had been another conference in the wardroom. All the squadron commanders were there with Stanhope Ring and the air staff. Waldron made his case again for giving his torpedo squadron fighter protection. He believed the Devastators needed at least one or two Wildcats to keep the Zeroes off them long enough to get rid of their torpedoes.

Waldron urged Ring to follow the approach used by Admiral Fletcher's carriers at the Coral Sea a month earlier, when half of the fighters went in low with the torpedo planes, and half stayed up high with the dive-bombers. Pat Mitchell, who commanded the *Hornet*'s Wildcat fighter squadron, continued to back Waldron all the way.

Pete Mitscher, who had been promoted from captain of the *Hornet* to admiral two days earlier, made the final decision. All ten of the *Hornet*'s Wildcat fighter planes would stay up to protect Ring and the dive-bombers. Waldron's squadron would stay in tight formation, but twenty thousand feet below the others. The entire air group would attack together when they found the Japanese.

Mitscher was convinced the Japanese would be keeping their Zero fighters at higher altitude, and would therefore focus their attacks on the dive-bombers. He made another point. At the Coral Sea battle, the Zeroes had proved faster and more maneuverable than the Wildcats. At higher altitude, the Wildcats would have more maneuvering room.

Waldron couldn't believe it. If the Wildcats couldn't duel with the Zeroes at low altitude, what chance would his Devastators have at less than half the Wildcats' speed, and particularly if they got caught alone?

The fight was over. Now he could only follow orders. Back in his stateroom, Waldron finished his letter to Adelaide, and began another one to his young daughter Anne.

In the Torpedo Eight ready room, Tex Gay was wrapping up his last assignment. As the squadron's navigation officer, one of his jobs was to make sure every pilot had a mimeographed copy of the charts covering the expected area of operations. Completing the chore, he went back to his stateroom.

Bill Creamer, his roommate, was sacked out in the upper berth. The stateroom desk was covered with their two latest projects. Creamer was carving a bowl out of koa wood. Tex's unfinished model of the new TBF Avenger sat next to it. Clearing the mess away, he sat down to write an entry in his daily diary.

> *June 3: Everybody is standing by ready. I have checked my plane until I know every bolt on it. It's in the pink. I hope I can get about forty-five inches of mercury out of it. I may need it. Got some spare rounds for Huntington and had Watson put the other 350 rounds in my fixed peashooter. Things are oiled and ready.*

In another squadron stateroom, Rusty Kenyon decided to take the Skipper's advice and write a letter home. Ever since the *Hornet* left Pearl Harbor, he had seemed increasingly nervous to some of the other pilots. They didn't know that his wife, Brownie, was about to give birth to their first child. When he was finished with the letter to her, he sealed it in an envelope.

Grant Teats had already written one to his parents. Upbeat and sensible, it took a different tone from some of the others. There was no hint of concern about his immediate future, only a quick squaring away of his affairs.

> *All my bills, every one, is paid . . . income tax, gas, insurance, O-club, are all paid. My bank account is located at Southern bank of Norfolk. . . . Enclosed you will find a check that will help out with incidentals. I was lucky in poker last night. . . . My*

*civilian clothes are packed in a large box belonging to Whitey
Moore. I guess this is about all. If I had a drink now it would be
a toast to the Japanese navy. Bottoms up. Write soon.*

*Love, Grant.*

At least one other pilot in the squadron was still awake, too.

Bill Evans had been busy organizing all of the material he had
written since starting flight training before Pearl Harbor: copies of
his letters, his poems, the whimsical sketches, everything. It made
up a thick packet, and he thought some of it was good. Finding a
mimeographed copy of an old *Hornet* Plan of the Day, he scrawled a
line on the back and placed it on top of the pile.

*Respectfully dedicated to those of the confused generation
who, being born during a world war, were taught that Peace was
the only touchstone to man's happiness; and fought another war
to make it so.*

He had finished his latest poem. He usually continued to make
changes to his work as he thought of more evocative words and
phrases. This time he decided to leave it alone. The essence of it was
there in a few of the lines from the longer poem.

## TRANSITION

*To this day have been given in perfect normalcy
Twenty-four hours, a sunrise, sunset, starlight,
Waking hours and sleep.
In all respects men walk quietly, speak as usual,
Draw breath with the same regularity that for every
Minute they have always breathed.
Magazines, poker games, and phonograph records;
Someone whistles "Stardust" because years ago
He learned to like a song and now
Its melody stays with him forever.*

*For this is forever.*
*In the past twenty-four hours,*
*All are facing for the first time,*
*Despite statements of a few to the contrary,*
*The magnitude of war . . .*

*Ahead, just beyond each wave that greets the bow,*
*A new life begins, newer than any*
*Can by the coldness of intellect imagine.*
*A life where nations play at gambling*
*For the World,*
*And each player antes its life blood.*

*Yesterday we were veterans of all the life behind,*
*Today some giant hand wipes clean the slate*
*And each is born in equal magnificence,*
*From which he may build or destroy himself . . .*

WEDNESDAY, 3 JUNE 1942
EASTERN ISLAND, MIDWAY ATOLL
TORPEDO EIGHT DETACHMENT
2200

Although he craved a few hours of sleep, Langdon Fieberling decided to walk over to the enlisted men's encampment. Arriving there, he asked the chief to bring together the enlisted crewmen who would be flying in the morning.

Up to that point, everything that Harry Ferrier had learned about their mission was through the rumor mill. That was enough to make some of the other men pretty apprehensive about their chances.

If Fieberling shared their assessment, it wasn't reflected in his words now. Standing tall in the darkness, he sought to put them at ease, his voice calm and reassuring.

Harry thought the lieutenant could almost walk on water. Not only was he a great pilot, but he was one of the few officers Harry had met who treated him as if his opinion had real value. Just a day earlier, Fieberling had confidentially asked Harry whether one of the enlisted men, Howard Pitt, was capable of fulfilling his duties as the radioman–tail gunner in Ozzie Gaynier's aircraft. Harry assured him Pitt would do a good job. The lieutenant accepted his advice.

Fieberling now told them that the enemy would arrive after dawn the next morning. As far as he knew, the forces they had on the island were everything there was to stop them. According to the briefing he had received, the American carriers were back protecting Hawaii.

"I would just ask you to do your jobs, and we ought to come out all right," he said.

As he talked, his confident attitude seemed to infuse itself into the little group. Harry could feel it, too. Tomorrow, he would be ready for whatever they came up against.

Across the encampment, Ozzie Gaynier was finishing a last letter to Rete. If anything did happen to him, he wanted her to know just how much she meant to him. He sealed it and buried the letter with the others he had written in one of the metal ammo boxes near his tent.

All of the men in the air squadrons had been told to bury their valuables. In the event the Japanese took the island, there was to be no evidence of which American units had been there.

◆ ◆ ◆

SITTING NEARBY, Ensign Vic Lewis tried not to dwell on what might happen to them at dawn. Like Gaynier and the others, he hoped to do his best, no matter what the risk. For most of his life, he had not been a risk-taker.

In some ways, Vic was like the innocent and determined young Jimmy Stewart in the movie *Mr. Smith Goes to Washington*. He was so earnest and polite that his mother would sometimes say, "Gee, I hope he has fun sometimes."

To earn the money he needed for college, Vic worked at the Howard Johnson's near his Randolph, Massachusetts, home, wearing a white shirt and tie, and washing dishes. After his ten-hour shift, he loved to cool off by going for a swim at a local pond.

There had been an accidental drowning death there a few years earlier, but most people had forgotten it. Not Vic. While other boys would plunge into the water and swim straight across, he would cautiously swim around the edge of the pond.

Few things could stop him when he set his mind to something. One Christmas Eve, the unplowed snow in Randolph was four feet high on the streets. Vic skied to the Episcopal church for the evening service, standing the skis up in the snow outside the door. He was one of the few people who made it.

Vic was raised on the virtues of tolerance and open-mindedness. His father, Maurice, was Jewish, and a traveling salesman for American Safety Razors. His mother, Serena, was Swedish Protestant.

Vic met Anna McGrory at Stetson High School, and they liked one another immediately. When they began dating, Anna's parents were less than thrilled with the match. Strict Catholics, they did not countenance her possible marriage to an Episcopalian, much less one whose father was a Jew. Yet they couldn't help but like him.

Vic and Anna continued dating all through college. In spite of her parents' objections to marriage, the two agreed they would work it out somehow in the future.

Flying had always intrigued Vic, but it seemed to go against his cautious nature when he announced to the family in January 1941 that he had applied to join the Navy flight program. During flight training, he was judged to be a good pilot, but one who always flew by the book.

After Vic had been assigned to Torpedo Eight at Norfolk, an incident occurred that changed his outlook on life. He was flying a training mission in an old Devastator. The plane had rubber flotation devices installed inside each wing so that if the plane was forced to ditch in the ocean, the flotation bags would automatically inflate and keep the aircraft on the surface long enough for the crew to escape.

The training mission called for Vic to drop twelve one-hundred-pound bombs on a practice target. His takeoff from Norfolk's East Field was routine, but as they climbed out over the sea, the plane began to yaw wildly to port. Machinist's Mate Bill Tunstall, who was riding in the middle seat, called out to Vic on the intercom that one of the flotation devices had burst free from its compartment and inflated.

Without hesitating, Vic kicked hard on the left rudder and dove toward nearby Chambers Field. As they came in for an emergency landing, Tunstall saw that a high sea wall protected the runway from the sea. Getting over it was going to be close. The unstable plane cleared the seawall by inches.

When the Devastator dropped to the runway, one wing slammed into the tarmac, dislodging the bombs from their racks as the plane skidded to a stop just short of several parked aircraft. After climbing down from the cockpit, Vic glanced around at the scattered bombs.

"Well, I'll be damned," he said.

Bill Tunstall and the other crewman came over to thank him for saving their lives. From that day on, Vic Lewis was no longer the young man who swam around the edge of the pond.

✪  ✪  ✪

ON THE OTHER SIDE of the Midway encampment, someone told Bert Earnest that they were selling beer over at the Marine supply shack. Before turning in, he and Charlie Brannon decided to find out.

The little ramshackle structure was nothing more than framing timbers covered with plywood. It was lit by two naked lightbulbs hanging from coated wire. Inside, Brannon's head almost brushed the ceiling.

A group of Marines were standing at a wooden slab countertop. Behind the counter were shelves with standard issue personal items like toothpowder, soap, razor blades, and socks. Several cases of warm beer were stacked along the back wall.

Right then, even warm beer looked good to Bert and Charlie.

"Two beers," said Bert.

"You got to have chits . . . sir," said the flat-nosed Marine behind the counter.

"I've got cash," said Bert. "Isn't that good enough?"

"I can't sell you beer without chits . . . sir," said the Marine.

"What is a chit?" asked Charlie.

Bert shook his head at the absurdity of it all. Here they were out in the middle of the Pacific Ocean, a thousand miles from nowhere and about to go into battle, and some young jarhead was giving him this bullshit.

"You got to buy a chit . . . sir," repeated the storekeeper. "Then I can give you a beer."

Bert glanced around at the other Marines. These boys weren't pilots. They had to be part of the defense battalion, Carlson's Raiders from the look of them. He realized this was probably their way of giving the Navy pilots a rib. In the Navy, the standing joke about a typical Marine's social ambitions consisted of getting "screwed, brewed, and tattooed."

He had no idea how much each chit was worth. Pulling out his wallet, he said, "Give me five bucks' worth."

The Marine counted out an inch-thick stack of coupons and handed them over.

"A beer costs one chit," he said.

Heading back outside, the two young pilots stood in the darkness and took their first sip of beer. It smelled like warm piss.

"It's a long way from the Top of the Mark," said Charlie.

On their last night in San Francisco, the two of them had gone to the Top of the Mark on Nob Hill, the traditional farewell spot for Navy officers heading overseas. After sipping ice-cold cocktails and watching the sun go down over the Golden Gate Bridge, they were about to go back to the ship when a group of businessmen came in. One of them struck up a conversation. After learning that the two pilots were shipping out in the morning, he offered to take them to a private nightclub in the city. It was called Cat's Eyes, he said.

When they got there, Bert and Charlie understood why. Tucked away in a discreet apartment building, the place was filled with high-class hookers. Although they were both offered the free services of one of the girls as a parting gift, Charlie laughed and said the offer had come a little too late. He had just gotten married, and Dorothy wouldn't approve. Bert added that he wasn't planning to do anything he couldn't tell his mother about, at least not yet. After watching the action for a while, they reported back to the *Chaumont*.

As they finished their beers outside the Marine shack, Charlie talked about Dorothy, and how she had given new meaning and importance to his life. Until he met her, he had had no idea what to do with his life when the war was over. Now he knew. He planned to go into business with his father in Montgomery, just as the old man had always hoped. Although they had only been married for two months, he hoped Dorothy was pregnant.

Bert still had no idea what he wanted to do. Jerry Jenkins said she would wait for him, but he didn't think he felt the same way about her that Charlie felt about Dorothy.

After deciding that one warm beer was enough for them, the two friends split up to go back to their bunks.

Charlie was sleeping in a tent with two other Avenger pilots. Bert had been invited to sleep on a real mattress in one of the permanent ready huts shared by Marine fighter pilots near the field.

He was walking along the edge of the runway under the pale moon when he happened to look down and saw what looked like a dollar bill lying on the surface of the hard-packed coral. He stopped and leaned down to pick it up.

Looking more closely, he saw it was actually a two-dollar bill. He had never seen one before. They sure didn't make very many. Maybe it was a good omen. Folding it up, he put the bill in his wallet.

# He That Shall Live

# This Day and See Old Age

**THURSDAY, 4 JUNE 1942**
**USS _HORNET_**
**TORPEDO SQUADRON EIGHT**
**0130\***

T
ex Gay awoke to the stabbing beam of a flashlight aimed into his eyes.

"Reveille, sir," came a disembodied voice from the darkness.

Through the open doorway, he could hear the other pilots being wakened all along the passageway. Sitting up, he realized he hadn't taken off his uniform before climbing into the bunk. Bill Creamer was getting out of the upper berth as Tex went down to the head to wash.

Most of the pilots were still groggy from interrupted sleep when they began trudging down to the ready room. A few detoured to the _Hornet_'s wardroom to revive themselves with a cup of coffee from the big urn near the door.

Once they were all there, no one seemed to have much to say. The big square reflector screen over the Teletype machine at the front of the room remained dark. They knew the Teletype keys would start chattering as soon as anything important happened. In the meantime, all they could do was wait. Whitey Moore immediately reclined the backrest of his chair and went to sleep again.

---

\*To integrate the complex action of the events that took place on the morning of June 4, 1942, the author chose to synthesize the time differences between the Japanese and American forces, and used local Midway time (Greenwich Zone + 12) for all of the forces concerned.

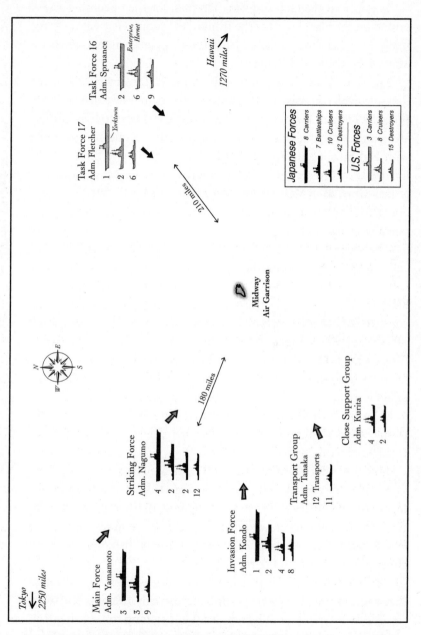

**JAPANESE AND U.S. FORCE DISPOSITIONS, JUNE 4, 1942**

Tex noticed the tactical formation plan for the upcoming attack posted on the blackboard at the front of the room. He went up to see if anything had been updated from the Skipper's original orders on May 28. Nothing had changed.

They would be flying in two divisions. Waldron would lead the first one, which consisted of eight Devastators in four two-plane sections. Lieutenant Raymond "Moose" Moore was next to him. Bill Evans would be flying behind the Skipper in the second section along with Hal Ellison. Lieutenant Jeff Davis Woodson and Bill Creamer formed the third section. Whitey Moore was in the last section, next to Jack Gray, a big Missourian with a fondness for Richard Wagner's operas. He often tortured his roommates by playing them on his portable phonograph.

The second division, seven planes, would be led by Jimmy Owens. Rusty Kenyon would be flying on Owens's wing, followed by George Campbell and Bob Miles, the tall, taciturn enlisted pilot who had been chosen to replace Frenchy Fayle. The third and last section consisted of Abbie Abercrombie, Grant Teats, and Tex. As navigation officer, Tex was bringing up the rear so he wouldn't have to waste time trying to stay in formation as he consulted his charts.

Tex felt calm, almost relaxed. Across the warm room, some of the pilots were talking in low voices about how close the *Hornet* needed to be to the Japanese fleet before an attack could be launched. Tex wasn't worried about it. Thankfully, that decision rested with the wise men up on the bridge.

Like the others, he knew their PBY patrol planes were spread out for hundreds of miles to the northwest of Midway searching for the Japanese striking force. When it was sighted, the Teletype keys at the front of the ready room would start clacking like mad. Having had less than three hours' sleep, he dropped into his cushioned chair, reclined the backrest, and dozed off.

Tex woke again to the sound of raised voices, and the realization that a few of the pilots were getting increasingly restless. Where are the goddam Japanese? Why was it taking so long to find them? At 0300, Jimmy Owens stood up and announced that they could go down to the wardroom for breakfast in groups of two or three.

EASTERN ISLAND, MIDWAY ATOLL
TORPEDO EIGHT DETACHMENT
0335

Bert came awake in his bunk to the rumbling blast of radial aircraft engines. Lying there in the hut, he decided they must be the B-17 Flying Fortresses warming up in their revetments across the airfield.

A few minutes later, he heard the Marine pilots getting up from their bunks and putting on their flight suits. Bert followed them out into the darkness. Checking his watch, he saw that it was almost 0400, about a half hour before dawn. The sky was full of stars. There was a light breeze coming off the sea.

While the Marine pilots headed over to the mess tent to grab some coffee, Bert decided to go straight to his Avenger. Although he hadn't eaten anything since the previous evening, he wasn't hungry or thirsty. When he got to the plane, Harry Ferrier and J. D. Manning were doing last checks on their weapons and equipment.

After carrying out his own preflight routine, Bert climbed up into the cockpit. Turning on his instrument lights, he went through the same steps he had automatically performed hundreds of times since leaving flight school, setting the fuel selector, confirming that the altimeter and the elevator tab were set on zero, adjusting the rudder tabs, moving the rudder with his feet, feeling the ailerons respond to the control stick in his right hand. Everything felt right.

When he was ready, he fired the engine, checking to make sure the oil pressure came straight up to its normal gauge setting, then feeling the familiar set of vibrations as the engine slowly began to steady. In the starlight, he could distinguish the outline of the Avenger ahead of his on the flight apron as its crew went through the same routines.

On one of the three runways, a B-17 was revving its engines in final preparation for takeoff. Letting go of the brakes, the giant bomber slowly gathered speed until it took off and disappeared into the dark sky. It was quickly followed by another one, and still another, until sixteen of them were gone.

Bert glanced at his watch again in the glow of the instrument lights. 0415. When it was obvious his engine was warm, he cut the power, and settled back in the cockpit to wait. One by one the rest of the Avenger pilots shut down their engines until things were quiet again. They would take off as soon as the Japanese striking force was spotted.

In the cockpit of the last plane, Darrel Woodside settled back, too. He was the only enlisted pilot flying in the detachment, and Darrel had mostly kept to himself since they arrived on the island, checking and rechecking all of the systems and equipment on his plane.

Until a year earlier, he had been a machinist's mate, just like the men who serviced the airplane now. In some ways, he felt like he was still one of them. Even though the officers in the squadron treated him as an equal, he often felt ill at ease around them. They were all college men. Darrel had barely finished high school.

After the Depression hit, he had often thought of quitting school to help out his family, but there weren't any jobs, at least not in rural Clearfield, Iowa, population one hundred seventy.

One morning he had come to school smelling like skunk. One girl noticed it as soon as he came through the door of their home-room. Then they all smelled it. No one said anything. The girls knew that Darrel was trapping small animals to help put meat on the family table, and then selling the tanned pelts for whatever he could. Every family in Clearfield did what they had to do to keep going.

The Woodsides' old frame house had no electricity or running water. No one else in Clearfield had it, either. Darrel's father, Leo, had been a wizard when it came to repairing small engines, but with almost everybody out of work, few people could afford to pay him for it.

After graduating from Clearfield High School in 1937, Darrel joined the Navy. Like his father, he had an almost instinctive sense about engines, small or large, and he was quickly promoted to aviation machinist's mate. After a year, he was recommended for flight training, which was extremely rare. The Navy had chosen well. After earning his wings, Darrel wrote home that he would rather fly than eat.

Darrel also had a secret he hadn't shared with any of the other pilots. The only guys in the outfit who knew about it were Billy Bragg and William Magee, two enlisted men back with the rest of the Avenger crews at Pearl Harbor. The only reason they knew was that they had been traveling with him when he was ordered up to the propeller school at Providence, Rhode Island.

That's where the singer Darrel was dating had been appearing with her band. Her name was Norma Egstrom and she often performed with the Benny Goodman orchestra.

At first it didn't seem possible to Darrel that she really liked him, but it turned out that she came from the same kind of family he had, and they just seemed to click. At twenty-two, Norma was a year younger than he was, and had grown up dirt poor on the plains of North Dakota.

Darrel thought he might be in love with her. He knew he wasn't alone. A lot of guys were in love with her. Her stage name wasn't Norma Egstrom. Somewhere along the line, it had been changed to Peggy Lee.

In the lead cockpit, Lieutenant Langdon Fieberling was wrestling with the most important decision he had ever made in his life. It involved the plan for their mission that had been finalized by Lieutenant Colonel Kimes, the Marine air group commander on Midway.

Under Kimes's plan, the Avengers, the B-26 Marauders, and the mixed force of Vindicator and Dauntless dive-bombers were all going to rendezvous above Midway and then proceed out together in joint formation. Once the Japanese fleet was located, the combined air group would make a coordinated attack.

Langdon Fieberling had serious doubts about the wisdom of the strategy. Sitting in the darkness, he was weighing the consequences of disobeying orders against his belief that Kimes's plan would almost guarantee failure.

For one thing, the group formation would be going out without fighter protection. Midway's fighters had been ordered to defend the islands against the incoming Japanese air strike that would inaugurate the battle.

Without fighter protection, the single advantage his Avengers had was speed. If they were going to have any chance to penetrate the enemy fighter groups that would be protecting the Japanese fleet and get in close enough to launch their torpedoes, speed was essential. The dive-bombers, particularly the old fabric-wrapped Vindicators, were as slow as molasses, and in any case they would be attacking from a much higher altitude.

Over the previous two days, Fieberling had gone back and forth on the subject with Kimes and his deputy, Major Verne McCaul, at the air operations bunker. At one point, Fieberling had been ready to concede the issue, and had informed the other Avenger pilots that they would all be attacking together. Now that he was facing the reality of it, he wasn't sure.

Fieberling wasn't the only one concerned about Kimes's ability to make sound tactical decisions. General Willis Hale, an Army Air Force brigadier who was sent to Midway to help plan the air defense, privately believed that Kimes was breaking down under the stress of preparing for the battle. Hale thought Kimes's deputy, Major Mc-Caul, was in no better shape. It wasn't a good situation.

Once they found the Japanese fleet, Fieberling had told his pilots, he would lead them toward the carriers. If there was only one, they would divide into two formations. Fieberling would lead one and Ozzie the other. One formation would aim for the carrier's port bow and the other, the starboard bow. Regardless of which way the ship turned, they would have a good chance to hit her.

If there was more than one carrier, each pilot would select the best target of opportunity presented to him. Fieberling strongly urged them to wait until they were close enough to the carrier to guarantee a hit.

As the approach of dawn slowly brought the other Avengers into clearer focus against the eastern sky, Fieberling continued to weigh his decision. He had been trained by Waldron to fight alone if necessary. This might be one of those times. Once they were airborne, his pilots would follow him wherever he led them. More than anything else, he wanted to give them the best chance to complete their mission and make it home safely.

USS *HORNET*
TORPEDO SQUADRON EIGHT
0440

After the Torpedo Eight pilots had eaten breakfast in the wardroom, Fred Mears thought they seemed a lot more animated, cracking jokes and fooling around in their usual way. A few minutes later, the keys of the Teletype suddenly began clicking. Everyone stopped what they were doing to watch the big reflector screen.

It wasn't the news they were hoping for. The laconic message simply stated that Navy PBYs and Army bombers had attacked an enemy force southwest of Midway. The pilots knew by then that it had to be the Japanese invasion force escorting the troop transports. The enemy striking force containing their big carriers would be coming from the northwest.

The plan was to destroy those carriers while their air groups were off attacking Midway, and before they could return to the ships. If the ambush was successful, hundreds of Japanese aircraft would be forced to ditch in the sea. Without air cover, the rest of their armada would be ripe for the plucking.

Glancing at his watch, John Waldron said, "It's almost dawn. This is when they will attack . . . if they're coming."

The pilots waited for another message to come through, but the Teletype machine remained stubbornly silent. Eventually, everyone began to settle down again. Rusty Kenyon was compiling a collection of limericks, and asked if any of them knew a good one. Fred Mears replied that he would be glad to contribute several, and began:

> *There was a young girl from Madras*
> *Who had a beautiful ass,*
> *Not rounded and pink,*
> *As you probably think,*
> *But with long ears, a tail, and eats grass.*

Rusty was furiously trying to write down all of the words as Fred spoke, but had to ask him to repeat it. Then Mears started on a new

one. The Skipper came over to join them. Grinning, he began to re-
cite one of his own favorites. Rusty copied the new limericks onto a
single sheet of paper and put it in the pocket of his flight suit.

EASTERN ISLAND, MIDWAY ATOLL
TORPEDO EIGHT DETACHMENT
0555

The eastern sky slowly turned a lurid orange.

Still sitting in his open cockpit, Bert tried not to think about what
might be waiting for them out there. It didn't matter anyhow. He
had joined the club. It was time to pay his dues. And it was impossible for him to believe that whatever the situation they found out
there, he couldn't find a way to deal with it.

He remembered when he was going through training and the
subject came up about the Japanese fighting capabilities in the air.
One of the instructors had said, "Forget them. They're nothing. We'll
take care of them in no time."

But that instructor had never met a Japanese pilot in combat.
Bert had never talked to anyone who had actually gone up against a
Japanese plane. It was all completely new.

Across the field, ground-support people were doing last-minute
checks on several of the Marine combat aircraft. Suddenly, a siren
began wailing and he looked up to see a jeep racing toward them
along the narrow apron at the edge of the runway. It stopped with a
squeal of brakes at Fieberling's Avenger.

A Marine officer jumped out and scrambled up onto his wing.
Bert could see them talking animatedly, and then the officer jumped
off. A few moments later Fieberling's engine fired.

Another Marine suddenly materialized at the side of Bert's
plane.

"Enemy force at 320 degrees, one hundred fifty miles," he shouted
up at him.

Lightly pressing the electric starter, Bert brought his engine to
life. Lieutenant Fieberling was already taxiing forward, and Bert fol-

lowed him out onto the runway. Charlie Brannon taxied along behind them, followed by Ozzie Gaynier, Vic Lewis, and Darrel Woodside.

The Marine fighter planes were taking off. Fieberling had to wait until the last of the twenty-four Buffaloes and Wildcats had climbed into the sky. Then it was their turn.

Bert listened to the comforting roar of his Wright Cyclone engine as he cut loose behind Fieberling down the runway leading north. In the tail section, Harry Ferrier hadn't bothered to put on a flight suit. He was wearing dungarees, a white T-shirt, and a blue baseball cap. Gazing through the Plexiglas, he watched the concrete surface of the runway separate from the rear wheel as their plane soared into the air.

The two sections of Avengers joined up in their designated formation, with Ozzie Gaynier bringing the second section into right echelon about a hundred yards behind Charlie Brannon, who was flying on Fieberling's right wing. Bert was on the left.

They climbed through the brightening sky to an altitude of two thousand feet and leveled off. When Bert looked back toward Midway, the B-26 Marauders and the mixed group of dive-bombers were still taking off from Eastern Island. Based on the plan, they were now supposed to circle at the rendezvous point until the rest of the air group joined up.

Instead, Lieutenant Fieberling turned straight onto a course of 320 degrees true, the heading that would take them to the Japanese fleet. Without any further signal, Fieberling goosed his speed up to one hundred sixty knots and led the Avengers northwest toward the distant horizon.

They had only been in the air a few minutes when the voice of Jay Manning broke in on Bert's intercom.

"They're hitting Midway, Skipper," he called out.

Behind them, the first air squadrons of the Japanese striking force had begun bombing the atoll. From his turret, Manning watched the explosions burst on Midway as tracers from the Marine antiaircraft batteries shot up at the Japanese planes.

Bert suddenly spotted a flight of aircraft speeding toward Midway. They had big red meatballs on their wings. One of them broke away to make a direct pass at him, but it veered off at the last moment without opening fire.

Fieberling kept the formation steady on its course, leading them up toward the scattered cloud cover at four thousand feet. As they were climbing, Bert glanced to his right. Charlie Brannon was over there grinning at him through his side windshield. They had just survived their first encounter with the enemy.

Bert grinned back. In perfect harmony, they raised their closed fists at one another in mocking tribute to Swede Larsen's "attack" signal. Then they each extended their middle fingers.

NORTHEAST OF MIDWAY ATOLL
USS ENTERPRISE
FLAG BRIDGE
0607

Rear Admiral Raymond Spruance, the commander of Task Force 16, which included the *Hornet* and the *Enterprise,* had been standing near the radio loudspeaker tuned to the frequency used by the PBY search pilots hunting for the Japanese fleet.

At 0603, he heard the startling message that two Japanese carriers had been sighted, and they were heading for Midway. While his excited staff began plotting the relative positions of the two fleets on their navigation charts, he waited in a corner.

Short and slender, he was dressed for the battle in the same informal uniform he had adopted since coming aboard the *Enterprise* a week earlier. Black shoes, khaki trousers, khaki shirt with the sleeves rolled up, no tie.

Prior to leaving Pearl Harbor, Admiral Nimitz had issued instructions on how Spruance was to employ his forces. The most important goal was to destroy the Japanese carrier force, but Nimitz had also warned, "You will be governed by the principle of calculated risk, which you shall interpret to mean the avoidance of exposure of your force without good prospect of inflicting, as a result of such exposure, greater damage to the enemy."

The meaning was clear. Under no circumstances was he to lose the carriers.

If Spruance decided to be cautious, he might deploy only a portion of his air squadrons in the first attack against the Japanese carriers, holding a reserve force in readiness in case of a reversal. If he decided to be bold, he could launch every available aircraft from his two carriers, and face the consequences. It was not in his nature to be bold.

Since coming aboard the *Enterprise*, Spruance had been carrying with him a small rolled-up navigational chart called a "maneuvering board." None of the members of the staff knew what was recorded on it, if anything, but many assumed it held secret navigational data provided by naval intelligence. Although the admiral took it everywhere with him, he never unfurled it.

Spruance was about to make one of the most important decisions in the Pacific war. He waited as the air operations officers continued to use their metal dividers and parallel rulers on the big chart tables, completing their calculation of the location of the Japanese carriers in relation to the American task force. When they were done, Spruance finally unfurled his little maneuvering board.

One of the staff officers was shocked to see that it was blank. Without asking for the air staff's navigational solution, the admiral calmly asked them to repeat the ranges and compass bearings they had used to make their calculations. After taking a few moments to plot the bearings on the maneuvering board, he used his thumb and forefinger to roughly estimate the distance between the two fleets.

"Launch the attack," he said in a soft voice.

The time had come to roll the dice. Spruance had decided to commit every available plane under his command to the attack, one hundred twenty fighters, dive-bombers, and torpedo planes from the *Hornet* and the *Enterprise*.

To the south, Admiral Frank Jack Fletcher, who was in tactical command of both carrier task forces from the USS *Yorktown,* was preparing to launch his own air squadrons.

Spruance was taking the extraordinary gamble that the rest of the Japanese carriers in the striking force were steaming in close proximity to the two that had been sighted by his patrol planes. If he was wrong, all hope of surprise would be lost, and the second group of enemy carriers would be free to launch a counterstrike against his badly outnumbered force.

NORTHEAST OF MIDWAY ATOLL
USS *HORNET*
TORPEDO SQUADRON EIGHT
0610

In the officers' wardroom, Rusty Kenyon had just finished a portion of baked beans, his favorite item on the breakfast menu, when all of the klaxons and bells in the ship seemed to go off together.

"General quarters!" came an earsplitting voice over the ship's loudspeakers. "Flight quarters! All pilots report to your ready rooms!"

Rusty ran back to Ready Room Four in time to see the reflector screen over the Teletype flash the message:

> *MANY ENEMY PLANES HEADED FOR MIDWAY BEARING 320 DEGREES.*

As they all stood riveted in front of the screen, the Teletype continued clattering out messages:

> *ALL FIGHTER PILOTS MAN PLANES ON FLIGHT DECK . . . HORNET BASE COURSE 240 DEGREES.*

The *Hornet* had more than doubled its speed and was heading southwest. Over the loudspeaker a voice declared, "The enemy main body is now attempting to take Midway. We are heading toward Midway to intercept and destroy them."

Soon the Teletype began chattering again.

> *PILOTS OF ALL SCOUT BOMBERS AND TORPEDO PLANES ON FLIGHT DECK, EXCEPT SQUADRON COM-*

*MANDERS, MAN YOUR PLANES. SQUADRON COM-*
*MANDERS AND GROUP COMMANDERS REMAIN IN*
*READY ROOMS FOR LATEST INSTRUCTIONS.*

Inside Ready Room Four, it was controlled pandemonium as the pilots rushed to gather the plotting boards, helmets, goggles, and survival gear stored in the compartments under their cushioned seats. While putting on the flight equipment, they kept their eyes intent on the messages streaming across the reflector screen.

Another message quickly followed.

*CORRECTION . . . DO NOT MAN PLANES UNTIL*
*DIRECTED.*

A groan of frustration greeted the new order. As the pilots waited for another message to head for the flight deck, the same modulated voice blared out from the ship's loudspeakers.

"We intend to launch planes at 0700 to attack enemy while their planes are returning from Midway. We will close to about one hundred miles of enemy position."

Standing at the front of the ready room, Waldron gave the pilots their final instructions, telling them that he thought the Japanese carrier task forces would "swing together" and retire just far enough so that they could retrieve their planes from the first strike. He told them not to worry about navigating, just to follow him.

"Maybe it's the Sioux in me but I have a hunch the Japanese ships will be in a different position than our reports have them," he said at the end. "I won't hesitate to run this squadron dry of gas in an effort to find them. In that case, we'll all sit down in the water together and have a nice little picnic.

"I have no doubt that we'll be back here by noon," said the Skipper, "but if we find ourselves alone and outnumbered by the enemy planes on the way into attack, we'll keep boring in toward the carrier. If there is only one man left I want that man to take his pickle in and get a hit."

With a sardonic grin, Moose Moore turned to Tex and said,

"You'll never get a hit, Gay. You couldn't hit a bull in the tail with a six-foot rake."

Stung, Tex answered, "I'll get a hit."

Hal Ellison leaned over and extended his hand to the Texan.

"Good luck," he said.

"Same to you," said Gay, shaking his hand.

Ensign Hank Carey, a fighter pilot aboard the *Hornet* who was not scheduled to fly in the first launch, came into the ready room to wish good hunting to several pilots who were his close friends. He heard Waldron's dramatic last words to the squadron.

There was a period of silence. Carey heard Waldron say, "God-speed." A few moments later, the order came that they had been waiting for all morning.

*"Pilots, man all planes,"* read the reflector screen.

As they crowded toward the door, another order came through the loudspeaker for the air squadron commanders to immediately report to the bridge. Pete Mitscher was waiting there when his four air squadron commanders assembled for the hasty conference. The first one to arrive was Pat Mitchell, the skipper of the fighter squadron.

Mitchell had gone up to the bridge resolved to make one more at-tempt to convince Mitscher that his ten Wildcats should fly cover for the torpedo planes. It would be the last chance for Mitchell to make his case.

Mitchell was no smooth talker, but he knew Mitscher respected him. He had handpicked him for this fighter command. And like Mitscher, Pat was all Navy. He had graduated from Annapolis in 1927. His brother Bill was Annapolis '24. The newly promoted Ad-miral Mitscher was standing with the members of his air staff when Mitchell came up and saluted.

Without preamble, he requested that his squadron be assigned to fly cover for Waldron's Devastators. There it was. He had said it. Not just part of his fighter squadron, or even half of it. All of them. With-out a pause, Mitscher shook his head and told Mitchell he would stay up with the bombers. His tone made it clear that the decision was final.

"You'll protect Commander Ring and the dive-bombers," Mitscher told him as the other squadron skippers arrived together on the bridge.

Along with Ring, the assembled group included Mitscher's air officer, Apollo Soucek, and his operations officer, John Foster, as well as Walt Rodee and Ruff Johnson, who commanded the dive-bomber squadrons, and the bridge watch officers.

With Mitscher looking on, Commander Ring said that he was planning to fly a course of 265 degrees, which was almost due west, and more than 30 degrees to the north of the Japanese fleet's last reported position, 234 degrees southwest.

John Waldron spoke up in immediate disagreement. He proposed a course of 240 degrees, which took into account the last fleet sighting, as well as the possibility that the Japanese had swung back to the north after launching their first strike.

In response, Mitscher told Waldron and the others to follow the course Ring had given them. Ensign Fred Mamer, one of the watch officers, stood transfixed as he listened to the heated argument.

NORTHWEST OF MIDWAY ATOLL
TORPEDO EIGHT DETACHMENT
0655

The six Avengers of Torpedo Eight flew northwest across an empty cobalt sea. Lieutenant Fieberling never deviated from his base course of 320 degrees. They remained at an altitude of four thousand feet.

The Marine back at Midway had said the reported distance to the enemy fleet was one hundred fifty miles. At their cruising speed of one hundred sixty knots, they should have sighted it already. Maybe someone had made a mistake.

From his position at the far left of the formation, Bert suddenly spotted the wake of a ship dead ahead of him. The ship was moving southeast, almost directly toward them. Bert had studied all of the recognition profiles of Japanese warships. This was no warship. It looked more like a transport. *A piece of cake,* he thought. Then he looked past the transport to the northeast.

Japanese warships covered the whole expanse of ocean as far as he could see. Bert had never seen a fleet before, not even an American one. This looked like the whole goddamned Japanese navy.

A battleship was in the first group. The damn thing was so huge it couldn't be anything else. Beyond the battleship was a big aircraft carrier. A second carrier was steaming along right beside it. They were surrounded by a phalanx of cruisers and destroyers.

Fieberling had led them straight to the enemy. Six torpedo planes against the whole Japanese striking force.

"Enemy fighters!" Jay Manning called out on the intercom from his turret gun.

Suddenly, the Zeroes were all around them, too many to count. Bert watched them hurtling past from every direction, high and low. They were astonishingly maneuverable, and so many that they seemed to get in each other's way.

A Zero skidded into his field of fire as it attacked Fieberling's Avenger. Bert pressed the firing button on his thirty-caliber nose gun. It didn't fire. He tried again. Nothing happened.

Behind him, he heard Jay Manning open fire with his fifty-caliber machine gun, raking the first flight of Zeroes as they made darting passes between the six torpedo planes.

Underneath the tail, Harry Ferrier clenched the hand grips on the thirty-caliber tunnel gun and waited for a target. Through the Plexiglas window, he could see Zeroes flying above and below the three Avengers behind them, firing quick bursts as they sped into range.

Bullets started hitting the metal skin of the fuselage on both sides of him. It sounded like the clatter of hard rain on a tin roof. As Harry waited for a chance to fire, his left hand was knocked free from the machine gun. The grazing bullet felt like a red-hot iron on his wrist. Ignoring the pain, he gripped the handle again.

A few seconds later, Jay Manning stopped firing up in the turret. Harry turned around to glance back up into the fuselage. The automatic turret had stowed itself, which always happened when the gunner's hands were no longer gripping the machine gun. A "dead man's switch" automatically brought the turret gun to its position facing aft, from which it offered the least air resistance.

Jay was hanging limp in his safety harness.

A twenty-millimeter cannon round had hit him squarely in the chest and blown him apart. Until Harry saw the crimson river flowing down into the radio compartment, he had no idea just how much blood there was in a man's body.

Through the tiny side window, he watched another plane overtaking and passing them. It was on fire. It happened so fast he had no way of knowing whether it was a Zero or one of the Avengers.

Bert watched Langdon Fieberling put his nose over and begin to dive.

Opening his own throttle to full power, Bert went after him. Still in tight formation, the Avengers hurtled downward at three hundred miles an hour toward the surface of the sea. As if they were part of the American formation, the Japanese Zeroes pursued them all of the way down.

Fieberling pulled out of the screaming dive at two hundred feet and headed directly for the first of the Japanese carriers. When he opened his bomb bay doors, the rest of them did, too. It cut down on speed, but in the event of a hydraulic failure, they would still be able to drop their torpedoes.

Bert was on the left, Charlie on the right. Glancing back, Bert saw that the other three were still in the same tight formation behind them. Lieutenant Commander Waldron would have been proud.

Then the air was filled with tracer bullets again, constant flashes, and Bert's plane started taking more hits from the maneuvering Zeroes. He could feel the dull thump of machine gun bullets slamming into the armor plating that protected his back.

A cannon shell exploded behind the cockpit and shrapnel suddenly burst through the side of the windshield. He felt a fierce rush of air swirl around his face and blood began spurting from his neck, quickly coating the instrument panel with a shiny red film.

A Zero slid into attack position behind him again, and the pilot fired a long burst with his machine guns. Kneeling backward in the tunnel, Harry was about to fire at the Zero when the tail wheel of the Avenger dropped in front of him, blocking his field of fire and making his gun useless.

He immediately realized that the plane's hydraulic system had been shot out, causing the wheel to drop. Harry could hear the bullets from the Zero behind them tearing through the metal skin of the tail compartment. He felt a hot stab of pain in his head, and fell away.

Although Bert was holding the control stick steady, the Avenger began to drop out of the formation. He attempted to regain altitude by pulling back on the control stick, but it was limp in his hand. The cables to the elevator controls had obviously been shot away.

A spread of machine gun bullets shattered his instrument panel, and one more red ball of fire burst on his left wing. They were going down. With his hydraulics gone and the elevator cables severed, there was no way the plane could stay up in the air.

Veering out of formation, he took a quick glimpse back at the others. They were all still there, Charlie Brannon, Ozzie Gaynier, Darrel, and Vic. Lieutenant Fieberling was leading them straight toward the nearest Japanese carrier.

NORTHEAST OF MIDWAY
USS *HORNET*
0714

On the flight deck, the takeoffs proceeded with almost agonizing slowness. The first launch had begun at 0700 with eighteen Wildcat fighters. Ten were going on the mission. Eight would remain above the carrier to provide protective air cover in the event of an enemy attack.

The fighters were followed up by thirty-four dive-bombers. While they were climbing off the deck, the ten fighters going on the attack mission began clawing their way up to twenty thousand feet. The Dauntless dive-bombers went after them.

Under Mitscher's orders, Waldron's torpedo planes were slated to take off last after the dive-bombers. Six of them had already been brought up from the hangar deck to the flight deck in preparation for takeoff.

Tex Gay's Devastator was one of the first in line. Lee Marona, Gay's plane captain, was standing alongside the aircraft when Torpedo Eight's pilots came out on the flight deck to board their planes.

Just twenty years old, Marona was a strapping six-footer from northern Alabama who had turned down a football scholarship from Auburn to join the Navy. During basic training, he had put up with a lot of ribbing about his birth name, which was actually General Lee Marona. He had worked all night to make sure Gay's plane was ready for combat.

Farther down in the line, Abbie Abercrombie climbed into the cockpit of his Devastator after wrestling a parachute onto his broad back. His plane captain, Bill Tunstall, helped to strap him in. Abercrombie checked his instruments as another machinist's mate cranked the engine. It roared into life.

"Good luck, sir," said Tunstall.

"Thanks, Bill," said Abercrombie. "See you in Kansas City."

Climbing off the wing, Tunstall walked back to the tail section to say good-bye to Bernie Phelps, Abbie's young radioman-gunner. Bernie was his best friend on the ship. They had enjoyed some great leaves together back at Pearl Harbor.

Bernie was holding his wallet out in his hand as Tunstall came up.

"Hey Bill, take this," he said. "If I don't get back, send it to my mother."

Tunstall didn't want Bernie to think he had any doubts about his coming back.

"Aw, Bernie, you'll be back in a few hours. Forget it."

Bernie put the wallet back into the pocket of his flight suit.

As Tex Gay's plane was being pushed into position for takeoff, he had a moment of sudden panic. Gazing toward the bow, it didn't seem possible there was enough room to get up in the air, particularly with a two-thousand-pound torpedo sticking out of the belly. He motioned the plane pushers to shove his plane back a little farther toward the stern.

At the edge of the flight deck, the takeoff control officer began rotating his colored signal flag above his head, which was the sign for Tex to begin revving his engine to full power while holding the brakes and keeping the tail down. As Tex waited to release the brakes, the signal officer gave him the cut signal.

After Tex throttled back, the TCO yelled up to him, "Twelve-minute delay."

From the cockpit, Tex could see the Skipper standing near an open hatchway at the base of the island superstructure beneath the bridge. He looked fit to be tied. Tex watched him stalk over to one of the metal-covered phone units that connected to the bridge.

Far above them, the eighteen fighters and thirty-four dive-bombers were still climbing up to their assigned altitudes. A nervous Tex Gay wondered whether they would wait for the Devastators to join the group formation.

NORTHWEST OF MIDWAY
JAPANESE STRIKING FORCE
FLAGSHIP CARRIER AKAGI
0715

Through his binoculars, Admiral Chuichi Nagumo, commanding the Japanese striking force, watched the attack of the five remaining Avengers from the bridge of his flagship, the carrier *Akagi*.

The torpedo planes were heading straight toward the carrier *Hiryu*, which was steaming southeast in a line parallel to his flagship. Both carriers had begun turning to port so that their starboard batteries could bring to bear a full barrage of antiaircraft guns against the Americans. Several other warships had already opened fire.

Seeing the black bursts of smoke, the swarm of Zeroes that had been attacking the Avengers immediately darted away to safety. Exploding antiaircraft shells began blooming black in the sky all around the torpedo planes. Still they came on.

Commander Mitsuo Fuchida, the pilot who had led the Japanese carrier attack against Pearl Harbor and who was recovering from appendicitis, watched from the *Akagi* as the Americans continued to press home their attack in the face of such overwhelming firepower.

Excited shouts from the *Akagi*'s lookouts warned that behind the five torpedo planes were four more American aircraft, also coming from the south. They were the B-26 Marauders.

Suddenly, one of the Avengers burst into flames. It cartwheeled into the sea and created a great geyser of foam. Moments later, Fuchida heard a spontaneous roar of exultation erupt from the hundreds of sailors standing at their battle stations.

Still, the four remaining Avengers came on through the hail of bursting shells.

Several of the Japanese Zero pilots boldly decided to brave the ongoing antiaircraft barrage, and sped in to make more passes at the remaining planes. One by one, the Americans began to fall. Through his binoculars, Fuchida saw two of them launch their torpedoes before they were hit, but the planes were still so far away from the *Hiryu* that the ship easily changed course to avoid them.

When the last Avenger became a flaming torch in the sky, another exultant roar swept across the flight decks of the two carriers, as if the Japanese sailors were enjoying a spectacle at the Coliseum in Rome.

They were gone. Ozzie Gaynier and Darrel Woodside. Vic Lewis and Charlie Brannon. And Lieutenant Langdon Kellogg Fieberling. He had chosen to follow his own course and had paid the ultimate price. The eternal sea closed over the small wisps of smoke that marked their final resting places.

Langdon Fieberling had lost his terrible gamble.

Or had he?

On his flagship, *Akagi,* Admiral Nagumo took pause. Fifteen minutes earlier, he had been handed a radio report from Lieutenant Tomonaga, who commanded the first wave of Japanese bombers that had attacked Midway.

"There is need for a second attack," was his message.

The primary objective of the first air strike had been to fully eliminate the American air strength on Midway. Clearly, Lieutenant Tomonaga did not feel the task had been accomplished. Watching the attack by American torpedo planes that had just unfolded before his eyes, Nagumo could understand why. The decadent Americans weren't supposed to fight like this.

He had been impressed by their almost samurailike ferocity. And hard on their heels had been the equally audacious charge by four B-26 Marauders. One of the Army planes had nearly struck the flag deck of the *Akagi* before it dove into the sea.

Now he had to make his first critical decision of the battle. Nagumo's superior, Admiral Yamamoto, had specifically ordered him to keep a strong reserve of his combat aircraft armed with antiship torpedoes to retaliate against any American carriers that might be lurking within striking range of the Japanese fleet.

Yet, Nagumo's search planes had been in the air for almost three hours searching the sky to the east for an American task force, and they had reported no sightings up to that point. If he was to accomplish his primary mission, Nagumo needed to win control of the air over Midway, even if it meant taking the risk that there were American carriers in the vicinity.

At 0716, he ordered that the ship-killing torpedoes be removed from the reserve aircraft on the *Akagi* and the *Kaga,* and that the planes be rearmed with bombs. It would take almost an hour to accomplish the task, but they would then be able to take part in the second bombing strike against Midway to eliminate its air defenses once and for all.

### NORTHWEST OF MIDWAY
### THE LAST AVENGER
### 0716

He was going down. Before he hit the water, there was only one thing Bert Earnest wanted to do, and that was to sink at least one of the warships still firing at him. He could never reach the carriers now, but glancing off to the left he saw what looked like a Japanese cruiser, obviously one of their escort vessels. The ship was firing at him with its antiaircraft batteries.

Kicking the rudder, he turned the crippled plane toward the warship, and punched the switches to launch his two-thousand-pound torpedo. He had expected an immediate surge in speed after it was gone, but there wasn't any. Not sure the torpedo had dropped, he pulled the emergency release lever.

The riddled plane was losing altitude quickly now, down to a hundred feet, then seventy-five, fifty, twenty-five, twenty. Tightening his shoulder straps, Bert was preparing to ditch when he did something purely reflexive, something he always did when bringing an Avenger in for a landing.

He reached down to adjust the trim tabs that were controlled by the little four-inch wheel next to the cockpit seat. By turning the wheel with his left hand, he could help to offset the Avenger's nose-heavy tendencies whenever he landed.

As he turned the wheel, the nose of the plane gently leaped up in front of him. When he continued to roll the tab wheel, the plane actually started to regain altitude. This meant that the trim tab cables, which were separate from the elevator control cables, were still intact. A surge of hope went through him as he realized he might still be able to fly the plane.

The Japanese cruiser he had aimed his torpedo at was no longer firing at him and he quickly discovered why. The enemy warship didn't want to hit the Zeroes that had come back to finish him off. They took turns firing short bursts into him with each pass.

Keeping one hand on the stick to control direction, and the other hand on the trim tab wheel, Bert felt the Avenger slowly gain altitude as he aimed it northwest away from the Japanese fleet. Although he was now flying at full throttle, there was no way to know how fast he was going because the air speed gauge had been shot out along with the rest of his instruments. With all the holes in the wings and fuselage, maybe the bird would fly faster, he thought.

He knew his neck was still bleeding, because the wind kept fogging blood around the cockpit, but so far he didn't feel faint. While the Zeroes kept firing at him, he tried everything he knew to avoid the coup de grâce, first side-slipping the plane, then jinking back and forth. He pulled back hard on the throttle to throw off their aim, and then gunned it forward again. The two Japanese pilots kept making their passes, firing into the shredded fuselage to either kill him or the engine.

Perhaps another minute went by. He felt another spray of bullets thud into the armor plate behind his back. The passing seconds seemed like an eternity. Wouldn't they ever run out of ammunition? Didn't they have to go back at some point to protect their goddamned fleet? Couldn't they be low on gas?

And then they were gone.

He was alone above the sea.

There was no time to ponder why the Japanese pilots had finally granted him a reprieve. He forced himself to focus on what to do next. He hadn't heard from Manning or Ferrier since the Zeroes had first attacked. Bert called them on the intercom. There was no response. With so many things shot out, he couldn't be sure if the intercom was even working. He tried again. Nothing.

He had never felt so tired in his life. Struggling to keep his mind clear, he paused to take stock. The wound under his jaw had stopped spurting, although he could feel hot warmth continuing to flow down his neck. He decided it couldn't be worse than a deep flesh wound or he would already be dead.

More than anything he wanted to sleep. Sleep was not an option. He needed to get the Avenger all of the way back to Midway. Checking his compass, he saw that the gauge was frozen in place. Turning around to look back at the tail, he saw why. The compass wire was attached to a flux gate on the vertical fin, and it was riddled with holes.

With the hydraulic system shot out, he couldn't close the bomb bay doors. That started him wondering again whether their torpedo had actually dropped. Ferrier and Manning were the only ones who could confirm if it had by looking through a small glass plate into the bomb bay section. Bert didn't want to think about trying to land the plane with his hydraulics out and a two-thousand-pound torpedo hanging from their belly.

All of the instruments were gone: the gas gauge, air speed indicator, altimeter, oil pressure gauge, everything. He continued to roll the trim tabs until the Avenger had climbed to about three thousand feet.

For the first time since they had attacked the Japanese carriers, he was able to focus on how he might actually bring the plane home. He had no idea what had happened to Fieberling and the others, but he couldn't go back looking for them.

Midway had to be his ultimate destination. As far as he knew, it was the only landing place within a thousand miles. That led to the next problem. He had no firm idea where Midway was.

Lieutenant Fieberling had brought them up from the southeast. The Zeroes had driven him even farther northwest. That meant the whole Japanese fleet stood between him and the tiny atoll. By the time he got there, if he got there, it was possible that they might have already taken it, but the only other alternative was to ditch in the middle of the Pacific. The chances of being picked up by a rescue plane seemed even more remote.

His best guess was that he must be at least two hundred miles, maybe more, from Midway. At least the engine was running fine, even with all the punishment the plane had absorbed. He would have to get back by dead reckoning. Live reckoning sounded better.

The sun had been up less than three hours. From its position off to the east, he knew which direction was south, and a southerly course would hopefully keep him away from Japanese planes. He would use the scattered clouds for cover wherever he found them.

The real trick would be deciding when to turn east again. If he went too far south before turning, there would be nothing but ocean ahead of him for a thousand miles or more. He hoped his self-sealing fuel tanks hadn't lost too much gas while swallowing all of those Japanese bullets.

USS HORNET
TORPEDO SQUADRON EIGHT
0734

As an anxious Tex Gay waited in his cockpit for permission to take off, he glanced over to see a leather-helmeted pilot climbing onto his right wing. It was Whitey Moore. The little West Virginian's plane was positioned right behind his in the line of Devastators on the flight deck. Moore's freckled face leaned into the open cockpit with a broad grin.

"You would think at a time like this they'd get things straight," he shouted over the roar of the engines.

Tex nodded in full agreement.

"Tell you what," yelled Whitey. "You test the weight and I'll test the wind."

His jesting words again reminded Tex Gay that he had never taken off from a carrier flight deck with a two-thousand-pound torpedo before.

"I'll do my best, Whitey," he responded with forced jocularity. "If I go in the drink, that means she's too heavy, so you can go tell the captain to speed up."

"Just keep your eyes above water," Whitey said.

Giving Tex a thumbs-up, he jumped down to the deck and jogged back to his plane.

Farther back in the line of Devastators, Bill Evans sat in his own cockpit. *My luck can't last much longer,* he had written in his letter home. Would this be his final day? Would they soon be playing taps for him while the rest of the crewmen stood quietly on the flight deck in a memorial service, just as he had stood in the sun to honor his dead friends after they had made that last far journey across the horizon? *I have had the unforgettable taste of the sea on my lips.* It was a line he had hand-copied from Saint-Exupéry's book. *It is not danger I love. I know what I love. It is life.*

Behind Evans, Commander Waldron's plane wasn't even spotted yet on the flight deck. The Skipper was slated to take off last out of the fifty-nine planes in the group. As each minute passed, Waldron's frustration and anger mounted. All hope of surprise had probably been lost by now. And while they stood around waiting, the *Hornet*'s fighters and dive-bombers were using up precious fuel.

In the sky above him, Ensign H. L. "Hump" Tallman, who was flying one of the Grumman Wildcat escort fighters, wondered exactly the same thing. They had burned a ton of gas reaching twenty thousand feet, and now they were just flying around in circles.

Hump was the "tail-end Charlie," the last man in the formation of ten fighters. So far, the visibility below him was almost crystal clear. All of the ships in the task force were spread out in a great tableau on the azure sea.

Flying in the same circular pattern a few thousand feet beneath him, Ensign Troy Guillory sat in the cockpit of his Dauntless dive-bomber and like Tallman wondered when the brass hats were going to get this show on the road.

Tex Gay watched as someone ran up to the takeoff control officer and yelled something in his ear. Turning away from him, the officer made eye contact with Tex and motioned at him with his black-and-white checkered flag.

Revving his engines again, Tex waited for the sign to take off. The control officer began wagging the flag faster and faster as if trying to keep up with the engine, and then swept it forward, which was the signal to go. Tex released the brakes. The Devastator rumbled down the deck and slowly lifted off into space.

He had made it. No big deal after all.

While waiting for the rest of the squadron to join him, he began to circle the carrier at an altitude of five hundred feet. One by one, the other fourteen Devastators came up after him. Waldron was the last.

On the flight deck, Lee Marona watched the Devastators circling above the carrier and said a silent prayer that they would all come back safely. A born-again Christian, Lee was a member of the Bible group that some of the enlisted men in the squadron had formed.

Across the flight deck, he saw his younger brother Jess as he stood with the other plane pushers watching the squadron depart. Their father had been killed in an accident when Lee was four, and he had practically raised Jess, convincing him to join the Navy after he did.

Once in the air, John Waldron led the squadron away from the carrier and its escort ships. Far above the Devastators, Ensign Lawrence French, who was flying one of the fighters providing air cover, saw Waldron head off to the west. As he watched, the rest of the *Hornet*'s air group stopped circling and headed west, too.

Just as planned, Waldron's fifteen-plane torpedo squadron had formed up in two divisions. The Skipper led the first four two-plane elements, followed by the seven Devastators led by Jimmy Owens. Tex Gay brought up the rear.

Cruising at nineteen thousand feet, Stanhope Ring signaled the *Hornet*'s high air squadrons to form up in a group parade formation, with his own section of dive-bombers at the pointed apex of a giant "V." From the deck of the *Hornet,* the formation looked like a massive flock of migrating geese.

Flying in the left wing of the "V," Troy Guillory was grateful that all he had to do was follow the man in the position ahead of him, like a slow-witted elephant in a circus ring.

He was already apprehensive about how much gas they had used up circling above the carrier. So far, the whole mission had seemed to be a confused mess. His friend, Ensign Ben Tappan, who was flying wing on Stanhope Ring in another Dauntless, was feeling the same concern.

Three thousand feet above Guillory and Tappan, the *Hornet*'s ten Wildcat fighters were forced to alternately speed up and then slow down as they tried to provide high cover over the whole air group without overrunning it.

Ensign John "Mac" McInerny was the fighter squadron's fuel expert. Based on the reported distance to the enemy carriers, the group would need to find the Japanese fleet pretty quickly if the Wildcats were going to be able to complete their escort mission and get back to the ship.

In the last fighter, Hump Tallman was checking his gas gauge, too. Their range was shorter than the dive-bombers', and like McInerny he was wondering why they had taken off first.

Aboard the *Hornet,* Lieutenant Commander John Foster, the Annapolis-trained air operations officer, stared down at a radar screen and tracked Ring's air group as it moved west on a course of 265 degrees away from the carrier. Although they were now no more than tiny blips on the monitor screen, the fifty-nine aircraft represented one-third of Admiral Nimitz's striking force against the Japanese fleet, the other two-thirds being the air groups from the *Enterprise* and *Yorktown.*

There were no further sighting reports on the location of the Japanese fleet as the *Hornet*'s air staff continued to track the progress of Ring's group on the radar screen. At sixty miles out, the group was still on Ring's original course of 265 degrees when the last blips disappeared.

The only way for the carrier to communicate with the air group now would be by radio. Foster wasn't expecting any transmissions, however, because the pilots were under strict orders to maintain radio silence.

Looking down from his Wildcat at the end of the fifty-nine-plane formation, Hump Tallman saw only an infinite expanse of ocean in every direction. Twenty thousand feet beneath him, he could see Waldron's squadron of Devastators following the same course they were, the torpedo planes so low at around fifteen hundred feet that they looked like they were skimming the surface of the sea.

At 0816, Troy Guillory was startled to hear a voice coming through the earphones of his cockpit radio. He recognized it right away. He had heard it enough times aboard the *Hornet*. It was the voice of Lieutenant Commander John Waldron. Guillory noted that he hadn't identified himself with his call sign.

They were heading in the wrong direction, Guillory heard Waldron say.

Flying on the wing of Commander Ring, Ben Tappan heard Waldron, too. When no one responded to his call, Tappan began to wonder if he might have imagined it. Every pilot knew the order about radio silence. He decided he had probably been wrong. Then he heard the voice again.

"I know where the damn Jap fleet is," said Waldron.

There was more silence before Troy Guillory heard another voice. He knew this voice even better than Waldron's. It was the *Hornet*'s air group commander, Stanhope Ring. He sounded angry.

"You fly on us," he said, also without identifying himself with his call sign. "I'm leading this formation. You fly on us."

Troy Guillory had been one of the duty officers the previous night. One of the many lousy jobs ensigns had was to serve as mail censors, and he had been the one to read Commander Waldron's last letter home to his wife. There had been nothing in it he had to censor, but he remembered that Waldron had written something about having Sioux in him. *What's going on here?* he wondered.

Aboard the *Hornet,* the air staff had monitored the same radio transmissions, but the words were garbled. They were outraged that someone would be stupid enough to potentially compromise the security of the mission. Lieutenant Commander Foster thought it had to be coming from pilots in the group off the *Enterprise.*

Ben Tappan was waiting intently for Lieutenant Commander Waldron's response to Ring's order to stay in formation. A minute or two passed before he heard Waldron's voice for the last time.

"The hell with you," he said.

It was 0825.

Richard Woodson, the gunner in Ensign Don Kirkpatrick's dive-bomber, looked down and saw the lead torpedo plane slowly turn off to the left. As Woodson watched, the rest of the pilots in the torpedo squadron turned to follow their leader. He called Don Kirkpatrick on the intercom to report the news.

Hump Tallman, flying the last fighter in the high cover formation, watched them go, too. He hadn't heard any of the radio transmissions, but prior to takeoff Hump had plotted the course they would need to follow to find the Japanese fleet based on its last sighting. He checked the heading he had written down on his plotting board. It was the same general direction Waldron was going. He wondered why they weren't all following him.

Troy Guillory was wondering the same thing.

### WEST OF MIDWAY ATOLL
### THE LAST AVENGER
### 0835

Amazingly, Bert's Avenger continued to fly. Just about everything inside the plane had been smashed, but so far the engine hadn't faltered. It had been the first one off the Grumman assembly line. Maybe it was charmed.

He tried calling Ferrier and Manning again over the intercom, but there was no response. After the pasting they had received from the Zeroes, he had to assume they were either dead or wounded. There would be no way to find out until he landed.

Since leaving Midway Atoll, they had been in the air for better than two hours. Checking his watch, he figured that he had gone sixty or seventy miles south since the Zeroes had left him alone. Dodging in and out of the scattered clouds, he hadn't seen another aircraft. Below him, there was only the trackless sea.

Back in the tail section, Harry Ferrier slowly came alive to the harsh scream of the wind through the shredded fuselage. He was still draped over the tunnel gun. It was red with his blood.

There was an awful raw coppery smell in the air, and he had a terrible headache. When he reached up to gingerly touch his wound, it felt like there was a hole in his forehead. There was. A bullet had torn through the bill of his baseball cap and creased the front of his skull.

Sitting up, he tried to regain his bearings. The engine appeared to be running strong, and the plane remained steady on a level course. Turning the switch on the intercom, he called up to the cockpit.

"Are you okay, Skipper?" he asked weakly.

Bert was overjoyed to discover that Ferrier was still alive.

"I'm fine. . . . How about you?"

"I'm wounded in the head, but I think I'll be all right," he said.

"What about Manning?" asked Bert.

Harry tried to blot out the mental image of what he had seen after looking up into the turret.

"I think Jay's dead," he said.

The reality of it slowly sunk in.

"I want you to see if the torpedo dropped," Bert said a few minutes later. "I don't want us to land with it hanging out of the bomb bay."

There was a small glass port in the floor of the radio compartment that allowed Harry to look into the bomb bay. It was almost directly under the gun turret. When he crawled over to check, Harry saw that it was covered by Jay's blood.

He reported to Bert that there was no way to see into the bomb bay. He then asked if it would be all right for him to crawl up to the middle seat behind the cockpit. Since their tail gun was useless, Bert told Harry to come up.

Staring into the distance, Bert suddenly saw another plane emerge from the cloudy haze. It was heading in the general direction of the Japanese fleet. He was in no shape for another showdown with a Zero, or any other enemy plane for that matter. Without waiting to confirm whether it was friend or foe, Bert slid inside the nearby cloud.

APPROACHING JAPANESE STRIKING FORCE
TORPEDO SQUADRON EIGHT
0908

Waldron's fifteen-plane squadron flew southwest in right echelon formation, the second division close in behind the first. At one point, Tex Gay looked up and saw the pale reflection of the moon centered in the middle of his cockpit windshield. It continued to hover there as the minutes slowly passed. Tex didn't know it, but from the point at which Waldron had broken away from the rest of the air group, the moon's azimuth was 234 degrees true.

The Skipper had always told Tex that as a navigation officer it was his duty to keep track of everything he could on their flights. He was in the process of trying to estimate the rate of their fuel consumption when Waldron's voice came through his earphones, taut and harsh.

"There's a fighter on our tail," he said.

The Japanese plane was well out to the right of them and moving fast in the same direction they were. To Tex, it looked more like a float plane, the kind that could be catapulted off a Japanese battleship or cruiser. It quickly overtook them and moved past.

The Japanese pilot was almost certainly radioing their position back to his fleet. It only made Waldron angrier. With even one Wildcat flying cover for them, they could have shot him down before he had time to set up a reception committee for them. Now any chance of surprise was lost.

Grant Teats was busy trying to solve a more immediate problem. His engine was leaking oil, and it had fouled his windshield. Leaning forward, he reached around the open cockpit with his left hand to clean it with a rag while continuing to fly the plane with his right.

Reversing hands, he inadvertently hit the trigger button on his nose gun and fired a short burst past Abbie Abercrombie. Abbie took it in good humor, melodramatically wiping his brow as if narrowly escaping death.

### NORTH OF JAPANESE STRIKING FORCE
### *HORNET* AIR GROUP
### 0910

Flying high cover with the rest of Pat Mitchell's fighter squadron above the *Hornet*'s thirty-four dive-bombers, Mac McInerny decided it was time to take matters into his own hands, even if that meant his own court-martial.

The son of a blacksmith, Mac had never been afraid to take chances. Sporting an Errol Flynn mustache and muscled like a steer, the big Irishman had a reputation as a hard-partying woman-chaser. The other pilots in his squadron also knew him as one hell of a fighter pilot.

McInerny had spent a lot of time studying the fuel consumption traits of the Grumman Wildcat, and he knew his plane was running out of gas. The fighters were at the point of no return, if they hadn't already passed it.

After taking off from the *Hornet,* he had firewalled his throttle and redlined the manifold pressure, but the settings for minimum fuel consumption didn't necessarily correlate with long-distance flights. And on this flight, the fighters had been forced to fly in "S" turns in order not to outrun the dive-bombers, which further wasted precious fuel.

It was time to do something. Gunning his engine, McInerny left his position in the formation and pulled up alongside Lieutenant Commander Pat Mitchell. Getting the squadron commander's attention, he pointed animatedly to his gas gauge. Mitchell slowly shook his head at him and resumed staring forward.

McInerny cut back on the throttle and dropped back into his position as wingman to Johnny Magda. After another five minutes of droning westward into the empty sky, McInerny had had enough.

Flying up alongside Mitchell again, he pointed to his gas gauge once more to convey that they were beyond the point of no return. This time, Mitchell reacted with visceral anger, waving McInerny back into his position in the formation.

The big Irishman went back just long enough to signal Johnny Magda that it was time to go. Banking his plane to the left, he began to swing around in a 180-degree turn to return to the *Hornet*.

As he was turning, he looked off to the south and saw what appeared to be a rising column of smoke from a fleet of ships. He briefly thought about radioing the news to the air group, but he had cotton stuffed in his ears against the engine noise, and they were flying under strict radio silence anyway.

When Johnny Magda peeled off to go after him, the other fighter pilots watched them go. Then, section by section, they turned to follow him. McInerny looked back one last time. Mitchell, who by then was flying all alone, was turning to come after them.

*I'm going to be court-martialed for this,* McInerny thought.

JAPANESE STRIKING FORCE
FLAGSHIP CARRIER *AKAGI*
0914

The laborious process of rearming his planes with torpedoes was finally completed. For Admiral Nagumo it had been a brutally frustrating morning. After the first attack by the six American torpedo planes at 0700, he had ordered his reserve aircraft armed with contact bombs for a second strike on the air garrison at Midway.

This process necessitated not only removing the torpedoes, but changing the mounting hardware on each plane, which was different for launching a torpedo than for dropping a bomb. It was hard, time-consuming work. There were a limited number of crewmen to carry out the tasks and a limited number of trolleys to carry the torpedoes off the deck and bring up the bombs. For much of the time, the flight crews had to stand around waiting for someone else to finish his part of the process.

Then came another piece of stunning news. Shortly before 0800, word reached Nagumo on the bridge that one of his search plane pilots had located an American task force of ten warships to the northeast of Midway.

There was no confirmation that the task force included aircraft carriers, but his chief of staff, Rear Admiral Kusaka, pointed out that it was highly unlikely there would be a task force in that area without at least one of them.

To Kusaka, it appeared to be another cruel twist of fate. The search plane pilot who had sighted the American task force had been delayed thirty minutes before taking off with the other search aircraft earlier that morning. If he had left on schedule, this new information would have arrived while Nagumo still had his reserve force of torpedo planes and bombers spotted on his flight decks and armed with ship-killing ordnance. Instead, they had been ordered below to be rearmed with contact explosives for the second Midway strike.

Nagumo acted immediately. Remembering Admiral Yamamoto's stern warning about keeping half of his air fleet in reserve for just such a development, he ordered his carrier crews to remove the bombs they had just attached to his planes, and rearm them with torpedoes.

While the new work went on, more attacks arrived from the American air garrison at Midway. After the 0700 attack by the torpedo planes, a group of American dive-bombers had arrived from Midway, followed by a flight of B-17s that harassed his carriers with bombs dropped from very high altitude. Although the dive-bombers had been driven off by his Zero fighters, and no hits were scored by any of the other American bombers, the attack had kept his fleet from landing their own planes right away after their first strike against Midway.

At 0820, the same search plane pilot who had found the American task force of ten ships reported sighting a carrier. Sinking the American carrier now became Nagumo's first priority.

All of these delays had been excruciating. None of his ships had been damaged, much less sunk, but it seemed as if fate was conspiring against him. If he hadn't decided to rearm the planes after receiving the attack by the six torpedo planes, he would have been able to launch his whole reserve force of one hundred aircraft against the American carrier.

Instead, he had had to stand on his bridge and wait. Now the process of rearming the reserve force with torpedoes was finally completed. He was prepared to launch his counterstrike against the American carrier as soon as his own planes from the Midway attack could be landed.

All but the last few were back aboard the four carriers by 0915. He only needed to order his fully loaded attack planes brought up to the flight decks, and then turn into the wind to launch them. If the striking force received no more threats in the meantime, his planes would quickly be airborne toward the American carrier.

JAPANESE STRIKING FORCE
TORPEDO SQUADRON EIGHT
0917

Staring into the distance, Waldron suddenly saw the wispy smoke columns dead ahead of them. The enemy ships began to take shape as dark silhouettes on the crystalline sea.

To Tex Gay, it looked like they almost covered the ocean. As the squadron closed in on the enemy task force, he could see three carriers in the first group, and a fourth following behind. There were battleships and cruisers and destroyers all over the place. Maybe all that guff about the Skipper's Sioux intuition had been right after all. He had gone straight to the enemy fleet like they had been on the end of a plumb line.

Waldron was on the radio again. He was attempting to contact Commander Stanhope Ring to let him know that they had located the Japanese carriers.

"Stanhope from Johnny One," Gay heard him say. "Enemy sighted."

There was no response.

"Stanhope from Johnny One . . . answer," he called again. "Enemy sighted."

Flying behind Commander Ring in the *Hornet* air group formation, Leroy Quillen, the radioman-gunner in the dive-bomber piloted by Ensign K. B. White, heard Waldron loud and clear.

"Stanhope from Johnny One," he repeated once more.

As Waldron continued leading Torpedo Eight toward the vanguard of the enemy striking force, Tex Gay observed that one of the four Japanese carriers was in the process of landing a plane. Remembering that the original attack plan called for hitting the carriers while their aircraft were off bombing Midway, his first reaction was, "Oh Christ, we're late."

Waldron was back again on the radio, this time talking to his men.

"We will go in," he said, sounding very calm. "We won't turn back. We will attack. Good luck."

The Skipper put his nose down before leveling off at about five hundred feet as he headed in. The rest of the squadron followed him in perfect precision, almost like synchronized swimmers. He had told them that they might have to go in alone, and now the worst had come.

His words gave Tex confidence that they had a fighting chance to get in and drop their torpedoes, then light out for home. A moment later, the sky around them was filled with Zeroes. The enemy fighters swung around in half loops and wingovers to gain better firing positions.

"Johnny One under attack," Waldron radioed.

From the bridge of the carrier *Akagi*, Commander Minoru Genda, Admiral Nagumo's operations officer, watched with almost detached fascination as the fifteen torpedo planes came on. The slow-moving Devastators reminded him of a flock of waterfowl crossing a lake. To Genda, it was sheer idiocy for them to attack without fighter protection, and a total violation of the first rule of war, which was to concentrate one's forces.

*At last they have come,* Genda thought to himself, having wondered when they would arrive ever since the American carrier force had been sighted. It puzzled him that they were coming in so low.

As the Zeroes swirled madly around the Devastators, it seemed to Tex Gay that he was flying in slow motion. The enemy fighters appeared to have three times his speed, and were darting in and out of their tight formation like backcountry prairie falcons.

Up ahead to the right, he saw one of the Devastators drop like a hurtling stone into the sea, its two-man crew gone in almost an instant. It happened so fast that Tex had no idea whose plane it was. A few seconds later, another Devastator went down on his left.

"Is that a Zero or one of our planes?" came Waldron's voice on the radio.

Tex radioed back that it was a Devastator.

The Zeroes were concentrating on the lead planes in the formation as Torpedo Eight continued boring in toward the nearest Japanese carriers. Tex tried to keep his Devastator steady and straight so that his crewman, Bob Huntington, had a clear and stable field of fire. That also made them easier prey.

He watched as another one of the Devastators blew up in a shower of flame and debris. They were past the airborne wreckage of men and plane a moment later. The dwindling formation was still miles from the carriers when yet another Devastator did a slow half roll and crashed into the sea on its back, disintegrating when it hit the water.

Bob Huntington came on the intercom.

"Let's go back and help, sir," he said.

There was nothing they could do to help. Tex could only press on with the attack, even if they were the last ones left. Those were the Skipper's orders. There would be time for mourning their losses later.

Two Zeroes moved in to attack him, one from behind and the other from the port side. He could feel machine gun bullets thudding into the armor plate behind his bucket seat. A second pattern raked his instrument panel and blasted several holes in the windshield.

He heard Bob Huntington cry out on the intercom. Turning his head for a quick look, he saw him slumped down in his seat, motionless. When he turned forward again, the Devastator that had been flying alongside him had disappeared.

In the distance, Tex saw that the carriers had all swung to the west, heading away from them to reduce their target profile. Shoving the throttle forward, he watched the air speed indicator slowly begin to climb. Waldron's voice was still coming through his earphones, fast and furious.

"There's two fighters in the water," the Skipper had radioed at one point. "See that splash . . . I'd give a million to know who done that."

In the tail compartment of his Dauntless dive-bomber far to the north, Leroy Quillen was listening to Waldron's excited words as they came through the radio. He wondered why no one in the group was responding to Waldron's calls.

"My two wingmen are going in," came Waldron's voice for the last time.

Then it was his turn.

The Skipper's plane was out in front of the remaining Devastators, all alone except for the attacking Zeroes. As Tex watched, Waldron's plane suddenly burst into flames. Fire quickly enveloped the fuselage, and the aircraft began gliding down toward the sea, trailing a thick cloud of smoke and fire.

The Skipper suddenly stood up in the blazing cockpit as if he was riding a fiery chariot. In the plane's final moments, he thrust his leg out onto the right wing. Then the plane hit the water and he was gone.

Bill Evans never knew which Japanese pilot had killed him. He probably would have wanted the chance to write down what those last seconds were like, the sounds of the screaming engine, the flashing images, the colors of the tracer bullets hammering into his fuselage. But he would never have the opportunity. At twenty-three, he had run out of time. A hint of smoke temporarily marked the place where he went into the sea. A few moments later, it disappeared.

Leroy Quillen wasn't the only one listening to Waldron's urgent radio calls. Lieutenant Commander Ruff Johnson, leading the *Hornet* dive-bomber squadron on the left wing of Ring's formation, was given word of the transmissions and realized that on their present course, they were on a flight to nowhere.

Using his plotting board, he quickly drew a southeasterly interception course based on a rough calculation of where he thought the Japanese fleet had to be. Swinging out of the formation, he led his seventeen-plane squadron in a turn to the southeast.

Ensign Roy Gee, a young pilot from Salt Lake City, was flying in the second section behind Lieutenant Commander Johnson. The resourceful Gee had monitored the group's course throughout the flight. Until his squadron began its turn to the southeast, the *Hornet* air group hadn't deviated from the course it had started out on almost two hours earlier. Gee hoped they might still find the Japanese fleet before it was too late.

Stanhope Ring watched them go. His fighters had already left. Of the fifty-nine planes that had originally made up the group, only the dive-bombers in Walt Rodee's squadron remained with him. He signaled one of his wingmen to fly over to Rodee and signal him to stay in formation.

They were all gone. Fourteen pilots, fourteen crewmen.

The indestructible Grant Teats, who would no longer have to worry about Diana's emotional distress. Rusty Kenyon, who would never have the chance to hold his unborn child. Whitey Moore, who would never have his mountain farm in West Virginia. Abbie Abercrombie, who would never return to his beloved Kansas City. And Bill Evans, who would never write his book on the meaning of their sacrifice.

All of their dreams were dead. Along with those of Moose Moore, Jimmy Owens, Bob Miles, Bill Creamer, George Campbell, Jeff Woodson, Hal Ellison, Jack Gray, and the Skipper. And Horace Dobbs, Tom Pettry, Amelio Maffei, Otway Creasy, Ronald Fisher, Bernie Phelps, Bill Sawhill, Frank Polston, Max Calkins, George Field, Darwin Clark, Ross Bibb Jr., Hollis Martin, and "Pic" Picou.

Tex Gay was the last one left.

With Bob Huntington dead or unconscious in the rear seat, there was no longer any need for Tex to fly straight and level in order to provide his gunner a stable field of fire. He began jinking the plane, sideslipping between the Zeroes' machine gun bursts, drawing ever closer to the nearest carrier. The words of the Skipper kept replaying in his mind. *If there is only one man left, I want him to go in and get a hit.*

Tex had just opened fire with his nose gun at one of the Japanese fighters when a machine gun bullet from the Zero attacking him from behind grazed his left arm. The hand immediately went numb.

Up ahead, the Japanese cruisers and destroyers screening the carriers opened fire with their antiaircraft batteries. As soon as the barrage began, the swarming Zeroes darted away out of the line of fire.

Black bursts began mushrooming on both sides of his wings as the tracers sought him out. By some miracle, none of the shells hit him. The plane was bucking like a wild horse in the turbulent air as he passed over the screening ships and bored in toward the nearest carrier.

Using his right hand, he reached over and pulled back on the throttle, slowing the plane to eighty knots, which Waldron had always said was the ideal launching speed. Since this was the first torpedo he had ever launched, he wanted to make sure he got it right.

As he closed to within a thousand yards of the nearest carrier, it began swinging to the right to avoid his torpedo. Remembering his plotting exercises, Tex swung to the ship's port side for a higher percentage shot. Cutting across the bow, he headed back around in a tight turn and took aim slightly forward of the carrier's port bow.

When he punched the torpedo release button, nothing happened.

The electronic controls had been shot out. With his left hand numb, he jammed his knees together to hold the control stick in place, and reached over to pull out the emergency cable release lever with his right hand. He ripped it out by the roots.

Tex hoped the torpedo had gone because the carrier was now dead ahead of him, filling the screen of his windshield. He saw Japanese sailors running in all directions as the Devastator came screaming in toward the port side, just clearing the flight deck with a few feet to spare. Glancing up toward the bridge, he saw a Japanese officer wildly waving his arms in the air.

He knew that the antiaircraft batteries on the starboard side of the ship were waiting for him to cross so they could knock him out of the air. If he went that way, the Devastator would be an easy target.

Banking to the right, he flew down the carrier flight deck toward the stern of the ship. The flight deck was dotted with planes, gas hoses, and bomb trolleys. For a split second, he thought about crashing into them and setting the whole carrier ablaze. A moment later he was past the fantail and banking left to make his escape.

Flying low above the water, he passed between two Japanese cruisers and out beyond the task force destroyer screen. Another flock of Zeroes was waiting for him as soon as he came through the ships' last barrage of antiaircraft fire.

The plane was staggering along when a twenty-millimeter cannon shell blew apart his left rudder pedal and passed through into the engine compartment, setting it on fire. He felt a jolt of searing pain in his left leg as flames came surging back through the torn firewall.

There was no hope for the plane now. He was going in. Using the elevators, he kept the nose up as the Devastator dropped toward the sea. Using his right hand, he reached over to the left to cut the power switches.

The tip of his right wing hit water first, and the plane cartwheeled forward, slamming the cockpit hood shut above him. Black water was already flushing around his waist by the time he had unbuckled his shoulder straps.

The plane was going fast. As the nose dropped beneath the surface, Tex fought to release the jammed cockpit hood. It wouldn't move. Sitting on the bullet-shattered instrument panel, he tried to shove the hood along its track with his one good hand, but it wouldn't come free. He was trapped.

### NORTHWEST OF JAPANESE STRIKING FORCE
### HORNET DIVE-BOMBING SQUADRON
### WALT RODEE
### 0940

Lieutenant Commander Walt Rodee had finally seen enough.

His squadron's dive-bombers were now running dangerously short of fuel. He decided it was time to go home. He signaled to the planes in his squadron to follow him as he turned out of formation. Coming around 180 degrees, he began leading them back on a reciprocal course toward the *Hornet*. Ring's wingman departed with them.

Stanhope Cotton Ring continued flying west at 265 degrees, all alone.

### TEX GAY
### CRASHED IN THE SEA
### 0942

The seawater was up to his chin. In panic, he stood on the instrument panel and drove his upper body up against the jammed cockpit hood. It slowly moved back two feet, just enough for him to slip through the opening and reach the surface as the plane started to disappear.

The Plexiglas hoods over the middle and rear compartments

were still wide open. As the fuselage slid beneath the surface, he reached into the rear compartment to see if Bob Huntington might be still alive. He began trying to unbuckle Bob's flight harness while watching the seawater around his young gunner's chest turn dull red. Still strapped to his seat, Bob slipped from his grasp and went down with the plane.

### WEST OF MIDWAY ATOLL
### THE LAST AVENGER
### 0944

Whatever intuition Bert Earnest still possessed had told him it was time to turn east toward the sun. The moment had occurred almost an hour earlier. It had just felt right to change course to the east. Without a compass or any other instruments, all he had to go on was instinct.

The consequences of being wrong were obvious. If he overshot the tiny atoll of Midway, the next mass of land ahead of them would be Pearl Harbor, more than twelve hundred miles away. He wasn't sure he had enough gas to even reach Midway.

Having turned east, he and Harry saw nothing but ocean for miles in every direction. On and on they flew, searching vainly for the wake of an American ship or the hint of a landmass on the far horizon. As time passed, he began to consider the increasing likelihood that they would have to put the plane down in the sea. Although the water looked calm, there was very little chance that search planes would come looking for them to the west of Midway.

In frustration, he decided to climb through the cloud cover to see if something might be visible from a higher altitude. Rolling the trim tab wheel with his fingers, he took the battered plane up to four thousand feet.

Breaking through the clouds, he and Harry began scanning the sky ahead of them. Bert felt a shiver of excitement as he looked toward the southeast and saw what appeared to be black smoke.

He headed toward it, dropping down through the clouds as they drew closer. Emerging beneath the clouds, he could see that the smoke was coming from a massive oil or gasoline fire. The island could only be Midway.

It looked like they were going to make it.

With his radio shot out, there was no way for him to contact the airfield on Eastern Island to identify himself. As he approached Midway, Bert carefully went through the designated recognition turns that would identify the Avenger as a friendly aircraft. After coming this far, he didn't want some trigger-happy Marine gunner to shoot them down.

He changed course to land on the north-south runway, the same one he had taken off from early that morning. A lifetime ago. With no flap controls, he throttled back the engine as the plane slowly descended. Next, he pushed the undercarriage lever to lower the landing gear.

Nothing happened. The mechanical indicators in the cockpit showed that both wheels were still in their recessed compartments. Reaching down to the emergency release lever at the base of the instrument panel, he yanked hard on it.

The mechanical indicator for the left wheel now indicated that it had dropped down into its locked landing position. The right wheel had apparently stayed in its compartment.

His first thought was to try to shake the wheel loose. He used the trim tabs to climb back up to two thousand feet and then put the plane into a dive, waiting for the g-force to build before pulling the nose up.

The right wheel didn't come down. He took the plane back up again and tried the maneuver once more. The wheel refused to drop. Worried that the strain of the dives would shake the battered plane apart, he tried to think of something else. There were two options.

He could ditch the plane in the lagoon, or try to bring it in on one wheel.

With less than a hundred hours of flying time in an Avenger, he wasn't thrilled about trying to landing it on one wheel, but after everything they had come through, it didn't seem right to put it in the lagoon, particularly if there was a chance Jay Manning might still be alive. He decided to land.

As he came in over the airfield, the landing officer next to the runway began furiously waving him off with his signal flag. Advancing the throttle again, Bert rolled the trim tab to regain altitude.

He guessed that the landing officer had waved him off after seeing their torpedo hanging out of the bomb bay. After making another circuit around the field, he came in for his next approach. Once more, the landing officer frantically waved him off.

The hell with this, he said to himself. I'm taking it in.

The landing officer at the edge of the runway was still waving his flag when Bert's Avenger roared past him. Dropping to the runway, Bert felt his left wheel connect to the concrete path. He thought it was a beautiful one-point landing until the Avenger began slowing down. Suddenly, the right wing tipped over, hitting the runway and setting off an explosion of fiery sparks.

The plane spun wildly in a 270-degree arc toward several aircraft parked alongside the runway. As Bert braced himself for a crash, the Avenger finally came to a stop on the coral apron that abutted the runway.

It was over. He had come through the fire and survived.

Bert cut the power switches, and the air was quiet again. Unbuckling his safety harness, he saw a crash wagon speeding toward the plane. Climbing out of the cockpit on unsteady legs, he dropped off the wing and knelt down to look inside the open bomb bay. Their torpedo was gone. Only the cables that had held it in place were hanging from the belly. He had worried for hours over nothing.

Suddenly, there were people surging all around the plane. Harry had managed to get the rear hatch open and crawled outside. He felt faint as he tried to stand up. Two Marines came over to steady him. Seeing that his face and T-shirt were covered with blood, they helped him into a waiting field ambulance. A few moments later, he was on his way to the hospital tent.

Bert declined treatment of his own wound. Tottering like an old man, he headed back toward the turret to check on Jay Manning. A big Marine came up and blocked his path. Staring at the blood soaking Bert's flight suit, the Marine said quietly, "You don't want to go back there, sir."

Two other Marines were already draping a big canvas tarpaulin over the shattered turret where Manning had died. Turning away, Bert looked across the apron of the runway where the six Avengers had been parked that morning. It didn't look like any of the others had come back.

Another man was calling to him. It was the landing officer who had waved him off with his signal flag. "We were radioing for you to bail out," said the landing officer. "We thought bailing out would be your best chance."

Bert didn't have the energy to explain that his radio was gone along with the rest of the instruments. He asked the landing officer how many of the Avengers had gotten back.

"You're the only one so far," he said.

### TEX GAY
### FLOATING IN THE CENTRAL PACIFIC
### 0945

As Tex floated in the sea, two things suddenly surfaced alongside him, freed from the Devastator as it took its plunge toward the bottom of the Pacific. One of them was providential.

It was the aircraft's deflated life raft. He remembered Bob Huntington placing it in the middle seat before they took off. Apparently, it had not been strapped down. The other object floating in the water was a black rubber seat cushion.

The Skipper had always told them that if they were ever in a tight spot to never throw anything away. Tex decided to hold on to the cushion, too. His burned leg was beginning to hurt when he heard a plane diving and looked up to see a Zero heading straight toward him with its machine guns blazing. The surface of the sea began erupting in tiny geysers of water.

Pulling off his goggles in case they reflected the sun, he grabbed the black seat cushion and held it over his head. Treading water, he waited for the Zero to finish its run. It didn't come back.

JAPANESE STRIKING FORCE
FLAGSHIP CARRIER *AKAGI*
FLAG BRIDGE
0945

With the American torpedo squadron completely annihilated, an ebullient Admiral Nagumo was now free to release his counterstrike against the American carrier force.

Since the attack by the first six torpedo planes at 0700, his Zero fighters and his ships' antiaircraft batteries had destroyed or driven off every enemy plane. Not one of the torpedoes or bombs launched at his ships had hit a target.

A few minutes later, a lookout on one of the screening vessels reported that a new formation of enemy aircraft was approaching Nagumo's striking force from the south. It turned out to be another squadron of the same slow-moving torpedo planes.

The news came as a minor irritant to Nagumo, who knew that each American carrier had only one torpedo squadron. That meant a second American carrier was probably out there somewhere. All the better. Yamamoto's Midway plan was based on the notion of luring the American carriers from Pearl Harbor for the final deciding battle. Now they would be destroyed sooner rather than later.

With the crude frontal assaults the Americans had employed, Nagumo was confident the new element would be dispatched as easily as the others. In the meantime, he suspended the process of bringing up his own attack aircraft to the flight decks of his carriers until the latest American threat was repulsed.

His Zero fighter patrols headed south to intercept the new intruders, which were the fourteen Devastators of Torpedo Squadron Six from Spruance's flagship *Enterprise*, led by Lieutenant Commander Gene Lindsey.

The Zeroes dropped down to intercept the Americans as they

came skimming in just above the surface of the sea, and the Japanese pilots quickly began shooting them out of the sky. In less than twenty minutes, most of the Devastators had been destroyed. The surviving aircraft retreated without scoring any hits.

"Launch aircraft when ready," Nagumo ordered his four carrier commanders.

The Japanese carriers were turning into the wind for their launch when yet another report came in from one of the screening vessels. They had sighted more planes coming toward them. It was Torpedo Squadron Three, led by Lieutenant Commander Lance Massey. They had come from the *Yorktown*.

The newly replenished fighter patrols flying cover above the four carriers immediately went down low again to converge on this latest threat. One by one, the Devastators began to fall.

Was it possible that there were three American carriers lying in wait for him, wondered Nagumo? In his exultant mood, it was still of little consequence. He had driven off every previous attack without the loss of a single ship. At the same time, it was wise to be prudent.

It was 1020.

"Hurry up preparations for the second wave," he ordered Commander Genda.

TEX GAY
FLOATING IN THE CENTRAL PACIFIC
1020

After being strafed in the water by the Zero, Tex decided not to inflate his rubber life raft. There was no point in drawing attention to himself, not with the Japanese fleet cruising by like it was the Easter parade.

The wakes of the Japanese warships had roiled up the surface of the ocean, but even from his lowly vantage point, he could see the distant silhouettes of three of the Japanese carriers, including the one he had attacked before being shot down.

They had now turned into the wind.

From high above him in the sky, he heard a distinctly familiar whine. It reminded him of the low keening wail that a dive-bomber made right after pushing off on a bomb run from high altitude. He had heard it during training flights plenty of times.

It suddenly dawned on him that it just might be a dive-bomber. Hell, there had been more than thirty Dauntlesses flying with the *Hornet* air group alone. As the low moaning wail turned into a full-throttle screaming roar, he knew what the noise had to mean.

Then he saw one.

The Dauntless was plummeting down from more than two miles high, completely unopposed by the Japanese Zeroes. A few moments later, it was joined by a second and a third. He realized there must be a whole squadron, if not more.

The first Dauntless was already pulling up after completing its plunge to less than two thousand feet. Tex heard a terrific thunderclap, and a few moments later, a curtain of fire rocketed up from the deck of one of the carriers like a giant Roman candle. The same ship took another direct hit, followed by a third, each new detonation sending up a thick cloud of smoke and flame.

Still more Dauntlesses were diving now. Free of any hindrance from the vaunted Zeroes, they plunged down toward the remaining carriers. As he watched, another colossal blast resounded across the water, and a second Japanese carrier erupted into a blazing firestorm. Flames were coming out of both the fore and aft sections of the second carrier like a two-headed blowtorch.

Kicking his feet, he began yelling a hoarse cheer of soggy defiance, but it was quickly squelched by a surging wave. As he treaded water, a third rumbling blast thundered across the sea, and a billowing spire of smoke belched up from the third Japanese carrier. Submerged up to his chest, Tex could feel the pressure of the detonations.

He wondered if any of the victorious dive-bombers had come from the *Hornet*.

NORTHEAST OF MIDWAY ATOLL
*HORNET* DIVE-BOMBING SQUADRON
WALT RODEE
1040

Walt Rodee continued to lead his seventeen-plane squadron east on the reciprocal heading of the course they had flown out on that morning. The whole mission had been a total mess. All of his Dauntlesses were still carrying their full bomb loads. None of the pilots had seen a single Japanese plane or warship the whole way out or back.

He couldn't imagine what kind of reception they would receive from Pete Mitscher when they landed. It wouldn't be long now. Rodee's radio homing gear was working fine. They were less than an hour from the carrier.

As they droned along, another aircraft slowly overtook them. It was Commander Ring's Dauntless. He was flying at open throttle, making no attempt to conserve gas. He passed them by, heading east toward the *Hornet*.

NORTHEAST OF MIDWAY ATOLL
*HORNET* FIGHTER SQUADRON EIGHT
PAT MITCHELL
1045

Pat Mitchell's ten Wildcats had now been in the air for almost four hours, and none of the pilots had any idea where they were. After departing from Commander Ring and the rest of the air group, they had headed in an easterly direction back toward the *Hornet*. Pat Mitchell's radio homing device wasn't functioning properly, and he had turned over navigational responsibility to Stan Ruehlow.

There was nothing but ocean as far as they could see. From what had once been a mission to destroy the Japanese carriers, they were now in a desperate struggle to survive. One by one, they started running out of gas.

The first to go was Ensign G. R. Hill, who was Stan Ruehlow's wingman. As some of the others watched, his propeller started windmilling. Seconds later he was gone.

The Wildcat was a well-designed fighter, but it had the gliding capacity of a concrete block. McInerny was the next to go, and Johnny Magda went with him. They landed a hundred yards from one another on a placid sea.

Frank Jennings and Hump Tallman went next.

One of the last to go down was Pat Mitchell. After hitting the water, his Wildcat sank before he could extricate his life raft. When the plane disappeared, he was wearing only his Mae West life vest.

Mitchell was confident the pilots who survived ditching would be picked up soon. The rest of the *Hornet* air group had seen them go. Some of those crewmen must have written down the approximate bearings when McInerny had turned the fighter squadron around. Once the battle was over, he knew that Navy search planes from Midway would begin looking for them.

That is, if the Americans won.

NORTHEAST OF MIDWAY ATOLL
USS *HORNET*
1100

On the bridge of the *Hornet,* Lieutenant A. H. Hunker was standing the deck watch when he received a report that "a large group of planes bearing 260 true, distant 56 miles" was being tracked by the ship's radar and heading straight toward them.

These were the planes of Walt Rodee's dive-bomber squadron, returning from the west on the reciprocal course to the one the group had flown out on three hours earlier. Preparations began to land the planes as soon as they arrived.

When the *Hornet* turned into the wind to bring them aboard, a crowd of excited crewmen rushed to the flight deck to welcome the returning air group from its mission against the Japanese fleet. Hopes were high for news of victory.

They were puzzled to see only one plane come in to land. When it came to a halt on the flight deck, Commander Stanhope Ring unstrapped himself from the cockpit and climbed down.

Without acknowledging the cheers of the crew, he disappeared into one of the passageways off the flight deck, and went to his stateroom. Mitscher was forced to wait for the arrival of Rodee's squadron to learn what had happened. Upon landing, Rodee was ordered to the bridge. When he got there, Mitscher demanded to know what had happened to his group.

Rodee couldn't tell him.

He had flown west on the designated course until reaching the point of no return, and had then turned around to come back on the reciprocal course. None of his pilots had seen a Japanese ship or airplane going out or coming back. Somewhere along the way, Waldron's squadron had disappeared, followed by Mitchell's ten fighters. Later on, Ruff Johnson had taken his squadron off. Rodee had no idea what had happened to any of them.

After being dismissed, Rodee joined the pilots of his squadron in the wardroom, where they were relaxing with coffee and sandwiches. At some point after the flight, he decided to put an important detail from the previous mission in his official flight log.

Each page in a pilot's flight log had space for the date of a flight, the names of the crewmen who flew with him, the duration of the mission, and a brief description of the flight. Rodee decided to write down the course the *Hornet* air group had flown that morning.

*265 degrees.*

Outside on the flight deck, Lee Marona was standing with the rest of the plane captains from Torpedo Eight. They were still scanning the empty sky for a sign of approaching aircraft.

According to the scuttlebutt, Midway was supposed to be the biggest battle of the war so far. *If it is,* Marona thought, *we haven't seen any part of it.* Not one of the *Hornet*'s guns had been fired in anger all day.

Up on the flag bridge, Mitscher and his senior air staff were increasingly worried. This had been Mitscher's first chance to demonstrate his experience and acumen in a carrier battle, and as far as he knew, none of the *Hornet*'s planes had found the Japanese fleet.

Mitchell's fighter squadron could no longer be airborne. By now, Johnson's and Waldron's squadrons would be running out of gas, too, if they were still in the air. Where the hell were they?

The stakes were enormous, not only for the battle itself, but for Pete Mitscher's reputation and career. He had come a long way since Annapolis, where he had been expelled in his second year for a hazing incident. After his father exerted influence, he had started over. It had taken him six years to finish, graduating just three places from the bottom of his class.

It had not been an auspicious beginning, but Mitscher had gone on to blaze a successful trail in naval aviation and earn the respect of both his peers and superiors. He had served thirty-two years in the Navy. The idea that his career as a combat commander might be over after one day was difficult to bear.

He and his staff were forced to face the hard truth. They had sent out fifty-nine planes, and their air group commander had come back by himself, followed by a single bomber squadron still carrying all its bombs.

Mitscher could only hope that the other two *Hornet* squadrons, Ruff Johnson's dive-bombers and Johnny Waldron's torpedo planes, had done some damage to the Japanese striking force.

NORTHWEST OF MIDWAY ATOLL
*HORNET* DIVE-BOMBER SQUADRON
RUFF JOHNSON
1120

Still heading southeast, Ruff Johnson had spent a frustrating hour trying to locate the Japanese carriers after receiving Waldron's last desperate radio transmission. He hadn't found a trace of them. Now his squadron was running out of gas. As the fuel situation became critical, he decided to turn northeast in the hope that they could still reach the *Hornet*.

Off to port, he spotted another aircraft. It was the first plane from outside his own air group that he had seen on the entire flight. Johnson quickly identified it as an American patrol plane, and signaled to its crew that they were lost. The PBY pilot used his blinking lamp to give Johnson a navigational course to follow to Midway Atoll.

Johnson signaled the rest of his pilots that they were to follow him. Ignoring Johnson's signal, Johnson's executive officer, Lieutenant Alfred Tucker, continued flying northeast in the general direction of the *Hornet*. Two of the pilots followed him.

Johnson continued southeast on the coordinates the PBY pilot had given him. Using his plotting board, he figured they were approximately one hundred twenty miles from Midway.

A few minutes later, Ensign Troy Guillory felt his engine begin to sputter.

He was one of the pilots who had been assigned to carry a thousand-pound bomb in the belly, instead of the five-hundred-pounder most of the dive-bombers were carrying. Even though he had conserved fuel, the extra weight had finally run him dry. His propeller began to windmill and Guillory started down. As the rest of the squadron continued flying south, he made a successful landing on a calm sea.

In the distance ahead of him, Ruff Johnson saw a huge black fire plume emerge out of the haze. It was Midway. A few minutes later, another one of his dive-bombers ran out of fuel and headed down toward the sea.

Johnson began to worry that some of his pilots would run out of gas while landing with live bombs aboard. He diverted course to jettison his own bomb on the reef protecting Midway Atoll. The other pilots dropped their bombs in the same place and followed Johnson in to land.

Believing they were under attack, the antiaircraft gunners on Eastern Island opened fire on the Dauntlesses as they came into range, hitting three of the planes. Another Dauntless ran out of gas and ditched in the lagoon before Johnson was able to contact the ground controllers and convince them he was friendly.

His men had finally been under fire, even if it was from American Marines.

JAPANESE STRIKING FORCE
LIGHT CRUISER NAGARA
1630

To Commander Mitsuo Fuchida, the indomitable air commander who had led the Japanese attack on Pearl Harbor, the three dying Japanese carriers looked like spewing volcanoes as they belched flames and smoke into the azure blue sky. Reduced to tears, he sensed that Japan's chance for the final victory was about to die with them.

At least the *Hiryu*, the last of the four magnificent carriers in the striking force, remained miraculously untouched by the Dauntlesses. After avoiding a rain of bombs that morning, she had launched a counterstrike against the Americans, and her attack planes had reportedly sunk one of their carriers.

The fires on the *Akagi*, the *Kaga*, and the *Soryu* had raged most of the day, with each one becoming a red-hot mass of twisted metal torn by explosions of aviation gas, bombs, and torpedoes. As Nagumo and his staff watched in mortified silence, the flames also incinerated two thousand of the empire's finest sailors and airmen.

Fuchida's own escape from the flagship *Akagi* had been nothing less than miraculous. Still badly weakened from appendicitis, he was standing on the bridge of the *Akagi* at 1025 when a lookout had screamed, "Hell divers!"

He immediately trained his binoculars skyward. Through a break in the high cloud cover, Fuchida could see three dive-bombers plunging toward the *Akagi*, their silhouettes growing larger as they plummeted straight down. Far above the first three, he saw more Hell Divers pushing their noses over to begin their own runs.

Fuchida had flown dozens of dive-bombing missions himself. Watching them come, he felt like a judo master observing a brilliant and wholly unexpected pinning move by a slow, dull-witted novice.

In those last fleeting moments before the bombs struck, Fuchida sensed that the battle was about to be lost. The carriers had been caught flat-footed, focused on the successive frontal attacks from the low-flying torpedo planes, and oblivious to the danger from this high-altitude threat. Without opposition from fighters or the concentrated antiaircraft firepower of the screening ships, the dive-bomber pilots might as well have been flying a training mission.

Like all the previous attackers, these pilots were undeniably brave, only letting their bombs go at the last possible moment to ensure the best chance of success. As they pulled out of their screaming dives, he watched three ugly black cigar shapes come slanting in toward the *Akagi*.

Knowing what was about to happen, he threw himself down behind a cushioned barrier near the bridge railing. A moment later, he felt the bone-rattling concussion of a direct hit, followed almost immediately by a second hit off to the port side of the ship. A third bomb struck somewhere close to the stern.

Daring to stand at the railing as splinters of hot metal flew in every direction, Fuchida found his gaze drawn to the enormous black hole in the flight deck. The fifty-foot crater was adjacent to the amidships elevator that lifted the *Akagi*'s planes up from the hangar deck. The elevator was completely wrecked.

Fuchida rushed down from the bridge to better survey the damage. Through the jagged hole in the steel plates, he could see the bodies of mechanics and armorers strewn near the wreckage of shattered aircraft along the hangar floor. Secondary explosions began going off deep within the ship.

Returning to the bridge through dense black smoke, Fuchida saw that the sky was now empty. The American dive-bombers had come and gone in a span of less than ten minutes. Perhaps they had missed the other carriers, he thought, as he trained his binoculars toward the rest of the striking force.

To his horror, he saw that the *Kaga* and *Soryu* were both spouting columns of black smoke. They, too, had taken direct hits. He could only hope that the damage wasn't mortal. Aboard the carriers were the Japanese Empire's finest pilots, the men he had personally led in the attack on Pearl Harbor.

One of the bombs had jammed the *Akagi*'s rudder, and the ship began to steam in a wide circle. At 1042, she came to a dead stop. Fire control teams stood with hoses ready to try to extinguish the fires beneath the flight deck, but there was no water pressure in the pumps to operate them.

Belowdecks, hundreds of men in the engine rooms were dead or dying, suffocated by the smoke that had been drawn into the ship's internal ventilation ducts. On the bridge, a communications officer reported that the ship's radio transceivers were no longer working. There was now no way for Admiral Nagumo to contact the other ships in his striking force.

Flames began surging up the closed passageways to the bridge, and the heat became almost unbearable. As secondary explosions continued to rock the innards of the ship, the bridge structure began to shudder.

Admiral Nagumo appeared to be in shock, and Commander Fuchida understood why. The admiral had never lost a ship under his command to an enemy force. Now he was about to lose his flagship, the jewel of the carrier fleet, and possibly the rest of his carriers, too, along with hundreds of their finest combat planes and crew.

It fell to a senior member of Nagumo's staff to respectfully suggest that it was time to transfer his flag to another ship. Fuchida waited along with the others for the admiral to respond. Nagumo stood frozen-faced, his powerful arms stiffly at his sides, staring out of a bridge window.

"It is not time yet," he said.

"You are the commander-in-chief of the first carrier striking force," persisted the staff officer. "It is your duty to carry on the battle."

Nagumo finally agreed to leave the sinking carrier, but by then, the passageways from the bridge were choked with fire and smoke. There was no way to escape except through a forward window.

Someone secured a line to one of the bridge stanchions and flung the other end of it through the open window. Nagumo went out first. A former jujitsu expert, he dropped smoothly to the gun deck before climbing down a monkey ladder to the flight deck.

Fuchida was one of the last to leave. In his weakened state, he could barely hold on to the smoldering straw line as he went down hand-over-hand to the gun deck. The monkey ladder that connected it to the flight deck was now red-hot.

There was no alternative but to jump the last ten feet. As he launched himself out from the railing, another explosion from the hangar deck hurled him even higher into the air. In the resulting fall, both his ankles were broken.

As he lay in agony on the fire-ravaged deck with ammunition exploding around him, Fuchida was sure it was the end. Seeing him in distress, two brave sailors raced across the burning flight deck and carried him to safety.

Medics strapped him to a bamboo stretcher, and he was put in the launch with Nagumo's staff before it was ferried over to the light cruiser *Nagara*, the admiral's new flagship.

All of that afternoon, Fuchida watched the carriers go through their death throes. The *Soryu* had gone first. Hit by three one-thousand-pound bombs, she had become a pillar of flame within twenty minutes of the attack, and had gone down with her captain, all of her aircraft, and seven hundred crewmen.

The flagship *Akagi* was abandoned early in the evening. By then, she was nothing more than a drifting hulk, waiting only for her final ignominious sinking at the hands of Japanese destroyers. The ceremonial portrait of Emperor Hirohito that graced the wardroom of every Japanese warship had already been removed from its place of honor and ferried over to the destroyer *Nowake*.

The burned-out carrier *Kaga* was also dead in the water after having received five direct hits in the morning attack. Eight hundred members of its crew were entombed inside when the orders were given for the Japanese destroyer *Hagikaze* to sink her, too.

And then came the crowning blow, the bitterest pill of all. Shortly before sunset, the American Hell Divers had returned, this time concentrating solely on the *Hiryu*, the final carrier in the Japanese striking force, the last floating platform for all its remaining pilots and planes.

When the Americans were finished, four bombs had penetrated deep inside the hull. Although her crew endured a horrific night battling the internal fires, the *Hiryu* joined her three sister carriers in the deep Pacific abyss. The only reminders that these once majestic ships had ever existed lay in the debris fields of dead sailors and wreckage scattered across a thirty-mile stretch of sea.

The *Hiryu*'s remaining aircraft were forced to land in the ocean, joining the hundreds already littering the bottom from the *Akagi*, the *Kaga*, and the *Soryu*. Japanese destroyers picked up as many of the pilots and crews as they could find.

For Commander Fuchida and the other senior officers watching the catastrophe from the cruiser *Nagara*, the lost carriers represented far more than four of their most powerful warships.

They were emblematic of Japan's national pride, the culmination of bone-wearying sacrifice over the course of three decades to build Japan into a world-class power. The fast carriers had formed the heart of their bold new military philosophy that airpower, not battleships, would win the war.

The carriers had led the way in destroying the fleets of the European powers across the Pacific, and conquering lands and territory beyond their wildest ambitions. Now they had been wiped out in a single day.

It had to be fate, Fuchida concluded, right from the first unsupported attack by the six torpedo planes that had persuaded Admiral Nagumo to rearm his reserve planes with bombs instead of torpedoes.

And when Admiral Nagumo was finally ready to launch his counterstrike, the next torpedo plane squadrons had arrived, beginning their crude series of frontal attacks that never allowed the Japanese time to launch their own coordinated response.

Yes, it was the martyrdom of those unsupported torpedo planes that had sealed the carriers' doom. The Zeroes had been so busy killing the hedgehog they hadn't noticed the lurking tiger.

# When the Sea

# Shall Give Up Its Dead

Bert's Avenger sat like a blue metal Lazarus where it had finally come to rest at the edge of the runway. As word spread of its condition, men came from around the field to look at it, pausing for a few moments to stare at the shredded fuselage and wonder how the plane had made it back to Midway.

Marines had removed Jay Manning's body from the turret, and reverently placed him in the back of a truck. He was transported to the edge of the lagoon where the rest of the dead from the morning attack had been laid out side-by-side under blankets and tarps.

Eastern Island was littered with bomb rubble, and the choking smell of burning aviation gas permeated the air. Personal belongings and pieces of equipment were scattered everywhere. The mess tent where the officers in Torpedo Eight had eaten their meals was leveled, along with the shack where Bert and Charlie Brannon had bought their warm beers with paper chits the previous night.

Only the atoll's natural inhabitants appeared oblivious to the destruction that had taken place that morning. With calm detachment, the gooney birds silently plodded around the wreckage of machines and buildings.

Bert still thought there was an outside chance that Fieberling and the other pilots might have had enough gas to make it back. As planes continued to land, he kept checking to see if any of them were Avengers.

An intelligence officer asked Bert to accompany him to the flight operations tent where they were debriefing the returning pilots. There, the officer asked him to describe what had happened on his mission.

Bert told him they had found the Japanese fleet about one hundred fifty miles out on a heading of 320 degrees, and that Lieutenant Fieberling had led them in against one of the carriers. He had no idea whether the others had scored any hits against the enemy ships or what had happened to them.

The officer never asked him why Lieutenant Fieberling had chosen to lead the six-plane detachment against the Japanese fleet alone instead of waiting for the air group to rendezvous. It remained a mystery to Bert.

Beyond the walls of the tent, he could hear military aircraft continuing to take off and land on the hastily repaired runways. It suddenly struck him that they might be short of pilots.

"You know, I'm checked out on dive-bombers, too," he said. "If you still need pilots, I can fly one of those."

The staff officer glanced at Bert's wound and said, "Why don't you have that taken care of first?"

At the hospital tent, one of the medics cleaned the wound and put a compression bandage on Bert's neck, holding it in place with his fingers while wrapping several layers of white gauze and tape around the back of his head and below his jaw. When he was finished, Bert looked like the apparition of Jacob Marley's ghost in *A Christmas Carol*.

Not knowing what else to do, he walked back to the plane. There, one of the Marines told him he had counted more than a hundred machine gun and cannon holes in the wings, fuselage, and tail section.

Bert heard someone call out his name. Turning, he was surprised to see several dive-bomber pilots he knew from the *Hornet* air group. They were from Ruff Johnson's bombing squadron, and said they had just landed on Midway after a mission from the carrier. That was when Bert learned that American carrier forces had been part of the battle.

When the Dauntless pilots got finished staring at his bandages and bloody flight suit, they began to look over the battered Avenger. Bert asked them whether they had found the Japanese carriers, and they shook their heads no.

"What was it like?" one of them asked him about his own flight.

5 JUNE 1942
FLOATING IN THE CENTRAL PACIFIC
TEX GAY

All of that first day, Tex had treaded water in the sea, afraid to inflate his yellow life raft for fear of attracting one of the Japanese ships that were still steaming back and forth to pick up survivors from the burning carriers.

When darkness finally descended, he took the chance of inflating it. The raft had been perforated with bullet holes, but the $CO_2$ canister filled enough of the airtight compartments to keep him afloat. He tried to patch the holes, but soon gave up.

That night, the temperature dropped and his wet flight suit gave him little protection from the cold wind. The burns on his left leg began to ache. Lying in several inches of seawater, he looked through the small survival kit that was attached to the raft.

It held no potable drinking water, but he found some candy, which kept saliva working in his mouth. He thought about discarding his wet boots, but they were Justin jodhpur riding shoes and he had paid a lot for them. They stayed on his feet.

The long night seemed almost interminable, and he never slept, keeping vigil against sharks and Japanese ships. As dawn broke, Tex saw that the enemy fleet had disappeared. He was alone on the sea, drifting through a field of floating wreckage. He decided to take off his flight suit to let it dry in the sun. Shortly after that, he heard the sound of a distant aircraft.

The plane flew almost directly over him, and he saw that it was a PBY patrol plane. Someone in the plane's crew must have seen his yellow raft because the plane began making a slow circle above him. When Tex spread his arms horizontally, which was the "roger" sign for being okay, the pilot rocked his wings before continuing his flight to the northwest.

He knew then that someone would be coming back for him. It was only a matter of time. He silently prayed that they would get there before a Japanese ship happened along.

Through all of that second day, Tex drifted across the vast debris field. Nauseous and dehydrated, he finally lost consciousness. Awakening, he saw the sun dropping in the western sky. His left hand had swollen up to almost twice its normal size.

Late that afternoon, he again heard the sound of an aircraft engine, and looked up to see the same PBY coming back from its long flight in search of the retreating Japanese fleet. The pilot brought it down on the calm sea, and taxied right up to his raft. A crewman was standing in the open hatch. He gently helped Tex inside.

Once in the air, they gave him water, but he couldn't keep it down. When he told the pilot, Lieutenant "Pappy" Cole, that he had seen three Japanese carriers burning, the plane headed straight for Midway. There, the island commander came to the aircraft to confirm what Tex had told the crew.

Tex was put aboard another plane to Hawaii and knocked out with a painkiller. At the naval hospital in Pearl Harbor, the first doctor asked him how he had kept the wounds so clean.

"I kept them soaked in salt water for thirty hours," quipped Tex with a weary grin.

In the thirty hours he had been in the sea, he had lost more than twenty pounds. After doctors removed the shrapnel from his hand and applied a clean dressing to his leg, he was wheeled back to his room. Tex was lying in bed when the door swung open, and an elderly white-haired officer walked in, followed by a group of staff officers. Tex recognized him right away from his newspaper pictures. It was Admiral Chester Nimitz, the commander-in-chief of the Pacific Fleet.

When Tex tried to come to attention lying down, Nimitz said, "Relax, son. How do you feel?"

Tex told him he was doing fine. Commander Ernest Eller, one of Nimitz's staff officers, was amazed that the young man could be so open and cheerful after everything he had just gone through.

"I'd like you to tell me what you saw out there, son," said the admiral. "Do you feel up to telling us about it?"

Tex told him everything that had happened from the time Lieutenant Commander Waldron sighted the Japanese carriers until he was shot down. When he told about seeing the three carriers being hit, the admiral questioned him closely about it.

"You're sure those three carriers sunk, son?" he asked.

"You don't have to worry, Admiral," Tex assured him. "From the way those ships were burning, they had to be going down."

WESTERN PACIFIC
JAPANESE CRUISER NAGARA
ADMIRAL CHUICHI NAGUMO

Aboard the *Nagara*, Admiral Nagumo's staff was worried that their commander might commit suicide before the ship reached its home-island port of Kure. They took turns watching him while the *Nagara* continued to retreat across the gray, rain-swept sea.

Farther to the west of the *Nagara*, Nagumo's superior officer, Admiral Isoroku Yamamoto, was steaming home aboard his own flagship, the battleship *Yamato*. The man who had planned a decisive victory over the Americans in the Pacific had instead presided over a deciding defeat.

After receiving the radio message that uncontrollable fires were consuming the *Akagi*, the *Kaga*, and the *Soryu*, Yamamoto had lapsed into stony-faced silence. When word arrived that the *Hiryu* had been sunk, he retreated to his flag quarters. Along with the rest of the high command, he reached the home islands determined that no word of the appalling disaster should reach the Japanese people.

On June 10, the Japanese radio networks trumpeted a great naval victory over the United States. The announcement was preceded by the playing of the "Battleship March," a song the Japanese people had come to associate with every grand military triumph.

The radio networks reported that the Japanese Imperial Navy had emerged victorious in a titanic battle near Midway in which two heavy American carriers had been sunk at the loss of only one Japanese ship and thirty-five combat planes. The triumph was celebrated throughout the home islands by an ecstatic nation.

When the crews of Nagumo's striking force arrived at Kure Naval Base, they were confined to their ships. Leaves were forbidden, and contact with anyone ashore was prohibited.

The shell-shocked survivors of the four lost carriers were disembarked at a remote pier at Yokosuka under armed guard and then taken in a convoy to the base hospital complex, where they were placed in segregated buildings and guarded around the clock.

Wounded officers were treated no differently. They were all sent to locked wards in various military hospitals. None were allowed visitors, not even their wives and families.

Commander Mitsuo Fuchida, the heroic leader of the Pearl Harbor attack, was no exception. Still weakened from appendicitis and with both his ankles broken, he was secretly removed at night from the cruiser *Nagara* on a covered stretcher. He recovered from his injuries in total isolation.

Sitting alone each day in his hospital room, Fuchida concluded that the catastrophic defeat at Midway was probably the turning point of the war. If so, the capitulation of the Japanese Empire was only a matter of time.

SATURDAY, 6 JUNE 1942
USS *HORNET*
FLAG BRIDGE

On June 6, the remaining ships of the Japanese Imperial Navy retreated out of striking range, ending the Battle of Midway. The fight to save the careers and reputations of the senior officers aboard the *Hornet* had just begun.

Stanhope Ring's calamitous mission on the morning of June 4 had resulted in the deaths of twenty-nine of the thirty men in Waldron's Torpedo Eight. All ten pilots from the *Hornet*'s fighter squadron were still missing. Although Rodee's squadron had come back intact, three Dauntlesses from Johnson's squadron had also been lost.

Of the fifty-nine planes that left the *Hornet* to attack the Japanese fleet on the morning of June 4, John Waldron's squadron had been the only one to locate and attack the Japanese carriers, and that was solely because he had disobeyed a direct order from Commander Ring.

If the thirty-four dive-bombers from the *Hornet* had followed the same course Waldron did, the combined air groups from the three American carriers might well have sunk all four Japanese carriers on the first morning of the battle.

Instead, the fourth Japanese carrier, the *Hiryu*, had escaped the morning attack and subsequently launched a counterstrike against the *Yorktown*, pounding it with three five-hundred-pound bombs and two air-launched torpedoes.

On the afternoon of June 4, there had been a good opportunity for Mitscher to make amends for the failure of the morning mission. After the *Hiryu* was sighted, Admiral Spruance ordered his two carrier commanders to mount a combined strike against the last Japanese carrier in the striking force with every available dive-bomber.

"Prepare to launch attack group immediately, information later," Admiral Spruance radioed the *Enterprise* and the *Hornet* at 1510. The two carriers then received a follow-up communication from Spruance indicating the location and course of the *Hiryu*.

As these messages were being received, firefighting crews aboard the *Yorktown* were fighting to save the ship. The carrier was in no condition to launch a retaliatory strike.

At 1542, the *Enterprise* launched twenty-five Dauntlesses to go after the *Hiryu*.

Thirty minutes later, the *Hornet* began launching its own dive-bombers. They were delayed because Mitscher decided to first land the planes from Ruff Johnson's squadron, which had just arrived from Midway Atoll.

Sixteen of Mitscher's Dauntlesses had lifted from the flight deck when two of the pilots suddenly signaled that they were having mechanical problems. As the two planes came in for emergency landings, half the *Hornet*'s dive-bombers were still aboard the carrier, waiting to take off on the attack mission. The pilots included Ring and both his squadron commanders.

As soon as the two malfunctioning planes were safely down, Mitscher ordered the *Hornet* to be turned out of the wind, ending the launch. It was another major foul-up. By the time it was discovered that Ring and his senior pilots were still on the flight deck, it was too late to launch them.

Mitscher's staff scrambled to find out who the senior pilot was among the fourteen planes already in the air. Lieutenant Edgar Stebbins, an engineer officer in one of the squadrons, was ordered to lead the mission against the *Hiryu*.

By the time Stebbins found the last Japanese carrier, it had already received four direct hits from the Dauntless pilots of the *Enterprise* and was a blazing inferno. Looking around for another target, Stebbins spotted an escort vessel and proceeded to lead an attack on it. Fourteen bombs were dropped in the face of antiaircraft fire. All of them missed. The pilots returned to the *Hornet*.

That night on the bridge, Mitscher and his senior staff reviewed the *Hornet*'s performance. By every measure, including Mitscher's own, the first day had been a complete fiasco. In his own assessment, he had "failed to deliver."

It was hard to believe that so much could have gone wrong. While the air groups from the *Enterprise* and the *Yorktown* had succeeded in destroying all four Japanese carriers, the *Hornet* had never scored a hit.

When the sun rose on June 5, the four Japanese carriers were at the bottom of the Pacific. With them had gone three thousand sailors, two hundred fifty-eight combat planes, and more than a hundred of the empire's finest pilots. It had been an almost unbelievable victory.

There were still plenty of targets left, however. Fragmentary sighting reports suggested that two Japanese battleships were maneuvering somewhere to the northwest. Admiral Spruance waited through most of the day for a sighting report before committing his remaining combat planes to go after them. The sighting finally came that afternoon.

Due to the projected distance to the enemy battleships, Spruance ordered that all the dive-bombers be armed with five-hundred-pound bombs instead of thousand-pounders to increase their range. The thirty-two Dauntlesses launched from the *Enterprise* were armed accordingly.

Another thirty-two Dauntlesses were launched from the *Hornet*. Commander Ring led the first element of eleven planes, all of them armed with five-hundred-pound bombs. Walt Rodee led the second element. Seven of his planes had been armed with one-thousand-pound bombs.

After a long, fruitless search pattern, Ring turned his element around to head back to the carrier. On the return flight, he encountered the Japanese destroyer *Tanikaze,* and led an attack on it. Ten of his eleven planes released their bomb loads, although none scored a hit. Commander Ring was unable to release his own bomb. It was still lodged in the bomb bay when he returned to the *Hornet.*

The second element of the *Hornet* attack group, led by Walt Rodee, was forced to curtail its mission when the seven Dauntlesses carrying one-thousand-pound bombs ran short of fuel. Afterward, Mitscher's staff falsely reported to Spruance that all of the *Hornet*'s Dauntlesses had been armed with five-hundred-pound bombs.

Upon landing back aboard the *Hornet,* Commander Ring complained to his plane captain that when he had attempted to drop his own bomb, it wouldn't release. Ring declared that he had kept pressing the button on his throttle handle but the bomb wouldn't drop.

Several of the *Hornet*'s dive-bomber pilots were on the flight deck to hear his complaint. Ensign Roy Gee, who flew in Ruff Johnson's squadron, was astounded when he heard about it, because that button did not release the plane's bomb. The button was used to transmit voice on the radio when a pilot was flying in formation.

Commander Ring apparently hadn't known that the bomb release mechanism was forward of the throttle, and was also unaware that there was an emergency lever to use if his bomb release failed.

Word of the incident quickly spread through the *Hornet*'s ready rooms. That same evening, Ring requested that Ensign Clay Fisher, one of his wingmen on the June 4 mission, come to his stateroom to explain to him exactly what he needed to do to drop a bomb in the future.

Aboard the *Enterprise,* Admiral Spruance was informed that Rodee's squadron of dive-bombers had returned before the *Enterprise* group, and Spruance demanded to know why. After requesting an explanation from Mitscher's staff, Spruance was informed that seven of Rodee's dive-bombers had been carrying thousand-pound bombs, contrary to orders. Spruance was already displeased that the *Hornet*'s dive-bombers had completely missed the enemy fleet the day before; now his opinion of Mitscher plummeted.

When dawn arrived on June 6, time was running out for Mitscher to redeem himself. A last opportunity presented itself later that morning as the three-day battle came to a close.

On June 5, two Japanese cruisers, the *Mogami* and the *Mikuma,* had accidentally collided with one another. The *Mogami*'s bow had been sheared off and the *Mikuma* began trailing a massive oil slick. They were the only significant enemy forces left to attack.

At 0800, Mitscher launched twenty-five dive-bombers under the command of Stanhope Ring. The air group commander found the crippled warships as they were making their retreat to the northwest.

Ring led the first element of dive-bombers in the attack on the *Mikuma.* Although he successfully managed to release his bomb this time, it missed the ship, as did the bombs in the rest of his element. Two of his Dauntlesses were shot down in the attack.

The *Hornet*'s second element finally hit pay dirt, scoring two direct hits on the second cruiser, *Mogami.* Unfortunately, there were no secondary explosions, and the Japanese crew was able to extinguish the fires after the *Hornet* air group departed. Arriving shortly afterward, thirty-one dive-bombers from the *Enterprise* put five hits into *Mikuma,* which sank later that day.

Mitscher launched a second strike of twenty-three dive-bombers as soon as the planes from the first strike could be fueled and re-armed. Later that afternoon, they found the *Mogami* and its escorts, scoring one hit on the cruiser and another on a destroyer before the two enemy ships escaped.

That attack was the last air action in the Battle of Midway. What would soon be recognized as the pivotal victory in the Pacific War was over. Late on the afternoon of June 6, Admiral Spruance ordered his forces to retire eastward toward Hawaii. Back at Pearl Harbor, Admiral Nimitz anxiously awaited his commanders' reports detailing everything that had occurred during the battle.

After a long and gallant effort to save the *Yorktown,* the carrier finally rolled over and sank one day later. By then Admiral Spruance had already concluded that if Mitscher's dive-bombers had found the fourth Japanese carrier on the morning of June 4, the *Yorktown* might not have been lost.

How could Pete Mitscher and his staff account for what had happened to the *Hornet* air group on the morning of June 4? Navy regulations were very specific on the subject of filing After Action Reports. The Bureau of Aeronautics required that After Action Reports "be filled out by a unit commander immediately upon landing after each action or operation in contact with the enemy." Commander Ring was required to file one along with each one of the four squadron commanders. They were supposed to accompany Mitscher's report on behalf of the carrier.

Ultimately, Mitscher and his staff decided that only one After Action Report from the *Hornet* would be submitted to Admiral Nimitz. It was prepared by the staff and signed by Mitscher. The report never stated the actual course his air group had flown on the morning of June 4.

"The objective, enemy carriers, was calculated to be 155 miles distant, bearing 239 degrees T. from this Task Force . . ." were the exact words in the report. The *Hornet* air group had followed "the prescribed bearing."

In section six, the following line was incorporated in the report:

*AFTER SEARCHING THE PRESCRIBED BEARING THE SQUADRONS TURNED SOUTH TO SEARCH IN THE DIRECTION OF ENEMY ADVANCE. AS IT TURNED OUT, HAD THEY TURNED NORTH, CONTACT WOULD PROBABLY HAVE BEEN MADE.*

Spurious "official" map of the flight of the *Hornet* air group
on June 4, 1942. Adapted from the *Hornet*'s After Action Report,
and reprinted with the permission of B. K. Weisheit. Note that times
on the map are two hours later than the time on Midway. (A map
showing the actual route of the *Hornet* air group is included in
Appendix One.)

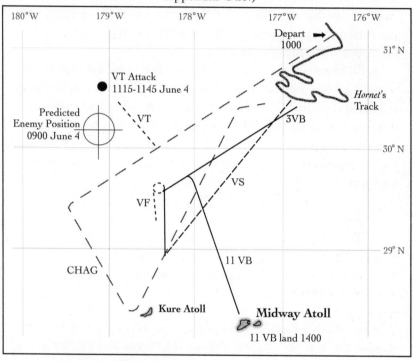

CHAG: Commander Stanhope Ring    — — — — — —
VT: Waldron's Torpedo Squadron    - - - - - - - - - -
VF: Mitchell's Fighter Squadron    · · · · · · · · · · ·
VS: Rodee's Bomber Squadron    — — — — — — —
VB: Johnson's Bomber Squadron    ——————

## HORNET AIR GROUP,
## JUNE 4, 1942

An accompanying map was prepared and included with the report. The map purported to show the courses flown by each of the four squadrons of the *Hornet* air group.

None of the officers and men who had actually witnessed the air group departing to the west or returning from the west would see the report. It would be classified secret as soon as it arrived at Nimitz's headquarters in Pearl Harbor.

The report and the map suggested that Ring had flown too far south of the Japanese fleet to make contact with it, and had only missed finding the enemy carriers by a hairbreadth. An honest mistake instead of a major blunder.

According to the map, John Waldron hadn't led his men southwest after breaking away from Ring, but to the northwest. The map indicated that Pat Mitchell's fighter squadron had turned north instead of east back toward the *Hornet* after McInerny led them away from the group.

And north of Midway was where the PBYs would begin searching for them.

FLOATING IN THE CENTRAL PACIFIC
*HORNET* FIGHTER SQUADRON EIGHT
MAC MCINERNY

If he ever made it back to civilization, the Navy was going to court-martial the hell out of him, thought McInerny as he floated in a raft next to his friend Johnny Magda. They might even accuse him of cowardice. After all, he had disobeyed orders and led the fighter squadron away from the group while the mission was still under way.

In the three and a half hours he had been in the air on the fourth, the only trace of a Japanese ship Mac had seen had been the smoke to the south of Ring's group when he had led the fighters away from it.

So far, they were in pretty decent shape. Between them, the two pilots had two canteens of water along with a small supply of dry rations that had been stored in the survival kit in each raft. The only fly in the ointment for Mac was what would happen to him after they were rescued.

Miles to the northeast of them, Lieutenant Commander Pat Mitchell drifted in the same calm sea with Stan Ruehlow and Richard Gray. They had gone the farthest of the ten planes in the squadron before running out of gas. In crash-landing, Stan Ruehlow had banged his head on the gun sight and split his forehead open. The wound was bleeding badly and he was in a lot of pain. He finally went to sleep after vomiting up seawater and blood.

Mitchell's life raft had gone down with his plane, and the three of them had to make do with the two rafts they still had. Dick Gray was the biggest man of the three. He took one raft, and the two smaller men shared the second one. Occasionally, one of them would switch off with Gray so that they could all sleep more comfortably.

Along with the survival stores in the two rafts, they had managed to salvage one canteen of water. Not knowing how long it would be before they were picked up, the three officers agreed to strictly ration the water.

As they waited confidently for rescue, the first day passed into darkness. When the sun disappeared, the air temperature dropped fifteen degrees. They shivered through the long night beneath a brilliant canopy of stars.

The next morning dawned clear. Mitchell set up a watch schedule so that one of them would always be awake to signal a passing ship or airplane. However, the sky and sea remained empty. All that day the sun beat down on them as they continued to drift across the trackless sea.

A shark arrived on the second night. It came right up under Mitchell and Ruehlow's raft, and the dorsal fin sliced through its thin rubber skin before knocking them both into the sea.

Ruehlow landed on the shark's back. Screaming in terror, he cut his hand shoving the shark's fin away as he swam to Gray's raft. Even though the shark disappeared, none of them slept for the rest of that night.

The next morning, Mitchell found a tube of cement and some rubber patches and crudely mended the long slashes in the damaged raft. Otherwise, the third day passed as uneventfully as the first two.

The water in their canteen ran out on June 7. By then, all three were weak and sunburned. Encrusted with salt, Ruehlow's split forehead was agonizingly painful. In the late afternoon, they suddenly heard the distant growl of a plane approaching. It was heading west toward the sun at very high altitude. They attempted to signal the aircraft with a hand mirror, but it kept on going. Later, a passing squall replenished their canteen, but as the fourth night approached, their optimism about being picked up began to wane.

Many miles to the north of them, Ensign Hump Tallman drifted along in his own life raft. He had successfully ditched his plane next to Frank Jennings, and the two of them had tethered their rafts together. Although they were unhurt, Jennings couldn't find his canteen in the cockpit before his plane went down. The one they had was only half full.

Tallman was bitter at what had happened on their flight to nowhere. He released some of his bitterness by writing down everything that had happened on the inflated panels of his raft with a lead pencil.

When he was finished, the yellow skin was covered with his scrawled account of the screwed-up mission. Even if he never made it back, he hoped someone would eventually find the raft and discover how and why they had been lost.

On their second night, a flying fish landed in Tallman's raft. He cleaned it with a pocket knife and the two pilots ate it raw. The water in the canteen ran out on the third day, and their tongues began to swell.

The sea slowly turned rougher, and waves swept over them. By the end of the fourth day, their eyelids were almost swollen shut from constant exposure to salt water. When Tallman heard the sound of an airplane engine, he had to part his eyes with his fingers in order to see it. Unfortunately, there was no signal mirror in either raft, and they had no way to get the pilot's attention.

Spread out across twenty miles of ocean, the remaining three pilots in the fighter squadron had all ditched alone. Ensign George Hill, the pilot who had run out of gas first, had gone down well to the west. Ensign Markland Kelly Jr. and Ensign John Talbot ditched within a mile of each other, but had then drifted apart.

Cut off as the men were from sight of one another, each hour in their rafts seemed excruciatingly long, particularly during the cold nights. Talbot, who was fair-skinned, suffered horribly from sun exposure, and after four days, the blisters on his face and neck had burst open.

They could only hope for a miracle.

On June 8, the fifth day after their ditching, Talbot's prayers were answered. Frank Fisler, the pilot of a PBY search plane, happened to spot his yellow raft floating on the surface of an empty sea and immediately landed to pick him up.

Airborne again, Fisler radioed news of the rescue back to Midway along with the coordinates of his position at the time of the pickup. The location came as a surprise. The PBY search pilots had been searching for the *Hornet* fighter squadron in an area almost two hundred miles to the west of where Talbot had been found.

After being provided with the new coordinates, the rest of the PBYs converged on the area where Talbot had been rescued, and hit pay dirt. One crew quickly spotted Mac McInerny and Johnny Magda, and landed to pick them up. Later that day, a third PBY found Hump Tallman and Frank Jennings.

By then, the sea had turned rough. The PBY was pitching wildly in the sea as the two exhausted men were brought aboard. Tallman attempted to ask one of the crewmen to save the raft with his notes on it, but could only watch as the crewman fired several bullets into it before shutting the hatch. His written account of the mission sank with it.

When darkness fell, the PBY pilots were forced to return to Midway. They were back early the next morning. In his first search pattern, Frank Fisler, the PBY pilot who had found Talbot the previous day, suddenly spotted the two rafts holding Mitchell, Ruehlow, and Gray.

A tropical storm was brewing, and thirty-knot gusts had whipped the surface of the ocean into a small tempest. After he made a rough landing, weather conditions deteriorated even further.

Although worried that the raging sea might dowse his engines on takeoff, Fisler concluded that the safest option was to get airborne again as quickly as possible. As the plane clawed its way into the air, a violent wave smashed into the PBY's metal hull, popping scores of

rivets and letting a small deluge of water into the forward compartment. Later, when he landed in the harbor at Midway, the hull began
leaking like a sieve and it was a close race to reach the shoreline before the PBY went down.

On June 10, the rescue planes flew out again to try to find the last
two fighter pilots, Ensigns George Hill and Markland Kelly Jr. The
weather was even more violent than the day before, and visibility
was extremely poor. For hours, the planes crawled along at an altitude of one thousand feet looking for a sign of them.

With light fading, the PBYs were forced to turn around to head
back to Midway. At that moment, one of the crewmen in Fisler's PBY
saw a yellow life raft careening across the surface of the wildly raging
sea. He called out the sighting on the intercom. A second crewman
confirmed he had seen the raft, too.

Fisler turned back.

Circling over the yellow raft, a crewman dropped a smoke canister to signal that rescue was near. When the other PBYs joined Fisler,
however, the pilots agreed it was far too rough to land. They flew
back to Midway as night fell.

Early the next morning they returned to the coordinates where the
raft had last been seen and fanned out in every direction. Although
they searched all day, there was no sign of the men or the raft.

Kelly and Hill were never found.

**USS HORNET**
**TORPEDO SQUADRON EIGHT**
**FRED MEARS**

As the *Hornet* headed back toward Pearl Harbor, Fred Mears was ordered to go through the personal effects of the pilots and men who
were lost in Torpedo Eight. It was the hardest thing he had ever had
to do.

*Seeing a girl's picture, an earmarked prayer book, or a wallet
with various cards in it made us realize how much each one*

*would be missed at home. It was a disheartening job. We also
had to skim through the letters each had received before we sent
them back to the nearest of kin, and in them we saw expressed
the love and good luck wishes that seemed so futile now. Many of
the officers and men had written last minute notes, as Waldron
advised, and in censoring these — which it was our duty to do,
much as we hated prying into them — we found the last heartfelt thoughts of brave men.*

Rusty Kenyon's letter to his wife was found in his empty
stateroom.

*Dearest Brownie,*

*This is another one of those letters which I hope never gets to
you unless I bring it myself, and give it to you from my own
hand. You might call it a note on thoughts before the first attack
from which I hope to return. This time the odds will be two to
one in the enemy's favor if we do tangle with them. The fight will
be out here off Midway Island.*

*I feel more at ease now with thoughts of a battle ahead be-
cause I know that even if I have to die I will know that soon you
will have a baby that is part of both of us. What love we have
consummated together. . . . I know that there is nothing greater
than love, and nothing finer. Everything I have is yours. You're
part of me, and I am part of you. . . .*

*The happiest moments of my life have been those that I have
spent with you. I love you sweetheart more than anything else in
the world, more than life itself.*

*With all my love, Rusty*

CORONADO BEACH
SAN DIEGO, CALIFORNIA
RETE GAYNIER

After her final farewell to Ozzie in San Francisco before the *Chaumont* sailed, Rete had driven down to San Diego with several of the other pilots' wives. She planned to stay there until the *Hornet* returned from the Pacific.

Along with Betty Miller, the wife of another Navy officer, she found a room to let in a Spanish bungalow on Coronado Island, about a mile across the strand from downtown San Diego.

Rete had immediately begun looking for a job, but the hunt proved futile. Since the Pearl Harbor attack, thousands had thronged the city to try to find work at the military installations. After leaving applications at dozens of offices, she could only hope that one of them would eventually contact her.

Her life was on hold. So far, the informal grapevine among the Navy wives hadn't picked up any news about the *Hornet,* or any of the other carriers out in the Pacific. Twice each day she waited for the postman in hopes of receiving a letter from Ozzie. It wasn't like him not to write. Rete's twenty-third birthday passed on June 2 without a word.

She felt one connection with Ozzie, and that was through the war news delivered nightly on the radio. The reporters' voices conveyed an immediacy that suggested they knew the details of each major event in the war as soon as it occurred. After supper, she and Betty would sit in their room and listen to the broadcasts on her portable radio.

The programs always seemed to focus first on the war in Europe. That week, the Russian stronghold of Sevastopol in the Crimea remained under siege from the German army. In North Africa, the Germans were claiming to have captured thousands of British soldiers at Tobruk. Prime Minister Winston Churchill had just arrived in Washington for another round of meetings with President Roosevelt.

Then it was on to the Pacific news, and the reporter announced that an important battle had apparently taken place near an island

Whitey Moore, Beaver High School, Bluefield, West Virginia, 1935. *(Senior photo, courtesy of Heber Stafford)*

William Evans Jr., Wesleyan University, 1940. *(Yearbook photo, courtesy of Charles Gillispie)*

Victor Lewis, Stetson High School, 1936. *(Courtesy of Nancy Lewis Willis)*

Grant Teats (*right*) with fellow teammate on the Oregon State championship track squad, 1938. *(Courtesy of Nancy Mahi)*

Unknown, Vic Lewis, John Taurman, Smiley Morgan, and
Bob Ries at the Bal Tabarin Restaurant in San Francisco,
May 20, 1942, the night Ries seduced the hatcheck girl.
*(Courtesy of Corwin Morgan)*

Lieutenant (JG) John Waldron
shortly after winning his wings,
1927. *(Naval Historical Center, courtesy of
Robert Cressman)*

Ozzie Gaynier with the puppy
"Tailspin," Ozzie's gift to his wife,
Rete, 1942. *(Courtesy of Rete Gaynier
Janiec)*

Smiley Morgan returning from a bombing mission over Japanese lines at Guadalcanal, September 1942. *(Courtesy of Corwin Morgan)*

James Hill Cook after his wedding to Marjorie, 1942. *(Courtesy of Edith Herring)*

Aaron Katz after his commissioning as a naval officer, 1941. *(Courtesy of Rick and Roger Katz)*

Aaron Katz, growing up in Cleveland, Ohio, 1931. *(Courtesy of Rick and Roger Katz)*

Bert Earnest's TBF Avenger after its amazing return to Midway on June 4, 1942. *(U.S. Navy)*

Captain Stanhope Ring on a visit to Naval Air Station, St. Louis, Missouri, February 2, 1944. *(National Archives and Records Administration)*

Bert Earnest and Harry Ferrier at Guadalcanal, September 1942. *(U.S. Navy)*

Frenchy Fayle, San Diego, California, August 1943. *(Courtesy of Rete Gaynier Janiec)*

Del Delchamps, USS *Yorktown,* 1942. *(Courtesy of Newton Delchamps)*

USMC Major Michael McGinnis Mahoney as a second lieutenant, 1931. *(U.S. Marine Corps History Division, courtesy of Bob Aquilina)*

Bill Magee during flight training, 1944. *(Courtesy of William Magee)*

Gene Hanson and Bob Evarts share a toast after returning from Guadalcanal, 1942. *(Courtesy of Gene Hanson)*

Evarts's Avenger about to sink on July 30, 1942. Ski Kowalewski shows his swimming ability after the crash. *(Courtesy of Gene Hanson)*

Smiley Morgan stands next to the cockpit of his TBF Avenger at Henderson Field, Guadalcanal, September 1942. Chief Machinist's Mate J. C. Hammond, who built Swede's "Frankenstein" fleet, sits on the wing second from left. Gene Hanson is fourth from the left. *(Courtesy of Corwin Morgan)*

Colonel Kiyonao Ichiki, the impetuous commander of the first force that attempted to retake Henderson Field on August 21, 1942. *(U.S. Marine Corps)*

Harold "Swede" Larsen after his promotion to commander following service at Guadalcanal. *(Naval Historical Center, courtesy of Robert Cressman)*

George Gay, second from right, hosts three of the Torpedo Eight widows at the New Paris Inn, San Diego, California, August 1942. Verna "Brownie" Kenyon is second from the left, Faye Ellison is in the center, and Rete Gaynier is on the far right. *(Courtesy of Rete Gaynier Janiec)*

Gary Cooper, Angela Greene, and Smiley Morgan at the Trocadero Nightclub, 1945. *(Courtesy of Corwin Morgan)*

called Midway. The Japanese news service was claiming that its navy had sunk two American aircraft carriers there. She wondered whether the *Hornet* had been involved, and whether Ozzie was part of it.

Soon, San Diego's morning newspapers were proclaiming a major American victory at Midway, although none of the initial news accounts was specific about which ships had participated in the battle.

Rete again turned to the unofficial Navy wives' network, but the security lid was still on tight. No one was talking about what had actually happened or which ships had been involved.

In the days that followed, she stayed close to the radio, monitoring each account of the battle, and hoping to hear news related to the *Hornet* and Torpedo Eight. More details emerged after a few of the senior naval officers stationed at Pearl Harbor were permitted to call their wives in San Diego to assure them they were all right. Word filtered down the ranks. It had been a carrier battle, all right, and the *Hornet*, the *Enterprise*, and the *Yorktown* had all been there.

Rete held on to the firm belief that Ozzie was safe. If he had been in the battle, she reasoned, he would have been aboard the *Hornet*, and the *Hornet* had come through all right. Her close friend Kate was the wife of Johnny Magda, one of the fighter pilots aboard the *Hornet*. Kate hadn't heard anything, either, but she remained confident that Johnny had made it, too.

Rete only became anxious as the days slowly passed without any word from him. Ozzie was a letter writer. He would never have missed writing on her birthday, or wiring her from Pearl Harbor as soon as it was permitted. She took solace in the fact that if anything truly bad had happened, the Navy would have officially notified her. In one sense, no news was good news.

Many other Torpedo Eight families were awaiting word from their loved ones, too. The delay was agonizing. On June 11, 1942, the mother of Grant Teats wrote him to express her anxiety.

JENNIE TEATS
SHERIDAN, OREGON

*June 11, 1942*

*Dear Grant,*
*I am anxiously waiting to hear from you since this big sea battle at Midway. I really feel that your carrier has seen action and I wonder if it is the one damaged. I hope and pray that you are all right. Everyone is talking about the wonderful victory at Midway and all ask if I know where you are and if I have heard. I can tell you I will be glad to get a letter from you. . . .*

FORD ISLAND, PEARL HARBOR
PETE PETERKIN

Distraught over the news of Lang Fieberling's death, Pete Peterkin had taken the responsibility for going through the items in his footlocker, the sum total of everything he had left behind. What he found seemed a pathetically small and melancholy reflection of his best friend's life, and he privately vowed to visit Laura Cassidy, Lang's fiancée, as soon as he returned to San Francisco. Fieberling's possessions were inventoried before being sent on to his parents. The list included:

Athletic Supporter (2)
Bags, Zipper Brown (1)
Athletic Shorts (1)
Ball, Rubber (1)
Caps, Cover, Khaki (1)
Caps, Officers (1)
Coats, Blue (1)
Coats, Khaki (4)
Drawers, Light (14)
Gloves, Handball (1)
Epilettes (2) (*sic*)
Shirts, Khaki (4)
Shirts, White (1)
Bedroom Slippers (pr)
Socks (7 pr)
Trousers, Blue (1)
Trousers, White (1)
Trousers, Khaki (4)
Undershirts, Heavy (3)
Undershirts, Light (8)

USS *HORNET*
FLAG BRIDGE
ADMIRAL PETE MITSCHER

As the *Hornet* drew closer to Pearl Harbor, Pete Mitscher wasn't sure what his next assignment would be, but he was hoping for a combat command in fast carriers. In the meantime, he finalized several decisions that directly affected the future of the *Hornet* air group.

Stanhope Cotton Ring was relieved as the *Hornet* air group commander. Mitscher decided to make him a senior member of his staff. Mitscher also recommended that Ring be promoted to captain and be given the Navy Cross for his performance in the Midway battle. Ironically, it was the same medal posthumously awarded to John Waldron.

After reviewing the After Action Report of the Midway battle prepared by his staff, Mitscher signed the report and forwarded it to Admiral Raymond Spruance. As the task force commander, Spruance was responsible for endorsing the report before it was forwarded to Admiral Nimitz.

Upon reading the *Hornet* report, Spruance chose to do something quite extraordinary for an admiral reviewing the combat performance of one of his new peers. On the endorsement page, Spruance wrote, "As a matter of historical record, the *Hornet* report contains a number of inaccuracies. The *Enterprise* report is considered accurate and should be relied upon for reference."

FRIDAY, 12 JUNE 1942
ROYAL HAWAIIAN HOTEL
WAIKIKI BEACH, HAWAII
MAC MCINERNY

After being picked up in the sea along with Johnny Magda, McInerny was flown to Pearl Harbor, where he was sent straight to the hospital. The fair-skinned Irishman's legs and feet were covered with painful boils. His face and upper body had been baked bright red.

As the days passed, Mac McInerny kept waiting for someone to come and arrest him for dereliction of duty in abandoning the June 4 mission, but no one said a word about it.

FRIDAY, 12 JUNE 1942
CORONADO BEACH
SAN DIEGO, CALIFORNIA
RETE GAYNIER

Rete arrived home from work at the naval air station to find the telegram.

> THE NAVY DEPARTMENT DEEPLY REGRETS TO IN-
> FORM YOU THAT YOUR HUSBAND ENSIGN OSWALD
> JOSEPH GAYNIER UNITED STATES NAVAL RESERVE IS
> MISSING FOLLOWING ACTION IN THE PERFORMANCE
> OF HIS DUTY AND IN THE SERVICE OF HIS COUNTRY
> X THE DEPARTMENT APPRECIATES YOUR GREAT
> ANXIETY AND WILL FURNISH YOU FURTHER INFOR-
> MATION PROMPTLY WHEN RECEIVED X TO PREVENT
> POSSIBLE AID TO OUR ENEMIES PLEASE DO NOT DI-
> VULGE THE NAME OF HIS SHIP OR STATION
> REAR ADMIRAL RANDALL JACOBS, THE CHIEF OF
> NAVAL PERSONNEL

She immediately called Ozzie's parents in Monroe, Michigan. They had already received a copy of the same telegram. They urged her not to worry, telling her that men often went missing and turned up safe.

Ozzie couldn't be dead, she decided. They were so close that she felt sure she would have felt it if he was gone. Men fell in battle, but not Ozzie. She remembered his last words to her. He had promised he would come back.

That night she tossed and turned in her room near Coronado Beach. Shortly before dawn, she must have fallen asleep, because it was still pitch dark outside when she awoke to see Ozzie beside her next to the bed. He was wearing his uniform. His face was calm and reassuring.

"I'm all right, darling," he said, his face close to hers. "I'm okay."

The next morning she decided that it couldn't have been a dream. It had been as vivid as anything she had ever experienced, and could only mean that he was still alive. He must have survived the mission, whatever it was. She knew the battle had been fought over ocean. Perhaps he had made it to an island somewhere, a place that wasn't even on the map.

For the first time since receiving the telegram, she felt renewed hope.

### U.S. NAVAL HOSPITAL
### PEARL HARBOR
### TEX GAY

Tex recovered quickly from his wounds.

One afternoon, he was put in a wheelchair and rolled out onto the front lawn of the hospital. He was still wearing his pajamas. A dozen press photographers were waiting for him there. A pretty nurse handed him a copy of the *Honolulu Star-Bulletin*. Its banner headline read, JAPANESE SMASHED AT MIDWAY. All the photographers took his picture.

On June 15, Admiral Mitscher came for a visit after the *Hornet* arrived back at Pearl Harbor. The admiral asked him to describe everything that had happened on the flight, after which he congratulated Tex on his almost miraculous survival.

A few days later, an officer came to see him from the Navy's public relations office. He told Tex that a lot of people back home were questioning what the Navy had been doing since December 7. Now the Navy had an answer for them. It was the resounding victory at Midway. The officer asked Tex if he would go back home and let the American people know what the Navy had accomplished.

Tex agreed to go.

He knew his status in the Navy had changed as soon as he boarded the cruise ship *Lurline* to go back to the States. That first night he was assigned to the captain's table for all his meals. And as he strolled around the promenade decks, people would point him out to their friends as if he were a movie star. Another group of reporters was waiting for him when he disembarked in San Francisco.

Within a few days, his photograph had appeared in almost every newspaper in the country. One headline read, ENSIGN GAY SOLE SURVIVOR OF TORPEDO SQUADRON EIGHT AT MIDWAY.

In Philadelphia, Grant Teats's fiancée, Diana, had finished one of her nursing classes when she saw the story and immediately wrote to Grant's sister Charlotte in Oregon.

> *The newspapers each day have so much news about the Pacific fleet. The Ensign Gay that was such a hero I thought was a boy in the same squadron as Grant, but when his picture came out in the paper, it didn't look like the person I knew. A girl from my hospital that dated him said it was, but now I can't figure it out. So that leaves me in a daze . . .*

Soon, Tex was being called upon to make speeches at business conventions, and he was invited to appear on Nelson Eddy's radio program. A week later, he received a musical tribute from big band orchestra leader Kay Kyser.

In each place Tex visited, they would give him a painted cardboard key to the town or city. Attractive women sometimes gave him the key to their hotel room. It was an amazing experience, hectic, crazy, and fun. He couldn't help but get caught up in the fanfare.

Pretty soon he was on the invitation lists of celebrities. Inside, he felt like the same down-to-earth guy he had been before it all happened, but now he was meeting movie stars. He began to receive fan mail and even marriage proposals. Twentieth Century Fox wanted to make a movie of his life. He turned them down.

Tex set aside time to visit the widows of the lost pilots in the squadron, including Faye Ellison, Brownie Kenyon, and Rete Gaynier. He did his best to allay their grief, although one of the other widows told him she thought he was getting too much attention.

That was before they put him on the cover of *Life* magazine, and he really became famous. "The Sole Survivor," they called him. Tex hadn't asked for all the public attention, and he knew it hadn't changed him. He was a little embarrassed about it all the same.

For some reason, the press seemed unaware of the gallant sacrifice of the eighteen men from Torpedo Eight who had made the first unsupported attack on the Japanese fleet from Midway Atoll. In fact, there was no public recognition at all for Langdon Fieberling and the others who had died with him.

It was particularly hard for the families who received a telegram stating that their sons were missing in action. A few attempted to cope with the uncertainty by communicating with each other.

### To the Parents of Ensign Albert Earnest

*Dear Friend:*

*Our son, Ensign Charles E. Brannon, was reported missing in action in the Midway battle of June 4. We are trying to find out something definite about him from someone who was an eyewitness, and thought perhaps Ensign Earnest could tell us something about it.*

*Since reading this week's* Life *I have no hope for Charles. Before I quite understood what they did I had a tiny bit of hope. But the Japs were taking no prisoners. Charles was 23 earlier this month. Would have been I should say.*

*We have no hope of ever seeing our son again, but since there is a slight possibility that he might have been taken prisoner, or drifted to some island without communications, we are so anxious to learn the details about this battle, that is the part he took in it.*

*We certainly hope Ensign Earnest came through OK and will come back to his loved ones after this dreadful war is over.*

*Very sincerely,*
*W. T. Brannon*

Bert Earnest's parents had no idea that their son had even been at Midway.

*Dear Mr. Brannon,*

*We received last night your letter, and beg to assure you of our heartfelt sympathy in your apparent loss. We are jittery every time the telephone rings for fear it will be a message from the Navy Department in Washington that Bert is missing, but fortunately for us up to this time no such message has been received.*

*We regret exceedingly that we have no information whatsoever from Bert about his activities in the Pacific. As a matter of fact, he has never even written us that he was in the Midway battle . . . We are not sure, but we are of the opinion that Bert and your son were roommates at the base in Norfolk because Bert frequently spoke of his roommate Charlie. Regretting we can give you no information whatsoever and expressing to you our sincere sympathy, we are,*

*Very sincerely,*
*Mr. and Mrs. James Earnest*

PEARL HARBOR
COMMANDER-IN-CHIEF, PACIFIC FLEET
ADMIRAL CHESTER NIMITZ

## United States Pacific Fleet
### Flagship of the Commander in Chief

In the name of the President of the United States, the
Commander in Chief, United States Pacific Fleet, takes pleasure in
presenting the GOLD STAR in lieu of the second NAVY CROSS to

ENSIGN ALBERT KYLE EARNEST, U. S. NAVAL RESERVE

for service as set forth in the following

CITATION:

"For heroic conduct and extraordinary achievement as pilot
of a torpedo-bomber airplane during the Battle of Midway on
June 4, 1942, when, having completed an unsupported torpedo
attack despite tremendous enemy fighter and A.A. opposition,
he flew his crippled airplane back to his Midway Islands base.
Ensign Earnest's return flight to his base is one of the epics
of combat aviation. Not only were all parts of his plane except the engine damaged by the seventy-odd machine gun bullet
and cannon-shell hits sustained, but his elevator control was
shot away (he flew and landed the plane by expert use of the
elevator trimming tabs), his bomb bay doors could not be closed,
his compass was inoperative, and one wheel of the landing gear
could not be extended. Despite all these material casualties -
himself wounded, his turret gunner dead - he flew some 200
miles back to Midway and negotiated a safe one-wheel landing.
This particular airplane was one of six engaged in the same
combat mission - the first time that this new and unproven
model had been subjected to combat. The other five failed to
return. Earnest's dogged determination to return this damaged
airplane to its base resulted in its being available for
thorough examination and study. This, coupled with his report,
has been of inestimable value in the preparation of data for
the improvement of this model and for future design. His
courage and skill in the handling of his plane were in keeping
with the highest traditions of the naval service."

C. W. NIMITZ,
Admiral, U. S. Navy.

EASTERN ISLAND, MIDWAY ATOLL
BERT EARNEST

On June 6, a brief memorial service was held for Jay Manning. Along with the other men who were killed during the Midway battle, his body was reverently ferried out of the lagoon aboard a PT boat and laid to rest at sea.

Orders arrived from Pearl Harbor that Bert Earnest's Avenger should be shipped back to Hawaii for an inspection by aeronautical engineers who hoped to determine how it had survived so much damage.

The battered plane was carefully hoisted aboard a seaplane tender that was taking Marines back to Hawaii, and it was strapped down to the deck. The first night out from Midway, the temperature in the compartments belowdecks turned brutally hot, and some of the Marines decided to go topside to sleep. As the ship slowly plowed eastward, it ran into a series of rain squalls, and they took shelter under the fuselage of the wrecked aircraft that was fastened to the deck.

They awoke to find their bedrolls soaked with blood. During the stormy night, hard rain had scoured clean the shattered gun turret in the Avenger. Jay Manning's remains had dripped through the bullet-riddled fuselage onto their bedrolls.

Ordered back to Hawaii on June 9, Bert said good-bye to Harry Ferrier and boarded a Marine R4D transport plane headed for Pearl Harbor. As the aircraft slowly climbed out over the Pacific, it was hard for him to believe that he had been out there for little more than a week and had already been part of one of the biggest naval victories in American history.

He began to think that he might even have earned a week or two of leave in Hawaii, relaxing on Waikiki Beach before he had to report back to duty. After the transport plane was in the air, he discovered that many of the men flying with him were heading stateside to enjoy extended family leaves.

That got him thinking about the same possibility. It was foolish to speculate, but who knew what was going to happen to him when he arrived back at Pearl? Maybe they would say, "Good job, Bert," and give him a chance to fly home to Richmond where he could spend some time with Jerry Jenkins.

He fell asleep thinking about all the wonderful possibilities.

When the plane finally landed, Swede Larsen was there waiting for him. After being congratulated on his Midway mission, Bert was told that Torpedo Eight was now under Swede's official command.

"Report to me at Luke Field," Larsen said. "We have a lot of work to do."

Sister Sara

Smiley Morgan sat in the cockpit of his silent Avenger, waiting for word on whether they were taking off at dawn. Swede's detachment of the squadron's remaining pilots and planes had been on alert since June 2, just in case the Japanese might still be coming their way.

Each morning, the pilots would be awakened in the darkness of the lanai at the old Bachelor Officers' Quarters. Still groggy, they pulled on their flight suits and walked over to Luke Field. There, they would warm the plane engines, shut them down, and wait in the gloom of the predawn sky at the edge of the runway.

Shortly after sunrise on the morning of June 5, a ground officer raced around in a jeep to tell them they could stand down again. Climbing out of the cockpit, Smiley walked back to the old BOQ to shave and shower. Then he headed over to the new BOQ to have the breakfast buffet: freshly sliced pineapple, melon, papaya, pancakes, waffles, eggs, ham, and bacon — all at a cost of twenty-five cents.

It was another magnificent morning, the only kind they seemed to have in Hawaii. After he moved far enough away from the sepulchral odors still coming from Battleship Row, the syrupy smell of exotic flowers seemed to fill the air.

Hawaii was stunningly beautiful, Smiley thought. Even the walking paths were lined with neatly trimmed hibiscus hedges, flaming red bougainvillea, and other exotic flowers he had never seen on the

Gulf Coast of Florida. Along with the profusion of color, there was constant birdsong from the jacaranda and poinciana trees. In some ways, it felt like a vacation. With his friends in Torpedo Eight out fighting the Japanese, he felt guilty about it.

By then, they all knew that something momentous was occurring a thousand miles to the west. Two days earlier, Smiley had run into a PBY pilot who had just returned from Midway. He had told him a big battle was brewing out there in the Central Pacific. The pilot said he had seen Langdon Fieberling's six Avengers at Midway, and that they were part of the air garrison defending the island.

That night, several more PBYs came in from Midway loaded with wounded Marines and Navy fliers. The pilots began passing the word that a major victory had been won against the Japanese fleet. At the same time, a crazy rumor began to spread that Torpedo Squadron Eight had been wiped out.

On the morning of June 6, Swede received official word through Admiral Noyes's office that all of Torpedo Eight's Devastators from the *Hornet* had been shot down, and that Tex Gay was apparently the only survivor. Tex had been flown back from Midway and was at the base hospital. Swede immediately went over to see him.

He came back with the confirmation that not only was the Skipper dead, but so were all the other pilots and crewmen except Tex. Swede brought the squadron together and told them that Langdon Fieberling was gone, too, as were all the pilots and crewmen in his detachment, except Bert Earnest and Harry Ferrier.

In the hours that followed, the remaining members of Torpedo Eight gathered in the hangar at CASU-5 to talk about what had happened. At first, the reality of it was almost inconceivable. How could forty-five out of forty-eight men from the squadron be killed in one day? It just wasn't possible. Not the Skipper. He had been larger than life. Not all the others, too, the friends they had trained with through the long winter at Norfolk, the guys they had joined on liberties, and shared so many memories with.

That same evening, Swede came back to say that they had been ordered to join the battle. The carrier *Saratoga* had just arrived from the West Coast, and was on her way out to intercept the remainder of the Japanese fleet. The squadron would fly their Avengers out to the carrier. "Now, we'll finally see some action," Swede assured them. This was their chance to help finish off what remained of the Japanese fleet.

Early the next morning they took off from Luke Field and landed aboard the *Saratoga*. Smiley was nervous about putting his Avenger down on a flight deck for the first time, but he came in as smooth as silk.

Once they were aboard and on their way, Swede brought the pilots together to give them the latest news. Apparently, the Japanese striking force was gone. They had hightailed it back to Japan. The battle was over. Admiral Spruance and the rest of the victorious task force were heading back to Hawaii.

Swede did not give the squadron time to celebrate. To become officially qualified on the Avengers, each pilot had to make eight carrier takeoffs and landings. Swede got approval from the captain for his pilots to earn their qualifications right away.

Smiley Morgan's first flight left him less than ecstatic. On a technical level, it went fine, and he made the first carrier landing without mishap. What he hadn't found enjoyable was the discovery that whoever had flown the plane before him had relieved himself in the pee tube beneath the cockpit seat.

Normally, the tube would have emptied itself during the flight, but there must have been a blockage of some kind, because when Smiley did a slow roll before returning to the carrier, he found himself drenched with the man's urine. He had to make seven more landings before he was able to head belowdecks to take a shower.

Otherwise, the experience of being at sea aboard a fast carrier was new and exciting. With the exception of one spell of bad weather, Swede kept them flying every day.

On June 11, Swede received orders to fly his ten Avengers from the *Saratoga* to the *Hornet,* joining the remaining officers and enlisted men of Waldron's Torpedo Eight as the ship returned to Pearl Harbor.

Once aboard the *Hornet,* Smiley quickly discovered that the atmosphere was dramatically different than on the *Saratoga*. Many of the pilots seemed subdued and even downcast. Smiley presumed it had to do with all the losses they had suffered.

When Swede brought his pilots together in Ready Room Four, everything was just as it had been left when Waldron had led the squadron out on their first and last combat mission. At Swede's request, Fred Mears and the other two replacement pilots who hadn't flown in the battle told them what they knew.

While they talked, Smiley couldn't help but notice the reminders of the doomed squadron's last hours aboard ship. A few of Waldron's instructions were still chalked on the blackboard. Some of the personal gear of the lost fliers was found in the compartments under their leather seats.

With the death of Waldron and all the senior pilots, the highest-ranking Torpedo Eight officer left aboard the *Hornet* was Lieutenant George H. Flinn Jr., the squadron's personnel officer. His job kept him deskbound, maintaining the records of every man serving in the unit.

A graduate of Yale, class of twenty-six, Flinn was the son of a construction magnate from Pennsylvania whose company had built the Holland Tunnel in New York City. Flinn didn't look much like a naval officer, with his rumpled uniform and his cap always askew, but he was proud to be part of a combat unit, and he had enjoyed being in temporary command of the squadron.

He had particularly liked taking care of the pilots, almost as if he were the housemaster of an unruly fraternity. After the squadron had taken off on June 4, Flinn went down to the galley and ordered the cooks to prepare roast chicken dinners for all fifteen of his pilots.

He had the chicken dinners delivered on trays to the ready room in anticipation of their return, and he had refused to allow the mess boys to take the trays away until long after it was obvious the guys were never coming back.

Flinn considered it his job to fill Waldron's shoes until officially relieved.

On June 12, Swede ordered the remaining officers and enlisted men in the squadron to assemble on the hangar deck. After the flight crews and support personnel had lined up in ranks, Flinn and Larsen walked to the head of the formation.

The physical contrast between the two men was startling. Flinn seemed almost clownish-looking with his cockeyed hat and baggy khakis. Standing beside him, Swede looked like a recruiting poster.

Flinn spoke first.

He told them that it was a privilege to be their commanding officer, and that he was proud to be leading a combat unit of American fighting men. His words struck some of the pilots as a bit odd. No deskbound officer could command an air squadron. When he was finished, Swede stepped forward. In his parade ground voice, he said, "You were the commander, George. I'm the commander now."

Smiley Morgan was reminded of what Langdon Fieberling had once said to him about Swede when they were about to fly their Avengers across the United States. Fieberling had referred to him as "the lion." That's what Swede reminded him of now, the king of the jungle marking his turf.

"You're no longer in charge of anything, George," Swede proclaimed, "unless I say so."

Smiley found himself feeling sorry for Flinn.

"Torpedo Eight still exists," Swede said next, "and the way I feel it exists is to get vengeance. That's how I see our job now, revenge.

"We're going to hit the Japs wherever we can," Swede went on. "We're going to blow into the heads of those Japs who pulled the trigger on us at Midway that their country would have been better off if they hadn't been born. . . . I want vengeance, and I think you want it, too. We've got a score to settle and a chance to settle it. Who can ask for more?"

No one cheered when he was finished. A lot of them were still in shock over what had occurred a week earlier. Bill Tunstall, the machinist's mate who had been Abbie Abercrombie's plane captain, was still regretting not having accepted Bernie Phelps's wallet so the money could be sent on to his family.

Back in his stateroom, Fred Mears expressed his own feelings on the subject of vengeance in his personal journal. He hadn't flown with the other pilots on June 4, but he had gotten to know them in the last days and hours of their lives. He had read their final letters and gone through their personal effects. He had listed the items belonging to each man, and had packed them in boxes to be returned to their families. Fred had a different take than Swede on what was important when they went into battle again.

> *In the Navy, and especially in wartime, you do what you are told to do, and if some of your comrades are killed in the process it's tough to take but it doesn't change you into a wrathful avenger. Eventually, it leads to a steadying cold determination to beat the Japs and win the war. But fancy words don't help. Any time a pilot says, "Thoughts of Jack or Joe will be riding with my next torpedo," he is just blowing or else he is emotionally unfit to be a combat aviator. The only thoughts which should be riding with a torpedo to make a hit are those of entry and departure, target angle, target speed, dropping point, avoidance of A.A. fire, and other matter of fact considerations.*

Fred Mears didn't confine his thoughts about Swede's call for vengeance to pen and paper. He brought them up to several of the pilots as well. Word of his reaction to Swede's speech got back to the new commanding officer.

Swede already harbored serious doubts about Mears. He was someone who never seemed to take things seriously, coming across as a rich playboy who was always talking about girls and parties. Like George Flinn, he was a Yale man. In fact, Pete Peterkin was, too. All of a sudden it seemed like there were more of these Ivy League guys in the squadron than Academy men. Swede was surrounded by them.

Mears lacked the avenging instinct Swede was looking for from the pilots in his squadron. He decided to transfer him out before his lackadaisical attitude infected the others.

SATURDAY, 13 JUNE 1942
TORPEDO SQUADRON EIGHT

As the carrier task force neared Hawaii, Admiral Spruance released the pilots and flight crews to fly back to their air bases in the islands.

They would then be given liberty to celebrate the triumph over the Japanese fleet.

The order didn't apply to Swede's detachment since none of them had seen action in the Midway battle. Swede gave his pilots a twenty-four-hour leave, after which they were ordered to report back to work on Monday, June 15. He had already laid out an ambitious flight schedule that would keep them flying daily training missions at Luke Field.

Later that morning, the carrier pilots from the *Enterprise* and the *Hornet*, as well as the surviving pilots from the *Yorktown*, flew back to Ewa Field, the Marine Corps installation on Oahu where most of them were stationed. There, they began preparing for liberty, using the telephones at the Officers' Club to book rooms at the Moana Hotel, the Royal Hawaiian, or one of the other resorts on Waikiki Beach. The lucky ones arranged for dates.

Before heading out, many of them gathered at the bar to toast their victory. The big room was filled with laughter and freely flowing scotch. Every few minutes, someone would loudly call for a toast to another flier in the room.

Ensign Johnny Adams was a Wildcat pilot aboard the *Yorktown*, and had shot down a Japanese torpedo plane that was attacking the carrier during the battle. Adams was enjoying a drink with his friends from the *Yorktown*'s fighter squadron when he heard a loud voice calling for another toast.

When the big room went quiet, he looked up to see Stanhope Cotton Ring, the *Hornet* air group commander, standing by the packed bar, his glass raised in front of him. Ring announced that he wanted to stand a round for every flier in the club.

Adams and his friends were astonished when none of the pilots from the *Hornet* got up from their tables. They remained where they were, some standing, others sitting, stone-faced. A few conspicuously turned their backs on Ring.

Johnny Adams and his friends from the *Yorktown* went up to claim their free drinks. Adams had no idea why the others were giving Ring the cold shoulder. He felt sorry for him. For his part, Ring seemed oblivious to the fact that the pilots who had flown with him during the battle were refusing to drink his liquor.

That night, the noise at the bar seemed deafening to Smiley Morgan. It was overflowing with fliers, not just Navy fliers but Army pilots, too. The Navy had taken over the Royal Hawaiian for the duration of the war, but it was now being shared by the Army Air Forces, including some of the pilots who had flown the B-17 Flying Fortresses in the Midway battle.

None of them had made a hit on a Japanese ship, but that hadn't stopped them from saying they did. It was the first time the Navy pilots learned that the Army public relations people were officially claiming that their B-17s had won the Battle of Midway. To rub more salt in the wound, the Honolulu papers were running stories that hailed the pinpoint accuracy of the Army pilots as one of the keys to the victory. Not only did some of these Army guys believe their own press accounts, but they were belligerent about it.

The Navy fliers deeply resented their claims. The carriers' torpedo squadrons had sacrificed their lives to buy the precious battle time that had allowed the Dauntless pilots from the *Enterprise* and the *Yorktown* to dive down and sink all four carriers.

Meanwhile, the B-17s had dropped their bombs from a height of nearly four miles, far above the antiaircraft fire and the attacks by the Zeroes. In fact, the only near hit made by a B-17 in the entire Midway battle was when a B-17 accidentally attacked the American submarine USS *Grayling*. The Fortress's flight crew was up so high they claimed they had sunk a Japanese cruiser.

A physical confrontation was inevitable, and fights broke out that night all over the Royal Hawaiian, erupting in the bars, hallways, and gardens, and leaving in their wake a trail of broken bottles, glasses, heads, and furniture.

As for Smiley, he had planned an enthusiastic search for an exotic Hawaiian girl who looked like Dorothy Lamour, a girl he could hopefully maneuver out to the palm trees that fringed Waikiki Beach.

Unfortunately, none of the Hawaiian girls he met looked like Dorothy Lamour.

Smiley had started the evening with his friend James Hill Cook, the earnest young flier from Grand Cane, Louisiana, who had given him his enduring nickname in a poker game. Over drinks, they had started reminiscing about Lieutenant Commander Waldron. One night back in Norfolk, the Skipper and his wife, Adelaide, had hosted a party for the pilots. Morgan and Hill had been standing in the doorway to the kitchen when Waldron came out of one of the bedrooms.

"Come over here," he had said to them. "I want to show you something."

He then led them back to the bedroom, where his two young daughters, Nancy and Anne, were curled up in their beds, asleep. "Did you ever see such pretty little girls?" he asked them with a father's pride.

Cook, who had married his fiancée, Marjorie, just before leaving for the Pacific, told Smiley that he hoped Waldron's daughters would always remember their father, and would come to know what an extraordinary man he was. Smiley recalled the time when Cook had been actually lovesick about Marjorie, and Waldron had given him emergency leave to get married.

"Go home and marry that girl," the Skipper had said, "so you can come back and do your work again."

Smiley decided to get drunk after Red Doggett came up to him at the table and handed him a ten-dollar bill. At first, Smiley had no idea what it was for. Seeing his confusion, Red said, "It's the money Darrel Woodside owed you. I'm just following through on what he promised you."

It only made him feel worse.

Smiley slept late Sunday morning, and then went to meet Mac McInerny. The big Irishman's face was still lobster red from exposure, and his scabbed feet were so painful that he was wearing tennis shoes without laces. The two of them spent the day together, sitting on the shaded terrace of the Halekulani Hotel and drinking beer.

McInerny was bitter. He told Smiley what had happened to the group on June 4, culminating in his decision to head back to the carrier after they had passed the point of no return. Ring was all show, Mac told him. He might look the part, but he was no combat leader. The one squadron commander who had known what he was doing was Waldron, and he was dead. There had better be a lot of changes in the air group or it would happen all over again, he warned Smiley.

Monday, 15 June 1942
Luke Field, Ford Island
Pearl Harbor
Torpedo Squadron Eight

At 0600, the pilots of Torpedo Eight reported for duty at Luke Field. They began the most intense training period the squadron had ever undergone. It included practice bombing runs on a fast-moving destroyer, simulated group attacks against the *Saratoga*, field carrier landings, gunnery missions, and practice torpedo runs.

On June 20, Smiley was diving at a target sleeve being towed in the water. He had just pulled out of the dive, which gave his teenaged tail gunner, Nicholas Chorak, a chance to rake the target with his machine gun. But Chorak never opened fire, and Smiley called the turret gunner on the intercom to ask him what was wrong. He said that Chorak was slumped over his gun. Smiley got on the radio to declare an emergency and immediately landed.

Except for the trickle of blood running out of his nose, the boy looked to Smiley like he was asleep. When a medical attendant told him Chorak was dead, Smiley turned away from the others and cried. Later, he learned that Chorak should never have been cleared to fly. James Hill Cook tried to ease his sense of guilt by saying, "You have to forget about it, Smiley. It's best not to look back until this is all over."

TUESDAY, 23 JUNE 1942
LUKE FIELD, FORD ISLAND
PEARL HARBOR
TORPEDO SQUADRON EIGHT

After roll call that morning, Swede Larsen introduced Lieutenant Bruce Harwood as the squadron's new executive officer. At thirty-two, Harwood had served in the Navy for seven years. He was from Claremont, California, and had graduated from Arizona State Teachers College. Like several of the pilots in the squadron, he had been inspired to fly after Lindbergh's solo flight across the Atlantic.

Harwood had been a fighter pilot aboard the *Hornet* in Pat Mitchell's squadron. At Midway, his division of Wildcats had flown the combat air patrols that defended the carrier against attacks from Japanese dive-bombers and torpedo planes.

Right from the start, it was clear that Harwood was different from Swede. For one thing, he rarely said a word. To some of the pilots, he seemed melancholy, as if he lived with some inner sadness. Whatever the reason, he made it clear that he had no time for idle conversation.

Aboard the *Hornet*, he had won a reputation as an unflappable flight commander. In the air, Harwood was a superb pilot. He quickly developed an almost instinctive sense of the Avenger's capabilities and limitations.

He was also the biggest man to ever serve in the squadron, a raw-boned 220 pounds on a six-foot-three frame. Seeing his body filling a doorway, one had to wonder how he had ever fit in the cockpit of a fighter. A man of immense strength, Harwood impressed one officer in the squadron by picking up a full fifty-five-gallon oil drum that had fallen off a truck and loading it back aboard.

Everyone wondered how he would get along with Swede. It turned out to be a good match. Unlike Swede, he never raised his voice. If someone made a mistake, he handled it man to man. He carried out Swede's orders with calm, self-assured authority.

Through the remainder of June, the squadron maintained an unrelenting work schedule, flying multiple training missions every day. On June 27 alone, they made thirty-six flights. Later, they began night training, flying dozens of missions over the blacked-out islands.

As the weeks passed, the men in the flight crews began to form judgments about the capabilities of every pilot in the squadron. Fairly or unfairly, the reputations usually stuck.

When it came to Swede, there was no question that he was a superb flier. The men had learned to stay out of his way. His temper had a low flash point, and none of them enjoyed being on the receiving end of one of his tirades, whether the infraction was real or imagined.

Lieutenant Jack Barnum, whom Swede had made the squadron operations officer, was a good pilot, but often complained about petty problems with the plane he was about to fly, almost as if looking for a reason not to go.

Ensign Bert Earnest was held in awe by the enlisted men, in part because of his legendary flight at Midway, and in part because he was unfailingly polite to his flight crew and his new plane captain, Bill Tunstall, who was responsible for keeping his Avenger in top condition. Earnest never had to order them to do anything; instead he just asked for whatever he needed in his mellow Virginia drawl. They would jump to the task.

Ensign Gene Hanson, the second-generation Swede from Iowa, was another popular and capable pilot, as were Smiley Morgan, James Hill Cook, and John Taurman, all of whom never "put on airs."

Ensign Bob Evarts was a gentleman, too, but he quickly became known as a hard-luck flier. Through no apparent fault of his own, his missions were often scrubbed because his planes had mechanical breakdowns.

Ensign Herb Jay was the only Jewish pilot in the squadron. Swede openly derided him as his "Brooklyn Indian." Jay seemed very cautious in the air, always flying "by the book."

Fred Mears was just the opposite. He sometimes tried to make the Avenger behave like a fighter, unnerving his flight crew in the process. Ensign Tex Grady was another pilot who seemed to take unnecessary chances.

Frenchy Fayle had returned to the squadron after missing the Midway battle because of his leg wound. He was considered a good pilot, but "flaky." On the ground, he would sometimes begin dancing by himself, pirouetting like a ballet dancer. Things like that didn't reassure the flight crews.

Red Doggett and Bill Dye, the two enlisted pilots in the squadron, were competent and well-liked. Tall and soft-spoken, Dye had blond, ringletted hair. It had led to the nickname "Curly Bill." He was the lowest-ranking pilot in the squadron, and had the most flying hours.

With Tex Gay having returned to the States and not expected to come back, there were now seventeen carrier-qualified Avenger pilots in the squadron, including Swede. That number was reduced to fifteen when Fred Mears and Herb Jay were transferred out on July 4.

Fred Mears was particularly happy to go. He had recently been on the receiving end of a lot of Swede's needling. Fred was joining the torpedo squadron on the "Big E," the carrier *Enterprise*. His new skipper was Lieutenant Commander John Jett, an officer he liked and respected.

He also felt fortunate when he was assigned his new flight crew. The turret gunner turned out to be none other than Harry Ferrier, the young radioman who had survived the Battle of Midway with Bert Earnest. The only visual evidence of the harrowing mission was a livid circular scar on Harry's forehead.

After Midway, Harry had been given the choice of returning to Torpedo Eight or transferring over to the *Enterprise*. Although he loved flying with Bert, he hadn't enjoyed serving under Swede. Once aboard the *Enterprise*, he requested to be assigned as a turret gunner.

Harry told Fred Mears he had learned something valuable in the Midway battle while watching the Japanese Zeroes attack the planes behind him. Several of the Japanese pilots had turned away when the fifty-caliber tracers from the Avengers' turret guns looped in close to them.

"I have no hankering to be an ace gunner," he told Mears. "All I want to do is put enough slugs in the air to keep the Zeroes off our tail."

TUESDAY, 7 JULY 1942
LUKE FIELD, FORD ISLAND
PEARL HARBOR
TORPEDO SQUADRON EIGHT

After reveille, Swede ordered a full muster of the squadron in the hangar of CASU-5. There, he announced that Torpedo Eight had been officially assigned to the USS *Saratoga*. The transfer of men and gear to the new ship was to take place that morning. "Sister Sara," as she was affectionately known, was considered a lucky ship, and the men were excited to be joining her.

Later that day, Swede reported to Commander Harry Don Felt, who commanded the *Saratoga*'s air group. Felt told Swede that the carrier was heading for an important assignment in the South Pacific. So far, the destination was secret.

On July 8, the *Saratoga* and its escort ships left the Hawaiian Islands. Six destroyers led the advance, followed by a screen of cruisers, including *Minneapolis, Astoria, Vincennes,* and *New Orleans.* Two oil tankers followed the *Saratoga*, indicating the task force had a long way to go before stopping to refuel.

That night in the officers' wardroom, rumors began circulating about their unnamed destination. In the wake of the Midway victory, everyone was excited at the chance to take the offensive against the Japanese for the first time in the war.

The carrier's air squadrons began conducting daily scouting and search missions, flying out on two-hundred-mile legs to make sure the sea-lanes were clear of enemy ships. As the task force continued south, the daily routine didn't vary, although conditions aboard the ship slowly changed.

After the carrier's freshwater tanks were depleted, water became increasingly precious. There were constant warnings about conserving the potable water produced by the ship's distilling equipment.

The quality of the food began to decline with each additional day at sea. Within a week, the fresh milk was gone, followed by the eggs and vegetables. Within two weeks, the fresh meat would be gone, too, leaving only cured meats like ham and bacon.

Official confirmation of their first destination came down from the flag bridge a few days into the voyage. They were heading for the Tonga Islands, which were friendly, and lay between Fiji and Samoa. There was still no hint of where they would be going after they arrived there. As they neared the equator, the cool northeast trade winds were replaced by the heat of the equatorial sun.

On July 12, the pilots returned from their regular pattern of search missions to discover that the *Saratoga* had crossed the equator, and in accordance with long Navy tradition, King Neptune would be conducting his rites of initiation for those who were crossing for the first time, a ritual in which "pollywogs" became "shellbacks."

Among the officers in Torpedo Eight, only Swede Larsen and Bruce Harwood had been initiated. The rest of the men in the squadron were fair game. As the veteran shellbacks compared notes on the indignities they had been made to suffer during their own initiations, the pollywogs from Torpedo Eight were led to a steel platform just beneath the flight deck. One by one, they were sent up the steel ladder through an open hatch.

Pete Peterkin was the first officer through the hatch to the flight deck. Emerging into the sunlight, he saw King Neptune sitting in a throne chair. Whoever was playing the role wore a massive crown of seaweed and was attired in smelly rags. Surrounding him was his motley court, their faces smeared with paint like Indian braves.

As he stepped onto the flight deck, Peterkin encountered a masked man wearing a cardboard sign that read DOCTOR. Pete was invited to swallow a large dose of foul-smelling liquid from a metal ladle. He did.

"Let the initiation begin," bellowed King Neptune.

Ahead of him, the crowd suddenly parted, forming a gauntlet of men that stretched across the flight deck. Before Pete could take off, a man wearing a sign labeled BARBER attempted to hack off a chunk of his already short hair with plumber's shears.

Then Pete was streaking down the open lane between screaming shellbacks, all of them whacking him with stuffed canvas clubs and wooden paddles. Shielding his eyes, Peterkin ran as fast as he could. At the end of the line stood the most effective "wallopers," giants who could lift a man right off the deck with the force of their blows.

He turned back to see the rest of the officers in the squadron running the same gauntlet, many of them laughing as they came through. They included Earnest, Barnum, Morgan, Evarts, Taurman, and Cook.

With the time-honored ritual concluded, the new shellbacks nursed their bruises as they celebrated their transformation with soft drinks, coffee, sandwiches, and ice cream.

TUESDAY, 21 JULY 1942
USS *SARATOGA*
OFFICERS' WARDROOM

They were enduring another day of sweltering temperatures when Commander Felt assembled the carrier's pilots in the wardroom to give them the word on where they were going.

The Japanese were building an airfield at a place called Guadalcanal in the Solomon Islands, Felt told them. Once it was constructed, the Japanese would be able to use their long-range bombers to cut off the Allied supply lifeline between the U.S. and Australia.

The Navy wasn't going to let them do it.

U.S. Marines were being sent in to take the airfield away from the Japanese. They would then hold it as a staging base against Rabaul, the Japanese-held fortress farther north in the Bismarck Archipelago. Along with Guadalcanal, the Marines would be landing at Tulagi, where the Japanese had a squadron of Zero floatplanes.

Felt pointed to a large map of the Solomon Islands and showed them where each place was located. Most of the islands were unfamiliar, with names like Santa Cruz, Isabel, and Malaita. The only island name Smiley Morgan recognized was Florida, but it wasn't his home state. It was a snake-infested island filled with native headhunters.

The proposed date of the invasion had been code-named "Dog Day." In mounting the offensive, the Navy was providing the transport ships that were carrying nineteen thousand men of the 1st Marine Division from their staging area in Wellington, New Zealand, to a rendezvous point where they were all headed.

On Dog Day, American carriers would be responsible for provid-

raised in a household with seven sisters. When he was fourteen, his father, Sam, who owned a scrap metal business, decided to send him to a yeshiva for the religious training that would prepare him to be a rabbi.

Aaron refused to consider the idea. All he wanted to do when he got old enough was fly airplanes, he told his father. After the inspiration of Lindbergh's flight across the Atlantic, he had begun going out to the Cleveland-Hopkins Airport to sit in the grass and watch the planes land and take off. He was ten years old.

Instead of going to the yeshiva, he told his father that he wanted to attend the Ohio Military Institute, a boarding school in Cincinnati. Sam Katz reluctantly supported his decision.

No one wanted to tell Aaron, but his family was convinced he had no chance to become a pilot. One just had to look at him to see how ridiculous the idea was. He had an astigmatism that required him to wear the kind of Coke-bottle eyeglasses that made his eyes look twice their normal size. Without the glasses, he was almost blind.

In 1931, he became one of the first Jewish boys to attend the Ohio Military Institute. He turned out to be both a good student and an accomplished cadet, winning his ceremonial sword upon graduation in 1935.

Somewhere along the line, his eyesight began to improve. No one in the family could understand why. He had never had surgery or other medical treatment. It seemed almost miraculous, as if Aaron had simply willed his eyes to become stronger.

After graduating from the University of Illinois with a degree in economics in 1939, he applied to become a pilot in the Army Air Forces. They rejected him. He then applied for active service as a naval aviator and was accepted. To the wonderment of his family, he passed the eye exam and was sent to Pensacola, where he won his wings.

Now Katz had the pleasure of serving under Swede Larsen. It wasn't the first time Aaron had confronted anti-Semitism, but it had rarely been delivered so blatantly. Usually, it was evident in things said or done behind a man's back. Swede Larsen was right up front with it. Aaron preferred it that way. As in the past, all he could do was try to win the man's respect by proving him wrong.

He had done it before.

MONDAY, 27 JULY 1942
TONGATUPU, TONGA ISLANDS
USS SARATOGA

In turbulent seas, the *Enterprise* rendezvoused with the *Saratoga* and the *Wasp*. They were soon joined by the massive convoy of transport ships carrying the nineteen thousand men of the 1st Marine Division, as well as the supply vessels carrying their arms, stores, and equipment.

Consisting of eighty-two ships, it was the largest American naval force yet assembled in the war. The pilots flying air patrol over the armada had the best view, with the ships stretching across the ocean as far as they could see.

In addition to the three carriers, the force included the new battleship USS *North Carolina,* with enormous sixteen-inch guns that could help to pound the enemy-held islands into submission.

The senior commanders of the invasion force came together aboard the *Saratoga* to finalize their plans. Rear Admiral Noyes was flown over from the carrier *Wasp*. Rear Admiral Thomas Kinkaid, commanding the *Enterprise* task force, came across on one of his escort destroyers. He was followed by Rear Admiral Richmond Kelly Turner, who commanded the amphibious forces of the invasion, including the transport and supply ships that would carry the Marines and their equipment to the landing beaches. Turner was accompanied by Rear Admiral John "Slew" McCain, who commanded naval air forces in the South Pacific, and Major General Alexander Archer Vandegrift, who commanded the 1st Marine Division, which would make the invasion and secure control of the islands.

Smiley Morgan had never seen so many brass hats in one place before. After they were all piped aboard, the commanders met for three hours to hash out the final details for the invasion, which was scheduled for August 7.

Planning efforts had been complicated by the fact that Guadalcanal was huge, fully ninety miles long from Cape Esperance in the north to Makina at its southernmost tip. In between were 2,700 square miles of tropical rain forest, numerous rivers, and hundreds of miles of beaches. To the north, the island was capped by an 8,000-foot-high mountain range.

The 1st Marine Division was understrength, and had had little time to train or become fully equipped. Prior to receiving his orders for the invasion, Vandegrift had thought he would be given six months to prepare his division for battle.

The most contentious issue between the senior commanders involved the length of time the three American carriers would remain in close proximity to the landing beaches after the 1st Marine Division was put ashore at Guadalcanal and Tulagi.

Both islands were inside the range of Japanese attack planes from Rabaul. Vice Admiral Fletcher was concerned that his carriers would be vulnerable to land-based air attack from Rabaul, as well as to enemy submarines.

Fletcher had commanded carrier forces against the Japanese at the Coral Sea and Midway battles in April and June. Two of them, the *Lexington* and the *Yorktown,* had already gone down. Fletcher was considered a hard fighter, but he was not about to see it happen a third time.

For his part, General Vandegrift was concerned about being left unprotected on the landing beaches before his men could solidify control. This would be no raid. It was a full-scale invasion with an entire Marine division.

Vandegrift requested that Admiral Fletcher keep his three carriers close enough to the landing beaches to provide air cover for at least four days, the minimum time he estimated it would take to put ashore all of their arms, equipment, and supplies.

Fletcher responded by saying that he planned to pull the carriers out on the third day. The danger from enemy planes, warships, and submarines was too great. To stay any longer, he insisted, would seriously endanger his carriers, which were the most important assets the Navy had in the Pacific.

There was no consensus on it when the meeting broke up. One of the things they did agree on was the need for their planned invasion rehearsal. It would hopefully resolve some of Vandegrift's concerns.

In his small office compartment belowdecks, Swede Larsen was conducting his own planning sessions with the officers of Torpedo Eight. He told Pete Peterkin that he wasn't satisfied with the condition of the squadron's Avengers. On almost every training mission, one of their planes had experienced a mechanical failure before take-off. They were getting a bad reputation, said Swede, and he wasn't having any of it. He ordered Peterkin and Chief Machinist's Mate J. C. Hammond to work on the planes around the clock if necessary until every one of them was prepared for Dog Day.

THURSDAY, 30 JULY 1942
KORO ISLAND, FIJI
USS SARATOGA
TORPEDO SQUADRON EIGHT

The invasion rehearsal off Koro Island quickly turned into a farce.

The engines on many of the Higgins landing craft proved to be unreliable, and a number of them broke down before they had even left the transport ships. Then it was discovered that treacherous reefs that could rip the bottoms out of the landing craft protected the simulated landing zones. They went no farther.

As the failures mounted, General Vandegrift became increasingly frustrated. Only a third of the Marines had disembarked for the exercise when the landing rehearsal was canceled.

For Torpedo Eight, the flight segment of the invasion rehearsal started just as badly. The second Avenger to take off in the flight exercise was to be flown by Bob Evarts, the so-called hard-luck pilot from Grand Forks, Idaho.

Twenty-one-year-old Zygmond "Ski" Kowalewski was strapped into the turret gun behind him. Prior to their takeoff, a group of sailors had gathered along the flight deck to give Ski a collective thumbs-up. They weren't there as part of the Ski Kowalewski Admiration Society. It was to protect their investment. Ski was carrying two thousand dollars of their cash in his flight suit. They had given him the money so he could bring back souvenirs for them from the Fiji island of Suva.

When Evarts got the signal to take off, he shoved the throttle forward and released his brakes. As he hurtled down the deck, the aircraft's tail hook, which normally remained locked under the Avenger's fuselage until released from its compartment prior to landing, accidentally dropped free.

Barrier wires had been stretched across the *Saratoga*'s bow and stern to catch the tail hooks of planes that had missed the arresting wires. The barriers were strung ten feet above the flight deck.

As Evarts's plane roared into the air, its tail hook caught the barrier wire and the Avenger came to a bone-jarring stop in midair. As the crowd of horrified sailors watched, the plane dropped out of sight off the starboard bow.

When the sailors ran to the edge of the flight deck and looked down, the first thing they saw was Ski Kowalewski swimming for all he was worth away from the side of the ship, which was streaking past the downed aircraft at thirty knots.

The USS *Phelps,* one of the carrier's escort destroyers, quickly came up to search for the flight crew after the plane disappeared. Along with Ski Kowalewski, Bob Evarts and the third crewman were also rescued.

Following the flight segment of the invasion rehearsal, in which more than a hundred aircraft from the carriers strafed and bombed targets on Koro Island, the big warships in the invasion force unleashed repeated salvos of cannon shells against a simulated enemy airfield. After they finished pounding the friendly island with twenty tons of explosives, the warships moved off.

Aboard the *Enterprise,* Fred Mears and his fellow pilots were watching the fireworks display as it drew to a close. "I guess that will teach those Japs a lesson," said his wise-ass friend Ensign Gerry Richey.

Fred had come to look at much of what happened aboard the carriers, especially with the big brass and their staffs, as something out of a Gilbert and Sullivan opera. The daily peccadilloes struck him and his friends as particularly ludicrous in the middle of a supposed fight for civilization.

As the invasion force steamed toward Guadalcanal, a dive-bomber from one of the other carriers had flown over to the *Enterprise.* When its passenger emerged from the second seat, he headed straight for the officers' wardroom and pronounced to one of the supply officers that his admiral's staff was planning to have omelets for lunch and they lacked enough eggs to feed everyone. When the staff officer's plea was refused, threats were exchanged before he was forced to fly back empty-handed.

That same afternoon, Fred Mears and his friend Ensign Dick Jaccard were scheduled to fly a scouting mission. Fred asked Dick which sector he would be searching. At Midway, Jaccard had been recommended to receive the Navy Cross for putting a direct hit on the Japanese carrier *Hiryu*. He was a pure warrior.

"Oh, my dear," he said. "I've given up that awful searching. It's so hard on the complexion! Besides, I must run over to Sara's and borrow a cup of sugar. Poor George will be so disappointed if I don't bake him a cake for dinner tonight."

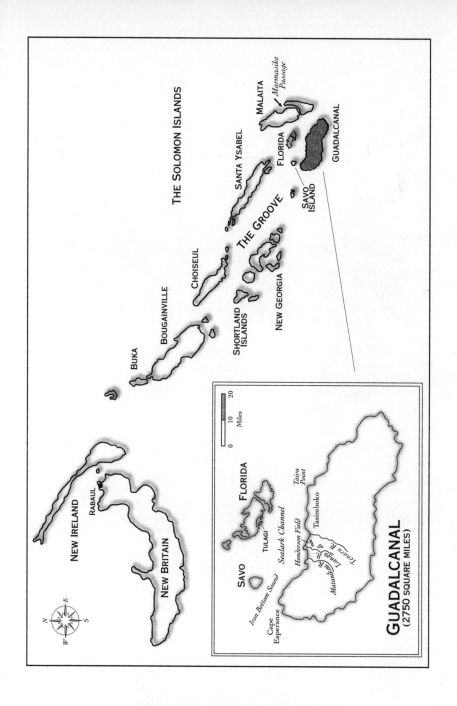

THE SOLOMON ISLANDS,
AUGUST–NOVEMBER 1942

Dog Day

The American invasion force crept slowly eastward in the pre-dawn darkness across an ebony sea. In the hot, overcrowded transports, nineteen thousand men of the 1st Marine Division prepared to disembark as soon as they reached their landing beaches at Guadalcanal and Tulagi.

Boredom from the long sea voyage was replaced with growing anxiety.

So far, their luck was holding. The previous day, August 6, had been gray and overcast, cloaking the eighty-two ships from the eyes of Japanese scout pilots. Late that afternoon, the sun had broken through, bathing the invasion force in golden light.

Aboard the *Saratoga* that evening, Commander Felt assembled his pilots in the wardroom to go over their assignments for the last time. After the briefing was over, a group of Filipino mess stewards attempted to play the latest swing music of Glenn Miller on their ukeleles. Most of the officers turned in early.

They were awakened about two hours before dawn, and the pilots assembled for breakfast in the wardroom. After more than a month at sea without reprovisioning, the *Saratoga*'s morning menu was re-duced to coffee, stewed tomatoes, toast, and powdered eggs. It didn't inspire a healthy appetite.

The pilots assigned to fly in the first wave of attacks headed straight to their planes, which were already spotted on the dark flight deck. Overnight, the seas had turned violent, and the wind was gusting at twenty knots. Standing in the darkness at the edge of the deck, Lieutenant Pete Peterkin silently prayed that all of the squadron's Avengers were ready to go.

In the weeks since Swede had ordered him and Chief Hammond to get the planes squared away, Torpedo Eight had continued to be plagued with mechanical failures and engine malfunctions. A number of its flights had to be aborted. In addition to losing Evarts's Avenger on the barrier wire a week earlier, several pilots had made rough landings aboard the carrier, resulting in further damage to their aircraft.

The sarcastic jibes from the other squadrons had gotten so bad that Peterkin and Hammond defiantly offered to bet any takers on the ship that all of their aircraft would have successful takeoffs on Dog Day. It was about pride, but the two of them stood to lose a lot of money if even one of the planes failed to get airborne.

At 0500, the blue flash of exhaust gas garishly lit up the flight deck as dozens of airplane engines were started and slowly warmed up. After ten minutes, they were turned off, and it was quiet once more.

Bert Earnest sat in the gloom of his cockpit and wondered why he felt so nervous. His Confederate ancestors in Virginia, at least those who had survived the Civil War, had sometimes referred to their first time under fire as having "been to see the elephant."

Whatever the words meant, he had been to see the elephant on his very first mission at Midway. Hell, he had seen a good-size part of the whole Japanese navy. So why should he be nervous now? He decided that nerves would probably be part of every combat mission he ever flew. It all came down to how much luck a man had. If fate was something like a cat's proverbial nine lives, he wondered how many he had already used up at Midway.

Far off on the port side of the carrier, he was startled to see a sudden eruption of brilliant flame in the inky darkness. The flash lasted only a few moments and was gone again. He knew there were escort ships in that direction, and wondered if one of them might have been hit by an enemy torpedo or bomb.

Waiting to take off behind him, Gene Hanson was nervous, too. Like most of the pilots in the squadron, this would be his first combat mission, and he was worried about taking off in the dark. There had been a sliver of a pale new moon earlier, but it had waned to nothing. He could barely see his hands in front of his face.

How would they find each other in the middle of it all? The seven Avengers in the first attack were supposed to rendezvous above the carrier and then Swede would lead them to their assigned target. That sounded fine except that dozens of planes would be taking off from the three carriers at the same time, all trying to join up in the crowded airspace.

They were under strict orders to maintain radio silence until the first Japanese targets were hit, so all he could do was follow the tail-lights of the plane ahead of him and hope they eventually found each other.

In spite of his nervousness, Gene Hanson felt confident and pre-pared. He was a thorough pilot, and had made a personal check of every important mechanical system on the aircraft. Using a flash-light, he had even inspected the bomb racks before getting into the cockpit. The armorers had loaded him with nine one-hundred-pound concussion bombs and three incendiaries.

His dad had been a machinist back in Burlington, Iowa, and Gene had grown up with a reverence for all things mechanical. Descended from Swedish immigrants, the stoic six-footer had started work at the John Deere tractor company in Moline, Illinois, right out of high school. He had lived in a cheap Moline rooming house while work-ing on an assembly line making threshers. After saving up enough money, he had put himself through junior college, and then joined the naval reserves. He had won his wings in December 1941, a week after the attack at Pearl Harbor.

Gene's best friend in the squadron was the unlucky Bob Evarts. He and Evarts were built almost exactly alike, and when their backs were turned, it was hard for the crews to tell them apart. They had both started out the war clean shaven, but in recent months Gene had nurtured what the other pilots scathingly called his "Clark Ga-ble" mustache. After sending his fiancée a recent photograph, he was waiting to find out whether she liked it or not.

Waiting behind Hanson on the flight deck were John Taurman, Red Doggett, Jack Barnum, Bob Ries, and Swede Larsen. Swede, who was leading his first combat mission, would be the last pilot in the flight to take off.

If Swede was nervous, it wasn't apparent to Yeoman Jack Stark, who was standing on the flight deck to watch as the squadron prepared for its mission. To Stark, Swede looked like an excited thoroughbred in the starting gate at the Kentucky Derby.

At 0530, the three American carriers turned southeast into the wind and began launching their aircraft. The Grumman Wildcats went off first, quickly followed by the Dauntless dive-bombers. Everything was going like clockwork until Ensign William Bell took off in one of the last dive-bombers aboard the *Saratoga*.

As Jack Stark watched in horror, Bell's Dauntless suddenly stalled in midair, hovering there for a moment as if in suspended animation. Then the plane and its three-man crew disappeared off the bow into the boiling sea. In the predawn darkness, there wasn't a chance of their being saved.

Torpedo Eight's seven Avengers moved up to take off after the last dive-bomber. As Bert taxied forward to the starting line, Pete Peterkin made his way to the plane across the slick flight deck.

After the tail-hook accident that had cost Bob Evarts's plane a few weeks earlier, Peterkin had decided to crawl under each aircraft just before takeoff to make sure that its tail hook was locked up. It was a dangerous job, particularly in the dark. The gusting force of prop wash from moving airplanes on a slippery deck had caused several deaths aboard the carriers, which was why Peterkin had assigned this job to himself.

One by one, the big Avengers roared down the flight deck and lifted off into the black sky, each pilot following the taillight of the man ahead of him. Swede was the seventh and last. As he came up to the starting point, Peterkin checked that the tail hook was stowed before scuttling back to join Chief Hammond at the edge of the flight deck.

Swede revved the engine to the straining point, and the takeoff control officer gave him the signal to go. Swede released his brakes, and the plane quickly began to pick up speed.

Suddenly, Peterkin felt a lash of spray on his face. It wasn't seawater. He smelled the reek of motor oil, and realized that Swede's engine was spewing it out of the breather pipe. He could now hear the engine misfiring, once and then again, as the plane continued lumbering down the deck.

Chief Hammond yelled out for him to cut the engine. If Swede reacted right away, there was still a chance he could stop the plane before it dropped into the sea like the doomed Dauntless ten minutes earlier.

But Swede never hesitated. With the engine at full throttle, his sputtering Avenger slowly clawed its way into the air. The dark shape of the aircraft briefly dipped below the bow of the carrier before finally disappearing into the murky sky above them.

The first seven had all made it. When the last one was gone, Peterkin and Hammond went down to the hangar deck to do a final series of checks on the eight Avengers that would go out in the second wave of attacks.

The dark sky above the carriers now held a confusing mass of pilots struggling to find one another. Planes from the *Saratoga* quickly found themselves entangled in formations from the *Enterprise* and *Wasp*.

In getting his own troubled plane into the air, Swede had lost contact with the rest of the flight. His windshield was covered by a film of oil, and it was impossible for him to see anything clearly.

The standing orders from Commander Felt were that no pilot should spend more than five minutes trying to locate the rest of his formation. If unsuccessful, he was to head off on his flight's preplanned compass bearing. Hopefully, the lost pilots would find the rest of their group once dawn broke.

After searching for the others, Swede gave up and headed east on his own. By then, the deputy flight leader, Lieutenant Jack Barnum, had assumed command and was headed toward their first target.

Torpedo Eight's initial objective was Florida Island, where aerial reconnaissance indicated that the Japanese had built a command installation. As Barnum's formation flew over the dark mass of Guadalcanal, Gene Hanson saw yellow splashes of light erupting out of the darkness far below him as bombs and tracer rounds from the first wave of fighters and dive-bombers hit their targets. With radio silence no longer necessary, his cockpit radio suddenly came alive with excited chatter.

Flying alone at full throttle, Swede followed them across the crowded sky over Guadalcanal. His engine was running fine now, and a brief rain squall had cleared his windshield. Dawn was breaking when he caught up with the rest of the squadron as they approached the western coast of Florida Island. Swede radioed to Jack Barnum that he was taking back command.

Their assignment was to destroy the Japanese headquarters at Point Purvis, which was located about twenty miles northeast of Guadalcanal across Sealark Channel. When they arrived there, it was light enough to see that the installation was already reduced to smoking rubble. A few smaller buildings were still standing, and Swede led the formation down in a low-level "flat-hatting" attack to destroy them.

Their second objective was on the coast of Malaita, a much bigger island to the east of Florida. The mission called for them to use their remaining bombs to destroy any enemy ships they found in the Maramasike Estuary.

Unfortunately, thunderheads blocked the passage leading to the estuary, and Swede decided to lead them up the western coast of Malaita to a point where they could cross a mountain range to reach their objective. Bad weather again forced them to turn back.

Swede decided to head farther north.

As they flew on through the lightening sky, Gene Hanson saw that Malaita was made up of different shades of green. There were the blue-green mountains, darker green jungle, and the pale green of its grassy fields and coconut palms.

After miles of uninterrupted jungle, Swede came to a small, sheltered harbor along the northwest coast. He immediately thought the place looked suspicious. The lagoon was large enough for Japanese torpedo boats and maybe even bigger ships. He then saw what appeared to be boat moorings dotted around the harbor.

Swede was now sure it was a Japanese torpedo-boat base disguised as a fishing village. The torpedo boats were probably hidden in the dense jungle along the shallow creeks that fed the lagoon.

To John Taurman, Bert Earnest, and Gene Hanson, the place appeared to be nothing more than a native settlement. A cluster of primitive huts ringed the lagoon. Tiny figures in canoes were paddling along the inlet that led toward the settlement. More canoes were beached along the shore line.

Swede didn't wait to hear their opinions. Over the radio, he ordered them to follow him down in another flat-hatting attack. Coming in low, he opened up on the huts with his nose machine gun before releasing his first bomb on the largest one in the clearing. He then went into a steep climb to give his machine gunners a better angle to strafe with their machine guns. Barnum, Ries, and Hanson followed Swede in, dropping their payloads on other huts in the settlement.

As he swept in behind them, John Taurman decided not to release his bombs. Heading in on his own run, Bert Earnest saw little stick figures running out of the huts in every direction. They didn't appear to be wearing clothes, much less Japanese uniforms.

"Knock off the firing," he called out on the intercom.

After two more passes, Swede ran out of ammunition and ordered the rest of them to form up behind him for the return flight to the *Saratoga*. It was now full daylight.

Flying back over Guadalcanal, Gene Hanson could see an American cruiser pounding the landing beaches with salvos of shell fire, the explosions tossing palm trees like match sticks into the air along with geysers of sand and debris.

Offshore, American transport ships were disgorging dark masses of men as Higgins landing craft idled in the water alongside them. Waves of landing craft were churning toward the invasion beaches, crammed with men and equipment. Farther inland, a long brown gash cut straight across the green landscape. It was the packed-earth runway of the Japanese airfield.

### USS SARATOGA
### 0800

Aboard the *Saratoga,* the second flight of Torpedo Eight's Avengers was preparing for its own mission. Bruce Harwood would lead the eight-plane formation. His orders were to find and destroy any enemy positions still left on Guadalcanal.

Sitting behind Harwood in the second seat was Clark Lee, a correspondent for the Associated Press. It was the first time a journalist had been given the chance to fly on a combat mission in the Pacific.

Lee liked the big, taciturn Harwood. In the midst of all the pandemonium on the carrier deck, Harwood had an almost uncanny sense of calm. Lee turned on the radio earphones in his flying helmet and heard the jumbled voices of pilots hitting targets on Guadalcanal and Tulagi.

Pete Peterkin and Chief Hammond watched nervously as one by one, the eight Avengers took off from the flight deck. After the last plane was in the air, he and Hammond celebrated their achievement by shaking hands. They would collect on their winning bets later.

Once airborne, Clark Lee could see the mountains of Guadalcanal rising through the clouds in the distance. He felt the plane shudder as Harwood had his flight crew test their machine guns before they came down over the north shore of the island.

Lee took in the panorama of the American invasion force.

A long line of landing craft was beached parallel along the dun-colored sand. Higgins boats full of men and equipment were waiting offshore to unload their cargoes when a free spot opened on the beach. Offshore, the transports were still untouched by enemy fire. They all faced bow-in toward the shoreline, steadily unloading more men and equipment into the landing craft.

As far as Lee could see, there was no serious enemy resistance on Guadalcanal. Apparently, surprise had been complete. Harwood led the formation in a pass over the newly constructed, packed-dirt airfield. A group of frame buildings adjoining the runway was already ablaze.

Smiley Morgan, who was flying on Harwood's wing, searched the landscape below them for possible targets. He watched as a Wildcat fighter went in low to strafe what at first looked like men on horseback trying to escape across the grassy plain. As their flight drew closer, he saw that the fleeing men were a panic-stricken herd of cattle.

Harwood received orders over the radio to bomb a section of dense jungle near the airfield where Japanese troops were thought to be hiding. As the explosions burst behind him from Harwood's five-hundred-pound bombs, Clark Lee scribbled into the open notebook on his lap, "Hit 'em. Hit the bastards. Kill the lousy Japs."

It was the first payback he had personally witnessed since Pearl Harbor.

### USS SARATOGA
### 1000

Aboard the *Saratoga,* Swede's flight had just landed. He ordered the squadron's planes to be rearmed and fueled. The pilots were given thirty minutes to relax before their next mission, and they headed down for coffee and sandwiches.

In the wardroom, Gene Hanson could see that John Taurman was incensed. The big pilot went straight over to Swede and told him they had just bombed a native village. Worried that a physical confrontation might land Taurman in the brig, Hanson joined them at Swede's table. When Taurman repeated the assertion, Swede heatedly denied it.

"What the hell were we shooting at?" asked Bert Earnest, coming up to join them.

"Didn't you see that Jap torpedo boat?" asked Swede.

None of them had. Swede said it might have looked like a native village, but it was actually a cleverly concealed Japanese torpedo-boat base. He had seen one of the boats lying camouflaged in a creek near the settlement.

The boat moorings in the lagoon were the tip-off, he said. Fortunately, they had taken out the base before the Japanese could use it to launch an attack on the invasion force. He would write it all up in his After Action Report.

Bert hadn't seen a torpedo boat or any moorings. The only thing he remembered seeing were the thatched-roof huts and the tiny stick figures running in every direction after the first bombs hit the settlement.

Taurman still wasn't convinced, and he was right in Swede's face. Gene Hanson got in front of Taurman and urged him to calm down.

They had another mission to fly and it was too late to do anything about it now.

Twenty minutes later, they were back in the air. Swede's orders were to again cross over the Maramasike Estuary on Malaita, and search it from end to end for enemy ships.

No longer hindered by bad weather, the flight made it through this time, but their search yielded no enemy ships or planes. Suddenly, they spotted a group of buldings at the edge of a small bay. Sweeping in low, they flew over a cluster of people standing in one of the clearings waving white objects at them.

The pilots waited for Swede's orders to go in, but he decided not to attack. After radioing the USS *Mackinac* that the estuary was clear of enemy ships, he led the flight back to the carrier.

### OVER GUADALCANAL
### 1400

Still searching for targets over Guadalcanal, Smiley Morgan finally met the enemy. At that moment, he had been lagging well behind Harwood instead of staying in the tight, well-ordered formation.

"Zeroes at eleven o'clock," someone called out on the radio.

Staring through his windshield, Smiley was shocked to see dozens of Japanese planes materialize out of the glare. Seeing that they all appeared to be heading in his general direction, Smiley quickly tucked the nose of his Avenger right behind Bruce Harwood.

The Japanese planes went straight for the American transports lying offshore. The American fighters were waiting for them. When the enemy dive-bombers dove to begin their attacks, the Grumman Wildcats went down after them. The Japanese Zeroes that were escorting the bombers went down after the Wildcats.

The first major air battle of the campaign was under way.

Harwood received orders to return to the *Saratoga*. As Smiley banked to the west, he saw one of the Japanese dive-bombers spiral down in flames toward the sea. Below him, an American transport ship was burning, the dull red flames rising into the sky inside a great cloud of black smoke.

**USS SARATOGA**
**1800**

The officers' wardroom was packed with happy and excited pilots, most of them still in sweat-stained flying clothes, all talking and gesturing with their hands to show how they had made an attack or shot down an enemy plane. Based on their own arithmetic, the score included at least twenty Japanese fighters and bombers.

The *Saratoga*'s wardroom mess staff had pulled out all the stops to celebrate the fliers' victories in the air. The cooks had come up with the delicacy they had been hoarding for just such an occasion. It was the centerpiece of the small feast, fried Spam sandwiches served on silver trays along with canned fruit juice.

It seemed to Smiley as if the fighter pilots thought they had shot down half the Japanese air force. He felt embarrassed at having only seen the enemy in the air, while these men had actually engaged and defeated them.

In truth, fifteen Grumman Wildcats had failed to return to the three American carriers, a stunning loss. Nine of the Wildcats had been shot down by Japanese Zeroes, while six others had crashed. The Japanese had lost twelve planes, two of them Zeroes.

One of *Saratoga*'s fighter pilots told Smiley he thought he had shot down one Zero, and possibly two. Although Smiley was happy for him, it made him feel even more left out.

He did receive one congratulatory boost from his best friend in the squadron, James Hill Cook. Cook laughingly recounted how he had seen Smiley tuck his plane in right behind Harwood after they had spotted the Zeroes. He told Smiley it was a magnificent example of precision flying.

Later, Swede gathered the squadron pilots together to say that although it had been easy pickings so far, the enemy would be back in the morning. Raising his clenched fist, he told them that this would be their first opportunity for vengeance. They were Torpedo Eight, he said, and it was time to begin settling the score for Midway.

That night in his stateroom, Gene Hanson lay in his berth and tried to erase the Malaita mission from his mind. In hindsight, he wished that he had spoken up to Swede about it, or, like John Taurman, refused to drop his bombs. But it was too late now. There was no way to undo it.

## GUADALCANAL
## 2300

On Guadalcanal and Tulagi, ten thousand newly landed Marines sat in their foxholes and stared into the unfathomable darkness, waiting for a Japanese counterattack. The cries of exotic birds and other creatures filled the moist night air.

Along with the unnerving sounds from the rain forest, land crabs the size of a man's fist moved everywhere just under the surface of the sand. The noise of the digging crabs reminded one young Marine of someone chewing pecans, shells and all.

Their imaginations ran wild.

Hearing a strange noise in the jungle, a Marine would fire at it, thinking that Japanese sappers were about to assault his position. When one man fired, it triggered off a chain reaction of echoing rounds from skittish Marines farther along the line.

In his command post under a copse of bomb-scarred coconut palms, General Vandegrift met with his staff to assess the day's results. It was raining hard as the staff told him what little they knew.

So far, things had gone well, at least on Guadalcanal. They had secured most of their assigned objectives although the terrain bore little resemblance to what they had been led to expect in the preinvasion briefings. Mount Austen had been described as a hill by one of the former plantation managers who had briefed them in New Zealand. To Vandegrift's staff, it looked more like Mount Everest.

The first captured prisoners from a Japanese construction unit assigned to build the airfield told the Americans that their army had fled into the jungle when the bombing and shelling began.

It had been a different story on Tulagi. There, the fighting had been horrific. The island was honeycombed with caves, and the Japanese had set up machine gun nests in them with intersecting firing positions. There were tunnels between the caves, and they were impervious to bombs. The only way to reduce the enemy strong points was for Marines to go into the caves with grenades and improvised demolition charges. A lot of Lieutenant Colonel Merritt Edson's Marine raiders had died trying.

The major concern for Vandegrift was getting his equipment and supplies ashore, particularly the field guns, tanks, food, and ammunition. At their preinvasion conference aboard the *Saratoga* on July 27, Admiral Fletcher had said he would give him three days before pulling out the carriers. Once the carriers were gone, there was no guarantee that Admiral Turner, who commanded the transports, would remain behind without fighter protection.

So far, Vandegrift estimated that they had received less than 20 percent of what was needed to hold the airfield and the islands. The supplies had come ashore much faster than the shore party of three hundred Marines could move them inland off the beaches. The Higgins boats had been forced to idle offshore waiting to bring in their cargoes.

There was no front ramp on the Higgins boats, and everything had to be manhandled out of them, carried up the beach, and distributed to the supply dumps set up farther inland.

In the brutally humid heat, things had quickly bogged down. The Marines had never felt anything like it. It quickly sucked the energy out of a man. But the only way Vandegrift could add men to the work details was to take them from combat regiments, and he still had no idea of the threat he might be facing from the Japanese.

As scattered gunfire continued to erupt along the perimeter, Vandegrift ordered that more Marines be assigned in the morning to the unloading task. It was critical that the antiaircraft guns and field artillery in the transports be brought ashore so that the Marines would be able to defend themselves after the Navy pulled out.

SATURDAY, 8 AUGUST 1942
USS SARATOGA
TORPEDO SQUADRON EIGHT
0600

Dawn was breaking under a leaden sky when Torpedo Eight took off from the *Saratoga* to attack Japanese-held positions on the small island of Tanambogo, located two miles east of Tulagi.

A garrison of several hundred Japanese defenders continued to hold out from the island's highest promontory, designated Hill 121. From its deep coral caves, the Japanese were pouring a withering stream of machine gun fire down on the Marines attempting to take the island.

When Swede's flight of twelve Avengers arrived at the designated target, they were ordered to drop their payloads onto the caves from which there was still resistance. Afterward, they returned safely to the *Saratoga*.

On Guadalcanal, the invasion continued to go smoothly. By noon on the eighth, Vandegrift's Marines had captured the airfield along with newly constructed machine shops, repair sheds, and underground storage tanks filled with fifty thousand gallons of gas and oil.

To the north of the airfield, Marines found a rich haul of food and supplies amassed by the Japanese in preparation for their imminent occupation, including a fully functioning ice-making plant. Within an hour, someone had erected a handwritten sign reading TOJO ICE COMPANY . . . UNDER NEW MANAGEMENT.

There were tons of bagged rice and stacks of tinned goods including Alaskan crabmeat cocktail, sliced beef, and exotic fruits and vegetables. When a Marine uncovered a large supply of beer and sake, it was immediately put under armed guard.

With most of their tactical objectives secured, the next challenge for Vandegrift was to hold the islands against the expected Japanese counterattack. It came swiftly from both air and sea.

The first fifty enemy attack planes arrived at almost precisely noon. The Japanese pilots had received orders to try to sink the carriers that were providing air support for the invasion force, but these were deployed too far offshore. Unable to locate them, the Japanese torpedo bombers headed for the dozens of stationary transport ships.

As they came in low across Sealark Channel, the planes came under a hail of disciplined antiaircraft fire from the American escort ships, but they still succeeded in sinking one transport and damaging a destroyer.

At 1800 that evening, Admiral Frank Jack Fletcher came to a decision that was to have profound consequences for the invasion. He decided to recommend the immediate withdrawal of his three carriers.

At the planning conference on July 27, Fletcher had told General Vandegrift that he would keep the carriers in close proximity to the landing beaches for three days. Unfolding events, however, not the least of them the loss of twenty-one Grumman Wildcat fighters in the previous twenty-four hours, had now caused him to change his mind.

Earlier that afternoon, he had spoken by short-range radio with Admiral Leigh Noyes, who was in tactical command of the three carriers. "In view of possibility of torpedo plane attack and reduction of our fighter strength I intend to recommend immediate withdrawal of carriers. Do you agree?"

"Affirmative," responded Noyes.

Admiral Fletcher based his decision on several factors. Almost the entire Marine amphibious force was now ashore, and they had achieved most of their initial objectives on Guadalcanal and Tulagi. There were no important ground targets left for his dive-bombers and torpedo planes to hit.

Unaware of Admiral Turner's unloading problems with the transports, Fletcher viewed the three carriers as more important than the invasion force itself. He also embraced the philosophy that carriers should be used to strike quickly and withdraw before the enemy could mount a strong counterattack. This situation seemed a perfect example of that philosophy. In his mind, the withdrawal was a temporary repositioning of his carrier fleet to confound the enemy.

Fletcher proceeded to inform Admiral Turner, whose transport ships were still being unloaded, of his decision to pull out. As darkness fell, Fletcher ordered the three carriers to head southeast in a long column away from the invasion area.

The withdrawal left Turner in a difficult position. More than half of the 1st Marine Division's supplies, including most of its heavy equipment, still remained aboard the transports. That material might be critical to their survival.

With Fletcher pulling the carriers out, however, there would be no fighter protection for his transports. The only defense against Japanese attack planes would be the antiaircraft guns on the escort force of cruisers and destroyers that remained under Turner's personal command.

The Japanese gave him little time to make a decision on whether to stay or go.

At 1900, shortly after Fletcher began his withdrawal, Turner received the news that an American search plane had sighted a Japanese naval force of seven ships, including at least four cruisers, heading south from Rabaul.

Based on the reported speed of the enemy force, Turner believed there was little possibility of their ships reaching the waters around Guadalcanal that same night. While the unloading of the transports continued, he deployed his escort force of eight cruisers and six destroyers to the north of his transports to block the Japanese from getting through.

Two American destroyers were sent on ahead to guard the approaches around Savo Island through which any Japanese force would have to penetrate to reach the landing beaches. Both destroyers were equipped with radar, and would warn the rest of the escort force as soon as the enemy appeared.

Late in the evening, Turner decided that without the carriers, his transports were simply too vulnerable to air attack. The following day, he would begin withdrawing them from the landing zones.

Turner radioed General Vandegrift on Guadalcanal, and requested that he join him on his flagship, the USS *McCawley*. Shortly before midnight, Vandegrift arrived to confer about the situation. Turner informed him that Admiral Fletcher had departed from the invasion area with the three carriers. Without air cover, Turner said he felt compelled to withdraw.

This news was a stunning blow to Vandegrift. He had hoped to have at least two more days to bring ashore the rest of his supplies and equipment. He persuaded Turner to give him an opportunity to find out the military situation on Tulagi before the admiral made his final decision.

Vandegrift was en route to Tulagi aboard the minelayer USS *Southard,* when the blackness of the northern horizon was lit up by a series of brilliant explosions. It sounded like distant thunder.

One of the ship's officers thought it might be heat lightning. Standing on deck, Vandegrift knew it came from heavy naval guns, and that a major naval battle was taking place to the north.

Aboard the *Southard,* sailors began cheering with each rumbling explosion, confident that the American and Australian escort force was dealing the Japanese a serious defeat. The explosions went on for more than forty minutes before the northern horizon went dark again.

For a sea battle, it had been the worst disaster in American naval history.

The two American radar-equipped destroyers had not detected the Japanese force as it approached Savo Island under the cover of the black, moonless night. After evading the American picket destroyers, six Japanese cruisers and one destroyer had closed on the rest of the unsuspecting Allied escort force.

First using their Long Lance torpedoes, which ran true for more than ten miles at a speed of fifty knots, and then using barrages of deadly accurate gunfire, the Japanese force sank the heavy cruisers *Astoria, Quincy, Vincennes,* and *Canberra.* Another cruiser, the USS *Chicago,* was heavily damaged.

In forty minutes, thirteen hundred American and Australian sailors had been killed, with hundreds more grievously wounded. Oil-soaked and delirious survivors floated for miles across what was soon to become known as "Ironbottom Sound."

Incredibly, the Japanese had not lost a single ship.

The only saving grace for the Americans was that after annihilating the Allied escort force, the Japanese naval commander made the wrong assumption that Fletcher's three American carriers were still protecting the transport ships at Guadalcanal. Not wanting to be caught in daylight by American dive-bombers and torpedo planes, he withdrew at high speed toward Rabaul, sparing the transports almost certain destruction.

SUNDAY, 9 AUGUST 1942
GUADALCANAL
1ST MARINE DIVISION
1800

Admiral Turner's transport ships sailed away from Guadalcanal late that afternoon, taking with them artillery pieces, antiaircraft guns, trucks, barbed wire, food, and ammunition.

The Marines stood alone.

General Vandegrift was enraged at what he viewed as a desertion by the Navy, first by the carriers, and now by the vital supply ships. The Marines on Guadalcanal and Tulagi were well aware of what had happened to the American forces in the Philippines just five months earlier. On Bataan, the Americans had been forced to surrender to the Japanese army when their food and ammunition ran out, after which thousands of Allied soldiers had died while being herded sixty miles at bayonet point into captivity. Now the Marines had to wonder if they would share the same fate. After inventorying what they had ashore, including captured Japanese supplies, Vandegrift's staff estimated that if each man was limited to two meals per day, there was a three-week supply of food.

Along the landing beaches, shell-shocked survivors from the sunken cruisers were still floating in on life rafts when Vandegrift brought dozens of his senior regimental officers together to brief them on what they could expect in the weeks ahead.

They sprawled out on the sand under a lashing rain squall, staring up at him with slack faces and bloodshot eyes. Vandegrift knew that if they were to survive, he needed to convince these men that they could hold the islands against whatever the Japanese threw at them until they were relieved.

It was too soon to know the final score from the naval action at

Savo Island, but the results didn't look good. As he spoke to his officers, the cruiser *Chicago*, its bow sheared off, slowly crawled past the beach on its way out of the invasion area.

This was no time to sugarcoat the truth. He decided to hold nothing back, telling them he had no idea when they might be resupplied, while assuring them that this was not going to be another Bataan or Wake Island, where the Americans would be forced into a humiliating surrender. Even if they had to fight on alone, the Marines were going to hold.

The first thing they needed to do was establish a coordinated line of defense to meet the all-out counteroffensive that would soon be coming at them by air and sea from the Japanese fortress at Rabaul. Their next priority was to finish the airfield so it would be ready for the Marine air group that was on its way to provide them with air support against the Japanese attack planes. The final priority was to disperse all of the supplies and ammunition from the landing beach to protected supply dumps that could withstand air attack by Japanese bombers.

They were in a tough spot, he said as his officers sat through the downpour, but Marines had fought and survived in a lot of tough spots before. They had everything they needed to defeat the Japanese as long as every man pulled together and did his job.

While Vandegrift was concluding the briefing, a patrol of the 5th Marine Regiment encountered Japanese troops on a jungle trail near the Matanikau River, a few miles to the west. In the ensuing firefight, a Marine officer was shot and killed.

The battle for Guadalcanal had begun.

SUNDAY, 9 AUGUST 1942
ADMIRAL ISOROKU YAMAMOTO
COMMANDER-IN-CHIEF, COMBINED IMPERIAL FLEET

When news of the American invasion of the Solomons reached him, Admiral Yamamoto immediately recognized the strategic significance of American control of the airfield on Guadalcanal, and made plans to expel them.

He ordered the advance force of the Japanese 2nd Fleet, as well as the carrier striking force of the newly created 3rd Fleet, to provide the naval muscle required by the Imperial Army to "clean out" the American ground and naval forces in the Solomon Islands.

The advance force of the 2nd Fleet was ordered to sail in forty-eight hours. It consisted of one battleship, five heavy cruisers, a seaplane carrier, and two destroyer squadrons. The carrier striking force of the 3rd Fleet, which would provide air support for the counteroffensive, included the Empire's newest heavy carriers, the *Shokaku* and the *Zuikaku*, along with the light carrier, *Ryujo*. The carriers had a combined complement of 127 combat aircraft, and would be escorted by two battleships, two heavy cruisers, one light cruiser, and ten destroyers.

The navy's success, however, would depend on an equally potent contribution by the Imperial Army. Unfortunately, its high command did not share Yamamoto's views about Guadalcanal's strategic importance. At that moment, the army was in the process of planning a ground offensive against Port Moresby in New Guinea, and considered the American thrust in the Solomons to be little more than an annoyance.

Initial reports sent to Rabaul led the army to believe the Americans were conducting a "reconnaissance in force" at Guadalcanal, not a full-scale invasion. Although Japanese pilots claimed they had sighted thirty transport ships in the invasion force, an army staff officer contended that due to the softness of American troops, they required twenty transports for a single regiment.

With no agreement on the size of the American ground force, the Imperial General Headquarters decided to allocate nine thousand troops from three different military units to retake Guadalcanal.

More than ten thousand Americans were already there. Another seven thousand held the island of Tulagi and the other initial invasion objectives. The lack of accurate intelligence by the Japanese would have serious consequences.

The only Japanese military unit available for an immediate counterattack was on the island of Guam. It was a detachment of three thousand seasoned troops commanded by an aggressive and highly decorated army colonel named Kiyonao Ichiki. He was ordered to immediately prepare his men for action.

SUNDAY, 9 AUGUST 1942
USS *SARATOGA*
TORPEDO SQUADRON EIGHT
1800

As the *Saratoga* continued steaming away from the invasion area, Swede Larsen was tallying the results of the previous two days of squadron operations. He commended Pete Peterkin and Chief Hammond for their roles in successfully preparing all the aircraft for combat. Not one plane had experienced a serious malfunction, and all of them had returned safely to the *Saratoga*.

In his After Action Report for the dawn mission on August 7, Swede described it as a "glide bombing and strafing attack on Langa Langa Harbor, Malaita Island, destroying observed sea plane and motor torpedo boat moorings and adjacent clusters of grass huts."

He made no mention in his report of having sighted a torpedo boat in one of the creeks. John Taurman remained convinced that they had attacked a native settlement. Commander Felt, the *Saratoga* air group commander, decided to recommend Swede for the Distinguished Flying Cross for his "heroism and extraordinary achievement in aerial combat against the enemy."

It was Swede's first combat citation, and the first received by the squadron for the Guadalcanal operation. That Sunday, most of the pilots on the *Saratoga* were simply grateful to have a chance to relax after two days of constant flying.

After forty days aboard ship without reprovisioning, their monotonous diet was temporarily enhanced when the officers' "Gedunk" bar began operating again, serving ice cream made from powdered ingredients as long as they lasted.

Smiley Morgan privately wondered whether the battle for the Solomons might already be over. It sounded to him like a lot of Japanese planes had been shot down in the first two days. Some of the fighter pilots were already declaring victory.

No one seemed to know why the American carriers were heading away from the Solomons invasion area, but the obvious reason was that they weren't needed there anymore.

# The Galloping Dragon

To some of the pilots, it felt as if they had suddenly been cut off from the war, from the world itself, and had become guests aboard a tourist ship cruising the South Pacific.

The *Saratoga* wasn't as elegant as a tourist ship. The food in the officers' wardroom continued to worsen. A typical supper would be boiled rice served with canned Vienna sausage. The next night, it might be chili beans served with rice and canned corn.

In the enlisted men's mess, those meals would have seemed like delicacies.

Each morning, Smiley checked in at the squadron office to find out if any missions had been scheduled. A few pilots from the squadron were flying daily air patrols, but he was never asked to fly one.

The task force was evidently in safe waters because the jarring klaxon of the general quarters signal had become a distant memory. Even the weather cooperated, with a succession of beautiful days in which the pilots spent hours sunbathing on the breezy flight deck.

Then the rumor mill started gearing up again. The word was that Fletcher was planning to ambush the Japanese carriers before their planned counteroffensive against Guadalcanal. John Taurman told Smiley that he thought Guadalcanal might be like Gettysburg, where no one expected a big battle to take place, but both sides kept raising the stakes after they got there until it became a deciding battleground in the war.

On August 17, Admiral Noyes flew over from the *Wasp* to confer with Admiral Fletcher. The latest intelligence from Pearl Harbor suggested that two and possibly three Japanese task forces carrying troop reinforcements had converged on Guadalcanal.

On August 19, the carrier USS *Long Island* arrived for a rendezvous at sea with the *Saratoga*. The *Long Island*'s flight deck was crammed with combat planes. It was the Marine air group that had been promised to General Vandegrift to defend Guadalcanal.

Fletcher ordered the *Saratoga* cleared for action. The two carriers headed north again, toward the Solomons.

THURSDAY, 20 AUGUST 1942
GUADALCANAL
1ST MARINE DIVISION

Since Dog Day, Vandegrift's Marines had done everything they could to prepare for the Japanese counteroffensive. By August 12, 2,600 feet of packed-earth runway had been completed at the airfield. It was a remarkable achievement. In just three days, his Marines moved 7,000 cubic yards of dirt to fill the long depression left in the runway. When they were finished, it was decided to name the field after Lofton Henderson, a Marine dive-bomber pilot who had been killed at Midway.

Vandegrift was concerned that the Japanese might assault the same landing beaches along the northern coast that his own men had used. He had the Marines dig in along the beaches' entire five-mile length.

On Dog Day, the Japanese army garrison on Guadalcanal had fled west across the Lunga River. He placed the 5th Marines along its banks to repel any counterattack from that direction. On the eastern perimeter, he put his defensive line along a stream called Alligator Creek. There he deployed the 1st Marines.

To the south of Henderson Field, there was only dense jungle. Along this less vulnerable part of the perimeter, he placed support troops, including the engineers, artillerymen, and construction units.

His most precious assets were the artillery pieces that had been unloaded before the transports left. There weren't many, mostly short-barreled howitzers, but they could stop a Japanese ground attack in its tracks. He placed the howitzers in a central position within the perimeter so their fire could be shifted in any direction. The few antiaircraft weapons were deployed north of the airfield to meet the Japanese bombers when they arrived from Rabaul.

Enemy air attacks had been constant. The Japanese came over whenever they pleased, day and night, dropping bombs and strafing positions around the airfield. At night, Japanese submarines would surface offshore and lob shells at the American positions. Without air cover, there was nothing for the Marines to do but endure it all in their trenches and foxholes.

On the night of August 12, tragedy struck. Colonel Frank Goettge, the division's senior intelligence officer, had led a twenty-five-man patrol to the far side of the Matanikau River after a Japanese prisoner indicated that a group of Japanese soldiers there were looking to surrender.

No word was received back from the patrol until early the next morning, when a naked and bleeding Marine crawled back into the American lines and reported that the patrol had been virtually wiped out. Another survivor claimed to have witnessed Japanese soldiers hacking wounded Marines to death with samurai swords. Vandegrift immediately sent a reinforced company to recover Goettge and his patrol. No trace of them was found.

The island itself had also begun to take a serious toll on Vandegrift's men. After one week ashore, his medical staff estimated that nearly 20 percent of the Marines were suffering from dysentery.

Another steaming hot day was coming to a close on August 20 when Marines at the airfield heard the distant drone of aircraft engines. At first, they assumed the planes were Japanese, although the enemy usually attacked at midday and from the north. These planes were coming from the east. When an officer with binoculars held them up to his eyes, he saw that the first plane in the formation had white stars under its wings.

Like Yankee fans watching a ninth-inning DiMaggio home run, the Marines started cheering. The raw-voiced howl spread across the length of the airfield and to the farthest corners of the defense perimeter as each man recognized what it meant and joined in.

When the first Dauntless dive-bomber braked to a stop in a cloud of dust at the edge of the packed-earth runway, Lieutenant Colonel Dick Mangrum, who commanded the Marine dive-bomber squadron, dropped down from the wing. General Vandegrift stepped forward to shake his hand.

"Thank God you have come," said Vandegrift, close to tears.

Behind Dick Mangrum's Dauntless were eleven more dive-bombers, followed by nineteen Grumman Wildcats under the command of Major John Smith. Now the Japanese could no longer fly over Guadalcanal without a fight. The Marines could finally hit back.

Prior to the invasion, American war planners had designated "Cactus" as the code name for Guadalcanal. Now, two weeks after Dog Day, the Cactus Air Force had been born.

That evening, Vandegrift personally celebrated its arrival by bathing with his men in the slow-moving Tenaru River. As he slathered himself with soap in the brown water, he glanced up to see a resolute young Marine on the riverbank cradling a thirty-caliber machine gun. Somehow it filled him with a transcendent confidence.

He went to sleep on the night of August 20 feeling secure that they were ready for whatever threat the Japanese could mount. The only remaining question was when the Japanese counteroffensive would begin.

It began five hours later.

FRIDAY, 21 AUGUST 1942
GUADALCANAL
1ST MARINE DIVISION
0200

The first Japanese attempt to retake Henderson Airfield came out of the darkness at the edge of Alligator Creek on the northeastern rim of the defense perimeter held by the 1st Marines.

The attack was led by Colonel Kiyonao Ichiki of the Japanese Imperial Army. His nine-hundred-man detachment of elite shock troops had been secretly delivered the previous night by six destroyers to a position several miles east of the American lines.

Ichiki was a veteran of China and Malaya. Dedicated to the code of Bushido, his martial philosophy allowed no pity for the enemy or for himself. Time and again, he had watched Allied troops retreat in panic in the face of his fierce "Banzai" charges.

Ichiki's orders were to attack only if he felt he had enough men to retake the airfield. Otherwise, he was to secure a position on Guadalcanal and await the reinforcements that would be delivered in a few days. Ichiki had no idea how many Americans were on Guadalcanal, but it didn't matter. They were the same decadent breed that had surrendered at Bataan. He didn't need reinforcements.

Ichiki's plan was simple. His men would burst through the American line with the concentrated force of a spear point, and then drive inland to the airfield. As soon as it was in his hands, he would radio for reinforcements.

Near the mouth of Alligator Creek, a sandbar ran parallel to the beach where the lagoon met the sea. It was here that he would launch his spear thrust. At 0200, a green flare exploded in the darkness over the sandbar. Under its garish illumination, Ichiki's first wave of shock troops came charging toward the Marine defense line shrieking, "BANZAI . . . BANZAI!"

Waiting twenty-five yards behind a strand of barbed wire at the western edge of the sandbar was a group of one hundred Marines. They were supported by three emplaced machine guns and a thirty-seven-millimeter gun. None of them had ever fought at night, or against an all-out assault by veteran troops. For most, this was their first combat action after two months of training in New Zealand.

Ichiki expected the Americans to break and run, just like the British troops had in the Malayan jungle. Instead, as his first wave of screaming attackers closed on the American line, the Marines sent back a concentrated hail of rifle and machine gun fire, cutting down many of the Japanese as they reached the string of barbed wire at the end of the sandbar.

A handful of attackers were able to breach the wire and run the last twenty-five yards to penetrate the American positions. There, the fighting became hand-to-hand until all of the Japanese were killed.

As the sound of the growing firefight reached General Vandegrift's command post, he waited nervously by his field telephone to learn the results of the first major action of the campaign.

Seeing the failure of his first assault, Colonel Ichiki ordered two more companies forward in a second Banzai charge. It too broke under the disciplined fire of the 1st Marines. Undaunted, Ichiki ordered another company to wade through the surf to get behind the American line. They were cut down with machine gun fire as they charged up the beach.

With hundreds of dead Japanese troops covering the sandbar, Ichiki fell back with the remainder of his force to a large coconut grove. In the morning, a reserve Marine battalion got behind him and cut off any further retreat. His last pocket of resistance was reduced with mortar fire, and four American tanks rumbled into the coconut grove to force their surrender.

The remaining Japanese refused to give up, even with the outcome no longer in doubt. They fought the tanks with rifles and pistols. A wounded Japanese soldier would wait for an American medic to examine him, then pull the pin on a hand grenade to kill them both. Ichiki's men gave no quarter, and expected none. The battle ended late on the afternoon of the twenty-first.

One Japanese soldier surrendered.

Between the sandbar and the coconut grove, nearly eight hundred Japanese soldiers lay dead, some of them half-buried by the pounding surf, others literally ground into the loamy soil under the treads of the tanks. Colonel Ichiki disappeared into the slaughter ground along with the rest of his men.

Forty-four Marines had been killed and more than seventy wounded.

For his part, General Vandegrift realized that the Japanese had underestimated the size of his defense force and the fighting caliber of his men. He doubted they would make the same mistake twice.

SATURDAY, 22 AUGUST 1942
USS SARATOGA
TORPEDO SQUADRON EIGHT
0600

The *Saratoga*'s air group was going back into action. They were heading north toward the Solomons to intercept the biggest concentration of Japanese warships since the Battle of Midway.

Smiley Morgan was the duty officer that morning as three of Torpedo Eight's Avengers prepared to take off on air patrol. Standing in a blustery wind on the flight deck, he watched the planes taxi up to the starting point.

The second pilot in line was his roommate, James Hill Cook. From his cockpit, Cook motioned Smiley to come over. Running across the flight deck, Smiley climbed onto the wing and leaned into the cockpit.

"I'm a little dry," Cook shouted over the roar of his engine. "You got any gum?"

Smiley found a pack in his shirt pocket and handed him two sticks. Cook unwrapped them and put the gum in his mouth.

"Thanks," he said.

Smiley jumped off the wing and ran back to the edge of the flight deck. The first Avenger was already taking off. Cook was next. When he revved his engines to the straining pitch, the control officer waved him forward, and the plane shot down the deck.

Smiley had watched hundreds of takeoffs. This one seemed no different from the others until he felt the ship canting over to port, and saw Cook's plane begin to drift left. Near the end of the runway, his left wing was extended out over the side of the ship. As he attempted to gain altitude, the plane lost headway, and went over the port side.

Smiley watched it hit the water, left wing first, and quickly go under. A few seconds later, he saw one member of the crew bob back to the surface. A destroyer following behind the *Saratoga* picked up the lone survivor.

It wasn't James Hill Cook. He had gone down with the plane, along with his tail gunner, C. E. Thompson. The next morning,

Smiley boxed up James Hill's personal property, including the desk photograph of Cook's wife, Marjorie. He remembered Cook's own words after Smiley's gunner Nick Chorak had died back at Ford Island.

"You have to forget about it, Smiley. It's best not to look back until this is all over."

It didn't make Cook's death at the age of twenty-four any easier to accept. Sitting in their stateroom, Smiley found the words to write a letter to James Hill's mother. He hoped it would give her some comfort to know that his last days aboard the *Saratoga* had been good ones.

SUNDAY, 23 AUGUST 1942
USS *SARATOGA*
TORPEDO SQUADRON EIGHT
1340

As the *Saratoga* headed northwest to engage the Japanese fleet, PBY search planes sighted an enemy task force of eight warships. It included heavy cruisers, destroyers, and transports, but no carrier.

Commander Felt assembled the pilots of the dive-bomber and torpedo squadrons in the *Saratoga*'s wardroom. "The Japanese are about to make a major effort to recapture Guadalcanal," he said. "The weather is very bad, but we will try to find them."

Felt told them he would be leading the formation of thirty-one Dauntlesses. Swede would lead the accompanying flight of six Avengers carrying torpedoes. Clark Lee, the AP correspondent who had flown with Bruce Harwood on Dog Day, received permission to fly with Swede.

While PBY search planes continued hunting for the Japanese carrier forces, the pilots waited in the wardroom. An hour passed. Frustration mounted as an hour and then a second one slipped past. The jarring sound of the telephone on the bulkhead wall finally broke the tension. Commander Felt listened to the message and replaced the phone.

"No carriers yet," he said. "We'll attack the cruisers."

At 1440, the *Saratoga* turned into the wind to launch the attack. Felt's thirty-one dive-bombers and the six torpedo planes formed up above the carrier and headed northwest. As they climbed through the dark overcast sky, Clark Lee noted that Frenchy Fayle was flying on Swede's port wing. Bert Earnest was on his right.

The planes broke through the first layer of overcast at about one thousand feet. Within minutes, they flew into a violent storm front with ferocious winds and torrential rain. Clark Lee lost sight of Fayle and Earnest in the murky gloom. He became terrified that Swede might collide with one of the other planes.

The turbulence continued to grow as the formation continued on the course that hopefully led to the enemy cruiser force. Lee had finally managed to calm himself again when they began encountering a sickening combination of updrafts and downdrafts.

One moment they would be flying along on a level course. The next moment the Avenger would be plunging straight down in free-fall. For the first time, Lee felt the physical sensation of having his heart in his throat. He clutched the steel frame of his cushioned seat and held on.

OVER THE PACIFIC
TORPEDO SQUADRON EIGHT
NEWTON DELCHAMPS
1500

As Commander Felt's thirty-seven-plane formation continued northward, Bill Dye and Bob Evarts were fighting southeast through the same violent sky, attempting to find the *Saratoga* after a two-plane flight from Guadalcanal.

Aviation Ordnanceman Third Class Newton "Del" Delchamps had never experienced anything like it before. Delchamps, a ruddy six-footer from Theodore, Alabama, was the tail gunner in Bill Dye's crew. A month earlier, he had celebrated his eighteenth birthday aboard the *Saratoga*. Some of the men thought he was a bit hot-tempered, but had plenty of guts. It was probably because he had pretty much raised himself after being orphaned before the age of ten.

Del had already seen enough combat to last him for a while. He had been aboard the *Yorktown* at Midway, and was one of the last men off the ship. An exploding bomb had trapped him in a badly mangled steel catwalk. He was still entwined in it when the announcement came over the loudspeakers: "All hands abandon ship." He had finally freed himself and slid down a line to the sea.

As a boy, Del had lived through the killer hurricanes that regularly battered southern Alabama. The storm they were now flying through was worse. From the tail, he couldn't see where they were going. He could only see where they had just been, and that was all over the goddamn sky.

Earlier that day, they had ferried Commander Walter Schindler, Admiral Fletcher's staff gunnery officer, from the *Saratoga* to Guadalcanal. Del had wondered why they were going over until he got inside the tail compartment and found the cargo of freshly baked bread, rolls, pastries, and a decorated layer cake. It struck him there was a big difference between the chow they served up in Admiral Fletcher's flag mess, and the crap the enlisted men had been eating for weeks.

A staff officer was waiting for them at Henderson Field. He had two Marines remove the precious cargo and stow it in his jeep. No one asked Del if he had sampled the baked goods.

It was afternoon when Bill Dye found Del at the mess tent and told him to prepare for takeoff. Commander Schindler had returned and they were heading back to the *Saratoga*. When Del climbed into the tail again, it no longer smelled like a bakery.

The compartment was crammed with Japanese military gear: Nambu pistols, rifles, helmets, swords, flags, and uniform jackets with brownish stains. Unlike the bakery, it didn't smell very good, although once they were headed down the runway, the fresh air streaming through the turret carried the odor away.

They ran into the storm front soon after leaving Guadalcanal. The vicious combination of updrafts and downdrafts made him sick to his stomach. One moment it was like he was on a rocket ship heading to the stars, and the next it was like the bottom had dropped out of the world.

The storm wouldn't have been quite so bad except for the Japanese souvenirs. Each time the plane hit a downdraft, the compartment would fill up with flying military gear. The helmets were the worst. He found himself punching at them as they flew up at him from the deck. It wasn't enough that he had to fight the Japanese while they were still alive. Now their junk was beating him to death.

Finally, he heard Bill Dye's voice on the intercom. They had been in the air for a long time, but Del had no idea where they were. Dye told Commander Schindler that they had marginal fuel to make it to the *Saratoga*, and adequate fuel to make it back to Guadalcanal. He was asking Schindler to make the decision.

"You're the pilot, Bill," said Commander Schindler. "You make the call."

Dye radioed Bob Evarts to say that they were returning to Guadalcanal.

OVER THE PACIFIC
TORPEDO SQUADRON EIGHT
SWEDE LARSEN
1630

Clark Lee was ready to give up flying altogether if they ever made it back to the *Saratoga*. He decided there were plenty of other good stories to cover in the war without ever getting in another combat plane.

So far, Swede had managed to fly through the blinding rain and fierce winds without colliding with any of the others. Personally, Lee thought it was a miracle. More incredibly, Commander Felt was still searching for the Japanese cruisers.

The weather had finally moderated a little when they arrived at the place where Felt expected the Japanese cruisers to be found. Descending through the clouds, the thirty-seven planes slowly circled in formation over the area. The ocean was empty.

Commander Felt radioed the group that he would lead them farther north, but ten minutes later they encountered a new storm front. Felt broke off the search and radioed that they would head for Guadalcanal instead of returning to the *Saratoga*. The rain and winds followed them as they flew south.

About an hour later, Lee, sitting in the seat behind Swede, heard his voice on the radio. Swede had spotted a landmass off to starboard and thought it might be Savo Island. The northern coast of Guadalcanal slowly emerged ahead in the rainy darkness. As they came in over Lunga Point, Lee could see that the Marines had lit bright flares along both sides of the runway. It was like a wonderful beacon welcoming them home.

The Japanese gave them a different welcome. The first Dauntless was coming in on its approach to the field when blue tracer bullets from enemy machine guns in the jungle near the field began arcing toward the plane.

Luckily, all thirty-seven planes made it down safely. A jeep came out to pick up Swede and he invited Lee to accompany him to the Pagoda, the one-story building constructed by the Japanese that had been converted to the Marine air group's headquarters.

There, Lee ran into Commander Schindler, whom he knew from his time aboard the *Saratoga*. Schindler had his own hairy story to tell about his aborted flight back to the carrier. He invited Lee to join him at General Vandegrift's command post for drinks.

Across the airfield, Del Delchamps was sitting on an empty gasoline drum under the wing of Bill Dye's Avenger and wishing he had a drink, too. As a curtain of warm rain fell in sheets off the lower edge of the wing, he wondered where he was going to sleep that night. It definitely wasn't going to be in the tail compartment with the smelly Japanese souvenirs.

Suddenly, he heard the distant boom of thunder. A few moments later, he saw a cannon shell explode in the trees north of the airfield and realized they were under attack. He ran for one of the slit trenches.

A Marine lying alongside him in the mud told Del that a Japanese submarine surfaced almost every night in Sealark Channel and lobbed shells into their positions. None of them came close, but Del didn't get much rest.

When Clark Lee and Swede Larsen came back from Vandegrift's headquarters after sampling some captured Asahi beer, Lee curled up in Swede's tail compartment, falling soundly asleep as rain hammered the metal fuselage above him. Swede slept in the cockpit.

JAPANESE BATTLESHIP *YAMATO*
ADMIRAL ISOROKU YAMAMOTO
2200

As his flagship moved through rain squalls north of the Solomons, Admiral Yamamoto issued final orders for the counterstrike that would wrest control of Guadalcanal's airfield from the Americans.

In the weeks since the landings, he had tried to convey the strategic importance of retaking the airfield to the high command of the Japanese Imperial Army, but with only marginal success. They did not fully share his views, and had committed only ten thousand troops in total to the effort. Convoys carrying the first reinforcements were on their way to Guadalcanal.

Yamamoto's goals were more ambitious than landing reinforcements. As he had planned at Midway, he wanted to destroy the American carriers. To hold Guadalcanal, he was sure the Americans would have to expose them, and he was ready.

Now converging on the Eastern Solomons were three Japanese naval task forces. They comprised the bulk of the remaining striking power of the Imperial Navy, and consisted of three aircraft carriers, a seaplane carrier, two battleships, fourteen cruisers, and twenty-four destroyers.

At dawn on August 24, Japanese scout planes would be launched to the east and south to find the American carriers. If their search was unsuccessful, the focus of Yamamoto's carrier attacks would be the airfield at Guadalcanal. Denying the Americans the use of the field was almost as valuable as taking it back. The carrier attacks would be supported by Japanese bombers and fighters flying from Rabaul.

Yamamoto's two big carriers, *Shokaku* and *Zuikaku,* would launch their full complements of ninety dive-bombers and torpedo planes, supported by thirty-six fighters. A third carrier, the *Ryujo,* would be sent on ahead of the other two, escorted by the cruiser *Tone* and two destroyers. If its thirty-three attack planes failed to locate the American carriers, they, too, were to bomb the airfield at Guadalcanal.

The *Ryujo* was a lucky ship. In English, the word meant "Galloping Dragon."

MONDAY, 24 AUGUST 1942
GUADALCANAL
NEWTON DELCHAMPS
0700

Overnight, the ferocious storm fronts had finally moved off, ushering in a torrid morning on Guadalcanal. Shortly after his breakfast of oatmeal and black coffee, Del Delchamps was told that the Marine air group on Guadalcanal was short of bombs, and that he was to remove the four five-hundred-pounders from Bill Dye's plane.

As an ordnanceman, Del had been taught the proper procedures to both arm bombs and safely defuse them. First, he needed a bomb hoist to place under the open bomb bay, so that the bombs could be safely unloaded when he finished defusing them.

When he asked a Marine sergeant where he could find a bomb hoist to remove the four bombs, the sergeant just laughed. They only had one, he said. A Marine slept with the goddamn thing, and it was a good stretch away on the other side of the field.

Forget the bomb hoist, he told him. Del should just disconnect the safety wires from the bomb shackles, get up in the cockpit, and pull the salvo lever. The bombs would drop five feet to the ground and then be carted off by the Marines.

It didn't sound good to Delchamps. He had been taught to do it the Navy way, and there had been plenty of warnings back at ordnance school of what could happen if a bomb accidentally fell out of an airplane, even if the plane was on the ground, and even if the bomb had been defused. And this was four bombs, all dropped together.

He looked around for Bill Dye to ask him what to do, but the pilot was nowhere in sight. Meanwhile, the Marine sergeant was yelling at him to get to work removing the bombs so the planes could be gassed for takeoff.

Getting under the open bomb bay, Del quickly removed the wire leads to each igniter. Then he climbed up on the wing and got into the cockpit. As he looked down at the salvo release lever, a horrible thought went through his mind of the bombs hitting the ground, exploding, and disintegrating him. Freak accidents happened all of the time.

After calling out for everyone to get clear, he was about to pull the salvo release lever when he heard a shout from just behind the wing. "What the hell are you doing up there?" screamed Swede Larsen. "Get out of that cockpit and come down here!"

The big eighteen-year-old climbed out and dropped down from the wing. He started to explain that there was no bomb hoist and that the Marine sergeant had told him to release the bombs onto the ground. Swede didn't let him finish.

"You're an idiot, Delchamps," he shouted. "Do you want to blow up all these planes?"

Del looked around for the Marine sergeant but he had disappeared. The crews from the nearby planes were grinning at him like hyenas as Swede continued to dress him down as a loser and a disgrace to the Navy.

"Go find the bomb hoist and do the job properly," Swede shouted.

In the middle of the tirade, Del had started feeling really hot. There was no need for Lieutenant Larsen to put him down in front of everybody, not when he hadn't even given him a chance to explain. It was suddenly all he could do not to swing at the son of a bitch. But Swede was already walking away.

After using the bomb hoist, Del found out that the Dauntless crews had been ordered to unload their bombs, too. With only one hoist available, most of them had toggled their bombs into the mud, just as the Marine sergeant had told him to do.

At midmorning, an American search plane sighted a new Japanese task force far to the north. It included a single carrier. Based on the search pilot's position, the enemy carrier was about three hundred miles north of the *Saratoga,* and still out of striking range. Thirty minutes later, the *Saratoga*'s air staff received a report that another PBY had spotted a second task force that included heavy cruisers and destroyers.

At 1100, Commander Felt arrived from Guadalcanal with the group's dive-bombers. Swede landed behind him with seven Avengers, including Bill Dye's plane, which was carrying Commander Schindler. Bob Evarts's Avenger had to be left at Henderson Field after it had a mechanical malfunction.

After arriving back aboard with Swede, Smiley Morgan had gone below to shower and change into fresh khakis. As soon as he got to the wardroom, he knew that something big was up. The word was that enemy carriers were coming at them from the north, bringing along half the Japanese navy.

Clark Lee sensed the excitement, too. "It was like the last few seconds before the gong rings to start a heavyweight championship fight," he wrote in his journal. "This was the day, and no mistake."

Aaron Katz had been assigned to fly in Gene Hanson's section, and Gene pulled him aside over coffee to let him know that he was fine with the decision. He thought Katz was a good guy, but that Swede's constant baiting and criticism might have taken something out of him. Swede's favorite expression for Katz was "Jew boy," and he said after Katz's arrival that he wouldn't fly with him unless the whole squadron was going out together.

Hanson felt bad for Katz, but there was little any of them could do except show their personal support, particularly in front of Swede.

Hanson had found Aaron to be modest and unassuming, the exact opposite of the way Swede claimed that all Jews were. Gene told him he was glad to have him flying with him. Aaron thanked him for his confidence.

Above them on the flag bridge, Admiral Fletcher continued to hold back his dive-bombers and torpedo planes in readiness for a solid sighting of the big enemy carriers. At 1320, the *Saratoga's* radar sets picked up a large formation of enemy planes headed for Guadalcanal. Fletcher's staff reasoned that they had to have been launched from a Japanese carrier.

Fletcher decided he could wait no longer. He ordered half the air group to locate and attack the carrier. The remaining dive-bombers and torpedo planes were to stay aboard as a reserve force in the event another carrier group was sighted later. When flight quarters sounded, the pilots assigned to the flight tore out of the wardroom to man their planes.

Swede was convinced that the mission was another wild-goose chase, just like the one the day before. The sighting report of the enemy carrier was several hours old and hadn't even been confirmed. Believing the real action would come when the main Japanese carrier force was sighted, he told Bruce Harwood to take the first flight.

Going with Harwood were Gene Hanson, Aaron Katz, Bert Earnest, Andy Divine, Tex Grady, Bill Dye, and Smiley Morgan. Remaining behind with Swede were John Taurman, Red Doggett, Frenchy Fayle, Jack Barnum, and Bob Ries.

**USS SARATOGA**
**1420**

Waiting to take off, Bert Earnest felt the same nervous tension he had experienced before every combat mission he had flown. He was almost ready to greet the thing as an old friend.

Something struck him as comical when the crews came out to board their aircraft. Maybe it was because the air group had just been on Guadalcanal and had seen Marines walking around with

Bowie knives strapped to their belts, but a lot of the pilots and crewmen were suddenly armed to the teeth.

Bert wondered what good a Bowie knife or a Colt forty-five would be if he went into the sea. Just more weight dragging him down. After his Midway and Guadalcanal missions, all he usually wore were khakis, his leather helmet, comfortable shoes, and a Mae West life vest. When he could remember, he carried a canteen of water.

The launch went off without a hitch. When the thirty-six-plane group had formed up, Commander Felt led them north, following the compass bearing given to him by the *Saratoga*'s air plotting staff to take them to the enemy carrier. The afternoon was brilliantly sunny and clear. That would help them spot the task force if they got close.

Thirty minutes into the flight, the engine in Bill Dye's plane began to stutter. Quickly losing oil pressure, he fell behind the others. The problem only got worse, and he radioed Bruce Harwood for permission to turn back. Harwood gave his approval, urging Dye to jettison his torpedo if he had problems maintaining altitude.

As they continued north, Smiley Morgan felt a sense of pure exhilaration. Part of it was the guttural roar of thirty-six combat planes flying in formation above the glittering sea. But there was something else, too. For the first time in his life he felt he was part of something really important.

Commander Felt radioed the group that they were approaching the area where he expected to find the carrier and told them all to keep a sharp lookout. They continued on the same course for another twenty minutes but the sea below them remained empty.

Felt changed course and led them west.

## USS SARATOGA
## 1602

The radar screens aboard the *Saratoga* suddenly registered a large formation of aircraft coming straight toward them from the north at a distance of about one hundred miles. They could only be Japanese.

The mutual game of hide-and-seek was over, and the Japanese had won.

The planes were from the Japanese carriers *Shokaku* and *Zuikaku*, and they had found the Americans due to the heroic sacrifice of a single Japanese scout plane pilot. Earlier in the afternoon, the pilot had managed to penetrate to within thirty-five miles of the American carrier force.

Although attacked by six Wildcats, the Japanese pilot kept going. With his aircraft on fire and going down, he radioed that he had spotted a large enemy force and was being pursued by enemy fighters.

When the message was delivered to Admiral Nagumo, who commanded the Japanese striking force, he correctly surmised that the pursuing American fighters had to be part of a combat air patrol protecting an enemy carrier. Based on the compass heading that the reconnaissance plane had been following, as well as its elapsed flight time, Nagumo's staff made a guess at the approximate location of the American carrier.

Nagumo was not going to wait and be surprised as he had been at Midway. This time, he would hit the Americans first. Gambling that all of the American carriers were in the same area, he ordered an attack by every plane he had.

Nagumo's gamble had been sound, although on the previous night Admiral Fletcher had released the carrier *Wasp* to head south for refueling. Now *Enterprise* and *Saratoga* could only send up their Wildcats in a defense screen and hope for the best.

OVER THE PACIFIC
TORPEDO SQUADRON EIGHT
SMILEY MORGAN
1605

Smiley had looked down at the dazzling blue sea and it was empty. A few moments later, he looked down and saw the wakes of ships in the distance. As they drew closer, he could see it was a Japanese task force, its still tiny ships heading southwest at flank speed. In the center of the formation was an enemy carrier.

It was the *Ryujo,* the Galloping Dragon.

It didn't have a ten-story-high island like American carriers, but it was just as lethal, with eight five-inch cannons and dozens of heavy machine guns emplaced around the perimeter of its deck. The carrier was a couple of football fields long, and Smiley could see a great red circle painted on its flight deck.

Steaming in formation with the carrier were a cruiser and two destroyers. The destroyers were racing through the sea on the carrier's flanks to keep pace with it while providing fire support from its antiaircraft batteries.

This was what they had come for.

Black bursts of antiaircraft shells began appearing above and below them as the *Ryujo*'s gunners attempted to bracket the group's formation. Commander Felt gave instructions to divide the group into columns. He ordered seven of his dive-bombers to go after the big cruiser escorting the carrier, and told Harwood to assign two Avengers to it, as well.

Smiley Morgan was section leader and Harwood ordered him to launch the torpedo attack on the cruiser, taking Andy Divine along as his wingman. Smiley was disappointed that he wouldn't have a chance at the carrier, but acknowledged the order.

The heavy cruiser he was about to attack was the storied *Tone,* which had participated in the Pearl Harbor attack. At Midway, it was *Tone*'s scout planes that had found Admiral Spruance's carrier force, and had then reported the position of Waldron's squadron as it approached the Japanese fleet on the morning of June 4.

While Felt was making his dispositions, a flight of Zeroes took off from the *Ryujo*'s flight deck, after which the ship accelerated again to flank speed and heeled over in a tight turn, its wake carving a broad white circle on the dark blue sea. Gun flashes erupted along its entire length as it sent up a solid screen of antiaircraft fire.

Bruce Harwood radioed the four remaining Avenger pilots that they would attack low in a "hammer and anvil" maneuver, launching torpedoes at the carrier from both the port and starboard sides at the same time. Whichever way the carrier turned, they would hopefully hit it with a spread of at least two torpedoes. Harwood would lead the starboard attack on the *Ryujo* with Earnest and Grady. He ordered Gene Hanson to lead the port attack with Aaron Katz on his wing.

Smiley peeled off from the rest of the formation and headed for the cruiser. As he circled above it, his first impression was that it was even faster than the carrier and braced one hell of a lot of antiaircraft guns.

Commander Felt ordered his dive-bombers to begin their runs on *Ryujo*. One by one, they nosed over from three miles above the carrier, screaming down in near vertical dives. The first five bombs missed badly, splashing far off to port and starboard. The *Ryujo* might have been nine years old, but her captain was skillfully putting her through a combination of tight skidding turns as the Dauntlesses made their runs.

The next five dive-bomber pilots found it equally impossible to get a hit. One of them mistakenly dropped his landing wheels and dove at slower speed. He was the only one who came close to hitting the carrier, sending a great plume of water up alongside it.

Eleven more dive-bombers dropped their payloads as the *Ryujo*'s captain continued to demonstrate his remarkable dexterity in ship handling. None of the bombs struck home.

Twenty-one misses in a row. It seemed the carrier had a charmed life. Still circling above the *Ryujo*, Commander Felt radioed the seven Dauntlesses and two Avengers that were preparing to go after *Tone* to come back and attack *Ryujo*.

Lieutenant Syd Bottomley, the flight leader of the seven dive-bombers, acknowledged Felt's instructions and broke off to return to the carrier. Smiley never heard the recall order. He assumed that he was still part of the nine-plane formation as he maneuvered into position to launch his torpedo attack.

He and Divine were alone.

Felt didn't wait for the arrival of his last seven Dauntlesses. He pushed over in his own run on the carrier, having taken note of its speed and turning power, and focusing his aim on the red rising sun painted on the flight deck. Going down, he maintained a good angle, almost 75 degrees, and was careful not to overshoot before releasing his bomb at two thousand feet.

The explosion briefly engulfed the ship in a tall plume of spray. It might have been a hit, but it hadn't caused any immediate damage. *Ryujo* continued its skidding turns at flank speed.

It remained for the last seven Dauntlesses and Bruce Harwood's five Avengers to try to bring the charmed carrier to bay. In his dive, Syd Bottomley waited to release his bomb until he was less than fifteen hundred feet above the flight deck. He was a veteran of the Midway battle, and had made a direct hit on Admiral Nagumo's flagship, the *Akagi*.

His bomb hit the carrier amidships, setting off a column of orange fire. Following him down, the next six Dauntlesses dropped their bombs toward the soaring pyre of flames and smoke. From Gene Hanson's vantage point, it looked like they had scored at least one more hit as the carrier continued wildly circling.

It was the Avengers' turn.

Hanson headed down to set up the port side attack. Aaron Katz followed on his left wing. The Zeroes were waiting for them at two thousand feet. The first one came directly at Hanson with its machine guns blazing.

If he turned away, Hanson was sure it would make him an easy victim. Instead, he pulled up the nose of his Avenger and aimed it at the oncoming Zero, firing his thirty-caliber nose gun as the two planes raced toward one another. For a few terrifying moments, he was sure they were going to collide. Then the Zero veered off to the right and passed under the Avenger's tail. He could hear his gunners Shorty Aube and Frank Balsely firing away at him as the next Zero appeared in front of him.

He heard Aaron Katz's excited voice on the radio. The Zeroes were aiming high, Aaron told him. He had seen the tracers. As the next fighter cut loose with his machine guns, Hanson once more aimed his plane directly at him, and the Zero sheered off.

When Hanson's Avenger began drawing antiaircraft fire from the *Ryujo*, the Zeroes disappeared. He led Katz down to two hundred feet and headed toward the carrier's port bow.

The carrier was turning away from him, which made launching

from a good firing angle even more difficult. He and Katz had to swing farther left before turning to head in for the attack. Closing, Hanson could see the Japanese firefighting teams trying to extinguish the fires from the bomb hits.

Opening his bomb bay doors, he pressed the switch to release his torpedo. He felt it drop, but didn't wait around to see the results. After shutting the bomb bay doors, he made a quick turn to port, temporarily exposing the underbelly and wings of the plane to the carrier's gunners. He felt the plane shudder as a hit from one of the *Ryujo*'s shells tore loose the vertical fin in the tail, and took a big chunk out of the rudder.

Aaron Katz was right behind him. He had attacked at an altitude of less than fifty feet in the hope that the *Ryujo*'s guns couldn't be depressed that low. The theory didn't seem to be holding water. The tracers followed him wherever he went. Turning away from the ship, he glanced back to see if his torpedo was running true. It was. He didn't see how it was possible for the thing to miss.

Bert Earnest had come under attack from a Zero as Harwood brought them into position to make their run from the starboard side of the *Ryujo*. As he remembered from Midway, the fighters were amazingly fast, darting in and out of range in a few heartbeats. In an incredibly difficult maneuver, the pilot of one Zero rolled on his back and pulled through to get on Bert's tail.

*Here we go again* was the only thought that ran through Bert's mind as he dove to their attacking altitude of two hundred feet. The Zero pulled away when the antiaircraft gunners on the *Ryujo* opened fire on him.

Black smoke now surrounded the wounded carrier. It was billowing in their direction, and Harwood was forced to abort two attacks because it completely obscured the ship. On the third try, he was presented with a perfect broadside opportunity when the ship turned toward him.

The smoke hadn't suppressed the *Ryujo*'s ability to deliver an intense barrage of antiaircraft fire. The destroyer steaming beside her on the starboard side was pouring it at them, too.

Harwood was the first to launch his torpedo. Grady's went next. Heading in last, Bert tried to jink and weave away from Japanese tracers as they danced toward him. He couldn't see an enemy ship in the port direction after launching his torpedo. Dropping to fifty feet, he swerved to port.

Circling far above them, one of the dive-bomber pilots observed a single torpedo drive into the starboard side of the ship. For a moment, the force of the explosion seemed to lift the bow out of the water, after which the ship quickly lost speed and came to a stop.

The attack on the *Ryujo* was over.

While it was still under way, Smiley Morgan had proceeded to attack the *Tone*, still having no idea that the seven dive-bombers had left and that he and Andy Divine would be going in unsupported.

He had assumed the dive-bombers were preparing to make their runs from a higher altitude, so he decided to go in first, hoping to draw some of the carrier's fire away from the Dauntlesses.

The Zeroes came after him and Andy Divine as soon as they descended below five thousand feet, spraying them with disciplined torrents of machine gun fire. Divine's plane was hit several times as Smiley moved into position for his run.

One Zero pilot stayed on Smiley, giving him repeated bursts of machine gun fire even after the cruiser let loose a salvo from its antiaircraft guns. The Zero finally swerved away when all the starboard batteries on the ship seemed to open up at once.

To Smiley, it looked like a solid wall of blazing fire. How was he going to get through it? He had been taught by Commander Waldron to avoid attacking in a predictable head-on rush that would allow them to draw a bead on him. He had been taught to essentially feint like a halfback, quickly jinking the Avenger back and forth, while corkscrewing it in a spiral motion.

The gunfire tracked him left and right as he flew toward it at two hundred miles an hour. In the intensity of the moment, time itself seemed to come to a standstill. When a shell exploded close enough to make the plane leap, he actually closed his eyes.

When he opened them again, he was still heading for the massive ship. Cutting the throttle to launch speed, he held the control stick in his right hand, and reached for the torpedo release switch with the left.

The cruiser filled his line of vision when he released the torpedo

264 · A Dawn Like Thunder

and veered off to the right. It had been a perfect run, and he was sure he had made a good hit if the damn Mark 13 torpedo exploded on contact as it was supposed to do. The antiaircraft fire continued to chase him as he made his escape.

When he was clear of the guns, Smiley looked around for Andy Divine, but didn't see him. He looked for the Dauntlesses, too, but the sky was empty. A few miles away, the carrier was dead in the water. Behind him, the *Tone* had definitely slowed down.

Then he heard Commander Felt's voice on the radio, calling the group to rendezvous southeast of the enemy task force. By the time he arrived, most of the others were already there. Smiley had shoved the throttle all the way open, and came up so fast that he saw one of the fifty-caliber machine guns swing around to aim at him. He quickly slowed down.

Amazingly, they were all there, even Andy Divine. As they began heading back to the *Saratoga*, Gene Hanson glanced back at the Japanese task force. A pyre of smoke rose almost twenty thousand feet in the sky above the stricken carrier.

## USS ENTERPRISE
## 1638

The first wave of thirty-seven Japanese attack planes from *Shokaku* and *Zuikaku* found the *Enterprise* first. She was hurtling southeast through the deep Pacific swells at almost thirty knots to present the smallest possible target to her attackers. Every gun battery on the ship was brought to bear in the direction of the approaching planes.

Ten minutes prior to the enemy's arrival, the *Enterprise* had managed to launch its full fighter defense screen, followed by a counterstrike group of nineteen Dauntlesses and Avengers, which had been ordered to go after the Japanese heavy carriers.

The *Saratoga*, which was ten miles to the south of the *Enterprise* and also fleeing southeast, had sent up its own fighter screen to meet the Japanese attack. In addition, five of Swede's Avengers and two

Dauntlesses were ordered to join the counterstrike group from *Enterprise* that was going after the enemy carriers.

Swede had been reviewing the latest sighting reports when the launch order came down. He suddenly remembered that he had left his plotting board belowdecks. It would be getting dark soon, and he didn't want to be caught in the middle of the Pacific without the chart board to find his way home. He ran to get his navigational gear.

The *Saratoga's* takeoff control officers were under strict orders to clear the flight deck before the Japanese arrived, with or without Swede Larsen. They waved the Avengers forward for an immediate launch.

John Taurman took off in the plane carrying Swede's flight crew. Frenchy Fayle went off with a different crew, too. Jack Barnum and Bob Ries didn't have their flight or navigational gear.

Running along the carrier's dimly lit passageways, Swede fought through a crush of sailors rushing to their battle stations. By the time he made it to the flight deck, the *Saratoga's* defense screen of Wildcats was already dueling with the first wave of Japanese attackers.

Swede was shocked to see that four of his five Avengers were already gone. Red Doggett's plane was the only one left. Red was at the starting line, and the takeoff control officer was winding up his black-and-white checkered flag to send him off.

Sprinting across the deck with his plotting board, he leaped up onto Doggett's wing. Red couldn't hear him over the noise of the thundering engine, so Swede just thumbed him out of the cockpit. The enlisted pilot unstrapped himself and got out.

Red wasn't happy about it. Swede would deal with that later. He revved the engine and took off into the crowded sky. The other Avengers, along with the two Dauntlesses, were waiting for him. They headed north to join the *Enterprise* counterstrike group.

USS SARATOGA
1640

Associated Press correspondent Clark Lee felt an unwelcome tremor of fear as the growing roar of airplane engines signaled the arrival of the Japanese bombers. He tried to reassure himself that this was why he had come out to the Pacific in the first place. To witness a great battle.

Standing with the lookouts and spotters, Lee had put on a Mae West life jacket in case he would be swimming shortly. The bombing attack unfolded above him in a kaleidoscope of brilliant color. He felt the deck shudder beneath his feet as the boom of the carrier's antiaircraft batteries reverberated in his ears, combined with the thundering salvos from the escort ships.

A few moments later, he saw one of the Japanese bombers falling through the sky trailing a long comet tail of reddish-black smoke. Another blossom of flame erupted far above him, followed by a second enemy plane plummeting down to the sea.

The burning sky turned orange, black, purple, and red, as the ships' batteries hurled up thousands of exploding projectiles. In some places, tiny shards of shrapnel came down like falling rain. Mingled with the astonishing array of colors came the screaming whine of the enemy bombers as they began their dives on the carriers.

Another enemy plane disintegrated in a ball of fire, but there were too many to shoot down. A few minutes later, one of them scored a direct hit on the flight deck of the *Enterprise*, sending an orange ball of fire high into the air. The explosion was followed by a second hit, and the carrier began trailing a billowing cloud of smoke.

Men were being killed and wounded in every direction Lee looked. As he watched, the already stricken *Enterprise* took a third direct hit through its already shattered flight deck.

"Dive-bombers overhead . . . coming out of the sun," the lookout standing alongside Lee on the *Saratoga* called out.

OVER THE PACIFIC
TORPEDO SQUADRON EIGHT
SWEDE LARSEN
1725

Unable to locate the nineteen-plane *Enterprise* group in the confused sky, Swede led his seven-plane formation north toward the previously reported position of the enemy carrier.

On the way, he radioed the other Avenger pilots to find out who was flying with him. The crews might have gotten mixed up, but it didn't matter. Things always went wrong in combat situations. He had spent months training them to do their jobs, regardless of the conditions.

Of more concern was the fact that he was the only pilot who had brought his plotting board to compute their course and direction. The C6B was primitive but effective, a little wheel inside a piece of plastic that a pilot could use to log in each course change as he went along. Swede told them to stick tight with him through the mission. After nightfall, they would be flying virtually blind, and the plotting board might be critical to their survival.

They had been flying north for more than an hour and the sun had dropped to the edge of the horizon when Swede looked down at the darkening sea and saw a warship coming toward them.

It was Japanese. More warships emerged beyond the first one. They were destroyers, eight of them in a forward screen. Behind them came a phalanx of cruisers, three light ones, then four heavy cruisers all abeam, followed by another three light cruisers.

One of the two Dauntless pilots flying above the Avengers radioed that he had sighted a battleship farther back in the column, and they were going after it. Not seeing a carrier in the task force, Swede ordered an attack on the four heavy cruisers.

Off to the northwest he spotted a large cloud formation. It was vivid purple in the glow of the rapidly setting sun. Swede thought it might give the Avengers good cover for a low-level attack. As he led Taurman, Barnum, Ries, and Fayle toward the cloud formation, a flight of Zeroes raced to intercept them.

The purple cloud swallowed the Avengers long enough to escape the Zeroes, and Swede led them back out of the mist close to the surface of the sea. To reach the heavy cruisers, the Avengers had to first penetrate the screen of destroyers and light cruisers, all of which began hurling salvos at them as they came in.

To Bob Ries, it looked like the Christmas lights in a city building all being turned on at once. His plane was buffeted back and forth and up and down as the massed gunfire reached out for him. His only advantage was that the sky was already dark between the ships, making it harder for the gunners to find his plane against the sea.

Each pilot was on his own, selecting his target and lining up the run. As the Avengers closed in, the heavy cruisers broke formation and scattered. After dropping their torpedoes, that's exactly what the Avengers did, too, scattering into the dusky gloom. If there were any hits, no one saw them explode.

### JAPANESE CARRIER *RYUJO*
### 1800

As sunset turned to darkness, the crew of the Galloping Dragon was still fighting desperately to keep the carrier afloat. After two hours, the ship's firefighting teams had finally managed to quell the fires set off by the direct hits from Commander Felt's dive-bombers.

With the fires out, there was still a chance to save the carrier if they could restore power to the engine room. Once the carrier was moving again, the *Ryujo*'s air group could be landed on the flight deck after returning from its attack of the airfield at Guadalcanal.

The torpedo launched by Harwood, Grady, or Earnest had struck aft on the starboard side, and set off flooding in the engine room, also immobilizing the ship's steering control. In spite of every effort to shore up the shattered bulkheads and stem the flood of water with auxiliary pumps, the ship continued to list ever further onto its starboard side.

When the *Ryujo*'s air group appeared overhead, it was impossible for them to land on the tilting flight deck. By then, the planes also lacked the fuel to reach another Japanese carrier or a Japanese-held land base. The air group had already lost seven planes to Marine fighters over Henderson Field. A number of crewmen had been wounded in the air battle and needed immediate medical attention.

As the sun disappeared over the horizon, the remaining twenty-one fighters and dive-bombers slowly circled above the carrier like exhausted birds until they ran out of fuel and were forced to ditch in the sea.

Unable to stop the flooding, Captain Tadao Kato concluded that the damage from the torpedo hit was mortal, and ordered his crew to abandon ship. Several dozen sailors refused to leave and were still belowdecks fighting to save her when the Galloping Dragon rolled over and sank.

**USS SARATOGA**
**TORPEDO SQUADRON EIGHT**
**1830**

He felt completely drained, but Smiley Morgan was back home and happy to be alive. As he sat in the wardroom and enjoyed his glass of powdered lemonade, he only wished he could celebrate the occasion by spiking it with a splash of whiskey.

On this twenty-fourth day of August, he had finally been to see Bert Earnest's proverbial elephant. The truth be told, the elephant had almost stomped him, and he hoped he would never have to confront such a concentrated barrage of shell fire again. But for the first time, he felt as if he truly belonged.

At one point, Commander Felt had come over to shake his hand. He told Smiley that his decision to attack the heavy cruiser with just his wingman for support was one of the bravest things Felt had ever seen. Smiley was compelled to tell him that he hadn't known it was just him and Andy Divine when he made the decision to go in.

It didn't seem to matter to Commander Felt, who told him that Syd Bottomley said he had seen one of their torpedoes hit the *Tone*, and that he was recommending Smiley for a Navy Cross.

Smiley was even happier when Doc Lewis gave him one of the small bottles of brandy he occasionally provided to carrier pilots for medicinal purposes after they returned from a hairy mission. The precious bottles were considered a badge of honor. Right then, he preferred it to the Navy Cross.

OVER THE PACIFIC
TORPEDO SQUADRON EIGHT
SWEDE LARSEN
2000

Swede and the other Avenger pilots had scattered in different directions as they escaped the enemy task force. By the time Swede radioed the others to rendezvous with him ten miles south, night was falling.

In the Pacific, darkness fell with the swiftness of a descending curtain. As they groped through the sky, Jack Barnum and Bob Ries heard Swede's message and quickly joined him at the rendezvous. The three Avengers began circling above the sea while Swede kept trying to contact Taurman and Fayle. Neither one responded.

Swede knew that leaving them behind without navigational gear was a possible death sentence, but there was no way to know whether they had even survived the attack. With the fuel situation becoming critical, Swede radioed the others it was time to go. Using his chart board, he led them through the black night back to the carrier.

As they approached the *Saratoga*, Swede relayed his recognition signal and requested permission to land. A landing officer radioed him that the *Enterprise* had taken several hits and had been unable to land many of her aircraft. They had stacked up on the *Saratoga*, and the flight deck was now jammed. They would have to wait.

When enough space was cleared, the three Avengers landed. After Jack Barnum's crew climbed out of their plane, it was discovered that Barnum's torpedo was still inside the bomb bay.

Swede couldn't believe it. He was livid. Their job was to sink Japanese warships. That was what he had trained them to do, regardless of the danger. Barnum had obviously punked out and then endangered the carrier by coming in for a dangerous night landing with a live torpedo on board.

In his defense, Barnum said it must have been a technical malfunction. While the pilots and crews stood waiting in the darkness, Swede ordered an ordnanceman to check Barnum's release mechanism. It was found to be in good working order. In the heat of the attack on the cruisers, Barnum had apparently forgotten to open the bomb bay doors.

Swede told Barnum the screwup was going into his After Action Report.

When Swede finally got down to the wardroom, it was packed with fliers, not just the *Saratoga* air group, but many of the temporarily stranded *Enterprise* pilots as well. They were all replaying the actions of the day.

Regardless of the final tally, one thing was certain: they had beaten the Japanese back, and had shot down a lot of enemy planes in the process. The *Enterprise* had taken three hits and survived. Commander Felt said he was sure his group had sunk the *Ryujo,* even though no one had been there to see it go down.

Seeing Swede come in, Clark Lee cornered him for an interview.

"What did you hit?" he asked, notebook in hand.

Swede told him about the mission to find the carriers that had led to the discovery of the enemy cruiser force. There was no way to know for sure if they had sunk anything, but one of the Dauntless pilots flying above the Avengers reported seeing at least one torpedo hit home.

A bone-weary Smiley Morgan was still savoring the afterglow of his brandy when Bob Ries came over to tell him that John Taurman and Frenchy Fayle had gone missing with their crews. Ries had just come back from the communications center, where someone had confirmed that the two missing pilots had not landed at either Henderson Field or on the *Enterprise.*

The news took a little time to sink in. His best friend, James Hill Cook, had been killed just two days earlier. Now Taurman and Fayle were gone, too, although it was possible they had survived a night landing in the Pacific. That was their only hope.

Later that evening, Swede sat down with Bruce Harwood to discuss the day's missions. Harwood told him about the attack on the *Ryujo,* and how they had left the carrier burning in the water.

"I think we got this thing licked," said Swede. "It will be a picnic. We'll go over them like ants over a picnic."

# Resurrection Blues

It had been the biggest naval battle since Midway. The opposing fleets had each positioned themselves to deliver a decisive blow with their heavy carriers, accompanied by the massive firepower of their battleships, cruisers, and destroyers.

When it was over, the *Enterprise* and *Saratoga* were heading southeast again, away from the Japanese fleet. The Japanese heavy carriers *Shokaku* and *Zuikaku* were heading north again, away from the American fleet. Aboard their respective flagships, Admiral Frank Jack Fletcher and Admiral Chuichi Nagumo were both convinced they had earned a hard-fought victory.

For the first time since his defeat at Midway, Nagumo was exultant, convinced that he had left behind two burning American carriers, and believing he had driven the American Navy out of the Eastern Solomons.

Fletcher held the less ebullient view that his ships had won a tactical victory over the Japanese at the cost of temporarily losing the *Enterprise*.

The Japanese didn't know it, but they had come close to sinking the *Enterprise* and winning a truly decisive victory. After the first wave of Japanese planes had completed their attack, the burning and battered *Enterprise* lost its steering control. With the rudder locked in the starboard position, she kept swinging around in a wide circle.

At that moment, the second wave of thirty-six Japanese planes from the *Shokaku* and the *Zuikaku* were just beyond the carrier's sighting range. As radar operators aboard the *Enterprise* nervously tracked their flight, the bombers came steadily closer.

The Japanese planes were no more than ten minutes from finding the wounded carrier when fate, as it had at Midway, again dramatically affected the fortunes of war. At the end of the Japanese air group's southerly search pattern, its commander turned west instead of east, missing the American task force.

Late that night, Admiral Nagumo reviewed the results of the battle with his senior commanders. His first wave of attackers claimed to have left two heavy carriers burning when they withdrew. They had only exaggerated by half. Although they had badly damaged the *Enterprise,* no hits were made on the *Saratoga.* Nagumo accepted their claim anyway.

It appeared justified because a phalanx of fast Japanese cruisers had spent the previous several hours trying to catch up to the American carrier force and it had disappeared, leading Nagumo to believe that the carriers had been sunk and the surviving escort ships were in full retreat after the beating they had received at the hands of his carrier planes.

One of his senior captains strongly urged Nagumo to go after them. The captain argued that the two Japanese carriers still had plenty of aircraft to deal the Americans a finishing blow. Nagumo considered the idea but rejected it, believing another attack was unnecessary.

The cost of the battle had been high. Nineteen of the twenty-seven Japanese bombers and six of the ten Zeroes in the first wave had not come back. And the *Ryujo* was gone, sunk with all its planes.

Early on the morning of August 25, Nagumo radioed Admiral Yamamoto that his air group had left two of the American carriers burning and presumably sinking, and that the Americans were now retreating from the Solomons. With victory won, he said that he was retiring back to Truk to replenish fuel, pilots, and aircraft.

Yamamoto took Nagumo at his word about the destruction of the American carriers. Together, he and Nagumo had suffered the humiliating defeat at Midway. Now they could jointly enjoy the retribution. Believing that the American Navy had been swept clear,

Yamamoto felt confident that the Japanese army now could destroy the Marines marooned on Guadalcanal.

Far to the south of Nagumo aboard the *Saratoga*, Admiral Frank Jack Fletcher was sifting through his own After Action Reports as he pondered what to do next with the forces under his command.

His air staff had collated all the battle reports, which indicated that fifty-two of the enemy bombers and fighters in the first Japanese attack wave had been destroyed. It was an optimistic assessment considering there had been only thirty-seven planes in the first Japanese attack group.

With all the turmoil of battle, it was inevitable that claims were exaggerated. Two pilots were often shooting at the same target, and both might claim the same kill. Antiaircraft gunners firing at the same plane might claim it, too.

The Americans had lost eight Wildcats, although three pilots had been recovered.

Commander Felt was still making a spirited claim that his air group had sunk the *Ryujo,* although the assertion was disputed by Fletcher's air staff. The *Enterprise* had taken three direct hits and was still afloat. Why not the *Ryujo*? Ultimately, they agreed to report to Nimitz that the *Ryujo* had been left "burning badly."

Fletcher's staff was also briefly encouraged by a report that four B-17s had made multiple bomb hits on an unknown Japanese carrier in Nagumo's task force. In truth, the target had been a Japanese destroyer, and the bombers had failed to hit it. After Midway, Fletcher had learned to discount the Army Air Forces reports.

Some of the day's triumphs had been astonishing. While the *Enterprise* was temporarily unable to land her planes, the *Saratoga* had safely recovered nearly eighty of her aircraft, many in total darkness with pilots who had never made a night carrier landing. It was an incredible achievement.

The report on the condition of the *Enterprise*'s air group was more depressing. In July, she had left Pearl Harbor with nearly forty fighter pilots. Twenty-two were still aboard. Seventy-six sailors had been killed in the day's air attacks, and more than a hundred wounded. The *Enterprise* would need major repairs.

Fletcher knew for certain that he was still facing at least two and possibly four Japanese carriers, including the undamaged *Shokaku* and *Zuikaku*. With the *Enterprise* heading to dry dock, there was no margin for error.

It was time to withdraw, he decided.

**USS ENTERPRISE**
**FRED MEARS**
**0700**

When he awoke that morning, Fred Mears was nursing the hope that the *Enterprise* would soon be heading back to Pearl Harbor, allowing him to swap the monotonous diet of rice, rice, and more rice for the delectable meals and other creature comforts of the Moana Hotel.

On the previous afternoon, Fred had flown one of the attack missions against the Japanese carriers. After returning from an unsuccessful search, he was approaching the screen of escort ships around the *Enterprise* when the antiaircraft batteries on the battleship *North Carolina* suddenly erupted and Fred realized the carrier force was under attack.

It was the first wave of Japanese dive-bombers from the *Shokaku* and *Zuikaku*. Moments later, he and the other returning pilots heard a radio message: "All friendly planes keep clear during the attack."

As Fred looked on, two enemy bombers came out of their dives and headed in his direction. He had never seen a Japanese plane up close before. One of them peeled off to make an attack on him.

Fascinated with its colors and markings, he just watched as the plane sped toward him. When its pilot opened fire, his reverie ended. Fred raised the nose of his Avenger and fired at it with his thirty-caliber nose gun.

The popgun didn't faze the Japanese pilot, who came back after him. Behind Fred in the turret, Harry Ferrier fired disciplined bursts of the fifty-caliber machine gun at him until the Japanese pilot finally moved off.

Over the radio, the Avengers received orders to jettison their pay-loads before attempting to land. By the time Fred flew over the burning *Enterprise,* no planes were being allowed to come in. Darkness was falling fast, and he got in line to land aboard the *Saratoga.* He was still waiting his turn when the *Enterprise* signaled she was again taking planes, and he made another approach.

Coming in to land, he saw that the aft section of the flight deck had been blasted upward by one of the bomb hits. As Fred's Avenger slowed to a crawl, a plane captain with a bandage around his head came up with a flashlight to help him taxi to the elevator.

Down in the wardroom, the pilots were briefing the intelligence staff on what they had seen and done. Fred was dying for a cigarette, but smoking had been prohibited because of the danger of fire.

He and his sardonic friend Dick Jaccard, the Dauntless pilot who had made a direct hit on the carrier *Hiryu* at Midway, were already thinking ahead. If the damage to the *Enterprise* was as bad as it appeared, she would soon have to head into dry dock. That meant returning to Pearl Harbor, to good food and pretty girls.

Deciding to look for themselves, he and Jaccard went up to the flight deck in time to watch a flight of Avengers approach the carrier for a landing. The second one slammed into the steel crane at the end of the island, flipping over and coming to rest on its back in a grinding shriek of metal. The two pilots decided to forgo the rest of their inspection tour.

Early the next morning, they headed topside again. The smell of smoke and cordite was still thick in the air. Repair crews were working to replace the ruptured plates on the flight deck. Through a hole near the aft elevator, Mears could see men working in knee-deep water, clearing wreckage around the ship's damaged steering gear.

A Japanese bomb had penetrated down to an ammunition compartment. When the powder had detonated, the explosion had destroyed two five-inch batteries. Fred went into a shattered gun gallery to view the carnage firsthand. In the months since Torpedo Eight had been wiped out at Midway, he had come to view death in the abstract. Later, he put his thoughts down on paper.

*Most of the men died from the concussion, and then were
roasted. They were blackened but not burned or withered, and
they looked like iron statues of men, their limbs smooth and
whole, their heads rounded with no hair. One gun pointer was
still in his seat leaning on his sight with one arm. . . . Other iron
men were lying outstretched, face up or down. Two or three lying
face up were shielding themselves with their arms bent at the el-
bows and their hands before their faces.*

Later that morning, it was announced in the wardroom that the
*Enterprise* would be heading back to Pearl Harbor. Fred and Dick
Jaccard began making plans for how they would spend their shore
leaves.

### WEDNESDAY, 26 AUGUST 1942
### USS SARATOGA
### TORPEDO SQUADRON EIGHT

Since June 4, the squadron had not lost a pilot. Now they had lost
three in two days. Frenchy Fayle would be remembered for his ec-
centricity. He had marched to his own drummer, all right, and flew
with a nonchalant attitude to danger. He was also capable of surprising the others with his practical knowledge.

A few weeks earlier, he had come up with an ingenious solution
to an ongoing problem with the bomb release shackles. As a reward,
Swede had a brass medal struck for him in the *Saratoga*'s machine
shop. He had pinned the "Medaille de Bomb Shackle" on Frenchy's
chest in a mock-formal ceremony.

The loss of John Taurman hit the rest of the pilots particularly
hard. After James Hill Cook, John Taurman was the best-liked pilot
in the squadron. He could do a devastating impression of Swede, and
would often use it to relieve tension after someone was on the receiving end of one of the lieutenant's rants.

A month earlier, when the squadron had been preparing for

Guadalcanal and tension was high, he had typewritten and distributed the "Gedunk Intelligence Report," a two-page explanation for
why morale was low among the pilots. According to the report, they
had been overdosing on ice-cream sundaes at the Gedunk bar.

Smiley Morgan wrote a letter to Taurman's fiancée, Peggy. Back
in May, when the squadron had crossed the Pacific aboard the
*Chaumont,* he and John had spent a lot of nights together on the fantail. Smiley had double-dated with them several times, and thought
she was terrific. He knew Taurman's loss would be devastating
for her.

Gene Hanson remembered how Taurman had stood up to Swede
after they bombed the native village on Dog Day. Taurman had had
a sense of right and wrong that he truly admired.

FRIDAY, 28 AUGUST 1942
USS *SARATOGA*
TORPEDO SQUADRON EIGHT

In the days after the attacks on the *Ryujo* and the Japanese cruiser
force, Swede kept everyone busy. The squadron had lost three Avengers, and several of the other planes required major repairs. The Torpedo Eight pilots continued to fly daily air patrols.

Returning to the carrier after flying a mission to Guadalcanal,
Smiley Morgan was having lunch in the wardroom when someone
yelled out, "Taurman's alive!" A PBY rescue plane had picked him
up along with his two crewmen on the northern coast of San Cristobal Island, to the east of Guadalcanal.

When he finally made it back, Big John had quite a story to tell.

On the night they had attacked the Japanese cruisers, Taurman's
plane had been hit by antiaircraft fire right after launching its torpedo. His radio had been shot out and he had been unable to retract
his bomb bay doors, which badly slowed the aircraft down. By the
time he had gotten through the destroyer screen, the sky was almost
pitch black.

He swung south to try to join up with the others, but with his radio shot out he never heard Swede calling him. The odds of locating the *Saratoga* alone without his chart board or radio were ridiculous. Taurman could only proceed south and hope that he might spot a landmass familiar enough to lead them back to Guadalcanal.

Aside from his instrument lights, nothing relieved the blackness of the void they were flying through. About an hour later, a hint of moonlight appeared above him. It gave Taurman the chance to distinguish sky from sea.

He began passing over several islands. Taurman had no idea if they were Japanese-held, cannibal-held, or uninhabited. As his fuel ran out, those issues seemed less important. He needed to ditch. Coming up on the next landmass, he carefully set the Avenger down in a calm, unrippled bay. His crewmen made it out safely, extracting the life raft before the plane sank. Taurman and his two crewmen paddled across the bay to a sandy beach.

Island natives must have seen the plane come down because three of them arrived in a hollowed-out canoe early the next morning. The natives were carrying long, machetelike knives. Taurman was worried they might be cannibals until the first one walked up and shook his hand.

They were lucky to have landed off the island of San Cristobal. Its natives hated the Japanese, and were ready to help those who opposed them. Taurman and his crew were taken in the canoes to a nearby village where the natives killed a wild pig in their honor. They feasted on it that night with taro and sweet potatoes.

Informed that a "white headman" was living in another coastal village, they paddled over to Kira Kira, where a plantation overseer named Foster entertained them with eggnog and brandy. While they waited for a rescue plane, Taurman taught Foster how to play hearts and gin rummy. By the time Taurman was finished with his tale, Smiley was looking forward to being shot down.

Swede asked Taurman what he was going to do. As the survivor of a ditching, he was guaranteed survivor's leave, which meant he could fly back to the States for a month of rest and relaxation. Or he could stay with the squadron.

Taurman thought about it and made a joke. "Why would I want to go back to the States?" he asked. The other pilots knew he had been hoping to marry his fiancée, Peggy, as soon as he got the chance.

"I'll stay," said Taurman.

SATURDAY, 29 AUGUST 1942
GUADALCANAL
35TH BRIGADE, JAPANESE INFANTRY
GENERAL KIYOTAKE KAWAGUCHI

The next phase of the Japanese counteroffensive began under the cover of darkness. Shortly before midnight, a flotilla of Japanese destroyers began landing troop reinforcements on Guadalcanal. They were the advance elements of Major General Kiyotake Kawaguchi's 35th Infantry Brigade, another elite army unit assigned to retake Henderson Field after the annihilation of Colonel Ichiki's detachment on August 20.

The new troops were put ashore at Taivu Point, where the impetuous Colonel Ichiki had landed ten days earlier. Unlike Ichiki, General Kawaguchi was not rash. A former member of the general staff, he had commanded the 35th Brigade in the invasion of Borneo, and then saw action in the Philippines. The Japanese high command had only one criticism of him. He was considered too soft-hearted after he had objected to the revenge killings of pro-American Filipinos by Japanese execution squads.

Kawaguchi was told not to launch his attack until he had a concentration of force sufficient to take the airfield. Still not sure how many Marines were there, the high command provided six thousand troops. Kawaguchi's orders were to reconnoiter the situation on the ground. If more men were needed, he had only to ask. Once the field was in Japanese hands, they would rush in even more reinforcements from Rabaul.

"I think our faith is our strength," Kawaguchi exhorted his men as they headed for Guadalcanal. "Men who fight bravely, never doubting victory, will be the victors in the long run."

At his command post near Henderson Field, General Vandegrift was drafting an urgent request to his superiors for more planes. In the daily air battles over Guadalcanal, his pilots had shot down dozens of enemy aircraft, but there were only eight serviceable Wildcat fighters left to meet the next attack.

SUNDAY, 30 AUGUST 1942
USS *SARATOGA*
TORPEDO SQUADRON EIGHT
1200

Yeoman Jack Stark was in the squadron office when the report arrived that another missing pilot had been rescued. It was Frenchy Fayle.

His survival tale was similar to Taurman's. After the torpedo attack on the cruisers, Frenchy had circled around the Japanese fleet. His radio wasn't working and he never heard Swede calling him.

Heading south alone, the plane was attacked by a Zero. In the ensuing air battle, Frenchy's gunner, Eddy Velazquez, used his machine gun to devastating effect, setting the Zero on fire. They watched it explode in the sea.

The pilot Velazquez had killed was Yoshio Iwaki, a Japanese fighter ace with eight victories. At Midway, Iwaki had claimed credit for shooting down three of the six Avengers led by Langdon Fieberling.

Frenchy continued flying south in the darkness until his fuel was nearly gone, and then ditched in the sea off the island of Nura. Before the Avenger sank, Velazquez attempted to save his machine gun in case they needed it on the island. Between the weight of the gun and the ammunition belt, he went down like a rock. Deciding the gun wouldn't be much help to him at the bottom of the Pacific, Velazquez let it go. After the crew made it ashore, they were fortunate to be spotted by an Allied coast watcher and then picked up by the USS *Gamble*.

Swede asked Frenchy whether he planned to take his guaranteed survivor leave or remain with the squadron. Frenchy promised to write from San Diego and let the other pilots know how the girls were.

It left a bad feeling with the rest of the men.

MONDAY, 31 AUGUST 1942
USS SARATOGA
0748

At dawn, the *Saratoga* was zigzagging at thirteen knots southeast of Guadalcanal in concert with the *Hornet,* which had replaced the *Enterprise* after the damaged carrier left for repairs at Pearl Harbor.

Bert Earnest was finally enjoying a good night's sleep after inheriting Frenchy Fayle's stateroom. Bill Tunstall was preparing to wash the dirty clothes in his locker. Pete Peterkin had just finished breakfast in the officers' wardroom and was walking up to the flight deck. Smiley Morgan was already on the flight deck watching "Bullet" Lou Kirn, who commanded one of the bombing squadrons, lead his pilots through morning calisthenics. Jack Stark was sitting in the enlisted men's mess with a plate of powdered eggs and rice on his lap because the tables and benches had been stacked against the bulkhead. Bill Magee had just spent several hours repairing a plane engine and was about to head down for breakfast. Lee Marona was climbing a gangway ladder from the hangar deck up to the flight deck.

At 0748, a Type 95 Japanese submarine torpedo weighing nine hundred pounds and traveling at fifty miles an hour slammed into the *Saratoga*'s starboard side.

Jack Stark watched his plate of powdered eggs and rice suddenly levitate off his lap and sail over his head. Lee Marona looked up the gangway ladder to see a cloud of snowflakes descending on him. They were loosened paint chips from the bulkhead above him.

The AP correspondent Clark Lee was fast asleep in his stateroom when he awoke to what felt like a severe earthquake. He watched several pill bottles tumble out of the cabinet over his washbasin and smash to the deck.

Del Delchamps had been climbing a ladder next to one of the starboard five-inch gun tubs. The surge of water from the exploding torpedo engulfed him as he hugged the railing.

Waking up in Frenchy's old stateroom, Bert Earnest could only think, *Oh shit.*

At 0753, the *Saratoga* came to a stop. The starboard compartment that was quickly flooding contained the ship's turboelectric drive machinery. With its engines shut down, the carrier wallowed back and forth in the long sea swells.

Pete Peterkin rushed to the side of the ship to see the damage for himself. Looking down, he was amazed to see hundreds of fish swimming in the water as a big oil slick began spreading out from the place where the torpedo struck.

Forgetting about breakfast, Jack Stark rushed to his battle station. Abovedecks, he could hear the distant rumble of depth charges as the *Saratoga*'s escort ships went after the Japanese submarine that had launched the torpedo.

Belowdecks, the ship's engineers worked hard to get the carrier moving again. Dead in the water, the *Saratoga* was an easy target for another torpedo. Forty minutes later she was under way, crawling along at six knots.

The ship was starting to list when the engines broke down again at 1100. Admiral Fletcher decided to begin flying off the *Saratoga*'s planes to the friendly island of Espiritu Santo, about three hundred miles away.

When Swede received his orders to send half the squadron ashore, he ordered Bruce Harwood to lead the flight. Smiley Morgan, Bob Evarts, Bert Earnest, Andy Divine, Aaron Katz, and Bill Dye would go with him. Swede would stay behind with the remaining planes and crews.

Harwood told the men to pack all their personal gear in the planes. Like the *Enterprise,* the *Saratoga* would probably be heading into dry dock as soon as she could muster sufficient power. There was no telling when they would be back.

Del Delchamps helped to load Bill Dye's plane with personal gear, supplies, and ammunition. He began to worry about the weight of all the cargo when he saw two sailors struggling to load the heavy toolboxes of the squadron metalsmith into his tail compartment. The metalsmith was going, too.

Shortly after 1300, the *Saratoga* was taken under tow by the USS *Minneapolis*. Between the limited power of her damaged engines and the towing strength of the heavy cruiser, the carrier was able to reach launching speed.

Bill Dye was lined up for takeoff when the pilot of the Dauntless behind him let his brake slip and plowed into Dye's plane. Del Delchamps looked up to see the huge propeller chewing up their tail.

The Avenger was too damaged to fly. They were ordered to remove everything in the aircraft and reload it in a spare plane brought up from the hangar deck. It took them more than an hour. By then, the rest of the flight had taken off. They would be flying alone the three hundred miles to Espiritu Santo.

No one told Bill Dye or his crew that the new plane they were flying had a torpedo stowed inside the bomb bay. In addition to everything they were carrying, the torpedo added two thousand pounds of weight. And it was live.

Dye knew something was wrong as they were rolling down the flight deck. At full power, he barely lifted clear. Looking out the tail compartment window, Del was reminded of being in a lake boat back in Alabama. The plane was barely skimming the surface.

Dye finally climbed up to an altitude of thirty feet. It was as high as they ever got. The altimeter read zero all the way to Espiritu Santo. When they landed on the dirt landing strip, Del discovered the live torpedo in the bomb bay. The crew agreed that it was a miracle they had made it.

Aboard the *Saratoga,* Swede was told to transfer his support personnel to the destroyer *Grayson,* which would take them to Espiritu Santo. The decision put Jack Stark in a quandary. He was responsible for all of the records of Torpedo Eight, including the men's service files, pay records, and the pilots' log books. He was not about to leave any of it behind.

Jack and Ed Dollard, the other yeoman in the squadron, picked up the big file cabinet containing the squadron records and carried it over to the place where a breeches buoy had been rigged up to send them across to the destroyer.

They watched as another yeoman was strapped into the canvas seat of the breeches buoy. The seat was connected by a steel ring to a stout rope suspended between the two ships, and operated by pulleys at each end. In rough seas, a transfer at a height of fifty feet was a hairy experience. Fortunately, the seas were calm.

Jack ran back to the squadron office to get his portable typewriter. It was the principal weapon he had to fight the war, and it was definitely going with him. When he got back to the breeches buoy, Jack refused to go until the sailors operating it agreed to send over his typewriter and file cabinet.

They resisted until he threatened to bring Swede Larsen down on their heads. Whether that made a difference or they just got tired of arguing, the sailors finally secured his file cabinet and typewriter onto the canvas rig and sent it over to the *Grayson*.

The morning torpedo attack had caused twelve casualties out of the two thousand men serving aboard the *Saratoga*. One of the injured was Admiral Frank Jack Fletcher, whose forehead had been split open when the torpedo struck. When the *Saratoga* began its long journey back to Pearl Harbor, Fletcher went with her.

Only two carriers, the *Wasp* and the *Hornet*, remained in the South Pacific.


SUNDAY, 6 SEPTEMBER 1942
ESPIRITU SANTO
TORPEDO SQUADRON EIGHT

The island of Espiritu Santo was located six hundred miles southeast of Guadalcanal. In early July, the Americans had begun constructing a sprawling naval base there to provide logistical support for the Guadalcanal invasion.

Across the island from the base, a naval construction team had bulldozed a section of jungle near the sea and built a primitive airfield. It now became home to Torpedo Eight and several other air squadrons.

Espiritu Santo was no South Seas paradise. Any visions of beautiful native girls fanning a weary Navy officer with palm fronds on a sun-kissed beach were quickly shattered. The surrounding rain forest was as dense as anything Pete Peterkin had ever seen. The ten-foot-high undergrowth was so thick that a man couldn't pass through it without bringing along a machete to clear a path. The jungle went right to the edge of the shoreline.

The airfield itself was no more than a landing strip. The Navy construction team hadn't had time to build dispersal areas, and there were no shops to repair aircraft or buildings to house the support personnel. The squadron's Avengers had to be parked alongside the runway. The crews refueled them with hand pumps from fifty-five-gallon drums. There was no electricity or running water.

"Where are we supposed to live?" was the most commonly repeated question when they first arrived.

Near the landing strip, the new arrivals were shown several mounds of supplies covered by waterproof tarps. The material included canvas tents, hand tools, jerry cans full of drinking water, and cartons of K rations.

Bruce Harwood quietly announced that they would have to build their own camp. The pilots and enlisted men would all pitch in together. The news was not greeted with enormous enthusiasm by Bert Earnest. Clearing jungle with a shovel to put up a tent in 100-degree heat was not what he had signed up for as an officer and a gentleman.

They began with the most important facilities first, the latrines. The enlisted men built their latrines at the edge of the ocean. The officers preferred the grassy hill near the airstrip.

The only clothing they had to wear was what they had brought from the *Saratoga*. There was no rain gear, mosquito netting, kerosene lamps, or cooking equipment. It was the wet season. Without warning, the skies would release a deluge of lukewarm rain as they worked to build the camp. It would start and stop as quickly as turning a faucet and reduce their newly cleared paths into muddy quagmires.

As soon as the latrines were set up, voracious flies descended on the encampment. Without a screened mess tent, the flies attacked their food as soon as it was ladled onto a plate or removed from a can. The men would eat with one hand while waving away insects with the other.

Within days, some of the men began having serious bowel problems. Pete Peterkin was one of the first. An initial bout of dysentery led to a loss of ten pounds, and it didn't stop there.

About fifty native men were living near the airstrip. They came from inland villages and worked under the direction of the Navy construction team. Except for the little leather cups they wore around their genitals, they were naked.

The squadrons had been warned that Espiritu Santo still had cannibals and headhunters within its native population. No one felt compelled to find out if any of the laborers still practiced their traditional skills.

Harwood had no idea how long they would have to stay there. The most active rumor was that they were going to be sent north to support the Marine air group at Guadalcanal.

Swede arrived with the rest of the squadron a few days later. He called everyone together to read them a statement written by Captain Ramsey of the *Saratoga* shortly before Swede had taken off for Espiritu Santo.

" 'Your record of achievements is a matter to the greatest pride to us and it is our fervent determination to rejoin you as expeditiously as humanly possible,' " read Swede aloud as they all stood in the sweltering heat. " 'In the meantime carry on as you have in the past. No one could ask more.' "

If the words had been meant to raise morale, they fell short of the mark. The different squadrons in the camp were already bickering. One evening, Lee Marona was helping to deliver a meal to the officers' mess tent when he overheard a senior pilot in a dive-bomber squadron accuse the enlisted men in Torpedo Eight of stealing food. Swede told the man to prove it or go outside with him. The other officer backed down.

On the afternoon of September 3, Fred Mears and Harry Ferrier flew onto the airstrip. The *Enterprise* had gone back to Pearl Harbor after all, but Fred Mears and his friend Dick Jaccard hadn't gone with her.

Like the air squadrons aboard the *Saratoga*, the *Enterprise* squadrons had been ordered to fly ashore and await further orders. After they landed at their first stop in the New Hebrides, Mears and Jaccard buried their disappointment by getting drunk on native wine and stealing an Army jeep to go joyriding on the dirt roads surrounding the airstrip. Fred was then ordered to join Torpedo Eight at Espiritu Santo.

Bert Earnest was down at the airstrip when Fred and Harry arrived. Bert and Harry had a chance to catch up as they walked over to the tent encampment. Mears was no happier to see Swede than Swede was to see him.

It wasn't quite up to the standards of the Moana Hotel, but Fred quickly embraced the reality of his new surroundings. The next morning, he worked with two other pilots to build the camp's first shower, using two fifty-five-gallon drums suspended over coconut tree logs.

Life on the island settled into a monotonous routine. Occasionally, the officers were invited to eat supper at a Marine officers' mess near the airfield. The enlisted men had to make do with K rations, along with local fruits and vegetables, including "island cabbage," which was boiled in a pot and smelled like a man's sweat.

Jack Stark hated the island cabbage. What he longed for most was milk from the ripe coconuts that rested so tantalizingly at the tops of the palm trees near their tents. They rarely dropped to the ground.

He finally decided to approach one of the native laborers. Using sign language, he got his message across. Holding a nickel in his fingers, he pointed to the top of a palm tree. In less than a minute, the native had climbed the tree, and tossed down a batch of ripe coconuts. After Jack had gathered the harvest, he gave the man his nickel.

He was sharing the milk with his friends when Swede Larsen came by and roundly chewed him out. Apparently, an officer in the Navy construction team had visited Swede to complain that one of his men was single-handedly screwing up the local economy. He had been paying the natives six cents a day and the workers were now demanding a raise.

# The Canal

Sitting at his headquarters tent in a steaming jungle clearing a few miles to the east of the Marine defense perimeter, General Kawaguchi decided he was ready to capture Henderson Field. As soon as he controlled the airfield, swarms of Japanese planes would land there and consolidate his gains.

Unlike the late Colonel Ichiki, who had believed he could take the airfield with one "spear thrust" through the American perimeter, Kawaguchi had created a complex attack plan. It left no matter to chance, and even included the site of the formal ceremony in which General Vandegrift would personally surrender to him near the airfield.

With twenty-seven hundred square miles of beaches and dense jungle to cloak their movements, the Japanese had succeeded in landing Kawaguchi's troops at their designated locations. The American Marines began to mockingly refer to the nightly deliveries as the "Tokyo Express."

On the night of September 4, a Japanese light cruiser and eleven destroyers put ashore nearly a thousand troops before swinging around to sink two American destroyer transports, killing both ships' captains and thirty-three sailors. The stunned survivors floated ashore the next day.

Believing that the American carriers had been driven from the Solomons, the Japanese high command was supremely confident that their upcoming offensive would be successful.

Kawaguchi believed that no more than two thousand Marines protected the perimeter around the airfield. With six thousand fully equipped soldiers, General Kawaguchi was content with what he thought was a three-to-one advantage, and ready to execute his plan.

Although more than ten thousand Marines actually defended the airfield, they were spread out along a twelve-mile front. The area to the south of the airfield was the most lightly defended, and that was where Kawaguchi planned to make his principal attack.

Kawaguchi's battle plan called for a three-pronged assault. The main force, which had come ashore fifteen miles east of the American positions at Taivu Point, would penetrate several miles inland, and then pivot to attack the airfield from the south. Kawaguchi would personally lead them to victory.

A diversionary force would simultaneously attack from the southeast, aiming its thrust toward Alligator Creek, where Colonel Ichiki's men had been wiped out on the night of August 20. Their spirits would thus be avenged.

His third force, which had been landed to the west of the American perimeter, would cross the Matanikau River and attack the Americans' southwest perimeter at the same scheduled time. The assaults would be supported by naval gunfire from Japanese warships offshore. Prior to the attack, an aggressive bombing campaign would be unleashed by land-based bombers flying from Rabaul to soften up the American positions.

By September 5, native scouts reported to Vandegrift that Japanese troops had occupied the village of Tasimboko near Taivu Point. Vandegrift decided he would not wait for them to attack. On the night of September 7, he sent the 1st Marine Raider Battalion, commanded by Colonel Merritt Edson, in a small flotilla of ships to make an amphibious raid behind the enemy positions.

At dawn the next morning, Edson's Marine Raiders came ashore in a driving rain. Near the landing beach, they came upon two unmanned thirty-seven-millimeter field pieces. The guns were brand-new. Unopened crates of ammunition were stacked next to each one.

Following the trails toward Tasimboko, Edson's men confronted the rear guard of General Kawaguchi's main force, which had already left the village on its march into the interior.

The Japanese had left behind several hundred troops to defend Tasimboko, along with Kawaguchi's field artillery, his entire supply of cached food and ammunition, and a well-equipped radio station that allowed him to maintain contact with the other two forces on the island.

Edson's men were incredulous after they had swept away the rear-guard soldiers and found the huge stockpile of supplies. It included five hundred thousand rounds of ammunition for Kawaguchi's machine guns, rifles, and field pieces, large stores of medical supplies, new uniforms, boots, knapsacks, and a small mountain of crated food, canned goods, rice, and other supplies. Based on what they had brought ashore, Edson estimated the size of the Japanese force to be at least four thousand men.

There was no time for his Raiders to haul everything away. With the exception of the medical supplies and a few cases of British-made cigarettes, he ordered the rest of the supply dump destroyed along with the radio station.

Some of the Marines felt compelled to disobey the colonel's orders. They weren't called "Raiders" for nothing. Accomplished foragers, they returned to the beach lugging more than twenty cases of Japanese beer and Kawaguchi's entire supply of sake.

For Kawaguchi, the loss of his supplies was a potential nightmare. If he didn't capture the airfield within a few days, his troops would have nothing to eat except what they could forage in the jungle. With the radio station destroyed, he was no longer able to communicate with the commanders of the other two forces except by messenger.

After Edson returned with his report, Vandegrift knew that a major attack was coming, but he still didn't know where. Native scouts sent back messages that Japanese units were on the move in several areas around the twelve-mile-long perimeter.

Edson and Colonel Gerry Thomas, the division's operations officer, told Vandegrift they thought they knew where the attack was going to come from. Unfolding a crude map, they pointed to a spot less than a mile south of the airfield.

It was a low ridge that ran for more than a half mile beneath the slope of Mount Austen. Most of it was parallel to the Lunga River, and dominated the surrounding terrain. The long hilly spine had four smaller ridges that projected out like legs and were matted with tall kunai grass.

Trusting Edson's and Thomas's instincts, Vandegrift deployed the Raiders on the forward spur of the ridge that extended down to the Lunga River. He also provided Edson with two companies of the 1st Parachute Battalion, and moved a battery of 105-millimeter guns into a position south of the airfield to provide artillery support.

While the Marines were digging in along the ridge, General Kawaguchi was leading his main force through the jungle, taking every precaution to prevent its discovery from American spotter planes.

Initially, they made good progress. Without native guides, however, several of the units became lost. Others got bogged down in the interior's muddy swamps, and were forced to go around them.

Kawaguchi's greatest advantage remained the fact that the Americans still didn't know the size and location of his force, or when he would attack. On September 11, Kawaguchi received a message from Colonel Oka, whose diversionary force was now west of the Marine defense line near the Matanikau River. Oka vowed he would make his assault at the same time Kawaguchi launched his own attack with the main force.

The attacks were scheduled for 2200 on the night of September 12.

At midday on the eleventh, forty-two Japanese aircraft from Rabaul strafed and bombed the airfield. In the course of the raid, bombs were also dropped on the positions where Edson's men were digging in, killing eleven Marines. It confirmed Edson's belief that his ridge was the place where the Japanese would attack.

Vandegrift was at his command post after the air raid when he was handed a message from Vice Admiral Robert Ghormley, who commanded all naval forces in the South Pacific under Nimitz. It was not good news.

"The situation as I view it is very critical," Ghormley wrote. "Our transportation problem increases steadily as the Japs perfect their blockade methods."

Because of the recent loss of two carriers, as well as his inadequate reserves of aircraft, transports, and warships, Ghormley concluded that he could no longer fully support the Guadalcanal operation.

The meaning of his words was open to interpretation, but Vandegrift became incensed at what he viewed as another example of the Navy's failure to actively back up his Marines.

That night, flares were dropped by Japanese spotting aircraft. The flares presaged a two-hour bombardment of the airfield by Japanese warships cruising unhindered offshore. When the shelling ended, the Marines waited all night in their foxholes for the expected ground attack. The lines remained quiet.

SATURDAY, 12 SEPTEMBER 1942
HENDERSON FIELD, GUADALCANAL
1148

As the noon hour approached, forty Japanese planes attacked the airfield, destroying three Dauntlesses on the ground before dropping bombs on Colonel Edson's positions along the ridge. The attack killed four Marines and wounded twenty-five more. The Cactus Air Force was successful in shooting down six of the attackers at a cost of two Wildcats.

With night falling, Colonel Edson's eight hundred men dug in again along the ridgeline. Earlier that day, Edson had strengthened his most exposed positions by running a single strand of barbed wire in front of them. Once more, the Raiders settled into their foxholes and waited.

At 2130, four Japanese warships arrived unhindered in Sealark Channel and began shelling both Henderson Field and Edson's Ridge. The cannonade lasted twenty minutes and killed three pilots at the airfield.

When the bombardment ended, there was a minute of silence in the hot, humid night. At his command post a few hundred yards from Edson's Ridge, Vandegrift suddenly heard the stutter of machine gun fire coming from the ridgeline to the south. It was followed by the boom of mortar shells and the chatter of small arms fire.

Vandegrift waited to see if the firefight grew in intensity, which would signal the beginning of a major assault, or whether the attack was a feint or a possible probing of the line.

In the dense jungle south of the ridge, General Kawaguchi's complicated battle plan had begun to unravel. Neither one of his diversionary forces had reached its planned objective or knew where it actually was in relation to the American lines.

Kawaguchi shared the same predicament. At the scheduled launch hour of 2200, only one of his three battalions had reached its assigned position. His men had struggled all day to cross deep ravines and almost impenetrable undergrowth to reach their objectives while staggering under the weight of rifles, mortars, ammunition, swords, grenades, and several days' supply of food.

Kawaguchi wanted to delay the attack, but without radio communication he had lost contact with the rest of the main force, and his messengers couldn't reach them in time. Only one of his three battalions began its attack at the appointed time. Over the course of the next two hours, confused elements of the other battalions went forward after fighting their way through the jungle. Kawaguchi's two diversionary forces never reached their launching point.

In spite of the disjointed nature of the attacks, Kawaguchi's men made good progress on the right flank of Edson's line between the ridge and the Lunga River. There weren't enough Marines to maintain a solid defense perimeter, and the Japanese slipped through the gaps between the strong points.

Three platoons were forced to withdraw before they were cut off and wiped out. In one engagement, seven Marines went missing, presumably captured and killed. The rest had to fight their way back to the ridge.

Standing in the darkness of his command post, Colonel Edson felt the Japanese attacks slowly peter out and die. He knew that the Japanese would regroup for another assault, and probably make it under the cover of darkness the following night. Edson began thinking about ways he could redeploy his men to give the Japanese a surprise.

He hoped he had enough men to stop them.

SUNDAY, 13 SEPTEMBER 1942
ESPIRITU SANTO
TORPEDO SQUADRON EIGHT
1100

Swede gathered his pilots and crews together to give them the word.

They had been on Espiritu Santo for almost two weeks. Although more men had come down with dysentery, they now had a potable water supply, and were getting hot chow.

It had been raining heavily for two days, and was still pouring when Swede brought them together to say that he had just received new orders. The Japanese were putting on a big push. The squadron was headed for Guadalcanal.

With the *Enterprise* and *Saratoga* gone, the Japanese now controlled the waters around Guadalcanal and the place was getting shelled almost every night by their warships. Every day, the airfield was bombed by planes from Rabaul, and the enemy was sending in thousands of troops, more all the time. It was shaping up to be the biggest battle of the Pacific War.

Torpedo Eight was going up to help stem the tide. Theirs had been the first and only torpedo squadron ordered in with the fighters and dive-bombers. The men should be proud of being chosen, he said. They were the best torpedo squadron in the Navy.

There was no telling how many of the pilots and crews would make it back when it was all over, he said. He didn't want anyone going with him who wasn't prepared to see it through to the end.

Swede said he would lead the first group of six Avengers up later that day once the planes were ready. The pilots and crews he had chosen should pack up all their personal gear and stow it in the airplanes. The five pilots were Gene Hanson, Bert Earnest, Jack Barnum, Tex Grady, and Red Doggett. The list included every pilot in the first division except Aaron Katz and Bob Evarts.

Espiritu Santo would remain their permanent base, said Swede. More pilots and crews would be rotated back and forth to Guadalcanal as needed. The Marines already had plenty of support people up there, so most of the squadron's machinist's mates and ordnance men would remain behind with the personnel staff.

Swede reminded the men that the squadron had a new motto after the Battle of Midway. *Attack with Vengeance,* he exhorted them. They had only one job to do, he said, and that was to kill Japs.

Standing with the enlisted men, Frank Balsley wondered what he would find up there. He was a fifty-caliber turret gunner, and a replacement member of Gene Hanson's crew. He would be going up in the first group.

At twenty-one, Frank had never thought of the enemy as "nips" or "Japs." Growing up in Gardena, California, his oldest friend was Japanese, along with half of his high school class, and he had liked them all. They came from good, hardworking families just like his, trying to get through the Depression like everyone else.

Frank's father had been a butcher and then run a small grocery store. The Japanese families were some of his best customers. It had come as a real shock to Frank when he realized that America was going to war against Japan. Now he rushed to get ready.

As navigation officer, Smiley Morgan made sure that each pilot had a map of the Eastern Solomon Islands to go with his chart board. He estimated that it would take them four or five hours to get there.

The rest of the pilots came out to the field to wish Swede and the others good luck. It was around noon when the six planes, heavily loaded with torpedoes, ammunition, and other gear, took off down the dirt airstrip and lifted off.

### GUADALCANAL
### GENERAL A. A. VANDEGRIFT

After stewing over the message he had received from Vice Admiral Ghormley about the withdrawal of naval support for his Marines, General Vandegrift pulled aside Colonel Thomas, his operations officer.

They were going to defend the airfield until it was no longer possible, come hell or high water, Navy or no Navy, Vandegrift told him. If they lost the airfield, he would lead the survivors up into the hills and fight a guerrilla war. Just to be on the safe side, he told Thomas to prepare a contingency plan in case they were overrun.

Vandegrift left his command post and went to the Pagoda to give the bad news to General Roy Geiger, who had just arrived earlier that week to take command of the Marine air group. Vandegrift told him that if it looked like they were about to be overrun, Geiger should fly out all of his planes.

At the same time, Colonel Edson was meeting with his senior officers at the ridge. He told them that he expected the Japanese to make an all-out assault that night, and that he was pulling most of them back from their original line to form a new one farther up the ridge. General Vandegrift had agreed to make available a reserve battalion to shore up any gaps that might develop during the battle.

Thirty-eight Japanese planes from Rabaul made an attack at around noon. Edson was visiting one of his units to tell the Marines what was at stake. If they failed to hold the ridge, he said, they would end up changing places with the Japanese, and would be reduced to eating lizards in the jungle.

### TORPEDO SQUADRON EIGHT
### 1750

The first thing Gene Hanson thought as they came in to land at Henderson Field was that it looked like a shallow bowl of black dust. The planes that had already landed were stirring up huge clouds of it as they taxied to the dispersal areas. Deep bomb crevices marked the edges of the runway like craters of the moon. Beyond the airfield, a grass field was littered with airplane wrecks.

Bert Earnest only noticed the American plane that had just been shot down over the airfield as they were coming in. The Dauntless dive-bomber plowed into the trees near the runway and exploded in a fireball.

As soon as they were on the ground, Marines came running up to tell them to get their gear out of the planes right away because they were expecting a shelling attack. Within a few minutes, they were walking toward a tent encampment concealed in a coconut grove north of the runway.

Frank Balsley felt something odd beneath his feet as he walked across the dark, gritty soil. It took a few moments to realize what it was. The earth seemed to emanate heat, as if there were a volcano down below the surface, waiting to blow.

The enlisted men were assigned tents, four to each one. A Marine showed them where to find the latrines and told them to familiarize themselves with the locations of the slit trenches around the camp before it got dark. When the shelling started, they needed to get to one right away.

Aside from four cots and mosquito netting, the tents offered no other comforts of home. Balsley stowed his stuff under his cot. By the time he went back outside, it was getting dark. Within thirty minutes, it was almost pitch black.

The officers were billeted in two-man tents. Bert Earnest was assigned to one with Jack Barnum. A big rat was waiting for them inside. The rat seemed to look at the tent as his assigned quarters and was in no hurry to vacate. Jack Barnum said he hated rats and asked Bert to get rid of it. When Bert advanced on the rat, it retreated under the back edge of the tent.

The mess tent was supposedly near the beach area, and the pilots were about to go looking for it in the darkness when a Japanese scout plane droned over Henderson Field and began dropping flares.

The sky was suddenly filled with light and sound as Japanese warships lying offshore began pounding the airfield and its surrounding installations with salvo after salvo of heavy gunfire.

Frank Balsley lay in his slit trench and wondered how men got through something like this every night. Being shot at by a Zero was one thing. He could shoot back. But all he could do now was lie there in the hot dirt and hope that one of the shells didn't land too close.

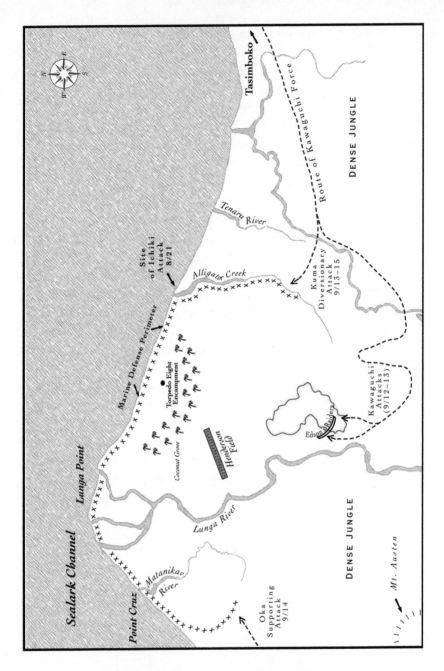

THE BATTLE OF EDSON'S RIDGE,
SEPTEMBER 12–14, 1942

SUNDAY, 13 SEPTEMBER 1942
EDSON'S RIDGE
GUADALCANAL
2100

In the middle of the shelling, Kawaguchi's men came charging out of the darkness below Edson's Ridge screaming, "BANZAI . . . BANZAI!" A few hundred yards to the north, Vandegrift listened to the growing crescendo of the battle and knew that this was no probing action. From the symphony of hand grenades, machine guns, automatic rifles, and mortar fire, he knew it was the all-out assault they had been waiting for since Edson found the supply dump at Tasimboko. Now it would come down to whether he had enough men to drive them back.

A Raider company on one of the knolls of the ridgeline absorbed the brunt of the initial attack. They held. A second column of Japanese troops broke through a gap in the line and swung around to cut off a platoon. The Americans had to fight their way back along the ridge for more than two hundred yards to hook up with another unit. Edson began calling in artillery strikes, directing the fire closer and closer to his own lines to break the thrust of the Japanese assault.

The strength of the attacks ebbed and flowed. During one lull at around 2300, Vandegrift's staff felt confident they had won. Then Kawaguchi's men came on again, fighting through the rain of artillery shells, taking over Marine foxholes, severing communications, and sowing confusion up and down the line.

From their newly gained ground, the Japanese began pouring a barrage of mortar shells onto the ridge. One of the shells severed the telephone line between Edson and the artillery batteries that were delivering targeted fire.

Another column of Japanese attackers came out of a smoke screen at the left end of Edson's line, many of them shouting epithets in English. One screamed, "Fuck Babe Ruth!" The Marines answered in kind.

The Japanese broke through the principal defensive line on Edson's left, and drove a significant wedge through the right. After hours of constant pressure, the ever-thinning line of defenders on Edson's left flank began retreating up the hill to make a last stand near one of the highest knolls along the ridge.

Two platoons that were cut off in the center of the line withdrew as well. Under continuous fire, the Marines dug in at the top of the knoll. Their last line resembled the outer rim of a horseshoe.

General Kawaguchi was within sight of victory. If he could drive the last group of Marines off the ridge, it was literally downhill the rest of the way to the airfield. Once he had it, Japanese troop planes were standing by to land at the field and solidify control.

In their encampment within the coconut grove, the newly arrived pilots and crews of Torpedo Eight could feel the ground reverberate beneath their feet with each salvo of the Marines' heavy artillery. The din was incredible.

At one point, another gun battle flared up east of the coconut grove. It was one of Kawaguchi's diversionary forces. The flight crews nervously wondered what to do if the Japanese broke through. Most of the pilots were carrying forty-fives but those wouldn't be much use against grenades and machine guns.

Shortly after midnight, they heard planes coming, and more flares went off over the airfield. The flight crews ran to reach the slit trenches as Japanese warships in Sealark Channel began another shelling attack.

The battle went on all night. At its most critical juncture, with Edson's men holding the last line on the knoll a half mile from Henderson Field, Vandegrift waited for the Japanese commander to deliver a coup de grâce. Victory or defeat hung in the balance. By then, his big howitzers had expended more than two thousand rounds of artillery shells on the Japanese positions and were running out of ammunition.

But the final attack never came.

One of Kawaguchi's three battalions had been poised to attack on the left side of Edson's line when the assault began. However, the battalion commander, Colonel Watanabe, became separated from his men in the jungle, and never arrived to lead them. Confused about their orders, his junior commanders remained unsure of where to go. Only a fraction of them got into the fight.

After seven hours of combat, with much of the fighting hand-to-hand, the slowly diminishing noise of battle signaled to Vandegrift that it was finally over. The Japanese had attacked twelve times, and the Marines had held.

At the pilots' encampment north of Henderson Field, one of the newly arrived fliers encountered a Marine officer at the mess tent near the beach and asked, "Hey . . . is it like this every night around here?"

MONDAY, 14 SEPTEMBER 1942
EDSON'S RIDGE
GUADALCANAL
0700

The Japanese lay everywhere in the kunai grass, hundreds of them in every pose of violent death, all the way from the knolls along the ridgeline down to the banks of the Lunga River. In a number of places, dead Japanese soldiers lay entwined with Marines.

At the knoll where the Raiders had made their final stand, a large cluster of dead Marines lay together in a roughly parallel line along the crest. Below them lay the bodies of the Japanese who had almost made it to the top.

In the morning, General Vandegrift was standing near his command post when three Japanese came charging out of the dense undergrowth. A Japanese officer rushed toward him waving a samurai sword. He was shot down after skewering one Marine.

The first count of enemy dead exceeded six hundred. It was impossible to know how many more had been killed in the shelling of the jungle beyond the Lunga, or how many wounded survivors the Japanese had taken with them.

The Marines had lost forty-nine killed, with more than two hundred wounded. The figure represented more than a third of the Raider battalion's strength before the battle.

In the brutal heat and humidity of Guadalcanal, it was necessary to get the bodies underground as quickly as possible. The American dead were gathered from all over the battlefield, brought to the cemetery, and buried under hand-lettered signs or simple wooden crosses. There was little time for ceremony.

There was none for the Japanese. For most of the morning, bulldozers moved up and down the slope of the ridge. They scooped up the bodies, deposited them in freshly excavated trenches, and covered them with soil.

Later that day, Torpedo Eight absorbed its first casualty on Guadalcanal. Swede had taken his Avengers up on two short flights to familiarize the pilots with the terrain of Guadalcanal and the surrounding islands. The flight didn't encounter any enemy planes or ships. After landing back at Henderson Field, there was an air raid, and Tex Grady fell out the back of a truck, injuring his elbow and knee. He was evacuated the same day.

Swede sent word to Espiritu Santo that he needed a replacement pilot for their sixth Avenger. That night, the pilots of Torpedo Eight sat in the darkness and listened to Gene Hanson's portable radio, freshly charged with a supply of flashlight batteries he had remembered to bring with him from the *Saratoga*.

The clearest station on the dial came from a Japanese radio network, and it featured the voice of the Japanese-American woman known as Tokyo Rose. Her soft mellifluous voice brought them the latest American swing bands. Between the musical selections, she talked seductively to the Americans serving across the Pacific. As Gene and the others listened, she made special mention of the men "cut off on Guadalcanal," and expressed her regret that they would soon be destroyed by the forces of the Japanese Imperial Army and Navy.

On their first two nights, the pilots and crews hadn't gotten much sleep. Their third night proved no different. They were lying in their tents under mosquito netting when enemy destroyers in Sealark Channel began lobbing shells into their positions again.

TUESDAY, 15 SEPTEMBER 1942
TRUK ATOLL
ADMIRAL ISOROKU YAMAMOTO

All through the night of September 13–14, the Japanese commanders on Rabaul waited for the radio message from Kawaguchi confirming he had captured the airfield. Reinforcements were standing
by to occupy the field as soon as it came through.

But the signal never came.

On the morning of the fourteenth, they sent a reconnaissance
flight over Guadalcanal to try to ascertain the results of the battle,
but the planes were shot down, indicating that the airfield was still
in American hands. On the morning of the fifteenth, the message finally came through from General Kawaguchi. He reported that he
had failed to capture the airfield, and was temporarily retreating to
regroup his forces.

Within hours of receiving Kawaguchi's report, Admiral Yamamoto issued new orders decreeing that the combined fleet's principal
objectives were to transport sufficient troops and artillery to take
back Guadalcanal, and to destroy the American airpower there.

He also approved plans to construct a new airfield at Buin on the
southern tip of Japanese-held Bougainville. That would cut in half
the distance his fighters and bombers had to fly between Rabaul and
Guadalcanal. He ordered his 11th Air Fleet to commence large-scale
air attacks on Henderson Field.

The chastened Japanese army quickly followed suit. On the same
day, they ordered the 2nd and 38th army divisions, totaling more than
17,000 troops, to embark for Guadalcanal with 170 artillery pieces.

A month earlier, one fully equipped Japanese infantry division
combined with heavy air and naval support would probably have
been enough to retake the airfield. But now the Americans were being reinforced, too.

USS *WASP*
1500

The American reinforcement effort suffered a catastrophic blow almost as soon as it began. On the same morning Kawaguchi began his retreat from Edson's Ridge, an American naval task force set out from Espiritu Santo, heading north for Guadalcanal. It was transporting four thousand men of the 7th Marines, along with their vehicles, guns, and equipment, to the landing beaches near Lunga Point.

The Navy had provided two heavy carriers, the *Wasp* and *Hornet*, along with the battleship *North Carolina* and ten other warships to escort the transports. On the afternoon of the fifteenth, the task force was one hundred fifty miles southeast of San Cristobal when it unwittingly passed through a screen of Japanese submarines. One of them fired a spread of nine torpedoes at the *Wasp*. Two exploded along its starboard side, piercing aviation gas tanks and powder magazines.

Within seconds, the escaping gasoline triggered a massive explosion. The heat of the flames ignited stores of bombs, powder, and ammunition, causing a rapid succession of new fires in the forward section of the ship.

With the *Wasp*'s water pipes shattered, it was impossible to contain the conflagration as it spread through the carrier. Oil and aviation gas set the sea around the ship on fire, further hampering rescue efforts.

At 2100, the *Wasp* went down by the bow, carrying 194 men with her. Fred Mears's closest friend, Dick Jaccard, the Dauntless pilot who had scored a direct hit on the *Hiryu* at Midway, was asleep in his stateroom when the torpedoes hit. He was trapped in his compartment and went down with the ship.

"*C'est la guerre*" had been one of his favorite expressions. "*C'est la vie, c'est l'amour.*"

Two of the torpedoes fired by the Japanese submarine narrowly missed the *Wasp* and traveled five more miles through the sea until one of them hit the destroyer *O'Brien*. The other smashed into the battleship *North Carolina*, which was forced to head for Tongatapu for repairs. The *O'Brien* sank before she could make it to Pearl Harbor, although most of her crew was rescued.

One thousand nine hundred forty-six crew members of the *Wasp* were picked up from the sea before the naval task force continued steaming north toward Guadalcanal carrying the 7th Marines.

# The Groove

G ene Hanson learned about the disaster when he heard another flier say that the *Wasp* was gone. His first reaction was, "Gone where?"

"Sunk," the flier said, adding that with the *Hornet* the only American carrier left in the South Pacific, the Japanese would have open season on them now at Guadalcanal.

That afternoon, Swede brought his four pilots together to say they were going out on their first mission early that evening. Their job would be to patrol the body of water between Bougainville and Guadalcanal through which the Japanese were bringing down their reinforcements.

The Marine fliers called it "the Slot." The Navy pilots had their own name for it.

The Groove.

In a briefing at the Pagoda, General Roy Geiger, the new commander of the Cactus Air Force, told Swede and the dive-bomber squadron leaders that they needed to take the battle to the Japanese. His Wildcat fighters would be responsible for knocking down the Japanese planes hitting Guadalcanal every day. He wanted the dive-bombers and torpedo planes to sink the ships carrying the Japanese troop reinforcements before they arrived.

The five Avengers took off at 1800. Each plane was carrying a two-thousand-pound torpedo. Near the runway, Jack Barnum taxied into a shell crater and damaged his landing gear. The other four took off and headed north in the company of thirteen Dauntless dive-bombers.

Near Gizo Island, they hit pay dirt on their first combat mission. Flying at seventy-five hundred feet, Swede spotted a group of enemy warships heading south: three light cruisers and four destroyers.

The dive-bombers went in first.

The enemy ships immediately sped up and began executing a series of evasive turns. Swede timed his own attack to begin between the seventh and eighth bombing runs. Diving to two hundred feet, he radioed the other Avenger pilots to go after the third cruiser in the column. They launched their torpedoes into the teeth of heavy antiaircraft fire at a distance of less than six hundred yards, and then headed for home.

Back at Henderson Field, the four pilots agreed that at least one of the torpedoes had struck the cruiser amidships on the port side, and that she had slowed down after taking the hit. Swede put it in his After Action Report. The Dauntlesses had succeeded in sinking a Japanese barge, but lost one of their planes when it failed to come out of its dive and crashed into the sea.

That night, another Japanese submarine surfaced in Sealark Channel and began shelling Marine positions near the beach. Although the pilots were getting used to it, they failed to get much sleep.

The next morning, Swede thought they might get lucky again if they went back to Gizo. There were no Dauntlesses available to accompany the Avengers, but Swede received approval for the mission.

Torpedoes were scarce, and so each plane carried four five-hundred-pound bombs. This time, all five Avengers took off safely. The evening sky was hazy, with limited visibility. North of Savo Island, Swede dove down to check out what he thought might be an enemy ship. By the time he regained altitude, he had lost contact with the others.

Near Gizo, one of Swede's gunners sighted two Japanese light cruisers heading down the Groove toward Guadalcanal. Turning west so that he could bomb them from out of the dipping sun, Swede headed down.

Within seconds, they were under attack from two Japanese floatplanes. His turret gunner, Ervin "Judge" Wendt, fought them off with short bursts of fire as the first came in high, and the second low.

At three thousand feet, Swede salvoed his bombs on the lead cruiser. Without waiting to see the results, he turned for home with the Japanese fighters in pursuit. Judge Wendt kept firing until one of them began smoking, and they broke off the attack.

The other four Avengers were already at Henderson Field when Swede landed. Somewhat sheepishly, they told him they had patrolled the same area around Gizo, but visibility was poor and they never saw an enemy ship.

FRIDAY, 18 SEPTEMBER 1942
GUADALCANAL
TORPEDO SQUADRON EIGHT
0600

To General Vandegrift, it looked almost too good to be true. In the gray murk of dawn, Sealark Channel began to fill with American ships, one after another, until the transports and tankers were anchored offshore with their precious cargoes of Marines, equipment, and aviation gas for General Geiger's Cactus Air Force.

In spite of losing the *Wasp* and the *North Carolina*, the Navy had kept coming, taking a chance that no Japanese carriers were lurking near Guadalcanal to wipe out the transports before they could be unloaded.

Early that same morning, the Japanese had mounted one of their largest air attacks of the whole campaign, but serious storms kept the sixty-four planes from reaching Guadalcanal after they took off.

Into the evening, the transports unloaded their cargoes, including four thousand Marines and tons of food, ammunition, guns, artillery, vehicles, tents, barbed wire, and spare parts. When they had finished, Higgins boats carried the wounded survivors of the Battle of Edson's Ridge out to the transports. As night fell, the task force weighed anchor and headed south.

Additional reinforcements for the Cactus Air Force landed that same afternoon. Swede was at Henderson Field to greet them when they landed. The flight of six Avengers from Espiritu Santo was led by Bruce Harwood.

Smiley Morgan and Bill Dye were there to stay. Harwood, Mears, Katz, and Evarts had flown up a new supply of torpedoes, and were flying right back to Espiritu Santo. However, the same fierce storms that had blocked the Japanese now led to the cancellation of their flight.

It gave Harry Ferrier, who had flown up with Fred Mears, a chance to catch up with Bert Earnest. Afterward, Bert approached Fred to say he needed a good turret gunner, and asked if it would be all right if Harry transferred into his crew. Fred said fine.

At around midnight, the pilots were asleep in their tents when a Japanese cruiser and four destroyers arrived in Sealark Channel and began shelling the coconut grove. Fred was sharing a tent with Aaron Katz. He awoke to the sound of an exploding shell, followed by the shout of a Marine as he ran past their tent.

"Hit your foxholes," he yelled.

Fred had no idea where his foxhole was. Besides that, it was raining like the deluge and he was wearing a new pair of blue-striped pajamas. He and Aaron talked it over and decided to stay in their cots. A few minutes later, a shell went off in the trees above them. It lit up the inside of their tent.

"Let's not be stupid about this," said Aaron.

Under the exploding shells, they ran to the closest foxhole. It was full of men. So was the second one. They kept running through the pelting rain until they saw a shallow empty trench. When both of them tried to squeeze into it, their arms and legs protruded over the edge. They remained there until it was over.

THURSDAY, 24 SEPTEMBER 1942
GUADALCANAL
TORPEDO SQUADRON EIGHT

For almost a week, violent storm fronts ranged across the Eastern Solomons, keeping most of the planes grounded at Guadalcanal and frustrating the goal of the Japanese air force to make the airfield permanently inoperable.

With no flights scheduled, the pilots and crews of Torpedo Eight caught up on rest. One morning, the rain stopped long enough for Smiley Morgan to decide to take a bath in the Lunga River.

When he got to the riverbank with his soap, razor, and towel, some Marines were washing their jeeps in it. Smiley had let his beard grow, and after soaping up he began shaving with his straight razor. One of the Marines yelled over not to nick himself or he would be certain to get dengue fever.

When Smiley asked what that was, the Marine said it caused an ugly red rash to break out all over a man's body, after which his cock would fall off. Even taking into account Marine exaggeration, Smiley decided he didn't really need to shave.

Food was being rationed at the order of General Vandegrift, and the men on the island were limited to two meals a day, the first one shortly after dawn, and the second late in the afternoon.

Smiley tried to eat whatever they put in front of him. Along with Pete Peterkin, he had come down with dysentery at Espiritu Santo. He had already lost fifteen pounds, and couldn't afford to lose any more. His "fluid drive" had persisted at Guadalcanal, and he had spent many hours sitting on the multihole throne chairs suspended over the latrine pits. If he didn't get his strength back, Swede told him, he would be grounded.

By wardroom standards, the meals on the island were barely edible. Once in a while they got hotcakes in the morning, but mostly it was plain unsweetened oatmeal ladled into their metal mess kits.

Even though the stuff had the texture of wallpaper paste, Smiley had learned to eat it fast. The big glob would start out white in the plate, but it would get darker and darker between bites. Every time a man walked by, his shoes would stir up swirls of the dark, loamy soil.

No matter how fast Smiley kept dipping his spoon, the bottom layer would usually be black by the time he got to it.

The afternoon meal was usually boiled rice. Sometimes it was served with canned sausage, other times with Spam. Occasionally, they got stew with real meat in it, or canned peaches and hardtack. What really kept them going was coffee. They drank it all day long. Sometimes, it was sweetened with condensed milk.

A thriving black market in Japanese war souvenirs had sprung up after the Edson's Ridge battle. The pilots were offered everything from bloodstained fountain pens to combat badges, medals, rifles, and pistols. Prices ranged up to one hundred dollars for a run-of-the-mill samurai sword.

Smiley didn't need bloodstained souvenirs to remind him of where he was. The whole island had a bad smell to it, from the rotting jungle that surrounded them to the scummy swamps near the river. His tent smelled of clammy, sweat-stained clothes.

A newly arrived pilot in another squadron had jokingly suggested they look at it like they were there on a camping trip. Smiley had camped out plenty of times in Missouri and Florida, but he had never chosen a place to camp where the river smelled like a sewer and contained leeches and poisonous snakes. His camping spots also didn't feature white ants the size of rosary beads that could devour a hunk of Spam in less than a minute. Or jungle rats as big as badgers that liked to nestle inside your overseas bag. He had never gotten hives, rashes, crotch rot, or dysentery on a camping trip, either. In some places, his skin was scraped raw from scratching.

Smiley was hoarding his small supply of cash to hopefully buy a bottle of whiskey, preferably scotch, if one were to miraculously appear. Liquor was at a premium on the island. Pilots would occasionally fly up a few bottles from Espiritu Santo. It disappeared fast. No one wanted to admit they had any, because it would be immediately stolen. The Marines were relentless foragers.

When General Geiger had arrived to take command of the Cactus Air Force in early September, he quickly put the fear of God in the men serving under him. Almost sixty years old, he was short and barrel-chested with cold, uncompromising eyes. A no-nonsense officer, he made it clear that he expected every man to toe the line.

After flying in, he had dropped off his personal gear at his guarded command tent and gone straight to see General Vandegrift. When they finished discussing the challenges they were facing, Geiger told Vandegrift he had brought a gift for him from Admiral Nimitz. His aide carried in a case of Johnny Walker scotch. But knowing that Vandegrift favored bourbon, Geiger said, "Archer, I have a case of bourbon and will trade you even up though mine are quarts."

Together, they rode back to Geiger's tent to make the swap. The case of bourbon was no longer there. Vandegrift gave Geiger two bottles of Nimitz's scotch but it didn't mollify him.

Three days earlier, Pete Peterkin had arrived from Espiritu Santo to take over as Torpedo Eight's engineer officer, bringing with him ten mechanics familiar with Avengers to help keep the squadron's planes in the air.

Swede invited Peterkin to share his tent, which was big enough for three men. It turned out to be fortuitous, because spare parts for their planes also had a way of disappearing on Guadalcanal. Pete kept the most important ones stored under his bunk.

On September 22, native scouts had reported that Japanese barges full of troops were being landed each night at Cape Esperance on the northern tip of Guadalcanal. That evening, Swede took Smiley up with him and they bombed the landing areas.

On the afternoon of the twenty-fourth, Gene Hanson was called up to General Geiger's headquarters and told that a group of enemy ships had been spotted northwest of Guadalcanal. Swede was down with fever, and Gene had been chosen to take a patrol out to try to intercept them.

His Avenger would be loaded with four five-hundred-pound bombs, and he would be accompanied by three Dauntlesses. At 2100, they took off from Henderson Field in the falling darkness, and headed out on a northwest compass heading.

They ran into the enemy ships almost immediately. He could see from the wakes that there were three ships in the formation. One was a light cruiser, and the other two destroyers.

The three Dauntless pilots each carried a single thousand-pound bomb, which they proceeded to drop in individual runs. None hit the enemy ships, which were making violent turns at flank speed.

Gene decided to try a glide bombing attack. He dropped down to fifteen hundred feet and headed straight into the barrage of antiaircraft fire that was pouring up from the cruiser. The first of his four bombs missed it, and he circled around for the next attack.

After Gene dropped the second bomb, Rube "Carpenter" Francis, his turret gunner, called on the intercom to say that it had missed, too. That only made the stoic Hanson more determined. On his third run, he was sure he had made a hit, but Francis said that it was only a near miss, exploding about thirty feet ahead of the cruiser.

Gene only had one bomb left. On his last run through the antiaircraft fire, he dropped it as close to the middle of the cruiser as he could. Francis told him it had exploded in the water within spitting distance of the starboard bow. As he headed back to Guadalcanal, the frustrated Hanson hoped it had fallen close enough to cause some damage.

After they landed, he went to the Pagoda to write up his After Action Report. General Geiger happened to be there. He listened as Gene described the mission, and the results of his four runs.

"You were taking on a cruiser, son," said the general. "Why didn't you just salvo all your bombs on the first run?"

Gene told him he wanted to make sure one of them hit home.

"I admire your guts, Hanson," said General Geiger, "but not your brains. Next time you're in a situation like that, make one pass and try to make it a good one."

"Yes, sir," said Gene.

As he made the long walk back to the encampment, he remembered the intensity of the gunfire from the cruiser and realized the general had been right. It was the dumbest thing he had ever done. He definitely wouldn't try it again.

Swede Larsen had escaped death again, although this time on the ground.

He had led a flight of eight Avengers two hundred thirty miles northwest toward Bougainville, but they found no Japanese warships coming down the Groove. Swede's backup orders were to bomb the new Japanese ground installations near Cape Esperance.

In near total darkness, Swede was unable to pinpoint any specific targets until the Japanese cooperated by sending up some antiaircraft fire, which allowed him and the others to strafe and bomb the gun positions.

After they returned to Henderson Field, Swede was visibly angry. He ordered several of the crews to remain behind while he reported the results of the strike. When he came back, Swede declared that a number of the gunners were not carrying their weight.

He focused his attention on Red Doggett's crew, and demanded to know whether they had strafed the target area after the bombs were dropped. J. D. Hayes, Doggett's tail gunner, spoke up, saying that he had. Swede called him a liar.

J. D. Hayes was just over five feet tall. Since the *Saratoga* had been torpedoed, he had tried to grow a piratical beard to make himself appear a bit more menacing. Swede didn't like beards. After continuing to ream Hayes out in front of the others, Swede ordered him to shave off the beard. He was walking away when the little gunner pulled his forty-five from his hip holster and raised it toward Swede's disappearing back.

Red Doggett was standing next to him, and shoved Hayes to the ground. If Swede heard the scuffle taking place behind him, he never turned around. The men who were there all wondered what punishment Hayes would receive for pulling the gun on him, but no charges were filed, and he remained on active flight status. He didn't shave his beard, either.

## MONDAY, 28 SEPTEMBER 1942
## GUADALCANAL
## TORPEDO SQUADRON EIGHT

There was no other way to describe it. Over the previous three days, General Vandegrift's Marines had taken a brutal beating from the Japanese. Their losses in killed alone had exceeded those in the two nights of desperate fighting on Edson's Ridge.

It had come at the hands of the survivors of the Kawaguchi force that the Marines had crushed two weeks earlier. Somehow, the survivors had managed to regroup to the west of the Marine defense perimeter near the Matanikau River. Seeking to expel them, Vandegrift had sent a battalion of nine hundred men from the newly arrived 7th Marines to confront the Japanese. In a fierce firefight, the Marines had been repulsed.

Vandegrift had then ordered Edson's Raider battalion to buttress the next advance. As the Marines went forward in another costly and unsuccessful assault, the Japanese air force attacked Henderson Field with fifty-six fighters and bombers from Rabaul. Although the Wildcats shot down three of them, two of Swede's Avengers were badly damaged on the ground.

Swede radioed Espiritu Santo for Harwood to bring up more planes. On the afternoon of the twenty-eighth, four more Avengers arrived. They were piloted by Bruce Harwood, Aaron Katz, Andy Divine, and Bob Ries.

As part of a rotation plan to make sure that the pilots and crews remained fit and ready for combat, Swede headed back to Espiritu Santo with Jack Barnum, Gene Hanson, and Bert Earnest.

**THURSDAY, 1 OCTOBER 1942**
**GUADALCANAL**
**TORPEDO SQUADRON EIGHT**
**0930**

Smiley Morgan was sitting in the squadron's ready tent on Pagoda Hill listening to the rain drumming hard on its canvas roof when a pilot rushed in to say he had just seen Admiral Chester Nimitz going into the Pagoda.

At first, the rest of them were skeptical. What would the most powerful American naval officer in the Pacific be doing there? But Smiley and the other pilots were watching from the tent when Nimitz walked back outside with General Vandegrift.

For a few moments, it looked like the two commanders might make the rounds of the ready tents. Smiley wondered what he would say if the admiral asked him how he thought the war was going. He never got the chance. Instead, the commanders got into their jeeps and drove away.

Along with the others, Smiley wondered what the admiral's visit might mean, or at least how it would affect their own lives in the days ahead. Clearly, something big was coming. The word was that the enemy was landing a thousand men at Cape Esperance every night. Smiley had flown two bombing attacks on the Japanese positions out there, but it had been so dark he wasn't sure he had hit anything.

The heavy rains finally started to slacken later that morning. By early afternoon, the runway began to dry out, and Bruce Harwood told the pilots that he would be leading a flight of five Avengers up the Groove to search for Japanese warships. Bill Dye, Bob Ries, Andy Divine, and a replacement pilot named Larry Engel would be going with him.

They took off at 1815, and headed north. Visibility was good under the scattered clouds as darkness fell. For more than an hour, they searched the waters northwest of Guadalcanal without sighting anything. Then one of the pilots spotted some white wakes on the black sea. He counted four warships, all destroyers, heading for Guadalcanal.

With the destroyers sending up a continuous screen of antiaircraft fire, Harwood radioed that they would go after the two leading destroyers. Harwood, Ries, and Dye would attack the first one, Divine and Engel the second.

Harwood saw Ries's torpedo explode against the starboard side of the first destroyer, sending a column of flame into the night sky. The ship was listing badly in the water as the pilots made their escape in the black night.

FRIDAY, 2 OCTOBER 1942
GUADALCANAL
TORPEDO SQUADRON EIGHT

While Harwood was leading his attack on the Japanese destroyers, Fred Mears had arrived at Henderson Field to rejoin the squadron after hitching a ride from Espiritu Santo on a B-17.

He was relaxing in his tent with Aaron Katz when a downcast Bob Ries came through the opening and told them that Bill Dye, Larry Engel, and Andy Divine had gone missing and were presumed lost on the mission they had just flown.

No one had seen or heard from them after the attack on the destroyers. As Mears and Ries discussed the crews' chances of survival, Japanese planes arrived over the field to drop flares in advance of another shelling attack. By now, Fred prided himself on being able to detect the first flash of an exploding shell, and reach his sandbag-protected foxhole before the next one hit. No one got much sleep again.

At dawn, Mears, Katz, and Ries took off to search the coast around Guadalcanal for the missing Avengers. In a three-hour flight, they spotted the wrecks of more than a dozen aircraft that had been shot down or crashed on the beaches, but found no trace of the lost pilots and crews.

They had just landed back at Henderson Field when the sound of an air-raid siren signaled another enemy air attack. Instead of their slower-moving bombers escorted by Zeroes, this time the Japanese had sent thirty-six Zeroes to fight a duel for air supremacy with the Marine and Navy fighters. Thirty-six Wildcats were scrambled to meet the incoming threat.

The Wildcats were at an immediate height disadvantage and the Japanese shot six of them down, as well as two Dauntlesses that were returning to Guadalcanal from a bombing mission. One Japanese Zero was destroyed.

### SARO ISLAND
### NEWTON DELCHAMPS

Del Delchamps, Jim McNamara, and Bill Dye drifted along in the sullen gray sea, wondering exactly where they were. After losing his way back to Henderson Field in the darkness the night before, Bill had been forced to ditch their Avenger in the sea before it ran out of gas.

As the plane came to a stop, Del and Jim McNamara climbed out onto the wings to retrieve the life raft. There was an access hatch on both sides of the fuselage. In a comedy of errors, the two teenagers began pulling on it from opposite directions. When they finally got the raft out, it wouldn't inflate. By then, the plane had sunk and they were treading water in the sea. Dye used an air pump to fill two of the chambers, and the three of them crawled into the raft.

The rain was coming down so heavily that two of them were forced to keep bailing with their bare hands. Since the raft kept leaking air, the third man pushed the hand pump. By dawn, they were exhausted.

At dawn, Dye could see the dark outline of a landmass through the rain. They slowly drifted toward it for most of the day. Del was the first to spot the speck on the gray horizon. As it slowly came closer through the rain, he could see it was a ship. It was too far away to tell if it was American or Japanese.

They had already heard plenty of stories about how the Japanese treated prisoners. All three of them were carrying forty-fives. After a brief discussion, they agreed to go down fighting.

For Del, the next twenty minutes were the most nerve-racking of his short life. From its forward silhouette, Dye finally decided it was a destroyer. As it came closer through the driving rain, the ship suddenly turned and they could see a red, white, and blue flag whipping on its fantail.

Bill Dye fired a flare in the air, then a second one. The ship turned again and came toward them. It was the USS *Grayson,* the same destroyer that had stood alongside the *Saratoga* to remove the support personnel of Torpedo Eight after the torpedo struck her.

When the three of them were aboard, they learned that Andy Divine, Larry Engel, and their crews had been picked up, too. The captain told them he would radio Guadalcanal that they were safe, and apologized for the fact that he would be unable to drop them back at Espiritu Santo for a while. Del didn't mind. He was enjoying the best chow he had had in weeks.

SATURDAY, 3 OCTOBER 1942
GUADALCANAL
TORPEDO SQUADRON EIGHT
0030

The nightly Japanese bombing and shelling attacks on Henderson Field usually didn't cause a serious loss of life, but no one could predict where they would land. A direct hit was fatal. The pilots and crews had learned it was better to be safe than sorry.

Pete Peterkin always made a point of scouting out a deep hole before it got dark. One afternoon he found a big crater made by a Japanese bomb that looked perfect. As soon as the nightly attack began, he ran and dove into it as the bombs started falling. He regained consciousness a few minutes later. A bulldozer driver had filled the hole earlier that evening.

Many of the men went to sleep wearing their shoes. They didn't want to have to search for them before running to their foxholes. The only shoes Smiley Morgan had brought with him were high-tops.

They were big and cumbersome. That night he had taken them off before crawling under the mosquito netting.

When the attack started, he was out of the tent and streaking toward his foxhole before giving any thought to the fact that he was barefoot. He tripped over something sharp, and felt a jolt of pain. By the time he was ensconced in his foxhole, his foot was bleeding badly.

He wrapped a towel around it when he got back to the tent. In the morning, he removed the bloody towel and saw that he had a four-inch gash from the pad to the heel. He went limping off to find the Marine dispensary. At one of the encampments, he stopped to ask a fat, grizzled Marine sergeant wearing a T-shirt for directions.

The man looked familiar, and Smiley thought he probably worked over at the airfield. The Marine asked him what the problem was and Smiley showed him his foot. The Good Samaritan helped him over to the medical tent. As a corpsman took him inside, the fat Marine urged Smiley to "keep your pecker up."

"Thanks, Sarge," said Smiley.

While the corpsman was cleaning the wound, he asked Smiley what he and General Geiger had just been talking about, and Smiley realized why the old Marine had looked familiar.

After his foot was sewed up, the doctor told Smiley that because of the danger of infection, he was temporarily evacuating him. Later that day, Smiley flew out of Guadalcanal on a transport plane bound for Espiritu Santo.

As he was leaving, three more Avengers were arriving at Henderson Field. The new aircraft had been flown up from Espiritu Santo by John Taurman, Red Doggett, and another replacement pilot, Bill Esders. Esders was one of the two survivors from the *Yorktown* torpedo squadron that had attacked the Japanese fleet at Midway after Torpedo Eight was destroyed. He was greatly admired. For John Taurman, it was his first return to action since he had crash-landed off San Cristobal.

Pete Peterkin was particularly grateful for their arrival. Between the planes lost on various missions and the ones damaged and destroyed in the Japanese bombing attacks, the squadron was running out of planes.

At noon, forty-two Japanese aircraft attacked Henderson Field. Unlike the previous day, when they had brought only Zeroes, this time there were fifteen bombers along, too. Coast watchers had given Guadalcanal an early warning, and the Wildcats were ready. They had a field day. When the dogfight was over, nine Zeroes had been shot down.

Later that afternoon Fred Mears, Bob Evarts, and Bob Ries went out on a mission to search for a Japanese cruiser and two destroyers that had been sighted 150 miles northwest of Guadalcanal. They had closed on the reported location when Evarts spotted the ships in the distance. As the Avengers began circling to make their attack, Fred Mears's gunner, George Hicks, saw Japanese fighters zooming up.

When Fred made his glide-bombing run on the carrier, one of them came after him. Fred could feel the plane's vibration as Hicks opened fire with the fifty-caliber machine gun. A bit later, Hicks calmly announced over the intercom that he had shot the plane down.

Fred was making another bombing run when he felt a blow strike the plane from one of the ships' antiaircraft batteries. It felt as if a giant had slapped his tail. George Hicks's voice was suddenly on the intercom, telling him that their tail gunner was seriously wounded.

Fred set course for Guadalcanal and pushed the throttle to maximum speed. He radioed ahead that he had a wounded man aboard, and an ambulance was waiting for them when they landed forty minutes later. Warren Deitsch, the tail gunner, was unconscious when they pulled him out of the plane. Later, a surgeon told Fred that he had three pieces of shrapnel in his brain and was not expected to live.

Prior to the flight, Fred hadn't been able to find his flying gloves, and he had asked Warren if he had seen them. Deitsch asked him if he was superstitious about wearing gloves on a mission. Fred admitted he was. "Well, I'm not," said the tail gunner, giving him his own. Fred had the gloves on when Deitsch was hit.

MONDAY, 5 OCTOBER 1942
GUADALCANAL
TORPEDO SQUADRON EIGHT
0130

Shortly after midnight, Mears was smoking outside his tent when an enlisted man came looking for one of the other pilots. He said it was for a "secret mission." Intrigued, Fred decided to go in his place. He put on his khakis and joined Evarts, Taurman, and Ries for the briefing by Bruce Harwood.

Harwood told them they were going to make a dawn attack on a Japanese reconnaissance base at Rekata Bay, which was about 140 miles north of Guadalcanal at the tip of Santa Isabel Island.

The *Hornet* was coming in with its whole air group to launch an attack on Bougainville. The last American carrier in the South Pacific was hoping to catch a lot of Japanese ships at anchor there and sink them. Torpedo Eight's job was to keep the reconnaissance planes that flew out of Rekata Bay from finding the *Hornet,* and radioing its location to Rabaul.

The five Avengers took off in total darkness at 0300, and headed north. They quickly ran into bad weather, which turned into the most ferocious storm Fred had ever flown through. Harwood began flying on instruments. The other four flew on contact, which meant that each pilot had to stay close enough to the plane ahead of him to see its flaming exhaust in the black, turbulent sky. They soon lost sight of one another in the grip of the storm.

When Fred had flown far enough and long enough to reach the coast of Santa Isabel, he was unable to see anything. The rain and heavy mist descended all of the way to the surface of the sea. He had no idea what had happened to the others, or whether they had made it.

Only the importance of the mission kept him from heading back to Guadalcanal. Climbing higher through the storm, he decided to circle around until the first morning light. Aside from flashes of lightning, he had no further contact with light or substance for two hours.

When dawn broke, he descended through the clouds. A landmass slowly took shape below him. He hoped it might be Santa Isabel, and after he flew along its northern coast for a while, the Japanese base finally emerged beneath the storm clouds in the distance. He told his crew to prepare for the attack.

One downed American plane was already burning in the sea as they came in. Up ahead, a Dauntless dive-bomber pilot was in the middle of his bombing run, and being pursued by a Japanese fighter. Fred called back to George Hicks and Ed Struble, his new tail gunner, to be ready for a fight.

As Fred was about to launch his bombs, a Japanese fighter attacked him from the left, raking the Avenger's fuselage and wings with machine gun fire. A Zero came up at him from below and to the right before opening fire.

A few seconds later, it was over. George Hicks had shot down the first fighter, and Struble had knocked down the Zero. On their way back to Guadalcanal, Fred discovered that his bombs hadn't released, but he decided it was a fair trade for two enemy planes.

After the long, arduous flight, all three men were pretty shaky when they reached the ground. Ed Struble, who didn't look old enough to have pulled the trigger on his machine gun, was apologetic about what he had done.

"Gee, Mr. Mears, I didn't mean to hit that plane," he said. "I just meant to scare him. But he just caught fire and blew all to pieces."

Putting on a stern face, Mears told Struble that "it would be all right this time."

General Geiger personally commended Harwood's pilots for making it to Rekata Bay through the storm. Fred was recommended for the Distinguished Flying Cross, while Hicks and Struble were put in for Air Medals.

The strikes on Bougainville by the eighty-six planes from the *Hornet* air group were marginally successful. After braving the same violent storm that had bedeviled Torpedo Eight, the *Hornet* fliers had found cruisers, destroyers, and transport vessels in the harbor, but succeeded in making hits on only two cargo ships and a seaplane tender.

TUESDAY, 6 OCTOBER 1942
GUADALCANAL
TORPEDO SQUADRON EIGHT
1800

General Vandegrift continued to receive daily reports that the Japanese were being reinforced with troops, field guns, ammunition, and supplies. The possibility of their bringing heavy artillery ashore, including 150-millimeter howitzers that could pound Henderson Field from several miles away, was particularly alarming.

General Geiger ordered another attack on the Japanese landing areas at Cape Esperance as soon as possible. John Taurman, Red Doggett, and Bill Esders were chosen to make it.

Later that night, they took off in fifteen-second intervals, circled the field, and headed north in single file. The flight distance was only twenty miles, but with low cloud cover and overcast skies, visibility was nonexistent. Each pilot followed the exhaust flame of the man ahead.

Pete Peterkin had already written about the depths of the Guadalcanal darkness in his journal. "It is impossible to believe how black the nights can be in these islands," he wrote. "Darkness closes in so tightly that it is almost suffocating."

When the three Avengers arrived over Cape Esperance, the pilots made their bombing runs at less than a thousand feet, hoping to drop the payloads where they would do the most good. As Esders pulled out of his run, a huge explosion lit up the area behind him. Apparently, he had hit an ammunition dump. The other pilots dropped their bombs in close proximity to it, and made their escape.

The black night closed in again as they headed for home. Esders and Doggett were flying together on a southerly course when Red radioed to say that he couldn't see a thing and was going to drop lower to regain his bearings.

He had already begun shedding altitude when Esders suddenly saw the glowing reflection of his exhaust flame on the surface of the ocean and realized they were already too low.

Esders was calling Doggett on the radio when Red's Avenger slammed into the ocean, careened upward about a hundred feet into the air, and then spun back down again into the dark sea.

Esders circled the area, waiting for a flare or other signal that the crew might still be alive. There was none. Doggett was dead, as were his two crewmen, Charlie Lawrence and J. D. Hayes, the little tail gunner who had pulled his forty-five on Swede Larsen less than two weeks earlier.

After his own bombing run, John Taurman became separated from the rest of the flight, and tried to make it back to Henderson Field alone. Aside from his compass, he had no navigational instruments to find his way.

Pete Peterkin was in the Pagoda when Taurman's voice came over the radio and Bruce Harwood tried to talk him home. Not knowing where Taurman was, there was no easy way to vector him back to the field.

Harwood had the airfield searchlights turned on and aimed in different directions, but Taurman couldn't see the lights from wherever he was. Harwood then decided to take off in his own Avenger to find him and lead him back to the field.

With Harwood in the air, Peterkin continued to talk to Taurman on the radio. Then radar operators picked up a Japanese air attack coming in toward the field. The searchlights were turned off, and Peterkin was forced to shut down radio communication until the Japanese were gone.

By the time Pete was able to reach Taurman again, Harwood had landed back at the field. Taurman had been in the air for five hours, and he sounded subdued. His voice was down to a whisper. At that point, he knew he was over the ocean, and thought he was near the southern coast of Guadalcanal.

In his last radio transmission at around 0315, he told Pete Peterkin that he was running out of gas and going to land in the water. He had experience doing that, he joked, so they should be all right.

At dawn, search planes went out looking for him and his crew, but found nothing. No word was received until a few days later when a member of Taurman's crew emerged from a native village to relate what had happened.

Taurman had put the Avenger down safely in the sea. He and his two crewmen, Russ Bradley and Johnny Robak, had inflated the raft and climbed aboard. As dawn approached, they heard a plane overhead and Robak, the radioman–tail gunner, attempted to fire a flare to reveal their position.

The flare gun discharged while pointed downward, putting a big hole in the raft and injuring Robak. When dawn broke, they found themselves two miles from shore. Bradley suggested that he swim in and send back help. Taurman, who was a strong swimmer himself, said he would stay with the injured Robak, who didn't know how.

That was the last time Bradley saw them. When he finally made it to shore, he fainted from exhaustion. By the time he got to a native village and they sent out canoes to search for the others, no trace of Taurman or Robak was found.

The other pilots were deeply saddened when the news arrived. John could have been back in the States on survivor's leave, and married to his girl, Peggy. Instead, he had chosen to stay with the squadron and had paid for it with his life.

Gene Hanson wrote a letter to Taurman's mother.

> *Somehow, in my own mind, I refuse to believe that John is lost. . . . I know that nothing I can say will alleviate your great anxiety and sorrow. But I share your loss as though John were my own brother. Having flown with him for almost a year, he is one of the greatest guys I have ever known or can ever hope to meet.*

THURSDAY, 8 OCTOBER 1942
GUADALCANAL
TORPEDO SQUADRON EIGHT
1700

At Espiritu Santo, Swede was recovering from a bout of dengue fever. It had kept him bedridden for days, but after receiving the report of the squadron's latest losses, he decided to fly back up to Guadalcanal immediately. Two replacement aircraft were ready to go. He told Bert Earnest to pack his gear. He would fly the second plane.

When they arrived at Henderson Field, Swede went up to the Pagoda to check in with the air staff. The message he received was clear. Their top priority was to sink the Japanese warships still bringing reinforcements down from Rabaul.

They also told Swede that General Vandegrift was planning to personally reward the next Avenger or Dauntless pilot who made a direct hit on an enemy ship with a Japanese ceremonial sword taken from the body of an officer killed during the Battle of Edson's Ridge.

That afternoon in the ready tent, Swede briefed the pilots going out with him. Along with the four Avengers, the group would include seven Dauntlesses and eleven Wildcat fighters. Flying with Swede were Bert Earnest, Fred Mears, and Aaron Katz.

It was the first time Swede had flown a combat mission with Katz, and he took the opportunity to needle him right up to takeoff. With everything they might be facing over the next few hours, it made no sense. Baiting Katz certainly wouldn't increase his confidence. Fred Mears concluded that his tent mate was Swede's anathema.

It was approaching dusk when the air group took off and headed northwest.

The Japanese warships were almost exactly where Geiger's air staff had plotted them to be. Coming up from the southeast, Swede saw the flotilla spread out in an open horseshoe configuration, with four destroyers surrounding what appeared to be a heavy cruiser.

As the dive-bombers began making their runs, Swede brought the Avengers in low to make their attack on the cruiser's port bow. In order to reach the bigger ship, they had to go through a screen of destroyers that were already throwing up heavy antiaircraft fire.

The cruiser was emerging from a thick smoke screen as Fred Mears came in for his approach. With his usual sense of detachment, he thought it looked like a dragon coming out of its cave. The antiaircraft fire the dragon was sending toward him was the most intense he had ever experienced.

Fred suddenly heard four sharp reports as machine gun bullets flashed by the cockpit. Then he launched his torpedo and took off with the throttle shoved wide open. Bert Earnest had followed him down. He waited to launch his torpedo until the side of the ship filled the cockpit windshield. Swerving away, he shoved his own throttle forward and escaped south. Together, he and Fred returned to Guadalcanal.

Back at Henderson Field, the pilots and crews assembled again to discuss the mission. Swede was livid at the lack of strafing fire. Turning to Katz, Swede demanded to know whether his crew had strafed. Katz's two gunners on the mission had been Bob Steele and Frank Balsley. Ordinarily in the turret, Frank had flown this mission as a tail gunner.

Balsley told Swede he hadn't strafed. Swede demanded to know why. Balsley explained that he hadn't been properly strapped in, and that because of Ensign Katz's good evasive maneuvers, he was bouncing all over the compartment.

"You're grounded," Swede told him.

*Grounded? That was a punishment?* Balsley wondered.

None of the dive-bombers on the mission had scored a hit. Three of the pilots agreed that Bert's torpedo had slammed into the side of the cruiser and exploded. Swede gave him credit for the hit and told Bert to go to General Vandegrift's command post to receive his reward.

Walking over, Bert felt as tired as he had ever been in his life. When he got there, they seemed to be expecting him. A colonel came up to shake his hand. Somehow, the colonel knew that Bert had gone to VMI, and said that he had gone there, too. Then he was being walked over to General Vandegrift, who was talking to several other members of his staff.

When they were introduced, the general smiled up at him, shook his hand, and said he appreciated what Bert had done in slowing down the Tokyo Express. Bert wasn't really sure whether his torpedo had exploded. All he knew was that he had lined up the approach pretty well and had made a good run.

The general proposed a toast to celebrate the hit. For the first time, Bert noticed a bottle of scotch whiskey on the table behind the general, along with some tin mugs. The general poured a small splash of the whiskey into each one and passed the mugs around to the officers. When everyone had one, he congratulated Bert again, and they all drank.

*This isn't half bad,* thought Bert. *I could do that again.* But the general didn't offer him a refill. Instead, he put down his mug, picked up a sword from the table, and handed it to Bert. "You earned this," he said.

The sword was a beauty. It was nothing like the ones the guys had bought as souvenirs after the September battles. This one was covered with medieval-looking mesh over the handle to protect the warrior's hand. The scabbard was made of polished leather, and there were shark's teeth embedded in the grip along with little hand-carved rosettes like chrysanthemums.

Someone had told the general that Bert had gone to VMI. "You know," he said, "my son went there, too." Bert remembered him. The general's son had been a first classman when Bert had been a rat.

"Keep up the good work," said General Vandegrift. Bert promised he would.

### SATURDAY, 10 OCTOBER 1942
### GUADALCANAL
### TORPEDO SQUADRON EIGHT

The squadron was now down to four planes. They had started out with eighteen. There were two left at Espiritu Santo. The rest were lying in the boneyard at the end of the runway, or scattered across the bottom of the sea. Swede had requested replacement planes, but there were none to be had.

On October 9, Swede radioed Gene Hanson and Jack Barnum to fly the last two Avengers to Henderson Field right away. That would give him six aircraft for what was shaping up to be the next big battle for control of the Eastern Solomons.

Later that day, he gathered his pilots in the ready tent to say that a big group of enemy warships had just been sighted coming down the Groove about a hundred seventy-five miles northwest of Guadalcanal. He told them that the Japanese were no longer waiting for darkness. They were coming down around the clock to put the last pieces in place for their upcoming offensive.

Torpedo Eight would be part of the largest strike group yet assembled from Henderson Field to go after the warships. It included fifteen Dauntlesses, twenty-three fighters, and all six of the remaining Avengers.

They took off at dawn and flew northwest. Near the island of New Georgia, the formation came up on a large enemy force. It included two light cruisers and four destroyers.

Their subsequent attack was an embarrassing failure. Although the Wildcats succeeded in shooting down four Japanese floatplanes that were flying high cover over the enemy task force, no hits were made on any of the warships in the ensuing dive-bombing attacks. After all the dive-bombers missed, Swede ordered the Avengers to launch their torpedoes against the port side of the first cruiser. When the ship suddenly turned to starboard, all of them missed, too.

One Dauntless and one fighter were lost in the strike.

SUNDAY, 11 OCTOBER 1942
GUADALCANAL
TORPEDO SQUADRON EIGHT

It was obvious to Pete Peterkin that the Guadalcanal campaign, or at least their part in it, would soon be coming to an end, one way or another. There were plenty of Dauntless and Wildcat squadrons at Henderson Field, but Torpedo Eight was the only torpedo squadron in the whole Cactus Air Force, and it was played out.

The remaining pilots were nearly spent, both physically and emotionally, after a month of air combat interspersed with the nervous strain of the nightly bombings and shellings. After taking daily doses of Atabrine to prevent malaria, their eyes had turned yellow, followed by their skin. Half of them were suffering from dysentery or ringworm, and from recurrent fevers.

The ground personnel weren't in much better shape. Although they didn't have to fly missions almost every night, the crews had worked around the clock to keep the battered Avengers in the air after they came back from missions with cannon holes in the wings and tails, with the radio or the hydraulics shot up, or with their instruments no longer working.

Swede had a simple policy when it came to a plane's airworthiness. He told Peterkin that if the engine was working and the controls weren't shot away, mark it "up," or available for a mission. That was becoming increasingly hard to do.

General Geiger's staff believed that October 11 would mark the beginning of the long-awaited Japanese offensive to wrest control of the Guadalcanal airfield from the Americans. All of their intelligence pointed to a powerful combination of land, sea, and airpower.

At around midday on the eleventh, the largest concentration of Japanese attack planes to ever hit Henderson Field came over the field in two waves of ninety aircraft. Coast watchers had failed to give early warning of their arrival, and the Wildcats were late in scrambling to intercept them. Fortunately, low cloud cover kept the enemy bombers from giving the field a devastating blow.

The first phase of the ground campaign began that day, too, with the Japanese occupying positions near the Matanikau River, from which they could launch artillery strikes on Henderson Field.

That night, the Japanese navy set in motion two operations designed to further support the upcoming ground offensive. In the first operation, they dispatched two seaplane carriers escorted by six destroyers to deliver another large contingent of troops along with howitzers, artillery pieces, antiaircraft guns, ammunition, and food supplies.

In the second operation, they sent three heavy cruisers and two destroyers to deliver a late-night shelling attack on Henderson Field, using shells with fuses designed to spray a lethal rain of shrapnel in every direction.

The American Navy, which had been reluctant to commit its depleted forces after the loss of the *Wasp*, decided to counter the nightly attacks. Gambling that the Japanese wouldn't be expecting them, they dispatched a task force of five cruisers and four destroyers to ambush the Tokyo Express.

The first Japanese operation went forward unhindered. Its task force's vital cargo of men and equipment was unloaded without incident near Cape Esperance. Shortly after midnight, the second Japanese task force arrived off Savo Island. It headed down Sealark Channel to begin its bombardment of Henderson Field.

The American cruisers and destroyers were waiting for them.

The battle lasted only thirty minutes. Firing salvo after salvo from their heavy gun batteries, the American cruisers delivered a rain of fire on the completely surprised Japanese.

Lying in his tent, Pete Peterkin heard the distant blasts, and ran down to the beach. At Lunga Point, he watched the continuous explosions of naval gunfire light up the sky near Savo Island.

When it was over, one Japanese cruiser was on the bottom of Iron Bottom Sound along with one destroyer. Two American cruisers and one destroyer had absorbed damage. One destroyer was lost.

The Japanese task force turned back without accomplishing its mission.

MONDAY, 12 OCTOBER 1942
GUADALCANAL
TORPEDO SQUADRON EIGHT
0600

Early the next morning, Swede said they were going out again, heading up the Groove to knock off more Japanese warships. Along with their six Avengers, the strike force would include seven Dauntlesses and fourteen Wildcats.

In addition to Swede, the pilots selected to go were Bert Earnest, Fred Mears, Gene Hanson, Bob Evarts, and Aaron Katz. Machinist's Mate Frank Balsley had been reinstated to duty after Swede grounded him, and was flying as Katz's turret gunner.

The strike group took off from Henderson Field shortly before 0630. As they passed over Savo Island, the pilots and crews could see oil slicks in the water from the ships that had been sunk in the previous night's battle, as well as a debris field full of bodies floating in brightly colored life vests.

The formation flew two hundred miles northwest under a clear blue sky. As they neared the southern coast of New Georgia, one of the pilots spotted two enemy warships. They were heading north away from Guadalcanal, and traveling at flank speed.

The fighters went down to strafe the ships' antiaircraft batteries to suppress their fire. Then the Dauntlesses nosed over and made their bombing runs, scoring several near misses.

Swede led his six Avengers down to their attacking altitude of two hundred feet. Splitting up, they bored in on the same ship from both port and starboard. If the fighters had suppressed the level of the enemy antiaircraft fire, it wasn't apparent to the Avenger pilots. They all began taking hits as they came within range of the naval guns.

Aaron Katz was flying on Gene Hanson's wing. They would be launching their torpedoes from the port side. Aaron suddenly heard a loud bang in the nose of his plane. Glancing at his instruments, he saw that his oil pressure was dropping. One of the cannon rounds had hit his engine. He immediately radioed Swede to report it.

Katz thought about breaking off the attack, and heading back to Guadalcanal. If he continued losing oil and his engine seized up while he was going in at an altitude of two hundred feet, they wouldn't have a chance. Even if they survived a ditching, the whole area around New Georgia was enemy-held.

He was still trying to make up his mind what to do when Gene Hanson turned away to make his attack. Aaron decided to follow him. His engine never faltered. It turned out to be a good run, maybe the best he had ever made, and he fired his torpedo at a distance of about seven hundred yards.

Still following Hanson, he swung the plane into a tight turn and tore away from the enemy ship. In the turret, Frank Balsley made certain he strafed the decks of the ship with his fifty-caliber machine gun as it receded into the distance.

Bert Earnest was looking back at the Japanese ship when he saw a torpedo explode against its port side. It was the first one he had seen actually detonate after striking the target.

"It's a hit," someone yelled on the radio. "She's coming to a stop."

Either Gene Hanson or Aaron Katz had put the torpedo into the ship, which was now dead in the water. To Aaron, it didn't matter either way. He was just grateful that the plane's oil pressure was holding steady.

The six Avengers made it back to Henderson Field about an hour later.

When they landed, Pete Peterkin checked out all of the planes with Chief Hammond. Five out of the six were in no condition to fly again, even by Swede's standards. They had been hit with dozens of rounds of machine gun bullets, piercing the wings, fuselages, and internal systems. It had been a miracle no one was wounded. Katz's plane was in the worst shape. His Avenger had absorbed a twenty-millimeter cannon round in the engine. It was still lodged inside.

Swede came over to Hanson and Katz to confirm that one of their torpedoes had made the direct hit. It was impossible to know for sure which one it had been, he said, so they would share the credit in his report. He solemnly shook both their hands.

### 1500

Swede spent the rest of the day brooding before he finally exploded. The eruption came in the squadron's ready tent on Pagoda Hill. Relaxing with the other pilots, Bert Earnest thought Larsen had gone nuts.

"We're going back for that cruiser," he suddenly bellowed at them.

After the ship had been torpedoed by Katz or Hanson, Swede had radioed the others that he wanted to stay and see it sink. Finally, Lieutenant Commander Kirn, who had been commanding the mission, told him it was time to go, particularly with so many of his planes shot up.

"Sink, you bastard!" Swede had yelled into the radio.

Back on the ground at Henderson Field, he couldn't let it go. As the hours passed, the thought of the ship sitting up there with the Japanese probably working to save it pushed him over the edge.

He angrily announced in the ready tent that they were going back up there to finish the job. Pete Peterkin was forced to tell him that five of the six Avengers were out of commission. Only one plane was in flying condition.

Swede ordered it to be armed with a torpedo. Later in the afternoon, he heard that a flight of five P-39 Airacobra fighters and eleven dive-bombers was heading up the Groove in the same direction. Taking the one undamaged Avenger, Swede tagged along.

When they arrived over the site of the morning attack, the warship was lying dead in the water exactly where Swede had left it. Three destroyers were circling the stricken vessel.

Swede did not care about the other ships. He only wanted to finish the cruiser. He radioed a request to the leader of the five Airacobra fighters that they make a strafing run with their machine guns to suppress antiaircraft fire while he went in low to launch his torpedo.

They were about to make a strafing run in support of the dive-bombers on one of the other ships, and moved off. Swede kept pleading on the radio for them to come back, but they never responded. As Swede angrily maneuvered his plane into position for the attack, he accidentally triggered the torpedo release, sending it harmlessly off in the wrong direction. It made him apoplectic.

"The cruiser," Swede called out to the dive-bombers. "Get the goddamn cruiser."

He watched as the rest of them pummeled one of the destroyers, which quickly sank. When Swede finally swung away to fly back to Guadalcanal, the ship was still floating calmly in the sea.

In truth, the Japanese never had a chance of saving it, with or without Swede. They had simply been rescuing the crew before it sank. By the time Swede reached Henderson Field again, the ship was at the bottom of Iron Bottom Sound.

The pilots in Torpedo Eight were convinced Swede had gone slaphappy.

Divine Fire

TUESDAY, 13 OCTOBER 1942
GUADALCANAL
TORPEDO SQUADRON EIGHT

No man who lived through the next twenty-four hours on Guadalcanal would ever forget them. The Japanese were prepared for the final showdown, and it started with another massive air strike on Henderson Field.

The first wave of forty-two attack planes arrived from Rabaul at around midday as a newly arrived convoy of American transports was in the process of unloading men and materiel. At that moment, they could not have been more vulnerable to a bombing attack.

The Japanese fighters and bombers ignored them.

In preparing for the upcoming offensive, their orders were to make the airfield inoperable, and they did their best to accomplish the task, destroying a B-17 and damaging twelve other aircraft, including four of Swede's Avengers, which were undergoing repairs. More important, one of the Japanese bombers made a direct hit on an aviation gas tank that held five thousand gallons of high-octane fuel. The resulting explosion could be heard over most of the island.

The next wave of Japanese planes, thirty-two Zeroes and bombers, arrived two hours later, and added to the day's damage total before returning to Rabaul. The Japanese lost only two Zeroes in the combined strikes.

Something even more threatening to Vandegrift's Marines was taking place at sea. A Dauntless dive-bomber flying a search pattern two hundred miles north of Cape Esperance came upon a large naval task force heading toward Guadalcanal. It was screened by eight destroyers. Behind the destroyers came six high-speed transports. The transports were carrying 4,500 Japanese troops, as well as more field guns, howitzers, tanks, antiaircraft guns, and ammunition.

The balance of forces on Guadalcanal was reaching another critical stage.

Pete Peterkin had been working all afternoon with Chief Hammond's mechanics to repair the four Avengers from the first bombing attack. Pete had taken a break to eat the afternoon meal in the mess tent when he suddenly heard an explosion on the airfield.

There were no planes overhead, and it was different than the loud *crump* of a bomb. He had plenty of experience with falling bombs. They made the earth tremble. This explosion didn't. A few moments later, there was another sharp blast, followed by yet a third. This one was definitely closer.

"Incoming artillery," someone shouted and they all headed for a nearby slit trench.

What Vandegrift feared most had come to pass. The Japanese had brought ashore 150-millimeter howitzers to shell Henderson Field, and the Marines had no long-range guns to hit back at them.

Vandegrift thought the artillery barrage might portend a full-scale ground attack. As night fell, he ordered a general alert. Around the twelve-mile defensive perimeter, sweating Marines waited in the darkness.

No attack came, but later that night a formation of Japanese aircraft came over, dropping bombs near the airfield and again sending the pilots and flight crews rushing to their foxholes. When the all-clear siren sounded, they wearily trudged back to their tents.

At 0130, a red flare ignited in the sky over the western edge of Henderson Field. A few seconds later, a white flare went off over the Pagoda, followed by a green flare over the eastern end of the runway.

The multicolored flares had been dropped by Japanese planes to provide the initial aiming points for the battleships steaming slowly down Sealark Channel less than a mile offshore. Admiral Yamamoto had sent two of the most powerful ships in the Japanese navy, the *Kongo* and the *Haruna*, both named after Japanese mountains, to eradicate the so-called Cactus Air Force once and for all.

The worn-out pilots and crews in the coconut grove slept straight through the flares. Suddenly, star shells began bursting over the airfield, bathing the encampment in an eerie light. That woke them up fast.

The star shells were followed by the first salvo of sixteen big guns from the battleships. Each of the gun barrels was fourteen inches in diameter. Each shell weighed more than thirteen hundred pounds.

Once the bombardment was under way, Japanese artillery spotters on Mount Austen helped to direct their fire. With almost clinical precision, the two battleships began walking barrages back and forth across the runway and dispersal areas containing the American aircraft and their support facilities. They moved on to the personnel encampments concealed in the coconut groves.

As Pete Peterkin heard the first salvo whistling toward them, he raced from his tent to an underground shelter. At least twenty men joined him there, including many of Torpedo Eight's support personnel. The dugout was about sixteen feet square, with a sandbagged roof of tree trunks reinforced with iron pipes. Peterkin had felt safe there under the past shellings. Crouching next to the others, he sensed that this one was different.

These explosions were of a totally different magnitude than what the men had become used to in the previous weeks. Like falling bombs, these shells not only made the ground tremble, but stirred the air in the dugout with black dust. In the past, the airfield had received the brunt of the shelling. These shells were hitting all over their encampment, too.

He could hear loud *crack-crack*s as the tops of palm trees above the dugout were severed from their trunks. They fell to the ground with resounding thuds. The men around Peterkin remained silent for the first fifteen minutes. However, unlike past attacks, the earsplitting noise and constant ground tremors never stopped. After half an hour with no letup in the bombardment, several men began weeping uncontrollably. One became hysterical and had to be subdued.

Bert Earnest had been lying in his tent when the first salvo of shells came in over the coconut grove. Glancing around in the sudden daylight, he saw Jack Barnum lying asleep in the other cot.

As Bert watched, two rats leaped from the ground onto Jack's cot and began frantically climbing his mosquito netting. Barnum, who hated rats, woke to them clawing wildly above his face and chest. Bert and Jack were both scrambling through the tent opening a few seconds later.

Earlier that morning, Bert had observed one of the other officers digging a foxhole between their tents. As the man worked and sweated under the sun to shovel out the dry, dusty soil, Bert had laughed at him.

Now he headed straight for the hole. He found it unoccupied, probably because it was still only half-finished. Nevertheless, the shallow hole looked incredibly inviting as the tops of the coconut palms in the encampment began snapping off above him, hurtling down like battering rams.

When he landed stomach-first in the trench, he felt something squirm underneath him. It was another rat. He stood up long enough to hurl it away, and then dropped down again. Hugging the earth, he made himself as small as he could as the shells came thundering in like an approaching freight train. He could hear shrapnel splinters tearing through the cloth of the tent he had just vacated with Barnum.

It was no different for the general commanding all of the forces on Guadalcanal. Vandegrift was now huddled belowground in his own foxhole across the airfield. The fourteen-inch shells played no favorites with rank or age. They dealt death wherever they landed.

There was nothing Vandegrift could do but take it. He had no artillery that could reach the battleships and there were no American warships nearby to confront them at sea. Gerry Thomas was trying to make light of the situation, saying to Vandegrift at one point in the middle of a furious barrage, "I don't know how you feel, but I think I prefer a good bombing."

"I think I do . . . ," began Vandegrift, when the shrieking blast of a near direct hit drowned out all other sound. The concussion of the bursting shell knocked him off his feet, and he came to rest on the plank floor of the dugout, temporarily in shock.

Major Gordon Bell, the commander of one of the Dauntless squadrons, was in a dugout close by when it took a direct hit. He was killed along with the rest of his senior officers.

Fred Mears made it to his own foxhole before the first salvo hit. Wearing his blue-striped pajamas, he had also remembered to put on his steel helmet. There were already a number of men in the foxhole ahead of him, all pressed together as far away from the dugout's opening as possible.

Each salvo came over with its own shrieking scream. Looking up, he watched the sky above him turn garish orange as the shells exploded. The ensuing cracks of thunder sent shrapnel flying in every direction. Above the raw smell of newly dug earth, the distinctive odor of cordite filled his nose.

After one of the shells detonated close to their foxhole, he could feel the man crouched next to him begin to shake. It was contagious. At the far end of the dugout, another man was trying to burrow under the men next to him.

One of the squadron's chief petty officers was sharing Fred's hole. With each mind-boggling roar of sound, he kept calmly repeating the same three lines over and over.

"Hell's fire," he would say first. "Holy balls" would follow the next burst. "A red-ass mule" was his finisher.

Bob Ries was squatting near Fred. When they caught each other's eyes, one of them started giggling. The other joined in, unable to help himself. At one point, Ries was brazen enough to say, "Don't worry, they haven't got our range yet." A few moments later, a coconut palm fell on the entrance to the dugout with a crash.

Forty-five minutes after it began, the shelling came to a sudden stop.

Fred warily crawled out of his hole to see a landscape that was dramatically altered. Most of their tents were gone, and the ground was covered with a thick layer of palm fronds from the shattered trees that had once towered over them. The reek of cordite was almost overpowering.

Beyond the coconut grove, fires were raging all over the airfield. An exploding ammunition depot set off a spectacular light-and-sound show all on its own. Airplanes were blazing like torches at their dispersal points, and the flames from burning aviation gas reached hundreds of feet into the air.

Fred heard an engine start. Across the encampment, he saw some men climbing into the back of a truck. Calling out to Ries, he started running toward it. Judge Wendt, who had been wounded in the back by flying shrapnel, managed to climb aboard along with Bert Earnest, Aaron Katz, and Gene Hanson.

Dozens of men were converging on the truck from all directions, including Pete Peterkin and the men from his dugout. The driver told them he was going to try to make it to the beach, where there were several well-protected air-raid bunkers.

Thirty or forty men were already crammed into the back of the truck's freight bed. At least that many were still trying to crawl aboard, climbing on top of the layers of men already there.

Another pinwheel star shell suddenly lit up the sky over their heads. The two Japanese battleships had only stopped firing long enough to turn around before coming back up Sealark Channel to deliver the second round.

Men were screaming to make more room in the truck as they frantically tried to claw a place aboard. By then, others were clinging to the roof of the cab and the front hood.

Machinist's Mate Bill Magee had seen that it was useless to try to get in the back. He draped himself over the left front fender, with his face pressed against the engine cowling, and his hands clutching the front bumper. *Maybe this is dumb,* he thought as he hung there. *What if the driver hits a tree?*

Frank Balsley was hanging on to the side of the truck's freight bed when the driver put the transmission in gear and began driving down the rough, debris-strewn road toward the beach. Men who couldn't find places on the truck ran after it, begging him to stop. Their voices could barely be heard over the deafening noise of the shells.

For Fred Mears, it was the wildest ride of his life, at least sober. The driver couldn't use his lights for fear of attracting shell fire, but he was soon doing forty miles an hour. The truck careened along the rough track, pitching and rolling with its wriggling cargo like a boat in a heaving sea.

As they neared the beach, the men at the top of the pile looked out across Sealark Channel to see the Japanese battleships as their blazing gun batteries unleashed another barrage.

When the truck came to a stop, the men began running toward

the shelters on the beach. Gene Hanson saw what looked like a welcoming underground pit, and leaped into it along with several other men. It took them only moments to realize it was a latrine. They weren't complaining.

At around 0300, the shelling finally came to a stop.

The battleships had launched 973 rounds of fourteen-inch cannon shells into the American positions. Rarely in the history of warfare had so much naval gunfire been concentrated into so small an area over so short a time. Looking down from Mount Austen on the flaming conflagration, Japanese artillery spotters joyfully radioed that they were looking at "a sea of fire."

The Japanese weren't finished. For the rest of that night, enemy bombers came over in small clusters to bomb targets lit by the fires that burned out of control on the airfield.

At 0530, the big Japanese howitzers opened up again on Henderson Field from their positions west of the Matanikau River. With everything they had already gone through, most of the pilots and crews slept straight through it in their bunkers and foxholes.

At dawn, a weary Fred Mears emerged from one of the shelters on the beach wearing his filthy blue pajamas and steel helmet. Aaron Katz had a raincoat on with nothing underneath.

The truck that had brought them down to the beach pulled up an hour later and unloaded two jerry cans filled with hot, sweetened coffee. It tasted better than any java Fred had ever enjoyed in the finest homes of New Haven, San Francisco, or Seattle.

WEDNESDAY, 14 OCTOBER 1942
GUADALCANAL
TORPEDO SQUADRON EIGHT

The dog-tired pilots and crews of Torpedo Eight returned to their encampment in the coconut grove to find that little had survived the shelling undamaged. The once soaring palm trees above their tents had been cut off at a height of about thirty feet. The palm boughs that had provided them with shade from the sweltering sun now littered the compound.

After a brief search, Pete Peterkin found the place where his and Swede's tent had stood. Some of the spare parts for the Avengers he had kept in it were still there, but they were scattered all over the ground. His personal belongings had disappeared. The only thing he decided to keep as a souvenir was a six-inch-long piece of shrapnel that had impaled his pillow and pinned it to the ground.

Bert Earnest and Jack Barnum's tent was gone, too, although Bert found his small, green carry-on bag. His Japanese sword had been lying under his cot, and it was still there in the black soil, partially buried. Otherwise, the only item he recovered from his personal effects was a shredded page from a letter he had been writing to Jerry Jenkins at Smith College.

"It's really not so bad here, darling" was one of the few legible lines.

Fred Mears found his tent intact, although punctured with dozens of splinter holes. He took the time to exchange his pajamas for shredded khakis. Outside his tent opening, he found the butt plate of a Japanese cannon shell. It was fourteen inches in diameter. He could have eaten a prime rib dinner on it, with room for mashed potatoes and Yorkshire pudding.

Ski Kowalewski's tent was also relatively undamaged. Inside his seabag was the small pocket Bible he always carried. It was embedded with several pieces of shrapnel.

Judge Wendt had had hundreds of dollars stashed in the bottom of a bag in his tent. Unfortunately, the tent was gone, along with the bag. The only thing he found was a small scrap of a twenty-dollar bill.

After they had surveyed the damage, Chief J. C. Hammond and Pete Peterkin went down to the airfield to take a look at their airplanes. The first Avenger they came to was totally destroyed, nothing more than a fuselage without wings.

As he was looking at the metal shrapnel from the big round that had smashed the plane to pieces, Pete noticed something unusual. Several rounds had been been made up of iron radiator caps, some of them clearly identified with the markings of their American manufacturer. It was the end product of the United States having sold so much scrap iron to Japan before the war.

The remaining five Avengers were riddled with steel splinters that had severed hydraulic lines, electrical circuits, and control wires. Several of the wing sections were damaged beyond repair.

Swede's quest for vengeance was clearly going to be delayed for a while. After examining the planes, Chief Hammond didn't believe any of them could be made to fly again.

As far as the rest of the Cactus Air Force, its striking capacity was reduced to almost nothing. There had been thirty-nine Dauntless dive-bombers in the dispersal areas around the field before the shelling. Only seven could still fly. With the Avengers gone, those seven dive-bombers were all that was left to attack the Japanese warships or bomb the enemy's rapidly expanding ground positions on Guadalcanal.

Forty-one men in the vicinity of the airfield had been killed, with many more wounded. Vandegrift's main radio communications center had been demolished. The Pagoda was half-destroyed, and was soon bulldozed. Almost all of the aviation fuel not already destroyed in the earlier bombing raids had gone up in flames, along with most of the ammunition depots.

General Vandegrift radioed that it was "absolutely essential aviation gas flown here." There was no time to wait for its delivery by ship. The fate of the Americans at Guadalcanal hung in the balance.

The only good news in the wake of the shelling attack was that twenty-four of the forty-two fighter aircraft at Henderson Field had survived. Once their stocks of aviation gas were replenished, they would be able to continue the aerial fight against incoming Japanese fighters and bombers.

Shortly after midday, a wave of forty-four Japanese fighters and bombers came over to bomb the field. They were unmolested by the American fighters, and dropped their payloads on several dozen aircraft, although most of them were already wrecks. An hour later, a second wave of attackers came over to hit whatever was left standing. This time, a handful of fighters went up to meet them, shooting down four of the bombers.

Later that afternoon, Swede brought all of the pilots, crews, and support personnel in Torpedo Eight together at the airfield. He told them that the Japanese ground campaign was probably going to begin any time now, and that a naval invasion force might arrive that same night.

They had no planes left to fight the enemy in the air, he said. In the days ahead, many of the men in the squadron would probably be sent back to Espiritu Santo. He wasn't sure when that would happen because the transports were taking out the wounded first.

Swede told them he planned to stay behind with a complement of officers and men in the hope that they might soon get replacement aircraft. In the meantime, every man in the squadron would be issued a helmet, a Springfield rifle, and plenty of ammunition.

He would now lead the squadron up into the hills, he said, and offer their services to the Marines on the front lines. If worse came to worst, and the Japanese took the airfield, maybe they could escape by boat from the other side of the island.

Taking along whatever they still had, the men began walking toward the ridges south of Henderson Field. As he plodded along with the others, Fred Mears came to the conclusion that the whole thing was pretty hopeless. If the war depended on how well he could aim and fire a Springfield rifle, they were in a lot of trouble.

They were about five hundred yards from the outer line of the Marine defense perimeter when Pete Peterkin saw a Marine officer coming toward them carrying a Thompson submachine gun. The Marine asked who they were and where they were going.

Swede explained their situation and said they were hoping to dig in with the Marines somewhere along the line. The officer told them he would be delighted to have them bivouac with his company along the ridge. Within an hour, the enlisted men were constructing canvas-roofed shelters inside the perimeter of his camp. Several tents were erected for Swede and his officers next to the Marine officers' own command tent.

That evening at supper, they learned that their host was thirty-six-year-old Major Michael McGinnis Mahoney, a Marine who had served eighteen years in the Corps, rising in rank from private to major while fighting in the jungles of Nicaragua and the Philippines.

Now he was in command of a special weapons company in the 7th Marines, which had arrived almost a month earlier. Each night, Mahoney sent out his men in small scouting parties to patrol beyond the more lightly defended parts of the line along the Lunga River. They had succeeded in stopping several penetrations by Japanese night fighters.

The Yale-educated Peterkin found Mahoney to be an amazing character, someone largely self-taught, who had earned his college degree taking correspondence courses. He was both passionate and knowledgeable about poetry and sculpture, among other pursuits not shared by most Marines. At the same time, his admiring men affectionately referred to him as "Machine Gun" Mahoney for his prowess with the Thompson.

Aside from the major's remarkable personality, Fred Mears was impressed with Mahoney's talents in training his company cooks. The evening stew, fashioned with the same materials provided to other units, was incredibly good. Afterward, Mahoney shared his dwindling supply of cigars with them.

When he went to bed that night, Fred's confidence was restored. He no longer had any doubts that the Marines would hold the field, even when Japanese ships began shelling the airfield again later that night. None of the shells came remotely close to their new positions, and Fred had his first good night's sleep in weeks.

Out of the Ashes

THURSDAY, 15 OCTOBER 1942
GUADALCANAL
TORPEDO SQUADRON EIGHT

In the fullness of dawn, six Japanese transport ships steamed into Sealark Channel and began disembarking thousands of troops within plain sight of the Marine defensive positions northwest of Henderson Field. Flying low cover over the enemy transports were dozens of carrier-based Zeroes.

It was a brazen reflection of the Japanese certainty that the Cactus Air Force had been obliterated. They were close to being right. Only six Wildcat fighters could be sent up to confront the Zeroes, and that was only by scavenging fuel from damaged aircraft. One Zero was knocked down for the loss of one Wildcat.

Up in the hills south of the airfield, Pete Peterkin started his first morning at Major Mahoney's camp with a plate of hotcakes. They were the best he had ever tasted. After finishing his coffee in the mess tent, he got together with Chief Hammond to discuss the possibility of repairing one of the wrecked Avengers.

The two of them hiked down to the airfield to take another look at the planes, only to discover that the Cactus air staff had written them off in a report they were preparing for General Geiger. They told Peterkin and Hammond not to waste their time.

Hammond spent the rest of the morning crawling through the five Avengers, detailing each problem with Pete taking notes alongside him. When he was finished, Hammond said there was an outside chance he could rebuild one plane from the remains of the rest.

As soon as they reported back to Swede at Major Mahoney's camp, he wanted to know how long it would take them to do it. A couple of weeks, maybe, said Hammond, if he had enough men to help him. Swede told them he wanted the plane ready for him to fly by October 22, one week away.

Two of Torpedo Eight's air gunners, Judge Wendt and Bert Edmonds, volunteered to go out on a sniper patrol with some of the Marines in Major Mahoney's unit. They went off carrying their new Springfield rifles, forty-five-caliber pistols, extra ammunition, and hand grenades.

An hour into the patrol, the two fliers had fallen behind on the narrow trail when a single shot rang out ahead of them. Wendt and Edmonds scanned the dense canopy around them, but didn't see anything. After waiting for a minute or two, they slowly went forward on the trail.

A dead body was lying ahead of them. When they came up to it, Wendt saw that it was one of the young Marines who had been leading their patrol. Wendt had flown plenty of dangerous missions as Swede's turret gunner, but the sight of the dead Marine terrified him.

Firing back at a Zero that was attacking him with machine guns blazing was one thing. This was another. When the other Marines came back to pick up their dead comrade, Wendt and Edmonds went straight back to camp. It was their last patrol.

In the afternoon, twenty-four Japanese bombers protected by a cloud of Zeroes made several runs on Henderson Field, ripping up the metal matting on the runways and damaging more planes on the ground.

The Americans did give the Japanese one bloody nose that day. Someone remembered that there was a buried cache of fuel drums near the airfield, and the precious aviation gas was used to launch a flight of Dauntlesses. They went straight for the transport ships that had been unloading men and equipment near the defense perimeter. Although the transports had unloaded most of their cargo, the Dauntless pilots sank three of them before they could return to Rabaul.

That night, two heavy cruisers and a destroyer squadron arrived in Sealark Channel to pound Henderson Field again. More than twelve hundred shells landed on the airfield and its support facilities. When Geiger's staff did its daily count of available aircraft early the next morning, the Cactus Air Force could mount only nine Wildcats, eleven newly patched Dauntlesses, and seven P-39 fighters.

FRIDAY, 16 OCTOBER 1942
GUADALCANAL
TORPEDO SQUADRON EIGHT

The work to construct a Frankenstein Avenger began early that morning. After breakfast, Pete Peterkin and Chief Hammond led a detail of men back to Henderson Field to get started.

Hammond selected the plane he thought had sustained the least amount of overall damage, and made an evaluation of everything that needed to be replaced or repaired. Its huge Wright engine was nothing more than twisted steel, and they would need to exchange it with a relatively undamaged engine from one of the other hulks. Of greater magnitude was the job of replacing one of its wings. The equipment needed to do both jobs had been destroyed.

While Chief Hammond considered those problems, mechanics began cannibalizing cockpit instruments, cables, hydraulic lines, and wiring from the planes that would never fly again.

Their work was hampered by the resumption of artillery fire from Japanese field guns to the west of the airfield. A few came uncomfortably close. At first, the men would run to a shelter whenever an incoming round whistled over. After noticing that Chief Hammond seemed oblivious to it, they tried to follow his example and keep working.

Later that morning, Pete Peterkin took a break from the work to say good-bye to the pilots of Torpedo Eight who were returning to Espiritu Santo. Bruce Harwood, Bob Evarts, Jack Barnum, Bob Ries, and Bill Esders were all leaving. Swede had ordered Gene Hanson, Bert Earnest, Fred Mears, and Aaron Katz to stay.

Katz was no longer the target of Swede's barbs. Perhaps it was because of his brave decision to make a low-level attack against the Japanese warship after his engine had been hit. Whatever the reason, Swede didn't bait him anymore.

A group of Torpedo Eight's enlisted personnel was also leaving that day aboard the destroyer *McFarland*, which had just arrived at Guadalcanal after bringing forty thousand gallons of aviation fuel to the beleaguered Cactus Air Force.

The destroyer would be heading back to Espiritu Santo as soon as its crew transferred the aviation fuel to an oil barge that was tethered alongside. While the crew pumped the gas to the barge through a fuel hose, the men from Torpedo Eight and the other squadrons were sent aboard.

Fourteen men were leaving from Torpedo Eight. Pete Peterkin shook hands with each one and wished him well before they boarded a Higgins boat for the ride out to the destroyer.

Once aboard ship, Bill Magee and Bert Edmonds, the young gunner in Harwood's crew who had accompanied Judge Wendt on the sniper patrol, found a place to sit together next to one of the iron bitts bolted to the deck. Ski Kowalewski found a place above decks next to the potato locker.

Walking back up the beach, Pete Peterkin was thinking that the men he had just seen off were damn lucky when he heard the sound of aircraft overhead. Nine enemy dive-bombers were nosing over to make bombing runs on the *McFarland*.

The *McFarland*'s crew had managed to transfer about half of the forty thousand gallons of gas to the barge. A crewman quickly used an ax to sever the fuel hose, and other sailors cut the lines tethering the vessels together.

As the *McFarland* picked up speed, the first bombs began to fall. Magee and Edmonds were sitting shoulder to shoulder. The last thing Magee remembered was Edmonds pointing up at an approaching bomber.

The first bomb landed directly on the oil barge, setting off an inferno and instantly cremating its crew of sailors and the Marines who were helping to transfer fuel. Another bomb fell on the fantail of the *McFarland*, detonating its rack of depth charges, and blowing the stern off the ship.

The intensity of the blast caused the bow of the destroyer to leap out of the water. Near the stern, a hailstorm of steel splinters killed twenty-seven men and wounded dozens more. Ski Kowalewski was one of the fortunate ones, protected from the blast by the potato locker.

When Bill Magee regained consciousness, he was lying on the deck of a PT boat. It was night. His chest hurt and he was hacking up blood. Someone came over to check on him, and Bill asked if he knew what had happened to his friend Edmonds.

The sailor didn't know, but said that they were headed for Tulagi, and maybe he would find him there. When they got to the island, Bill found out from one of the other men that Edmonds had been killed by flying shrapnel.

*Why him and not me?* wondered Magee.

WEDNESDAY, 21 OCTOBER 1942
GUADALCANAL
TORPEDO SQUADRON EIGHT

Swede had assigned eighteen men to build his new plane, and Hammond worked them in twelve-hour shifts. With the airfield blacked out at night, canvas tarps were draped over the Avenger, allowing mechanics with lanterns to continue working inside.

In just five days, the aircraft had been stripped of its damaged parts and put back together again with pieces from other planes. Pete Peterkin had found a Japanese truck with a hoisting apparatus mounted on its rear bed. The hoist was used to remove an undamaged Wright engine from one of the Avenger hulks and swung into position for the connection to be made to the engine housing of the new creation.

One of the plane's wings had been smashed. After they cut away what remained of it, Pete rounded up fifty Marines to lug a replacement wing from one of the wrecks and brace it in position while Hammond's mechanics fastened it to the wing root. The plane also needed a new tail, control wires, bomb release wiring, and a host of other components.

When, on the afternoon of October 21, Hammond announced that he was finished, he warned Swede that he didn't think the plane was safe to fly. Most of the instruments didn't work. The new wing was definitely out of kilter. It hung perceptibly lower than the other one, and he didn't have the tools to correct the problem.

Swede looked at the homely creation as if it were a golden chariot. "Don't worry," he told them. "I'll make the thing fly." When it was fueled and ready for a test flight late that afternoon, the engine ran fine.

After revving it to full throttle, Swede took off down the bomber strip. He climbed into the air long enough to set it down on the fighter strip at the other end of the field. Peterkin and Hammond followed him over in the Japanese truck.

The out-of-kilter wing definitely affected its performance in the air, Swede said, but he could adjust for it. Otherwise, the plane seemed fine. He told Peterkin and Hammond to prepare it for a bombing mission the next day.

Fred Mears had spent the day watching the aerial dogfights over the field between the Wildcats and the Zeroes. One of the encounters had been fought so low that he had to jump into a foxhole to avoid the machine gun fire.

Things were no less dramatic up at Major Mahoney's camp to the south of the field. At supper, Mahoney predicted that the all-out Japanese offensive would begin in a few days. There was no telling from which direction the Japanese might launch their assault, although it would definitely be delivered at night. General Vandegrift believed it would come from the west beyond the Matanikau River, where he thought the Japanese were mostly concentrated, but there was a chance Mahoney's unit might see action along their own southerly positions. Mahoney's only concern was that the defense line on the southern perimeter was stretched thin.

Torpedo Eight would do its share, Swede told him.

Early the next morning, he ordered the squadron's enlisted men to begin preparing foxholes along the Marine defensive line. When they finished digging the holes, he told them to bring up the thirty-caliber machine guns from the wrecked Avengers. Those would definitely give them a good edge.

Gene Hanson expressed the concern that all their machine gun ammunition had tracer rounds in its belts for use in aerial combat. Firing from their foxholes would immediately give away their positions. Swede told him not to worry about it.

**WEDNESDAY, 21 OCTOBER 1942**
**GUADALCANAL**
**JAPANESE SENDAI DIVISION**
**GENERAL MASAO MARUYAMA**

The Japanese were now poised to unleash their most ambitious attempt yet to retake Guadalcanal. Fully committed to the undertaking for the first time, the Japanese Imperial Army had chosen the Sendai Division to make the principal assault against the American Marines.

Also called the "Courageous Division," it had been trained under the stern, unyielding commander, General Masao Maruyama. One of the most storied units in the army, the Sendai Division had been formed in 1871. It had fought well in the Russo-Japanese War, and more recently in Manchuria and the Dutch East Indies. Maruyama's men had been trained to deal with privation, and particularly excelled at night fighting.

The division had been delivered at night by the destroyers and transports of the Tokyo Express. As they regrouped ashore, General Maruyama became concerned that they would be infected by what he viewed as the sense of defeatism displayed by the troops already there. "Do not expect to return to the homeland," he told them, "unless you are victorious."

On October 11, two of his division's staff officers were reconnoitering the American defense perimeter from the foothills of Mount Austen and spotted what they believed were undefended positions to the south of the airfield. The positions were almost directly in line with the ridges occupied by Major Mahoney's special weapons unit and other elements of the 7th Marines.

The observations of the Japanese staff officers led to a plan that called for a surprise night attack from the south. Nine battalions of the Sendai Division would roll over the lightly defended sectors near the Lunga River and then drive for the airfield. All they needed to do was capture it, after which reinforcements would immediately be flown in to consolidate their bridgehead.

Surprise was the key to the strategy, and so far, they had managed to achieve it. Their engineers had constructed a road through the jungle that would allow the Sendai Division to reach its staging area by October 22. In anticipation of the road's historic importance in the pantheon of great Japanese victories, it was named Maruyama Road after the division's commander.

General Harukichi Hyakutake, the newly arrived overall Japanese commander on Guadalcanal, issued an announcement. "The time of the decisive battle between Japan and the United States has come." His staff began to make preparations for accepting the American surrender.

By the twenty-first, the Japanese had amassed more than seventeen thousand troops on Guadalcanal for their final drive to retake the airfield. Although outnumbered by the more than twenty-two thousand Marines, they rivaled the Americans in effective strength. The freshly arrived Sendai Division was ready to go forward with unmatched zeal.

Vandegrift's Marines were not filled with unmatched zeal. Most of them had been on the island for two and a half months. They had fought two major battles and dozens of firefights and skirmishes in the sweltering heat and the putrid jungle. They had been subjected to constant shelling and aerial bombardment, poor food, bad water, jungle rot, dysentery, rat bites, snake bites, leeches, and trench foot. Many had refused to take Atabrine to prevent malaria because of rumors that the pills might make them sterile. Now many of them had contracted malaria.

The Japanese had another advantage. In addition to their massive infusion of troops, their navy had provided them with scores of field guns, 150-millimeter howitzers, heavy machine guns, heavy tanks, light tanks, and nearly two hundred tons of food, ammunition, and other supplies.

Most important, at the point of attack in their major ground assault, they would outnumber the Marines by a margin of about four to one.

THURSDAY, 22 OCTOBER 1942
GUADALCANAL
TORPEDO SQUADRON EIGHT
1350

Swede and his metal Frankenstein were ready for the squadron's first mission since October 12. In the previous week, the number of flyable Wildcat fighters had dropped to seventeen, and the Cactus Air Force was increasingly desperate for replacements.

Swede's Avenger had been loaded with twelve one-hundred-pound bombs, and the air staff had given Swede the coordinates of several suspected Japanese concentrations near Henderson Field.

Shortly after 1400, he accelerated down the runway and took off into a clear sky. From the air, the field was like an oasis in a sea of enemy-held jungle. One minute's flying time in any direction took them over Japanese positions.

Swede's turret gunner, Judge Wendt, looked for possible targets as they flew over the thick jungle canopy at an altitude of eight hundred feet. Wendt knew they had found a good place to bomb when antiaircraft fire began putting holes in the Avenger's newly replaced wing.

Swede swung around for a glide-bombing attack and then delivered a full salvo of twelve bombs on the spot where Judge Wendt had told him he had seen the enemy gun position. The resulting explosion set off several fires.

When they returned to the fighter strip, Chief Hammond expressed his worry about the shrapnel damage to the new wing structure. The wires and cables were all chewed up inside, he said. "Just make it fly," Swede told him.

By the time the Avenger had been loaded with another complement of bombs, Japanese artillery pieces had again begun raining shells down on the airfield, and flight operations were suspended.

Swede's next mission would have to wait until morning.

## JAPANESE SENDAI DIVISION
## GENERAL MASAO MARUYAMA

Maruyama had hoped to be in a position to launch his attack at precisely 1800 on the twenty-second, but his troops had become bogged down on the Maruyama Road over the previous four days. Calling it a "road" was a bitter exaggeration for the men who had to contend with its eighteen-mile length to the staging area. The road was nothing more than a narrow trail cut through jungle, swamps, and deep ravines, and barely wide enough for a man carrying a pack.

General Maruyama had decided he needed artillery support for his assault, and his staff ordered the men to dismantle the guns and hand carry them to the staging area. General Kawaguchi, who now commanded the right wing of Maruyama's force, found that he was encountering exactly the same difficulties that had led up to his own defeat on Edson's Ridge a month earlier. He did not want to be part of another defeat, and began expressing his concerns about the assault plan.

By the time Maruyama's men reached the staging areas for the assault, it was already evening, and too late for them to make a coordinated attack. Recognizing that he needed more time to properly organize the two wings of his force, General Maruyama postponed his assault until the following night.

At dawn, the Japanese resumed their artillery bombardment of Henderson Field. Later that morning, a flight of American transports was expected to arrive carrying critically needed spare parts from Espiritu Santo. Swede was asked to try to suppress the artillery fire by bombing a few of the closest Japanese positions.

Pete Peterkin watched him take off from the fighter strip. The Japanese were so close to the field by then that he could visually follow the plane through its entire flight. After lifting off, Swede headed west toward the Matanikau River. Making a slow circle, he came back and dropped a full salvo of bombs. Peterkin watched a flock of white birds suddenly soar up from the jungle canopy to escape the exploding havoc. The Avenger was back on the fighter strip in less than fifteen minutes. The American transport planes arrived safely shortly afterward.

At 1130, nearly fifty Japanese fighters and bombers arrived to attack the airfield, and thirty-two fighters went up to do battle with them. Seven enemy planes were shot down.

When the sky was clear again, Swede took off to go after other Japanese artillery positions near the Matanikau River. For this mission, he had been given specific map coordinates by the operations staff. He attempted to put the bombs directly on the assigned targets.

Going in on the first attack, the Avenger attracted heavy ground fire, but made it through unscathed. Swede dropped two bombs and then accelerated away as Judge Wendt strafed the position. On their second pass, the antiaircraft fire was more accurate. Judge Wendt felt the plane shudder as it took hits from one of the antiaircraft batteries. When Swede dropped his second salvo, there was a massive secondary explosion. At the same time, Wendt felt a searing pain down his arm from a shrapnel wound.

Judge radioed on the intercom that he had been hit and Swede flew straight for the runway. After Wendt had been taken to the hospital tent, Chief Hammond warned Swede that with the additional shrapnel damage to the wing, the plane should be grounded. Swede ordered it fueled and rearmed for the next mission.

### JAPANESE SENDAI DIVISION
### GENERAL MASAO MARUYAMA

The ongoing Japanese artillery bombardment from west of the Matanikau River had finally convinced Vandegrift's staff that it was from the west that the Japanese would launch their major ground assault. As the bombardment continued, however, the Sendai Division was actually far to the south of Henderson Field.

Surprise would have been complete, but Maruyama's plan had hit a snag. When his advance units had arrived at the staging area the previous night, they had been told the American lines were only four miles away.

In the light of day, it became obvious this wasn't the case. General Kawaguchi's men were mired in trackless jungle. A scout informed him they were actually eight miles from the American perimeter.

Early in the afternoon, Kawaguchi informed Maruyama that only one of his three battalions would be in position to attack that evening. Maruyama ordered him not to deviate from his original plan. When Kawaguchi protested that he couldn't adhere to the plan, Maruyama removed him from command.

The Americans still had no idea that the Sendai Division was there. The almost impenetrable jungle canopy prevented observation by spotter planes. As the afternoon dragged on, the Japanese continued slogging north toward the American lines.

### TORPEDO SQUADRON EIGHT
### 1500

Gene Hanson volunteered to fly the next mission against the Japanese positions west of the Matanikau. To acquaint himself with the idiosyncrasies of Hammond's patchwork plane, he flew it out over the jungle for a few minutes without drawing any fire.

Back on the ground, Hanson said he was comfortable with the plane's handling ability. Judge Wendt was back from the hospital with a bandaged arm, and wanted to go out again. Wendt was the best gunner in the squadron, and Gene said he was grateful to have him.

American ground spotters had located a Japanese artillery battery, and provided the map coordinates. In the air, Gene went up to a thousand feet and closed on the target. He released the bombs squarely over the battery and returned without receiving any damage.

JAPANESE SENDAI DIVISION
GENERAL MASAO MARUYAMA
1700

The Japanese ruse to persuade the Americans that their main assault would come along the Matanikau was still working perfectly. Vandegrift's staff had begun moving men and guns from other parts of the line to face the assault when it came. When they were finished, nine artillery batteries faced west, and the Marine defensive line there had been strongly reinforced.

Those same decisions left the southern perimeter weakened. Lieutenant Colonel Lewis Puller would be defending a line almost one and a half miles long with just his 1st battalion of the 7th Marines. The line ran roughly east to west, and traversed open fields separated by deep ravines and dense jungle. It was anchored near the Lunga River by Edson's Ridge, where Kawaguchi's force had been defeated a month earlier.

The sun was setting in the jungle to the south of Edson's Ridge when Colonel Shoji, the officer who had replaced Kawaguchi, was forced to send a message to General Maruyama that his right wing was still not prepared to make the attack that night.

An enraged Maruyama briefly considered his options before finally recognizing he had none. At 1715, he once more postponed the main assault until the following night. He also issued orders to postpone the two diversionary attacks along the Matanikau River that were timed to begin at the same hour as the Sendai's assault. Unfortunately, those orders did not reach the units involved.

The attacks went forward after another artillery bombardment on the Marine positions east of the Matanikau. Vandegrift's new operations officer, Colonel Merrill Twining, concluded, "It looks like this is the night."

From out of the jungle west of the Matanikau, two waves of Japanese tanks rumbled forward followed by Japanese infantry. The Marines waited for them in their positions east of the river.

### TORPEDO SQUADRON EIGHT
### 1835

The mounting roar of massed artillery, tank, and mortar fire reached the pilots at Henderson Field. Gene Hanson was waiting by the Avenger when Swede received the orders to bomb and strafe the enemy forces surging across the Matanikau near Point Cruz.

Gene volunteered to go up. Judge Wendt's arm wound had sent him back to the infirmary, and Rube Francis said he would replace him. Jim McNamara manned the tail gun.

Hanson was going through his final flight check in the cockpit when he glanced up and saw Swede standing on the wing. Swede hadn't said anything to him, or made any move to come over. It struck Gene as odd, but he was too busy to ask.

In fact, Swede had just said good-bye to Major Michael Mahoney after strapping him into the second seat. Mahoney thought he could provide important intelligence to General Vandegrift's staff if he had a chance to observe the enemy force dispositions from the air with his own trained eye. Swede had given him permission to go. He didn't inform Gene. As far as Hanson knew, he and his two crew members were the only ones aboard.

Taxiing onto the runway, Hanson shoved the throttle open and headed down the flight path. As he was pulling back on the control stick to lift off, an artillery round exploded on the runway to the left of the plane, shaking it hard before Gene got it in the air.

The Avenger had been armed with twelve one-hundred-pound bombs, and as Hanson approached the target area near Point Purvis, he remembered General Geiger's warning that it was idiocy to make individual bomb runs against well-defended targets. Gene planned to salvo all of them where they would do the most good, and live to fight another day.

Arriving over Point Purvis, however, he saw good targets just about everywhere. To the right, Japanese tanks were on the move, firing their guns into the Marine defense line. Beyond the tanks, he saw infantry coming on. To the left, he could see exposed Japanese artillery batteries near the river. He decided to drop his twelve bombs one by one.

The plane started taking fire as soon as Gene headed down. He was at eight hundred feet when he released the first bomb on a cluster of Japanese troops heading toward the American line. Regaining altitude, he saw a heavy field gun open up and headed straight for it, dropping his second bomb. He kept turning in tight circles to drop his bombs where they would help break the momentum of the Japanese attack.

Rube Francis called him on the intercom to say they had taken a bunch of hits in the fuselage, but there was no serious damage yet, and he and McNamara were getting in good strafing runs.

Gene had swung around to make his seventh pass when a burst of flame erupted in the nose of the plane. The engine immediately began to lose power. A few seconds later, it burst into flames. He could feel the growing intensity of the heat in the cockpit as fire licked toward him.

The Avenger was rapidly losing forward thrust. Gene needed to get clear of the battleground before they went in. Looking down, he saw he was near the neck of Point Cruz and turned to swing out over Sealark Channel.

He was turning to come back in for an emergency landing when the engine suddenly died, and the plane began to drop like a deadweight toward the sea. He tried to keep the nose up as they went in.

A shell blast had dislodged the left wheel from its compartment, and when they hit the sea, the Avenger flipped over onto its back. Submerged underwater, Hanson struggled to unstrap himself and fight his way to the surface.

He came out of the water to see Rube Francis and Jim McNamara floating nearby. He didn't understand why they both began diving under the fuselage as the Avenger sank beneath the surface.

After the plane disappeared, Francis told him that Major Mahoney had been in the second seat. He had probably been knocked unconscious in the crash landing. Unlike the flight crew, he had no training in how to survive a rough ditching.

The three of them treaded water for several minutes, but Mahoney never came up. Hanson was distraught at the thought of the major dying in his plane without his even knowing he was there. He wondered what he might have done differently if he had known. Why hadn't Swede told him?

It started to rain, a light drizzle that soon became a torrential downpour as they slowly swam toward shore. By the time they neared the beach, it was pitch dark. Gene had no idea which forces held the section of shoreline they were approaching. Hearing American voices on the beach, Gene took the chance of yelling out, "What's the password?"

"Lucky strike," came back a low voice. It was the correct password.

Back at Henderson Field, Pete Peterkin knew something had gone wrong when darkness fell and the plane didn't return. He went to the operations tent and was told that three airmen had crashed in the sea and were on their way to the hospital.

When Pete got there, Gene and his crew had just arrived. In the lantern light, Francis and McNamara looked all right to Peterkin, but Hanson seemed to be in shock. He couldn't stop talking about the fact that Mahoney had been in the plane and was still down there now.

Peterkin took them back to camp in a jeep he had borrowed. It was raining so hard that the airfield had flooded, and the jeep kept sinking up to its wheel base in the lower sections of the path.

The airfield was still being shelled, and Pete had to cross it to get to Mahoney's camp. He was circling the field when the jeep broke down in a flooded gulley. They abandoned it and went forward on foot.

Arriving at the camp, Peterkin told Captain Lew Aronson, Mahoney's executive officer, that Mahoney was dead. The news spread quickly, and cast an immediate pall on the whole company. Mahoney's men had admired him as Torpedo Eight had once revered John Waldron. Gene was worried that some of the Marines would harbor hard feelings toward him, but no one said anything.

They could still hear the sound of Japanese artillery fire. Captain Aronson told them that all the battle action was taking place along the Matanikau, but to be on their guard because snipers had infiltrated the southern perimeter.

Later that night, the rain finally stopped, and a pale moon came out. Fred Mears and Aaron Katz were trying to sleep through the bark of distant artillery and machine gun fire when someone slipped inside their tent.

"Sir, I think there's a sniper outside," a Marine whispered.

Fred grabbed his forty-five, pulled back the slide, and cocked it. Putting on his steel helmet, he slowly crept toward the tent opening, and crouched down to see what was happening outside.

He couldn't see anything beyond the cluster of tents, but could easily imagine a sniper in the trees above him. Suddenly, a loud shot went off within a few feet of his ear. It was the young Marine who had given him the whispered warning, apparently firing at a Japanese sniper.

Turning around, Fred saw Aaron Katz moving behind him in the shadows of the tent, pointing his own cocked pistol in Fred's direction. It wasn't enough to have snipers inside the perimeter. Now his tent mate was aiming at him. He suddenly got mad.

"Goddamn it, Katz, put that pistol away or I'll blow your head off!" he snarled.

Outside, cooler heads prevailed along the perimeter line. Orders were given to refrain from firing unless the shooter was certain that the target he was shooting at was an enemy soldier.

SATURDAY, 24 OCTOBER 1942
GUADALCANAL
TORPEDO SQUADRON EIGHT

In the morning, Swede demanded that Chief Hammond make him another Avenger. Hammond said he couldn't promise anything, but would get his mechanics to work on the remaining hulks in the boneyard.

Gathering the rest of the men together, Swede announced that Torpedo Eight would now do its fighting on the ground. The word was that there would be an even bigger push along the Matanikau River that night. Although Torpedo Eight was in a rearguard position, he warned them that anything could happen, and they needed to be ready.

After breakfast, he led them down to the front lines of the Marine perimeter. Dividing them into groups, he assigned the men foxholes that had been prepared under the direction of one of Major Mahoney's platoon officers earlier in the week.

Their section of the line had been dubbed "Bloody Knoll" after the September battles. Torpedo Eight's foxholes were dug into the side of a ridge that looked down into a ravine covered with solid undergrowth. Beyond the ravine was an almost endless vista of thick jungle.

Swede decided that some of the men hadn't dug their holes deep enough, and ordered them to go deeper. He then had the squadron's thirty-caliber machine guns placed between sandbags in the forward foxholes. Finally, he inspected the firing positions, making sure every man had a Springfield rifle with plenty of ammunition and a small supply of hand grenades.

More than one of the pilots wasn't thrilled with the idea of fighting the Japanese from foxholes. Their job was to fly airplanes. They had already begun to question why Swede was keeping them there when there had been only one plane to fly, and that one for only two days since the big shelling attack.

Now there were no planes at all, and Swede had not asked to be relieved. Instead, he had them digging foxholes. They were pilots, not badgers. They had not been trained for this kind of combat. The

Navy pilots could no more go hand-to-hand against a Japanese soldier than a Marine could climb into the cockpit of an Avenger and launch a torpedo into the side of an enemy warship. With no planes to fly, the obvious answer was for them to go where there were some.

Some of the enlisted men in the squadron were no happier about the idea than the officers. They were mechanics, machinist's mates, radiomen, and metalsmiths. A number of them had never fired a rifle, much less tossed a hand grenade.

Now they were part of Swede's private army, one grumbled. None of the complaints mattered. Swede was in command of the squadron, and he said they were going to fight.

As darkness fell, the men had their second meal of the day before heading out to their foxholes. Pete Peterkin was sharing one with Chief Hammond. It had begun to rain again, and Hammond was resourceful enough to have fashioned a roof shelter out of a ground tarp supported by wooden stakes. Others just hunkered down in their ponchos and let the rain drub on their helmets.

As uncomfortable as he was in a water-filled foxhole, Fred Mears concluded that it was probably a lot worse for the enemy soldiers slogging through the jungle. He didn't have long to find out.

Lieutenant Colonel Puller, commanding the southern perimeter, was standing in his command shelter when a Marine sergeant in an advance outpost beyond the perimeter whispered through his field phone that he was surrounded by thousands of Japanese soldiers, and that they were heading Puller's way.

Minutes later, the main assault by five thousand soldiers of the emperor's Sendai Division was launched against a line held by the seven hundred men of the 1st Battalion, 7th Marines, and anchored at Bloody Knoll by the thirty-one naval personnel commanded by Lieutenant Swede Larsen.

Infiltrating the Marine positions, teams of Japanese sappers began cutting the barbed wire in Puller's front. Puller grabbed his field phone and ordered, "Commence firing."

The rain-filled black sky suddenly turned bright with the explosion of flares, mortars, machine guns, and grenades. Under the brief glow of the flares, the Marines could see hundreds of Japanese coming out of the jungle on the run, most of them attacking near the center of Puller's line.

The line might have been thin, but it was embedded with nests of machine guns, sixty-millimeter mortars, antitank guns, and Browning automatic rifles. Puller's machine gunners kept firing belt after belt of ammunition as the waves of Japanese troops charged toward them. The fury of one attack would end with a stack of bodies in front of their positions. Before they could drag them away to clear their field of fire, the next wave would be coming on.

The Marines fired mortar rounds as fast as they could load them to break the momentum of the Sendai charges. Yet, the disciplined Japanese kept coming, hurling hand grenades and shouting epithets as they fought their way toward the defensive line and pushed it back up the ridge.

At the far end of the line near Bloody Knoll, Gene Hanson heard the dull explosions of mortars and hand grenades, followed by the rattle of automatic weapons as the Japanese launched their assault. He and the others watched the dark sky light up to the east of them like a Fourth of July fireworks display.

He wondered how they would do if the Japanese attack came their way. Wiley Bartlett was wondering the same thing. Half-Cherokee and from Lenox, Alabama, he had earned a reputation as one of the most gifted machine gunners in the squadron. The Marines had strung a single strand of barbed wire in front of his position, and he didn't think it would stop a billy goat, much less a Japanese soldier.

As the fighting continued unabated, Lieutenant Colonel Puller received a call on his field phone from Colonel Arthur Sims, his regimental commander, demanding to know what was going on. Sims was immediately skeptical that Puller's battalion was being hit by anything more than a diversionary attack, and still convinced that the main assault would be coming from the west along the Matanikau.

"If you want to find out what's going on, come and see," Puller growled into the field phone.

By then, dozens of Japanese had penetrated the defense line, one of them planting a Japanese flag inside the perimeter. Puller called an artillery position in the rear on his field phone and asked for fire support.

"If they get through here tonight there won't be a tomorrow," said Puller as the attack waves kept coming out of the jungle to the left and center of his line. The artillery commander promised him everything he could deliver.

As the firing got increasingly louder, it became obvious to Gene Hanson that the enemy attack was moving in their direction. A few minutes later, the men in the forward foxholes began pouring fire down into the ravine below them.

The attacks kept coming all night long. At one point, Puller was grateful to receive reinforcement from a green Army unit, the 3rd Battalion, 164th Infantry, that had just arrived at Guadalcanal. Puller fed them piecemeal into his most depleted positions. They made a difference.

Shortly before dawn, the attacks finally came to an end.

The Japanese had driven a lodgment into Puller's line that was more than a hundred yards deep and two hundred yards wide, but at terrible cost. In the first sickly light of day, Puller's Marines looked out on the narrow expanse leading down to the edge of the jungle and saw the Japanese dead lying as if in windrows, a thousand of them, maybe more. More than two dozen Marines had paid the ultimate price to stop them.

Japanese snipers had worked their way through the holes in the line, and were now settled into hiding places in the trees and undergrowth, waiting for the opportunity to kill as many Marines as possible.

SUNDAY, 25 OCTOBER 1942
GUADALCANAL
TORPEDO SQUADRON EIGHT

As coffee was being carried in jerry cans to the foxholes, a few of the enlisted men in Torpedo Eight took their Springfields down into the ravine below their position. They found the bodies of several Japanese soldiers. There were blood trails leading back toward the jungle.

Pete Peterkin didn't know who was responsible for killing the

Japanese attackers, but he was proud of the way the men had kept their heads. After a breakfast of K rations in their foxholes, Captain Aronson informed the squadron that there would probably be another attack along the perimeter that night.

Swede told Peterkin and Hammond to take his mechanics down to Henderson Field to begin work on his new plane, and to be back before dark. Fred Mears went with them.

At 0800, a twin-engine Japanese plane came into Henderson Field as if it was planning to land, and was shot down by Marine machine gunners. Inside the aircraft, the Marines found several dead Japanese officers in dress uniforms.

Apparently, a Japanese radio operator on Guadalcanal had erroneously relayed a message to Rabaul that the Sendai Division had captured the airfield. The officers in the plane had been part of the advance guard that had been sent down to officially congratulate Maruyama on his success.

But Maruyama's men had not captured Henderson Field, and that fact became quickly apparent to the first wave of Japanese planes, which had expected to find Japanese flags welcoming their arrival. Instead, they faced withering antiaircraft fire.

They immediately radioed back to Rabaul that the field was still in American hands. The additional troop deployments planned by the high command were temporarily canceled, although the Japanese navy's carrier planes were ordered to continue strafing and bombing the American positions in preparation for the next attack by the Sendai Division.

When Fred reached the airfield it was quickly apparent to him that Japanese carriers had to be close by, because he had never seen so many Zeroes before. When one wave would finish strafing and move off, another was coming in to hit the American positions.

He was standing in an antiaircraft position near the field when a group of Japanese dive-bombers arrived. A young Marine holding two forty-five-caliber Colt pistols was standing alongside him when one of the dive-bombers nosed over to make its run. In apparent support of the antiaircraft guns, the boy raised his pistols and opened fire, blazing away with both barrels as the plane came hurtling down at them.

As the pilot pulled out of his dive and tore away, the young Marine swung the forty-fives across Fred's chest, and continued firing past his right ear. Fred decided it was safer back in his foxhole on Bloody Knoll.

Kept idle by the daylong strafing and bombing attacks, Peterkin and Hammond had been unable to continue work on the plane, and went back, too. While they had been down at the field, Roy Williams, a Torpedo Eight ordnanceman from Texas, had shot and killed a Japanese sniper in a coconut palm near their position. As darkness fell, Swede sent the men back into their foxholes.

Farther down the line, Lieutenant Colonel Puller's Marine battalion, now reinforced by the 2nd Battalion, 164th Infantry, waited in the darkness for the Sendai Division to make its next move.

The Japanese had one more surprise in store. Instead of immediately launching the attack by the Sendai, they commenced another artillery bombardment along the Matanikau River, where Vandegrift had initially expected their major assault to take place.

A few minutes after that bombardment began, a separate barrage of artillery fire exploded along the southern perimeter. With Japanese heavy machine guns providing additional covering fire, the Sendai Division charged out of the jungle to launch its second assault.

Again, they came in waves, some with as few as twenty-five men, others with more than two hundred. With dogged determination, they hurled themselves at the reinforced positions in a desperate attempt to break through to the airfield.

As the Sendai Division attacked from the south, Japanese troops also charged the western perimeter at the Matanikau, taking an important section of high ground before being dislodged in a counterattack.

But as on the previous night, Japanese bravery and discipline were no match for presighted mortar positions, well-spotted heavy artillery, intersecting machine gun fire, and thirty-seven-millimeter field guns.

Once again, small groups of Japanese soldiers succeeded in penetrating the perimeter, attempting to outflank the defensive positions, but they were too few to break through to the airfield. Near dawn, the Japanese began to withdraw.

MONDAY, 26 OCTOBER 1942
GUADALCANAL
TORPEDO SQUADRON EIGHT

There was no doubt about the margin of the previous night's victory. It could be found on the blades of the bulldozers that scooped up more than two thousand rapidly decomposing bodies along the perimeter before burying them in mass graves.

Swede pulled Torpedo Eight out of the line later that morning. Some of them hadn't left their foxholes for two days except to relieve themselves. They hadn't fought off the main attack of the Sendai Division, but they had held the section of the line assigned to them. Pete Peterkin told them it was the first time an American carrier squadron had ever fought on a front line against an attacking enemy.

By then, the sailors even looked like Marines. Their original clothing was long gone, either shredded in the October 13 shelling or rotted from mildew and dampness after six weeks on the island. Most of them wore Marine-issue dungarees.

And like the Marines, their clammy faces were yellowed with Atabrine, they had ringworm and dysentery, and their nostrils were full of the stench of rotting Japanese corpses. They were jaundiced, bone-weary, and fed up with Guadalcanal after weeks of combat action in the air, followed by the daily bombings and shellings on the ground.

Fred Mears yearned for the simple release of a good night's sleep, devoid of the sound of machine guns and artillery fire, a sleep undisturbed by the knowledge that thousands of men out in the jungle were planning to kill him.

With no planes left to fly, Bert Earnest, Fred Mears, Gene Hanson, and Aaron Katz were in full agreement. It was time to go. They wouldn't have another serviceable aircraft to fly until Chief Hammond and his mechanics built one. If they even could. One plane for five pilots. It made no sense.

TRUK ATOLL
ADMIRAL ISOROKU YAMAMOTO

Yamamoto was undeterred. He had attended the U.S. Naval War College and Harvard University. Yamamoto loved baseball and American movies, particularly westerns. He knew all about cowboys and Indians.

When he committed his forces to retaking the airfield at Guadalcanal, it was because he was convinced the American Navy would try to dash to the rescue, much like the cavalry riding to save the settlers. Instead of the cavalry, he believed they would send their carriers.

Whoever controlled the air and sea-lanes would eventually win the battle. Yamamoto now planned his own ambush. Lying in wait for the Americans would be four Japanese aircraft carriers, two battleships, ten cruisers, and more than twenty destroyers.

For Admiral Nimitz, the key to defeating the Japanese in the Eastern Solomons was to hold Guadalcanal, but to do so, he needed to be able to resupply it from the air and sea. The American carriers and their aircraft were the critical tools needed to maintain his supply line to the beleaguered island.

He had only two available. Steaming near Santa Cruz Island to the northeast of Guadalcanal were the *Hornet* and the *Enterprise*. The *Enterprise* had just returned after undergoing five weeks of repairs from the hits she had received on August 24, the day Torpedo Eight had helped sink the *Ryujo*.

The two carriers were escorted by the new battleship *South Dakota*, along with six cruisers and fourteen destroyers. From sighting reports, the American commanders knew that Japanese carriers were lurking somewhere to the north. As at Midway, they hoped their search planes would find the Japanese first.

Shortly after dawn, Japanese and American search plane pilots found each other's fleets at almost exactly the same time, and radioed the sightings. The Americans drew first blood when at 0740, two unescorted Dauntless scout bombers bravely attacked the light carrier *Zuihō*, making two hits on the flight deck, and preventing it from launching or landing aircraft for the remainder of the battle.

At 0830, the two opposing air armadas passed in full sight of one another, 73 American planes going one way, and 125 Japanese planes going the other.

Shortly after 0900, the planes from the *Hornet* and *Enterprise* attacked the principal Japanese carrier force, damaging the big carrier *Shokaku* with three bomb hits, as well as two of her escort ships.

At the same time, Japanese air formations commenced their attack with a ferocity the Americans had never seen before. In the span of two minutes, three bombs landed on the *Hornet,* two of them penetrating the flight deck. One Japanese bomber pilot, his plane on fire, deliberately crashed it into the *Hornet.*

A few minutes later, two Japanese aircraft fired torpedoes into the *Hornet*'s side, knocking out her engines, and bringing the ship to a dead stop. As she lay still in the water, the pilot of another burning Japanese bomber flew it into the ship, igniting the carrier's aviation gas tanks.

With the *Hornet* dead in the water, a flight of Japanese bombers moved on to attack the *Enterprise,* hitting her with two bombs, one of which exploded through the hangar deck, killing dozens of sailors.

TUESDAY, 27 OCTOBER 1942
GUADALCANAL
TORPEDO SQUADRON EIGHT

The first unverified rumor came from a pilot who had just arrived at Henderson Field. There was no official confirmation, but more details emerged as word spread. It turned out to be true.

The *Hornet* had gone down.

If Torpedo Eight could have considered a ship its own, it had been the *Hornet.* On the day the carrier had been commissioned back in Norfolk, the pilots of Torpedo Eight had stood proudly on her flight deck, arrayed in dress whites as she was welcomed into the fleet.

For the men who had been aboard that day, including Swede Larsen, Bert Earnest, Chief J. C. Hammond, Judge Wendt, and Gene

Hanson, the memories started with Lieutenant Commander Waldron and the others who had been lost since: Grant Teats, Bill Evans, Ozzie Gaynier, Whitey Moore, Vic Lewis, and so many others. Twenty-two of the original thirty-five pilots were dead, along with thirty crewmen.

Now the *Hornet* had been sunk with great loss of life in another carrier battle. At one point, Bert Earnest realized that his uniforms and most of his personal gear were still aboard her. They would always be.

With the major Japanese ground offensive beaten back, Swede brought together his four pilots, Earnest, Hanson, Katz, and Mears, to tell them his plans. They were the last of the seventeen squadron pilots who had flown with the Cactus Air Force. Between them, the five pilots had been recommended for seven Navy Crosses for uncommon valor.

Swede told them he was going to stay on the island until he was officially relieved. He thought that Guadalcanal was where they needed to be. He told them he had ordered Pete Peterkin to stay behind along with all of the enlisted men.

Chief Hammond thought he would have a plane ready to go in a week, Swede said. If the Japanese mounted another ground assault, the squadron would go back into its positions on the line until the plane was ready to fly.

He wasn't ordering them to stay. The ones who wanted to go back to Espiritu Santo were free to do so. The pilots who wanted to remain with him were welcome to stay.

The four of them talked it over. There would be only one plane to fly if Hammond was successful, and Swede would be the one flying it. What was the point? All four left that day aboard a transport plane for Espiritu Santo.

# Swede's Refrain

TUESDAY, 3 NOVEMBER 1942
GUADALCANAL
TORPEDO SQUADRON EIGHT

After the Japanese ground offensive was crushed, there was no serious fighting for almost a week. The Japanese stopped sending planes down from Rabaul to attack the airfield. The Tokyo Express no longer came down the Groove every night.

Swede continued to wait for another Frankenstein to fly.

Chief Hammond had put all his men to work on it. Between the new materiel that was now flowing into Henderson Field, and the spare parts he was able to scavenge from the boneyard, he made steady progress. A rebuilt Wright engine was transferred to the plane's engine root. Both wings were replaced. Slowly, it came together.

On Halloween, Swede took possession of his new creation and rumbled down the runway to see if it would fly. This one was far more unsteady than the previous plane, but Swede got it in the air, circled the field, and brought it back in.

He immediately pronounced the Avenger airworthy and told Peterkin to prepare it for a bombing mission the next morning. He then ordered Hammond to begin putting another plane together as soon as possible.

Returning to their camp, Peterkin discovered that Mahoney's special weapons company was moving out to a new position. Peterkin looked around for a new place to pitch their tents, and found one about five hundred yards farther along the ridgeline. It was in a thick copse of trees, and well concealed from a possible strafing attack. He also made arrangements for Torpedo Eight to eat at the mess tent of a newly arrived Marine unit. He reckoned they had now eaten with five different units since arriving on the island.

On November 1, Swede made his first attack in Hammond's new Avenger. It was in support of General Vandegrift's drive to push the Japanese back from their positions west of the Matanikau, and shove them out of artillery range of the airfield.

Flying alone, Swede looked for Japanese troop concentrations in the jungle below him. He couldn't see any, and purposely flew lower to draw their fire. The Japanese did not rise to the bait. He finally released a full salvo of twelve bombs over an area he thought looked suspicious. Back on the ground, he told Peterkin and Hammond that the plane was acting balky and to get the kinks out of it.

On November 2, he took off again to support the new Marine push. From the air, the Japanese appeared to have gone underground, and Swede was again unable to find any obvious targets. He went up alone again that same afternoon. Under low clouds, he dropped his twelve bombs in a jungle clearing.

That night, reports came in that a small force of Japanese troops had landed near Koli Point. The next morning, Swede flew low over the area, dropping twelve bombs on what looked like another suspicious site. In the afternoon Swede took off alone again, heading for the same sector he had bombed earlier that day. This time, his tail gunner reported he had seen small-arms fire coming from the jungle floor. Swede reversed course and dropped his twelve bombs where his gunner thought he had seen the muzzle flashes.

Pete Peterkin was having misgivings about the importance of the contribution they were making. He wrote a letter to Bert Earnest at Espiritu Santo, asking how the rest of the squadron was doing, and confiding his concerns about the mental and physical condition of the enlisted men left on Guadalcanal. He concluded the letter by asking Bert's opinion of why Swede would be keeping twenty men there when they were down to one plane. The letter went out on one of the daily transport planes.

Receiving Peterkin's letter, Bert Earnest wrote back that the only reason the men were there was because of Swede's personal ambitions. The letter went up to Guadalcanal on a supply flight. When it arrived, Swede happened to be present for mail call. He decided to open the letter, even though it was addressed to Peterkin. After reading Bert's comments about him, he passed along the opened letter to Peterkin without a word. Pete wrote to Bert, warning him that Swede had read his private comments.

When Swede returned from his third bombing run on November 3, Lieutenant George Flinn, the squadron's personnel officer, was waiting for him at their new camp. He had just arrived from Espiritu Santo with important news. The squadron was going to be officially relieved by a Marine torpedo squadron that was already in New Caledonia, and would soon be arriving at Guadalcanal.

That evening, an excited Peterkin shared the news with the twenty enlisted men. They were elated. Just a few more days and they would be headed out of Guadalcanal to join the rest of the squadron.

Flinn also told Swede that a new Avenger had just been delivered to Torpedo Eight at Espiritu Santo. It was supposed to go to the *Hornet* before she was sunk. Swede ordered it flown up immediately. He also told Flinn to radio a request for volunteers to return to Guadalcanal.

WEDNESDAY, 4 NOVEMBER 1942
ESPIRITU SANTO
TORPEDO SQUADRON EIGHT

For Fred Mears, the days at Espiritu had floated by in a sunny haze. The Navy's construction teams had made a lot of improvements since his first visit back in August. After clearing the malarial jungle, they had built a complex of frame buildings beneath the tall coconut palms near the airstrip.

The pilots were living at the edge of the bay in small wooden cottages that were clean and cool, with screened porches that faced out on the water. At night, it was quiet, with only the background noise of takeoffs and landings at the airstrip that were part of every pilot's life.

With the exception of a desirable woman, the place had most of the things a man could appreciate as he regained health and strength. The food was good, and thanks to the Navy's eradication efforts, there were fewer flying insects to swat away while they ate it. Whiskey and beer could be easily acquired.

The pilots and crews relaxed in different ways. Some headed over to the big naval base across the island to try to pick up nurses. Others played poker or Chinese checkers or cribbage, or just sat in their cottages near the bay with a paperback novel.

Guadalcanal had aged the pilots of Torpedo Eight. After the intensity of what they had gone through, their eyes and mouths were etched with furrows, and they had the sallow complexions of men who had been ill with dysentery and malaria. Fred Mears's hair was falling out. His reflexes had gotten slower.

Only one incident threatened to disrupt Fred's first week of relaxation. Lieutenant Benny Grosscup, the squadron's gossip-fed intelligence officer, informed the pilots that a carrier had just arrived at the big naval base and was supposedly short of torpedo pilots. He claimed to have it on good authority that they would all become part of the carrier's new torpedo squadron. It was a false rumor.

George Flinn radioed them from Guadalcanal that Swede wanted a crew to fly the new Avenger up there right away. Swede was also looking for volunteers to pilot the next Frankenstein plane Chief Hammond was building for him from the boneyard. Strong feelings were expressed about the idiocy of their commanding officer, particularly since the Marine torpedo squadron that was relieving them would be arriving in a day or two.

Bruce Harwood, who was required to remain with the squadron in Espiritu Santo, finally convinced several of the pilots who had been among the first evacuated from Guadalcanal to go back up.

Friday, 6 November 1942
Truk Atoll
Admiral Isoroku Yamamoto

In the wake of his dramatic victory over the American carrier forces off Santa Cruz, Admiral Yamamoto had begun preparing his next offensive to retake the airfield at Guadalcanal.

The stakes were inestimably high. As one of his confidential staff documents put it: "It must be said that the success or failure in recapturing Guadalcanal Island, and the vital naval battle related to it, is the fork in the road which leads to victory for them or us."

After the successive defeats of Ichiki's detachment in August, Kawaguchi's force in September, and then the Sendai Division in October, the Imperial Army had concluded that only one path led to assured success. For the next stage of the campaign, they pledged to commit thirty thousand additional troops and three hundred field guns to batter the Americans into final submission.

As always, the key to getting the troops there lay in controlling the air and sea-lanes around Guadalcanal. Admiral Yamamoto was now hard-pressed to guarantee that he had enough available naval forces to do it, even though he believed the remaining U.S. carriers had been destroyed at Santa Cruz.

Although the Japanese had won a clear victory when they sank the *Hornet* and badly damaged the *Enterprise,* the cost of the victory had been steep. Two of his carriers had been forced to return to Japan for repairs. Yamamoto had also sent the undamaged carrier *Zuikaku* home to regroup after it lost many of its experienced air crews.

In the Battle of Santa Cruz, one hundred fifty Japanese pilots and crewmen had been killed, including five squadron commanders from the torpedo and bombing squadrons, and eighteen section and flight leaders. The losses represented 49 percent of the torpedo bomber crews, 40 percent of the dive-bomber crews, and 20 percent of the fighter pilots.

Yamamoto's remaining carriers were operating with severely depleted air groups. In order to assure the safe delivery of the army's thirty thousand new troops, he would need to use more land-based aircraft from Rabaul. The first contingent of Japanese troops would be delivered by the Tokyo Express on November 7.

SATURDAY, 7 NOVEMBER 1942
GUADALCANAL
TORPEDO SQUADRON EIGHT

In the afternoon, American search planes spotted eleven enemy warships coming down the Groove north of Florida Island. The Cactus air staff was confident they were carrying Japanese troop reinforcements, and readied an immediate counterstrike.

At 1600, Swede briefed the newly arrived Bob Evarts and Andy Divine on the mission. Chief Hammond had completed reconstruction of a third Avenger that he hoped was ready for combat. Swede would fly the new replacement plane, Evarts and Divine the patchwork Avengers.

They would be part of an air group consisting of three Avengers, seven Dauntlesses, and thirty Wildcats. It would be a coordinated attack, with the fighters going in first to strafe the antiaircraft batteries, followed by the dive-bombers from up high and the torpedo planes down low.

Under scattered cloud cover, the group took off at 1630 and headed north to intercept the Japanese task force. Packed aboard the eleven destroyers were troops, artillery pieces, food, and ammunition.

The attack went exactly as planned. Although all three Avengers were hit by antiaircraft fire, Swede and Bob Evarts were able to launch their torpedoes from less than eight hundred yards away. They each claimed a hit, although Andy Divine, flying the newest patchwork plane, was unable to release his torpedo. After repeated attempts, he finally gave up. Pursued by Japanese fighters, one of his gunners was hit four times and critically wounded, but all three planes made it back safely.

For leading the attack, Admiral William Halsey awarded Swede the Distinguished Flying Cross. It was the second DFC Swede had

388 · A Dawn Like Thunder

received since taking command of Torpedo Eight. He had also been recommended for a Navy Cross for leading the mission against the Japanese cruisers on August 24, the day the squadron had helped sink the *Ryujo*.

WEDNESDAY, 11 NOVEMBER 1942
GUADALCANAL
TORPEDO SQUADRON EIGHT

For four days, heavy storms and howling winds pummeled the Solomon Islands, preventing Japanese air attacks from reaching Guadalcanal, and giving the pilots of the Cactus Air Force a chance to regroup. Most of them welcomed the opportunity to relax in their tents out of the gusting wind and rain.

Not Swede. Pete Peterkin was worried that his commanding officer was finally getting ready to blow. He thought a number of the squadron's enlisted men were ready to blow too, but for the opposite reason. They were desperate to leave. Swede wanted to stay and fight.

Like Earnest, Hanson, and most of the other pilots, Peterkin wondered why it was necessary to expose the crews to any more risk now that they had only three planes, two of them virtual cripples, and relief was imminent. Personally, he thought they had already pushed their luck too far.

On November 8, VS-71, the last one of the Navy's Dauntless squadrons in the Cactus Air Force, was evacuated. Torpedo Eight, with its two officers and twenty-one enlisted men, was the only naval air squadron left.

Even the award of the DFC did not seem to improve Swede's disposition. In spite of the bad weather, the Tokyo Express had continued to deliver troops and supplies every night. On November 10, Swede had tried to lead his three Avengers up the Groove to attack them. A violent storm had forced him to turn back.

His temper wasn't helped by the radio message from Benny Grosscup that the eighteen Avengers of Marine Torpedo Bomber

Squadron 131 had just arrived at Espiritu Santo. The first element of six planes would be flying up to Guadalcanal the next day to relieve him.

In two raids on the eleventh, seventy-seven Japanese planes attacked Henderson Field. In the aerial melees above Sealark Channel, nine Wildcats were shot down while destroying eleven of the attackers.

Swede knew that the next Japanese air and ground offensive was imminent. The word was that it would be the biggest one of the whole campaign, and he wasn't about to miss it.

### THURSDAY, 12 NOVEMBER 1942
### GUADALCANAL
### TORPEDO SQUADRON EIGHT

The first Avengers from the Marine air squadron nearly didn't make it to Guadalcanal. They arrived at the same time that a convoy of American transports was disembarking men and materiel to reinforce Vandegrift's depleted garrison.

The transports were escorted by five cruisers and eight destroyers. Fearing a Japanese air attack from Rabaul at any moment, their antiaircraft gun crews were being particularly vigilant.

At 1000, the six Avengers of the Marine squadron approached the southeastern coast of Guadalcanal. They were flying at low altitude, and the gun crews aboard the American warships decided to take no chances. They opened up on the unidentified intruders, raking the Avengers with machine gun fire as the Marine pilots kept trying to radio Henderson Field that they were friendly. Before the firing stopped, one Avenger had been damaged badly enough to be exiled to the boneyard as soon as it landed.

TRUK ISLAND
ADMIRAL ISOROKU YAMAMOTO

At Shetland Harbor near Bougainville, ten thousand Japanese soldiers, one-third of the newly committed troop reinforcements, began boarding a flotilla of transports for the run to Guadalcanal.

In conjunction with their arrival, Admiral Yamamoto had ordered two Japanese battleships, the *Hiei* and the *Kirishima,* to conduct another bombardment of Henderson Field. It would repeat the success of the battleships *Kongo* and *Hiruna* when they had destroyed most of the Cactus Air Force in a similar bombardment on the night of October 13.

The shelling would hopefully disrupt American air operations long enough to assure the safe delivery of the ten thousand reinforcements reaching Guadalcanal that same night.

FRIDAY, 13 NOVEMBER 1942
SAVO ISLAND
JAPANESE BATTLESHIP *HIEI*
0030

The battleships arrived in post-midnight darkness, approaching Guadalcanal from Savo Island after passing silently over the graves of the many American and Japanese warships that now littered Iron Bottom Sound.

The fourteen-inch gun batteries of the *Hiei* and the *Kirishima* were loaded with the same delayed-fuse bombardment shells that had wreaked such havoc on Henderson Field exactly one month earlier. The two battleships were escorted by the cruiser *Nagara* and eleven destroyers.

American search planes had spotted the two battleships heading toward Guadalcanal the previous evening. Unfortunately, the American Navy had no battleships to face them on equal terms, although a blocking force had been hastily assembled that consisted of two heavy cruisers, the *San Francisco* and the *Portland,* three light cruisers, and eight destroyers.

The Americans headed north to meet the enemy knowing this would be strictly a naval battle, its outcome determined by gut-busting gun batteries and ship-launched torpedoes rather than the carrier planes that had usually decided the previous encounters.

The task forces collided at 0150 south of Savo Island. The opposing ships quickly became intermingled, swinging wildly about in the darkness, opening fire at one another at almost point-blank range.

On Guadalcanal, the booming reverberations brought hundreds of men down to the beach. Pete Peterkin watched in awed silence as star shells lit up the northern horizon.

In the first few minutes, the American cruiser *Atlanta* was hit by a salvo of fourteen-inch shells from the *Hiei,* followed by a Japanese Long Lance torpedo that knocked out its engines and brought the ship to a dead stop.

A Japanese destroyer was then hit by a salvo of American fire. It blew up and sank, quickly followed by an American destroyer, which exploded as its crew was abandoning ship.

Still without power, the *Atlanta* unwittingly drifted into the line of fire of the cruiser, *San Francisco.* In the chaotic melee, the gun batteries of *San Francisco* fired into the *Atlanta,* killing Admiral Norman Scott and most of his senior officers on the bridge. It was the coup de grâce for the sinking cruiser.

Three American destroyers bored in on the battleship *Hiei.* Although their five-inch shells could not penetrate the behemoth's armor shield, they were able to rake her bridge and superstructure, slightly wounding Admiral Hiroaki Abe, who was commanding the Japanese task force, and knocking out several of the battleship's antiaircraft batteries.

The American heavy cruiser *Portland* was then struck by a Japanese Long Lance torpedo. It slammed into her stern, blowing off the starboard propeller, after which the ship could only steam in clockwise circles.

When the *San Francisco* came within range, the *Hiei* fired successive salvos at her with its fourteen-inch guns, smashing the bridge and superstructure, and killing the overall American task force commander, Admiral Daniel Callaghan, as well as the ship's captain, and many of its senior officers. Other shells knocked out the ship's control networks, and disabled several of her guns.

Before retiring, *San Francisco* was able to fire a desperate salvo back at *Hiei*. One of the shells hit home at a vital spot, penetrating the battleship's armor plate and flooding its aft steering room, which dramatically reduced her speed and maneuvering ability.

The savage engagement came to an end just forty minutes after it began. In the final moments, three more American destroyers were blasted out of the water, and the American light cruiser *Juneau* was hit by two torpedoes. She slowly crept away from the scene of carnage.

By any measure, it was another Japanese tactical victory. The Americans had lost a cruiser, four destroyers, and more than a thousand men. Without its starboard propeller, the *Portland* was crippled. Later that morning, the *Juneau* was torpedoed by a Japanese submarine and went down with an additional loss of six hundred men.

Only the light cruiser *Helena* and one destroyer now prevented Admiral Abe from completing his mission to deliver the devastating bombardment to Henderson Field. Once the Cactus Air Force was suppressed by a rain of his fourteen-inch shells, nothing could prevent the Japanese transports carrying the ten thousand Japanese troops from safely unloading their precious cargo.

Admiral Abe's second battleship *Kirishima* was undamaged. In concert with the cruiser *Nagara* and four destroyers, he could still carry out the massive bombardment of the airfield virtually unmolested. He had a conclusive victory within his grasp, and one that could potentially alter the entire Guadalcanal campaign.

Instead, Abe, his will apparently sapped by the intensity of the night battle, lost his nerve. He decided to abandon his mission and withdraw the task force. Transferring his flag to the destroyer *Yukikaze*, he left the damaged *Hiei* behind to retreat after the rest of his ships at a speed of just five knots.

Upon learning of the withdrawal, an enraged Admiral Yamamoto ordered that Abe be immediately removed from command. With the Cactus Air Force unsuppressed by the battleship's devastating bombardment, Yamamoto reluctantly ordered the convoy carrying the ten thousand soldiers to return to Shetland Harbor before daylight.

### HENDERSON FIELD, GUADALCANAL
### 0600

Swede wanted the stricken battleship.

Just before dawn, a Wildcat pilot had taken off to see the results of the night naval action. Beyond the sinking ships he saw near Savo Island, he reported sighting a damaged Japanese battleship attempting to retire north.

Although Swede had not been officially relieved yet, he had already discovered that Captain George Dooley, the Marine officer commanding the first six Avengers from the Marine squadron, was no pushover.

From the moment Dooley arrived, Swede hadn't been shy in attempting to lecture him on everything a new squadron needed to learn before it could make torpedo hits. Implying that Dooley and his pilots were too green, Swede offered to lead the first strike against the battleship off Savo Island.

Dooley was not about to kowtow to anyone. A veteran flier, he had once nearly died in a midair collision, and been forced to endure repeated operations to rebuild his horrifically burned face. He was no less resolute than Swede, and determined to make his mark as a combat aviator.

When orders were issued for the strike, it was Dooley, not Swede, who was given the first opportunity to go after the *Hiei,* and he took off in command of a four-plane formation of his unblooded Marine pilots. They followed five Dauntless dive-bombers.

Flying through the gloom above Savo Island, Dooley could see the burning hulks of American and Japanese destroyers drifting aimlessly across the debris-littered sea. The crippled *Portland* continued to steam in a slow circle. Hundreds of survivors of the *Atlanta* were floating in their life jackets off Lunga Point.

The pilots quickly came up on the gigantic *Hiei* as it crawled northward from Savo Island under reduced power. She was escorted by five destroyers, which immediately began throwing up a screen of antiaircraft fire as the planes came in to attack.

At 0615, a Dauntless made the first hit on the *Hiei,* its thousand-pound bomb landing directly amidships and setting off a tremendous explosion. Dooley's four Avengers went in next. One of their torpedoes also hit home, further slowing down the battleship.

After Dooley's flight returned, Swede requested to go up with the three Avengers still under his command. The request was denied. As soon as Dooley's planes were rearmed, he led the next mission. In his second strike against the now burning *Hiei,* Dooley was again successful. Penetrating to within five hundred yards, his torpedo slammed into the battleship's midsection, igniting another column of flame and debris.

At 1015, another group of Avengers dispatched from the carrier *Enterprise* arrived off Savo Island, and launched their own attack. The carrier's torpedo squadron claimed three more torpedo hits on the battleship.

They were followed by a group of B-17s. The Fortresses dropped fifty-six bombs from high altitude, earning one near miss for their efforts. At 1120, six Dauntlesses from Henderson Field attacked the *Hiei.* Those pilots claimed three more hits.

As midday approached, the *Hiei* was barely making headway in its desperate quest to escape. Fires burned everywhere above the waterline and the ship was covered in a dense cloud of black smoke.

At 1145, Swede was finally given his chance. He led up a flight of six Avengers, two of them piloted by Captain Dooley's Marine pilots. Dooley had allowed Bob Evarts to fly one of his squadron's new aircraft. Larry Engel had arrived and would pilot the fourth.

Swede went in first from the port side. His torpedo made a direct hit amidships, sending up a great cloud of debris. Bob Evarts scored, too, although the two torpedoes in the patchwork Avengers failed to drop.

Swede had done it. Regardless of what happened afterward, he had helped to nail a Japanese battleship. Returning to Henderson Field, he celebrated his mission with the other victorious pilots.

The air attacks continued until bad weather forced the field to shut down. Later that night, under the cover of rain and darkness, *Hiei*, a ship that had once been honored by the presence of Emperor Hirohito at the last grand review of the Imperial fleet, succumbed to everything it had endured, and sank to the floor of Iron Bottom Sound.

SATURDAY, 14 NOVEMBER 1942
TRUK ISLAND
ADMIRAL ISOROKU YAMAMOTO

Admiral Yamamoto knew that time was not on the side of the Japanese Empire. He fully appreciated America's rapidly growing industrial capacity to wage war. He knew it was critical that the thirty thousand Japanese troops and their equipment reach Guadalcanal as soon as possible. The campaign would be doomed without them.

Even as the *Hiei* was still fighting its death struggle, Yamamoto issued new orders to complete the mission Admiral Abe had failed to carry out the night before. On the night of November 14, the battleship *Kirishima* would deliver a crushing bombardment of Henderson Field in concert with two heavy cruisers. That same night, Yamamoto's twenty-three-ship convoy carrying the first ten thousand men of the Japanese 38th Infantry Division from Bougainville would arrive at Guadalcanal.

HENDERSON FIELD, GUADALCANAL
TORPEDO SQUADRON EIGHT

To the applause of the men assembled at the airfield, Swede Larsen accepted the official relief of his squadron by Lieutenant Colonel Paul Moret of Marine Air Squadron 131. In "surrendering the reins," Swede vowed that he would soon be back on Guadalcanal to take up the fight again, and that when he did, he planned "to see it through."

He was the only one to make the pledge. The others were grateful to finally be going home. They never wanted to see Guadalcanal again.

Chief Hammond turned over the squadron's three aircraft. After inspecting the two patchwork Avengers with their out-of-kilter wings, jury-rigged control systems, and missing instruments, one of the Marine mechanics openly wondered how the planes had ever gotten into the air. Both planes were officially decommissioned and sent to the boneyard to be cannibalized for spare parts.

Swede and Pete Peterkin were packing to fly back to Espiritu Santo when the news arrived. Something big was developing up the Groove. A search plane pilot had reported sighting an enemy task force of four cruisers and three destroyers just 140 miles northwest of Guadalcanal. Another search plane pilot who was flying farther north over New Georgia spotted a convoy of twenty-three enemy ships, including eleven heavily laden transports. The big Japanese push was on, and they were coming in broad daylight.

In a whirlwind of activity, every flyable Dauntless, Avenger, and Wildcat was armed, fueled, and sent off. Their first target was the cruiser and destroyer force less than an hour's flying time away.

Swede could only wait in frustration as reports came back that the Cactus fliers had succeeded in sinking one cruiser and badly damaging a second one. As soon as the attack planes returned, they were refueled and rearmed by ordnance men for the next strike.

As badly as Swede wanted to go up again, he knew his request would be rejected. It was an all-Marine show now. He no longer commanded a single plane. He and Pete Peterkin could only watch the Dauntlesses, Avengers, and Wildcats take off from Henderson Field to intercept the transport ships.

The air group found the twenty-three-ship convoy near New Georgia Island. Its twelve escort destroyers sent up an intense barrage of antiaircraft fire as they made smoke and zigzagged wildly to try to confuse the attackers. The slower transports, their decks crammed with thousands of soldiers, couldn't maneuver easily.

The fighters went down to strafe them while the Dauntlesses and Avengers got into position to launch their attacks. One by one, the transports were hit by bombs and torpedoes. The *Nagara Maru* went down first, followed by the *Canberra Maru*. When the air group withdrew after expending its bombs and torpedoes, more than a thousand Japanese soldiers lay floating in the oil-covered sea. Five hours still remained before the convoy would be hidden under the cloak of darkness again. Five hours to determine the course of the Guadalcanal campaign.

A second strike was organized as soon as the planes returned to Henderson Field. They were on the ground less than thirty minutes. Flying back up the Groove, they found the troop convoy continuing resolutely toward Guadalcanal. This time they sank the *Brisbane Maru*.

As soon as they withdrew, eight Dauntlesses launched from the newly repaired carrier *Enterprise* intercepted the convoy and sank the *Shinanogawa Maru* and the *Arizona Maru*. The attacks continued without respite all afternoon. The *Nako Maru* went down with the setting sun.

For a hundred miles along the convoy's tortuous route, debris fields full of dead and dying soldiers and sailors covered the sea. When darkness fell, six of the eleven transports had been sunk or abandoned. A seventh, the *Sado Maru,* the ship carrying the 38th Infantry Division's senior army officers, had been so badly damaged that it had fled northward.

Only four transports were left.

Admiral Yamamoto remained intransigent. At 1740, the Japanese convoy commander received orders from combined fleet headquarters to continue on to Guadalcanal, disembarking the troops and equipment as soon as they arrived.

SAVO ISLAND
JAPANESE BATTLESHIP *KIRISHIMA*
2200

At midnight, the battleship *Kirishima* and its escort force arrived off Sealark Channel to begin their bombardment of Henderson Field. Lookouts aboard the Japanese ships in the vanguard of the formation were startled to observe what appeared to be two American battleships in their path.

Admiral Kondo, who commanded the fourteen-ship Japanese task force from the bridge of the heavy cruiser *Atago*, refused to believe that American battleships could be there, stubbornly holding to the view that they must be cruisers.

To Kondo, heavy cruisers were of little consequence to a Japanese main body that included the *Kirishima*, his own heavy cruisers *Atago* and *Takao*, the light cruisers *Nagara* and *Sendai*, and nine destroyers.

But Kondo was wrong. The battleships USS *Washington* and USS *South Dakota* were there. They had just arrived after steaming at flank speed for almost four hundred miles to intercept the Japanese bombardment force.

The two American battleships had a combined complement of eighteen sixteen-inch guns, and their armor-plated sides were virtually impervious to the *Kirishima*'s smaller fourteen-inch guns. Four destroyers were escorting the battleships, the *Benham, Gwin, Walke,* and *Preston*.

Yet, the Japanese drew first blood.

Their fire was far more accurate. A combination of guns and Long Lance torpedoes quickly sank the *Preston* and *Walke*. The *Gwin* and *Benham* were hit with a combination of shells and torpedoes and forced to retire, the *Benham* mortally damaged. Their withdrawal left the two battleships to confront the fourteen-ship Japanese task force.

Still convinced that he wasn't facing enemy battleships, Admiral Kondo ordered the battleship *Kirishima* to head toward Lunga Point to begin the bombardment of Henderson Field.

The *South Dakota* was firing its first telling salvos when a powerful searchlight on one of the Japanese cruisers found the battleship, exposing its distinctive lines. The five Japanese cruisers and destroyers within firing range began pouring fire at her.

Although *South Dakota*'s armor plate prevented serious damage to the hull, the shells disabled the ship's radar-controlled guns, and ignited major fires on its superstructure. The *Washington* attempted to divert some of the Japanese fire, but after sustaining further damage, *South Dakota* swung away from the battle area.

The *Washington* now faced the fourteen-ship task force alone.

While the Japanese were concentrating their fire on the *South Dakota,* the *Washington*'s Captain Glenn Davis skillfully maneuvered his ship closer to the *Kirishima,* unleashing his sixteen-inch guns at nearly point-blank range.

The resulting damage was devastating. The *Washington*'s barrage disabled two of *Kirishima*'s four gun turrets and pierced her hull belowdecks, jamming the battleship's rudder to starboard, and flooding the steering compartment.

Aboard the *Atago,* Admiral Kondo ordered his escort vessels to pursue and destroy the *Washington.* Over the next hour, Captain Davis continued to maneuver away from them, narrowly avoiding a succession of Long Lance torpedoes, while keeping the Japanese from completing their mission to bombard Henderson Field.

As Kondo sifted the reports from his ships' commanders, he became convinced that his ships had sunk one battleship, four cruisers, and two destroyers. A second battleship was reportedly sinking. As a result, he concluded that the Japanese transports bringing the soldiers of the 38th Infantry Division could now disembark the remaining troops without serious interference.

Canceling Admiral Yamamoto's explicit order to shell Henderson Field, Kondo withdrew his entire force. While retiring northward, he received the unwelcome news that *Kirishima* was no longer capable of full power. Her engines were operating, but as with the *Hiei* two nights earlier, one of the American shells had flooded her steering compartment. The ship could barely make headway.

Kondo left a screening force of destroyers with her, and continued north.

In spite of heroic efforts by *Kirishima*'s crew to contain the fires that had been ignited deep inside her by the *Washington*'s sixteen-inch guns, the flames continued to spread. When they approached the ammunition magazines, they were flooded. However, the battleship continued listing to starboard until it rolled over and sank at 0325.

Far to the south of *Kirishima*'s grave, the last four Japanese trans-port ships raced toward the northern shore of Guadalcanal, desperate to disembark their precious troop reinforcements before daybreak.

There was no time now for the transports to stand offshore for the orderly transferral of troops and equipment to the beaches. Dawn was only two hours away, and the convoy commander radioed or-ders to the captains of the transports that they should run their ships aground.

At 0400, the four transport ships rammed into the shoreline west of the American positions at Lunga Point. A frantic effort began to unload the men and hundreds of tons of supplies and equipment from the hold of each ship.

Twelve miles away at Henderson Field, the pilots and crews of the Cactus Air Force waited in the darkness for their opportunity to de-stroy them.

SUNDAY, 15 NOVEMBER 1942
HENDERSON FIELD, GUADALCANAL
0550

At the first hint of dawn, eight Dauntlesses took off down the bomber strip. The Japanese transports were so close that the dive-bombers were pushing over into their attacks almost as soon as they were in the air.

To one of the pilots, the beached transport he was diving on looked like a disturbed ant hill as hundreds of Japanese sailors and soldiers scrambled for safety. There was no ground fire to deter the dive-bombers, and they quickly delivered direct hits on the first two transports with thousand-pound bombs.

Their flight was followed by Avengers carrying five-hundred-pound bombs. All four transports were wreathed in flames when another five Dauntlesses arrived with thousand-pounders to con-tinue the destruction.

It was like a turkey shoot with sitting ducks.

By 0900, the carnage was over. There were no targets left. The four transports were flaming infernos. The unloaded piles of ammunition, equipment, and supplies had been blown up alongside the ships.

Eleven transports had left Shetland Harbor near Bougainville carrying ten thousand Japanese troops, thirty-two thousand artillery shells, tons of food and medical supplies for thirty thousand troops, and hundreds of tons of military equipment.

When the Japanese made an inventory of what had actually reached Guadalcanal, it consisted of fifteen hundred bags of rice, two hundred sixty boxes of artillery ammunition, and two thousand dazed, unequipped soldiers. In carrying out the mission, the Japanese navy had lost two battleships, one heavy cruiser, three destroyers, and ten transport ships. Its army had lost many thousands of Japan's premier shock troops, along with all of their equipment.

Although the Guadalcanal battle would require several more months of hard fighting before it reached its conclusion, the strategic question had finally been decided. The Japanese would initiate only one more major air attack on Henderson Field before abandoning their effort to retake it in February 1943. From that date to the moment of their surrender in August 1945, the Imperial Japanese forces were in constant retreat across the Pacific.

HENDERSON FIELD, GUADALCANAL
TORPEDO SQUADRON EIGHT
0930

Swede needed one more mission, one last chance to wreak vengeance on the enemy. Unfortunately, Lieutenant Colonel Moret, who commanded the new Marine torpedo squadron, refused to let him fly one of his planes. Larsen had been officially relieved. It was time for him to go.

Swede had requested that he be allowed to stay on as an air operations officer so that he could put all of the experience he had gathered to good use in winning the Guadalcanal campaign. His request was rejected.

Pete Peterkin made arrangements for the ten men left in the squadron to fly back to Espiritu Santo in a B-17 on the morning of

November 16. Of the ten men, there were only two fliers left, Swede and Larry Engel. Pete was the only other officer. The remaining seven were Chief J. C. Hammond, Roy Williams, Hugh Lawrence, Basil Rich, Wiley Bartlett, Charles King, and Ridgeway Liccioni.

After the Cactus air group had come back from destroying the four beached transports, search planes flying a sector northwest of Guadalcanal reported sighting several more enemy vessels, drifting and apparently abandoned. They had been part of the troop convoy wiped out the previous day.

Swede decided to go after them. He knew it was pointless to ask Colonel Moret for the planes to do it. Instead, he went to see Navy Lieutenant Al "Scoofer" Coffin, who commanded the *Enterprise*'s torpedo squadron, and had been operating out of Henderson Field since the *Enterprise* had made its air attack on the battleship *Hiei* two days earlier. Coffin was waiting for orders to return to the carrier.

Swede asked him if he could borrow two of his Avengers for a quick run up the Groove to finish off the last transports. Coffin said sure. Maybe a couple of his own guys would want to go along, too.

Taking Larry Engel and two of the *Enterprise* torpedo pilots with him, Swede led the four Avengers up the Groove one last time. When they arrived over the still burning transports, the ships were drifting without power in the middle of a debris field dotted with rafts, small boats, and floating wreckage. If any Japanese remained alive, they weren't manning the ships' antiaircraft batteries, which were silent.

Swede went in to attack at two hundred feet. As he approached the ship to launch his torpedo, he suddenly saw a Japanese sailor dive headfirst off the stern into the sea. Perhaps the sight of the man affected Swede's aim. Coming in behind him, Larry Engel saw Swede's torpedo run wildly off course.

Engel's torpedo hit the transport amidships and set off a fiery explosion. The pilots circled overhead as the ship settled by the stern and sank within a few minutes. After it was gone, they went down to strafe the rafts and small boats until their ammunition was expended. Then they flew back to Henderson Field.

It was the last attack in the war made by Swede Larsen's Torpedo Eight.

Homeward Bound

MONDAY, 16 NOVEMBER 1942
HENDERSON FIELD, GUADALCANAL
TORPEDO SQUADRON EIGHT
0700

On their final morning at Guadalcanal, Lew Aronson, who now commanded Mahoney's special weapons company, invited Swede and the men of Torpedo Eight to have an early breakfast with him at his new camp.

During their first stay with the unit, Pete Peterkin had fallen in love with the hotcakes Mahoney's Marines ate almost every day. After enjoying them again that morning, he asked the company cook for the recipe. When he checked his watch, Peterkin was shocked to see that they were late for their scheduled departure aboard the B-17 he had lined up for them.

They left the camp on the run, but by the time the men arrived at the airfield, the B-17 was airborne and on its way to Espiritu Santo. When Peterkin checked at the operations tent, he was told there were no other planes large enough to take the men and their gear. It left the group in a sour mood.

At around 0930, Peterkin was making arrangements for where they would stay that night when the low rumble of multiengine aircraft could be heard approaching the field. He looked up to see six transport planes coming in to land.

It took a good deal of persuasion, but one of the transport pilots agreed to take them to Espiritu Santo without official orders. After the plane's cargo had been unloaded, the men of Torpedo Eight came forward to board with their personal gear.

When Wiley Bartlett approached the plane with a Nambu rifle he had found after the October 24 battle, the pilot told him he couldn't bring it on the plane. A few of the other men were also carrying guns and swords. Their pleas to keep the booty fell on deaf ears. Faced with the possibility of being left behind, Wiley Bartlett threw his rifle on the ground and climbed aboard. The others added their weapons to the pile.

Pete Peterkin decided that he wanted to be the last man in the squadron to leave Guadalcanal, and waited until the others got in the plane. When he saw Hugh Lawrence jump down to the runway to enjoy a last smoke, Pete jumped out after him, waiting until Lawrence was back inside before climbing back in himself.

The transport arrived at Espiritu Santo five hours later after an uneventful flight. When they were taken by truck over to Torpedo Eight's camp, Peterkin was impressed with all of the new facilities that had been constructed in the two months he had been gone. Bruce Harwood invited him to stay in the screened bungalow he shared with George Flinn at the edge of the sea.

For some reason, the calmness of the facility seemed to put Swede in a foul temper. He began loudly criticizing the "goldbrickers" who had stayed behind in plush quarters while the squadron was up fighting the real war on Guadalcanal.

A converted cargo ship, the USS *Kitty Hawk*, had been designated to carry the squadron back to San Diego. Everyone tried to stay out of Swede's way as the hours ticked down to the departure time on the eighteenth.

Swede brought the officers together and told them that, unlike the enlisted men, they had two options for getting home. The first was to return with the rest of the squadron aboard the *Kitty Hawk*, which would arrive in San Diego in about two weeks.

The second was to take their chances hitching a ride on one of the many aircraft heading back to Pearl Harbor through New Caledonia. At Pearl, they might catch a faster ship or maybe even find a seat on a plane heading stateside.

The pilots talked it over that evening. The word was that the *Kitty Hawk* would be packed with nearly a thousand men. They would be crammed like sardines into the staterooms and compartments, the facilities would be poor, and the food undoubtedly monotonous. On the plus side, the *Kitty Hawk* was steaming straight to San Diego. Therefore, it was highly unlikely they would be waylaid to join some other understrength torpedo plane squadron.

The option through Pearl Harbor gave them a chance of getting home sooner, but they also were more likely to be press-ganged into a unit that was heading back into harm's way. None of them were anxious for that to happen until they had enjoyed the pleasures of a home leave.

It was a gamble.

Pete Peterkin had no doubt about his choice. Not being a pilot, he was unlikely to get shanghaied along the way. He was going to fly to Pearl Harbor and then try to catch a plane to San Francisco where his wife, Jane, would hopefully be waiting for him.

Smiley Morgan was ready to take his chances, too. From Pearl Harbor, he envisioned getting aboard a converted cruise liner like the famous *Lurline* that George Gay had taken back after the Midway battle. It would be filled with lovely nurses who would be thrilled to meet a young Navy combat flier who had been recommended for the Navy Cross.

After Smiley spoke persuasively about his great expectations, Bob Ries decided to go with him. The thought of spending two weeks stuffed into a compartment with ten guys did not hold the same allure as returning aboard a cruise liner with several hundred nurses to choose from. Andy Divine thought about it awhile and said he wanted to go, too.

Bruce Harwood was flying back to San Diego on a higher travel priority to arrange the stateside transition for all of the men in the squadron before they got there. The rest of the pilots, Bert Earnest, Gene Hanson, Fred Mears, Bob Evarts, Aaron Katz, and Bill Dye, opted for the *Kitty Hawk.*

Fred Mears had become addicted to playing Monopoly. Aboard the *Kitty Hawk,* they would be playing for high stakes, and he was confident that he would be a good deal wealthier when they reached San Diego.

TUESDAY, 17 NOVEMBER 1942
ESPIRITU SANTO
TORPEDO SQUADRON EIGHT
0700

After spending the night in Bruce Harwood's cabin, Pete Peterkin hitched a ride the next morning on a B-25 heading to New Caledonia. At one point during the flight, the plane experienced a mechanical malfunction, and the pilot sent back word for everyone to put on parachutes and prepare to jump.

Pete couldn't believe that after coming through two months of green hell, he would now be forced to jump out of an airplane in the middle of the Pacific. He stood in the navigator's compartment and silently prayed they would make it. When they finally arrived, he quickly caught another flight headed to the island of Nandi in the Fiji Islands. This plane was outfitted with bunks, and he soon fell asleep.

Smiley Morgan, Bob Ries, and Andy Divine had gone out to the airstrip in the morning, too. They got seats on a PBM amphibious plane that was going to New Caledonia. When they got to their first destination on the island of Suva, the two PBM pilots, who were contract fliers from Pan American Airlines, refused to go any farther. They didn't like to fly at night.

The three Navy pilots walked around town, hoping to buy an exotic souvenir to bring home with them, but the shops were empty. Everything good had been sold at outrageous prices to the crews of the American ships that regularly put in there.

They discovered that some of the Polynesian women were more than six feet tall and weighed two hundred pounds. Even Bob Ries was intimidated. The three of them had lunch in one of Suva's seedy hotels.

The food was served by native waiters in black tuxedos. The ambience was slightly undercut when Smiley looked down at the packed-dirt floor and noticed that the waiters were barefoot.

ESPIRITU SANTO
TORPEDO SQUADRON EIGHT
1300

Newton "Del" Delchamps was cleaning his Colt pistol when Aviation Ordnanceman First Class Gordon Comstock, the leading mate in the shop, stopped by to tell him that Swede had called for a final muster of all the enlisted men to hand out promotions for meritorious conduct during the Guadalcanal campaign.

"I think you're going to get a promotion, Del," Comstock told him.

At eighteen, Del had already survived the sinking of the *Yorktown* and had made it through a succession of hairy combat missions before he crash-landed in the Pacific aboard Bill Dye's plane. He hadn't claimed credit for shooting down any Japanese planes, but he thought he deserved a promotion to aviation ordnanceman second class.

He put down the forty-five and walked out to the clearing in the coconut grove where the men were gathering in a big circle. Swede was already there, standing alone in the middle of the group. Del took a place in the circle between his pilot, Bill Dye, and Dye's original turret gunner, Wiley Bartlett, the eighteen-year-old half-Cherokee from Alabama. When Judge Wendt had been wounded, Swede had chosen Wiley as Wendt's replacement.

Once they were all assembled, Swede announced that he was going to reward those men who had earned promotions at both Espiritu Santo and Guadalcanal over the last two months.

Jack Stark was standing in the circle opposite Del Delchamps. Swede's announcement came as a surprise to him. He and Ed Dollard had faithfully kept all of the records of the squadron members' individual actions at Guadalcanal, as well as the daily activities of the men who had remained at Espiritu Santo. He assumed that once they were aboard the *Kitty Hawk*, Swede would ask him for the documentation he and Ed had prepared on each enlisted man in the squadron before making his recommendations for promotion.

From inside the circle, Swede walked up and stood in front of the first man.

It was a radioman–tail gunner who had brought down a Zero

floatplane during one of the Guadalcanal air battles. After telling the man he had performed well in the air, Swede promoted him on the spot.

He then began working his way around the interior of the circle, sometimes stopping to promote a man, sometimes passing a man by without a word. He stopped in front of Bill Tunstall.

Tunstall was the man Swede had accused of trying to kill him by failing to fill his gas tanks before a training flight back at Norfolk. A machinist's mate second class, Tunstall had never gotten up to Guadalcanal. At Espiritu Santo, he had been responsible for preparing the Avengers that were sent to fight up there, and worked on the ones periodically flown back down for maintenance and repair. He was considered one of the best plane captains in the squadron.

"No promotion," said Swede without further elaboration.

As Swede continued to go down the line of men, Jack Stark realized that he was making the determinations solely on the basis of his personal assessment of each man, rather than the man's actual record. He thought it was particularly unfair to the ones who had remained at Espiritu Santo. Swede couldn't know which men had worked the hardest to keep the squadron strong.

Farther down the line, Swede stopped in front of another machinist's mate who had stayed behind on Espiritu Santo. Jack knew him to be unreliable and lazy. Swede promoted him.

Swede had walked past more than half the men in the circle when he came face to face with Newton Delchamps. Stopping, he grinned up at the strapping six-footer. Thinking the smile must bode well for him, Del grinned back. He was a third-class ordnanceman. Being promoted to second class would mean a nice pay raise.

"Delchamps," Swede began, "it says in the Bible that God looks after widows and fools. You better hope so because you're goddam worthless."

Still grinning, he moved on to the next man in line.

Del couldn't believe it. Just as Swede had done back at Guadalcanal when he had ordered Del to salvo the four bombs into the sand, Swede had humiliated him in front of every man within earshot. Shaking with anger, he grabbed for his forty-five, but realized he had left the pistol back in his quarters.

With his right hand, he reached down and grabbed Wiley Bartlett's pistol from his hip holster. In one motion, he pulled back the slide and cocked the hammer. The distinctive sound of a forty-five shell being loaded from the magazine into the firing chamber drew the eye of every man in the circle. Harry Ferrier couldn't believe it was happening.

No one said a word.

Swede turned to look back at him as Del raised the pistol to his chest and yelled, "I'll kill you, you son of a bitch!"

A moment later, Bill Dye grabbed Del's right arm with both hands, and someone else was wrestling him to the ground. Dye forced the pistol out of his hand as Del dropped to his knees under the weight of the man on his back. Sometime later, he could hear Bill Dye asking him if he was all right, and he nodded.

The rest of the men watched as Del was led away. No one else in the circle had moved. Swede was still staring after Delchamps as Bill Dye took him over to a tall coconut palm at the far end of the clearing and sat him down.

"You stay here," he ordered.

Inside the circle of men, the silence seemed to last for a long time. Finally, Bruce Harwood said that they were dismissed. Harwood began talking with Swede as the rest of the group broke up and went back to their quarters.

Del was still sitting under the tree an hour later. By then, he had cooled off enough to know he was in big trouble. He could be facing a general court-martial for the attempted murder of his commanding officer. Dozens of men had witnessed it. If convicted, he would be facing twenty years in a military prison. They could even hang him.

Del knew one thing for sure. If they hadn't tackled him, he would have shot Swede dead. He was still sitting there alone when one of the pilots came over to him. Without saying a word, he reached down to shake his hand, and walked away.

By the time Bill Dye came back to get Del, a whole bunch of the officers and enlisted men in the squadron had come over to shake his hand or whisper, "Way to go, Del." One pilot told him he only wished Del had finished the job.

Dye asked him if he had finally settled down, and when he said yes, Dye told him to go back to his quarters. Del asked if he was under arrest, and Dye said he didn't know. Del returned to his tent and saw that someone had taken away his pistol.

That night, even more men sought Del out to give him a thumbs-up as they packed for the trip back to the States the next day. It struck Del that he wouldn't be going home with them now. Although he didn't have any close family waiting for him in Alabama, it made him sad to think he might not ever see his friends again.

WEDNESDAY, 18 NOVEMBER 1942
ESPIRITU SANTO
TORPEDO SQUADRON EIGHT

Del was talking to a man in the ordnance tent the next morning when Bruce Harwood came by looking for him. His face was grave. Here comes bad news, Del decided.

"Let's you and I take a walk together," said Harwood.

They headed up the apron next to the bomber strip as planes landed and took off alongside them. Del waited for him to say something, but Lieutenant Harwood never said a word the whole way to the end of the runway. They were almost halfway back when Harwood finally spoke.

"I guess you know that was a very foolish thing you did yesterday."

"Yes, sir," said Del.

"I would like to help you if I can," said Harwood.

Del thanked him.

Harwood told him that he had a friend who had just arrived in command of a new Dauntless squadron that was heading up to Guadalcanal. He said that he could get Del a transfer into his friend's outfit. He would tell him that Del was interested in dive-bombers. Nothing would ever be said about what had happened in the clearing.

Del might have been only eighteen, but he wasn't afraid to speak his mind. He thanked Lieutenant Harwood for trying to help, but said he had no interest in dive-bombers, and that he had spent enough time on Guadalcanal to know that he wouldn't be much help to anyone up there right now. All he wanted to do was go home with the rest of the boys in the squadron, he said. Then the Navy could do anything it wanted with him.

They walked along a little farther.

"All right," said Lieutenant Harwood, finally. "But I want you to promise me something, Del. That the next time the skipper makes you as mad as he did yesterday, you'll count to ten before you do anything else."

"Yes, sir," said Del. "You have my word."

Harwood told him that no action would be taken against him, and that he would be free to board the ship with the others. When Del went back to his quarters to pack his things, the other men were amazed to learn that he wasn't going to face punishment.

It wasn't until he was aboard ship and had thought a good deal more about the whole thing, that it struck him that maybe Swede Larsen didn't want anyone outside the squadron to know what had happened in the clearing any more than Del did. At the time, he also didn't know that he was the second man in the squadron who had tried to shoot the skipper.

## USS KITTY HAWK
## TORPEDO SQUADRON EIGHT

The *Kitty Hawk* left Espiritu Santo with a brilliant sun setting in its wake, homeward bound at fifteen knots on the first leg of its long voyage across the Pacific to San Diego.

As had been predicted, the ship was packed with officers and men, more than eight hundred of them in compartments and staterooms designed to hold two hundred fifty.

Fred Mears had been assigned a cot on the open deck, and he was a lot happier to be up there than in the airless compartments belowdecks. At night, the ship was blacked out, and the men gathered in the lounges and staterooms until they were ready for sleep.

He began his first game of Monopoly.

Swede Larsen spent time aboard the *Kitty Hawk* undertaking a sad responsibility that many of the men would have been surprised to know he thought was important. He was writing letters to the parents of the men in the squadron who had been killed in action over the previous months.

They weren't just the customary few lines to each grieving parent or widow. These were individual letters, incorporating his personal recollections of each man. The letter to Chastian Taurman, John Taurman's father, was three single-spaced pages, and deeply poignant in its depiction of John as an extraordinary young man. The letter culminated: "We in the squadron miss John terribly and nothing in the world would give me more pleasure than to be able to send you some good news concerning him. With very kindest regards, believe me, Very respectfully yours, H. H. Larsen."

Later on, Swede sat with Jack Stark and dictated the finishing touches to what would be the final entry in the war diary of Torpedo Squadron Eight. The diary had an entry for every day the squadron had been in the Pacific, commencing with its time aboard the *Hornet*, and continuing through its fateful day of destruction at Midway, its weeks of combat action aboard the *Saratoga*, and its two harrowing months on Guadalcanal.

"This entry completes the war diary of Torpedo Squadron Eight," Swede dictated to Jack Stark. "The spirit, the history, and the tradition of this squadron will never die. It was a pleasure and a privilege to have operated with so fine a group of officers and men against the Japanese forces. H. H. Larsen, Lieut., USN, Commanding."

SATURDAY, 21 NOVEMBER 1942
PEARL HARBOR
SMILEY MORGAN

Smiley had been waiting at a transit center in Pearl Harbor for four days, hoping to be assigned a berth on one of the many ships heading stateside, but all of the ones sailing in that direction were already packed to overflowing. He, Bob Ries, and Andy Divine had been told they would have a better chance of finding single billets, so they had split up to improve their chances.

It had taken three days just to get to Pearl Harbor, and Smiley was beginning to worry that his thirty days of home leave would be over before he ever got there. After spending most of each day at one of the transit centers, he would go back to a temporary transit barracks where the junior officers slept ten cots to a room.

On the fourth morning after he arrived, Smiley came down to the front desk to find a message ordering him to report later that day to an admin building at the submarine base. It sounded suspicious. One of the officers at the barracks suggested that it might mean a transfer to one of the new carrier units being assembled to go back out to the South Pacific.

He finally decided to follow orders, even if it meant a transfer. Once the Navy bureaucracy tracked you down, there was no escaping its wheels. When he arrived at the submarine base, it was to discover that his recommendation for the Navy Cross had come through. It was for the mission in which he had led Andy Divine against the Japanese cruiser *Tone* on August 24, and it was going to be presented in a medal awards ceremony that very afternoon.

The ten officers who were slated to receive awards for valor were assembled in a line on a small drill field near the sub base. As a band began playing "Anchors Aweigh," Smiley watched an officer in dress whites approach the line. The officer looked familiar to him, and a moment later he realized why. He had seen him once before on a rainy morning at Guadalcanal.

It was Chester Nimitz, the commander-in-chief of the Pacific Fleet. Following at his feet was a small dog. At first glance, it looked to the veterinarian's son like a collie mix. The dog halted when the admiral came to a stop in front of the first man in line. A staff officer read a brief citation, and the man was awarded the Distinguished Flying Cross. After pinning it on, Admiral Nimitz exchanged a few words with him, and moved on to the next man. The admiral's pet took a few more steps and sat down again. Smiley thought that the dog must have attended these ceremonies before.

Then it was Smiley's turn.

"'For extraordinary heroism as pilot of a torpedo plane,'" the staff officer began reading.

Smiley kept staring forward. Admiral Nimitz had a friendly, benign smile on his face. To Smiley, he looked more like one of the kindly parish priests he knew back in Florida than the commander of the Pacific Fleet.

"'. . . Lieutenant Morgan, defying terrific fire from hostile antiaircraft batteries and Japanese Zeroes, launched a vigorous and determined attack which scored a direct hit on an enemy cruiser.'"

When the staff officer finished reading the citation, Admiral Nimitz stepped forward and pinned the Navy Cross to his chest.

"Congratulations, Lieutenant," he said, shaking Smiley's hand.

Then he was on to the next man, the small dog following along in his wake. The ceremony was over in less than thirty minutes. Smiley briefly celebrated back at the BOQ before returning to the transit center to await news of a ship heading back to the States. Now that he had received the Navy Cross, he thought that the admiral's staff might pass the word along for him to receive a stateroom on the *Lurline* or one of the other passenger liners.

Five days later, his name was finally called for a berth aboard a ship that was leaving Pearl that night. It was bound for San Diego, the same destination as the rest of the squadron aboard the *Kitty Hawk*.

This ship was named the *Sacramento*. The name sounded good to him.

Smiley asked what kind of ship it was, but the sailor in the transit center didn't know. He only told him that the ship was anchored out in the harbor, and that a coxswain would take him out to it in a motor launch later that night.

It was pitch dark when the launch pulled away from the wharf and motored out into the mooring area where all of the troop and transport ships stood silently at anchor. Aside from Smiley, there were a few officers going out to board other troop carriers.

Pearl Harbor was still under blackout restrictions, and as they chugged slowly between the shadowy outlines of the darkened vessels, the coxswain kept calling out the name of the ship they were trying to find.

When there was an answering call, the coxswain brought the launch close to a boarding ladder that rose into the darkness far above them. Once the other officers were aboard, the launch continued in its search for the *Sacramento.*

"*Sacramento . . . Sacramento,*" the coxswain kept hollering into the black night.

Smiley finally heard an answering cry.

"*Sacramento* here," came a voice out of the darkness.

The voice hadn't come from very far above them, as with the previous ships. It sounded more like the sailor had been hailing them from the pier of a dock. When they pulled up next to the *Sacramento,* there was no boarding ladder to climb, just a quick set of steps leading to an open wooden deck. As the launch chugged away into the darkness, Smiley's heart sank.

This was no converted passenger liner, and it wasn't filled with returning nurses. The *Sacramento* turned out to be an old gunboat that had seen long duty in China, and was barely larger than a garbage scow.

The ship was under way almost immediately, and a sailor escorted Smiley to his small cabin. He was relieved to see that he had it all to himself, what there was of it. The cabin was just large enough to hold a single bunk the size of a large dog bed and a built-in wooden cabinet with a tin pitcher and bowl for washing.

Smiley went out to explore the rest of the ship. Pulling aside the blackout curtains to enter what he had been told was the main passenger lounge, he was surprised to see several military policemen armed with rifles standing guard inside.

The reason was quickly evident. They were guarding a group of American men in fatigues who were congregated at the back of the lounge. Some of them had their hands and feet manacled together. A big white "P" was painted on the backs of their shirts.

The *Sacramento* was taking them back to the States for incarceration in military prisons and stockades. The group included deserters, rapists, thieves, and murderers. A few of them glared back at him with obvious contempt. Instead of beautiful nurses, they were to be his principal dinner companions. Aside from the crew, Smiley was one of the few non-prisoners aboard. *This is going to be a long voyage,* he thought.

It was.

In spite of the fact that the thirty-year-old ship had once been known as the "Galloping Ghost of the China Coast," her best days were clearly behind her, and she wallowed along at barely ten knots.

It also turned out that most of the toilets for the ship were located just on the other side of the bulkhead from his own cabin. Day and night, the men in the johns would flush the toilets using a jet of sea water from high-pressure foot pumps. Smiley thought that each effusion sounded like a belching walrus.

Once they were out in the middle of the Pacific, things took a turn for the worse. They began to run into heavy weather, and it persisted for days. In rough seas, the little gunboat pitched and rolled like a cork. The sound of men retching and the commodes flushing became an almost permanent anthem.

Surprisingly, the food was pretty good, at least by Guadalcanal standards, and Smiley usually enjoyed the meals, particularly when he could keep them down. It took the *Sacramento* almost two weeks to reach San Diego. By then, there had been an outbreak of fever among the prisoners, and Smiley contracted it, too. He spent the first week of his leave recovering at Balboa Park Hospital.

Upon finally reaching his parents' home in Florida, Smiley found mail waiting for him. The Navy communication stated that Torpedo Squadron Eight had been officially decommissioned, and Smiley was being assigned to a new unit being formed in Seattle, Washington. It made him sad to think he would never again see many of the men he had served with during the most exciting seven months of his life.

Torpedo Eight had written its final chapter in the skies over the Pacific.

# Epilogue

Today, Midway Atoll's airfield on Eastern Island, the place from which Langdon Fieberling led the first six aircraft that attacked the vanguard of the Japanese fleet on June 4, is an eerily desolate place, a windswept landscape primarily left to the gooney birds and sand crabs. There is little hint of what occurred there during one of the pivotal battles of World War II.

The carrier USS *Hornet*, from which Lieutenant Commander John Waldron and his men went gallantly to their deaths, rests in an unfound grave at the bottom of the Pacific. The USS *Saratoga*, "Sister Sara," from which Bruce Harwood's flight of Torpedo Eight took off to sink the Japanese carrier *Ryujo* on August 24, 1942, was assigned in 1946 to become part of Operation Crossroads, in which it was used to test the effect of an atomic bomb blast at Bikini Atoll. The ship now lies at the bottom of the lagoon there.

Guadalcanal's Henderson Field, from which Torpedo Eight made its important contribution to stopping the Japanese advance in the Pacific, is now named Honiara International Airport, after the capital city of the Solomon Islands. It would be unrecognizable to the men of the Cactus Air Force who fought there, and is now the center of an important economic hub.

Torpedo Eight earned a unique record of achievement in the annals of the United States Navy. In the Midway and Guadalcanal campaigns, the squadron was officially credited with sharing in the destruction of two enemy carriers, one battleship, five heavy cruisers, four light cruisers, one destroyer, and one transport, along with numerous enemy aircraft.

Torpedo Eight sustained the highest number of casualties of any naval air squadron that fought in the Midway battle, as well as of all the naval squadrons that flew with the Cactus Air Force on Guadalcanal. At Midway, forty-five of the forty-eight officers and men serving in Torpedo Eight were killed. At Guadalcanal, seven of the remaining squadron members were killed and another eight wounded.

Its thirty-five pilots won an astounding thirty-nine Navy Crosses. The enlisted men in the squadron earned more than fifty medals for bravery in action, including multiple awards of the Distinguished Flying Cross, the Silver Star, and the Air Medal. Although official Navy records of military awards are not maintained on a squadron-by-squadron basis, Torpedo Eight might well have been the most highly decorated air squadron of the war.

Torpedo Eight earned another distinction that was unparalleled among the naval squadrons operating in the Pacific in 1942. It was the only unit to be awarded two Presidential Unit Citations from Franklin Delano Roosevelt, the first for the squadron's contribution to the victory at Midway, and the second for its distinction at Guadalcanal.

With the decommissioning of the squadron, the survivors of Torpedo Eight each received thirty days of home leave, after which they were ordered to join new units. For those readers interested in what happened to some of them, a brief account of their subsequent lives follows.

## BERT EARNEST

After returning to the states aboard the *Kitty Hawk,* Bert Earnest went home to Richmond, Virginia, looking forward to renewing his relationship with Jerry Jenkins, the Smith College student whose name he had scrawled on the instrument panel of the Grumman Avenger he had flown at Midway. At Guadalcanal, he had named his second plane in her honor as well. When it was destroyed, he had "Jerry III" inscribed on the fuselage of his third aircraft. That one suffered the same fate as the first two.

The recipient of three Navy Crosses, the Purple Heart, and numerous other medals for his bravery at Midway and Guadalcanal, Bert became one of the most honored early heroes of the war. This didn't seem to impress Jerry Jenkins, who waited for him to come home to announce that she had been engaged to someone else. He ruefully concluded that she probably wasn't the right girl for him anyway. He also decided to forgo naming any of his combat aircraft in the future.

In January 1943, he was assigned to a composite squadron, VC-31, a Navy innovation made up of both Avenger torpedo planes and Wildcat fighters, and based in Seattle, Washington.

On temporary leave in San Diego, he met and fell in love with Millie McConnell, the beautiful daughter of Navy Captain Robert McConnell, who had commanded the carrier USS *Langley* at the start of the war. In 1944, Millie and Bert were married at St. Alban's Cathedral in Washington, D.C.

Bert's new composite squadron was assigned to the aircraft carrier *Manila Bay*, and he left for the Pacific again in January 1944. During his second overseas tour, he flew more than a hundred missions supporting the invasions of Kwajalein, Eniwetok, and Majuro, as U.S. forces closed in on the Japanese home islands.

Returning to the States, Bert was recruited to make test flights of captured enemy aircraft, including a Messerschmitt 262, the first jet-powered fighter in the German Luftwaffe. On his first takeoff in the ME 262, an engine caught fire and the burning jet crashed into the dense copse of trees beyond the runway, stripping away both wings before finally coming to a stop. Incredibly, Bert stepped out of the remaining section of the fuselage uninjured. The two-dollar bill he had found on the runway at Midway was still in his wallet.

When the war ended, Bert became a Navy "hurricane hunter," logging more than a thousand hours in a B-17 as it gauged the wind speed of the fiercest hurricanes that assaulted the Eastern seaboard. He went on to enjoy a successful thirty-year career in the Navy, commanding an attack squadron, an air group, and an amphibious command ship.

He and Millie raised two children, Kathryn and David.

After completing a stint at the Naval War College in Newport,

Rhode Island, Bert received a three-year posting in Paris on the staff of the Supreme Allied Commander of NATO. In the late 1960s, he commanded the Naval Air Station at Oceana, Virginia.

Bert retired from active duty as a captain in 1972.

The shredded Grumman Avenger that Bert flew at Midway in what Admiral Chester Nimitz called "an epic of combat aviation" was shipped back to Pearl Harbor, where it was studied by aeronautical engineers to determine how it could have possibly survived all of the damage it received. The analysis comprised eight single-spaced pages, including each enemy projectile's size, point of entry, vertical angle, and horizontal angle. Considerable attention was devoted to the fact that the engine and all three propeller blades had received numerous hits and yet the plane had continued to fly.

All told, the engineers counted at least seventy-three separate holes from machine gun bullets and cannon fire. They conceded that there were so many large holes in the aircraft, as well as so much shrapnel inside, that the number of actual hits was considerably higher. Every component in the plane, including the fuselage, wings, tail, cockpit, windshield, turret, engine cowling, wheels, elevators, stabilizers, and instruments, had been perforated by bullets or shells. After the inspection was completed, the "metal Lazarus" was put aboard another transport ship and shipped to San Diego, where it was stored in a Navy hangar. Later in 1942, a base maintenance officer ordered it sold for scrap.

Bert's best dress white uniform from his first Pacific tour remains in the laundry of the USS *Hornet* at the bottom of the Pacific. His only keepsake from his time on Guadalcanal is a rusted cockpit chronometer that he keeps in his study. The captured Japanese ceremonial sword that he was awarded by General A. A. Vandegrift is now on permanent display at the Virginia Military Institute Museum in Lexington, Virginia.

At least two Grumman Avengers have been preserved for future generations. One is at the Pensacola Naval Aviation Museum in Florida, and another at the Admiral Chester Nimitz World War II Museum in Fredericksburg, Texas.

When the two exhibits were first opened to the public, both museum curators chose to honor Bert Earnest's combat achievements in the Pacific by inscribing his name on the cockpits. He was the only pilot honored in this way. After George W. Bush was elected president of the United States, Bert's name was removed from the aircraft at Pensacola, and replaced with the president's name. Bert's name remains on the Avenger at the Nimitz museum in Texas.

Millie Earnest passed away in 2007, and Bert lives in quiet retirement in Virginia Beach, Virginia. Whenever he drives his car, the ninety-year-old Bert carries the two-dollar bill he found on the runway at Midway on the night before his first combat mission.

## Smiley Morgan

Smiley Morgan returned to Florida to discover that the news accounts of Admiral Nimitz personally awarding him the Navy Cross had preceded his arrival home. The story of his unescorted attack against the Japanese cruiser *Tone* appeared in every newspaper across southern Florida.

This new celebrity made no more difference to his girlfriend, Caroline, than Bert's heroism had to Jerry Jenkins. Caroline gently informed him that she had fallen in love with another man while he was away.

After completing his convalescent leave, Smiley reported to Composite Air Squadron VC-35 in Seattle, Washington. Like Bert's newly created unit, it was composed of both Wildcat fighters and Avenger torpedo planes.

Following a brief training period, the squadron was assigned to the escort carrier *Chenango,* and its pilots were ordered to fly their aircraft to San Diego, California, where they were to be deployed aboard the ship. Near El Centro Marine Air Base north of San Diego, the engine in Smiley's Avenger caught fire. Trapped for almost a minute in the smoke-filled cockpit, he was the last one to bail out before the plane crashed and burned.

While on leave in San Diego, Smiley enjoyed a brief reunion with Bert Earnest, whose squadron was awaiting its own deployment to the Pacific aboard the *Manila Bay.* They were having drinks in the bar of the Del Coronado Hotel when a mutual friend, Charles De Bretteville, invited them to a cocktail party in the penthouse of the hotel his family owned.

There, Smiley met a famous married couple who would become his lifelong friends. They were the film star Gary Cooper and his wife, Veronica "Rocky" Shields Cooper. After the party, the Coopers asked Bert and Smiley to join them for dinner, and at the conclusion of the meal, Gary invited them to spend their next leave at the Coopers' home in Los Angeles.

Once Bert met Millie McConnell, his leave time was taken up with preparations for their wedding. Unattached, Smiley was virtually adopted by the Coopers, and joined them for every leave he enjoyed during the rest of the war, often traveling to Sun Valley, where he fished and went trap shooting with Cooper, Ernest Hemingway, and Clark Gable.

Back in Los Angeles, Rocky took him under her wing and introduced him to the young actresses who came to their regular dinner parties, including Ingrid Bergman, Sonja Henie, and the teenaged Lauren Bacall, who could only talk to Smiley about Humphrey Bogart.

One night, Rocky asked Smiley to escort Mary Livingston, the wife of comedian Jack Benny, to the premiere of the film, *Thirty Seconds Over Tokyo*, which starred Spencer Tracy and Van Johnson. Smiley wore his dress blues, and sat directly behind Van Johnson. When Rocky introduced the two of them before the movie started, Smiley mentioned that he had served aboard the *Hornet*, and had enjoyed meeting the real Jimmy Doolittle, who was being portrayed in the film by Spencer Tracy.

At the end of the movie, which was a powerful and stirring account of Doolittle's raid on Tokyo early in the war, the stars of the film were treated to a long, standing ovation, almost as if the actors themselves had flown the missions that helped turn the tide of the Pacific War. As the cheering continued, Van Johnson stood to acknowledge the audience's ovation. When he turned to wave up at them, he noticed the Navy Cross on Smiley's chest and was mortified.

"This is really embarrassing," he said with an apologetic grin.

In October 1943, Smiley returned to the Pacific aboard the

*Chenango,* flying close air support missions in the battles of Tarawa, Kwajalein, Eniwetok, and Okinawa. After being promoted to commanding officer of his squadron in March 1944, he had the fuselage of his plane painted with the name "Maria," after Gary and Rocky's only child. In the invasion of Guam, his plane was hit by enemy antiaircraft fire and he was forced to ditch in the Pacific. Picked up by the destroyer USS *Kidd,* he continued to fly combat missions at the Battle of Leyte Gulf.

Smiley returned to the States after fourteen months aboard the *Chenango,* having won the Distinguished Flying Cross and three more Air Medals. Shortly before the war ended, Smiley was introduced by his friend Chuck Spalding to another Navy officer who was in Los Angeles receiving treatment for a back problem he had exacerbated out in the Pacific. His name was Jack Kennedy. They hit it off and Kennedy invited Smiley to stay with him at the Beverly Hills Hotel whenever he was in town. The friendship led Smiley into less platonic encounters with Hollywood starlets.

When the war ended, he decided to stay in the Navy, and was assigned to a tactical development unit, COMFAIR West Coast. Afterward, he oversaw the training of reserve pilots at the Naval Air Station in Atlanta, Georgia.

In 1949, Smiley was on duty at the Naval Air Station in St. Louis when he met the young woman who would become his wife and soul mate. Nancy Corrigan was twenty. Smiley was thirty-two. They were married on September 24, 1949.

Smiley left the Navy with the rank of commander in 1954 to become an executive with the New England Mutual Insurance Company in St. Louis. He and Nancy had five children during a long and happy marriage. Eventually, they moved back to Florida.

In 1995, shortly before Nancy's death from cancer, she and Smiley made a visit to Hawaii, where they spent a day vacationing with Bert and Millie Earnest. While there, they visited the National Memorial Cemetery of the Pacific, in which the names of Bert and Smiley's friends from Torpedo Eight are forever engraved on the Punchbowl monument.

On the day before they were due to return to the States, Nancy asked Smiley if he would take her out to see the USS *Arizona* memorial. He had not planned on seeing it again. His memories of the doomed ship were deeply emotional. He could remember the smell of the sunken battleships as he had sailed slowly past on the day Torpedo Eight had arrived in Pearl Harbor aboard the *Chaumont*. That day had also been the precursor for the three long years he had spent flying combat missions in the Pacific.

Since it was their last afternoon in Hawaii, he agreed to escort Nancy out to the memorial in the National Park Service launch. At the entrance to the facility, he went to the ticket counter, just one more elderly, white-haired man shuffling up on bad knees. There, he was told by the young park service attendant that all of the tickets for the final launch of the day had already been sold. "I'm sorry," she said, pointing to the large tour group waiting to board. When Smiley looked over, he saw that it was a large party of Japanese sightseers.

Without rancor, he escorted Nancy back to their hotel.

In 2002, driving from the wedding ceremony of his youngest son, Chris, to the reception, he suffered the first of several heart attacks. Smiley Morgan's great heart finally gave out on April 3, 2007. He passed away at Tampa General Hospital, survived by his adoring children, Richard, Chris, Mimi, Markey, and Nancy.

## THE TORPEDO EIGHT SURVIVORS

The author has tried to garner as much information as possible about all the officers and men of Torpedo Eight who came back with the squadron from Guadalcanal. Over sixty-five years, the trail has unfortunately run cold for many of them. What follows are brief accounts of the postwar lives of some of the squadron's veterans.

### FRANK BALSLEY

After returning to San Diego aboard the *Kitty Hawk*, the young turret gunner's goal was to follow in the footsteps of Darrel Woodside, Red Doggett, and Bill Dye, and become an enlisted Navy pilot. He applied for flight training and was accepted into the program.

After winning his wings, Frank Balsley eventually logged more than ten thousand hours in the cockpits of nearly every aircraft in the Navy arsenal. Retiring from military service in 1965, he flew another fifteen thousand hours as a civilian, many of them for a private airline in Laos and Saigon during the Vietnam War.

The man whose closest friends growing up were Japanese-Americans remains a three-handicap golfer as he approaches the age of ninety. Today, he lives in San Jose, California.

### JACK BARNUM

Barnum's tour in the Pacific as a pilot with Torpedo Eight was enough to last him a lifetime. After he returned to the States, he turned in his wings.

### WILEY BARTLETT

After contracting a severe case of malaria on Guadalcanal, Bartlett nearly died aboard the *Kitty Hawk* as it headed home across the Pacific. Following convalescent leave, he was assigned to a new composite air squadron.

Shortly after reporting to the carrier *Manila Bay*, he discovered that Bert Earnest was one of the pilots in the squadron. "You're going to fly with me," Bert told him, and Wiley did. Through dozens of missions at Kwajalein, Eniwetok, and Majuro, Wiley flew as Bert's turret gunner, earning two Distinguished Flying Crosses and seven Air Medals for bravery in action.

In 1944, Wiley became a bombardier on the Navy version of the B-24 bomber. Flying out of the Philippines, the squadron flew twelve-hour missions every two days to Japanese targets inside China.

He turned twenty years old as the war ended. Marrying his sweetheart, Rolande, who was then serving in the women's naval volunteer service, he spent twenty years in the Navy, retiring to go to work for the Lockheed Corporation, after which he and Rolande bought and operated a commercial fishing boat in Monterey, California.

Wiley lives today in Repton, Alabama.

### NEWTON DELCHAMPS

Shortly after returning to San Diego with the rest of Torpedo Eight, Del Delchamps passed the test to become an aviation ordnanceman second class, and received the promotion that Swede Larsen had denied him on Espiritu Santo.

One night on home leave in Alabama, he met a pretty young woman named Effie Bishop, whose date for the evening had unfortunately become drunk. Del and Effie danced and talked until three o'clock in the morning. He left to go back to the Navy with the understanding that she would wait for him.

During his next Pacific tour, he was assigned to Torpedo Squadron Six aboard the USS *Enterprise*. There, he was selected to be a member of the flight crew of the commander of the carrier's air group, James "Bucky" Lee. When Commander Lee left the air group in October 1943, Del joined the crew of the carrier's next group leader, the legendary Lieutenant Commander Edward "Butch" O'Hare, the first naval aviator in the war to win the Medal of Honor. At one point, Del confided to O'Hare that he would someday like to be a pilot himself, and O'Hare cut him orders to attend flight school.

Heading to the States, Del was shocked to pick up a newspaper and read that Butch O'Hare had been killed while flying a night mission from the *Enterprise*. Del counted him as the finest pilot he ever flew with in the Navy after Bill Dye.

On New Year's Eve 1943, Del and Effie were married in Gulfport, Mississippi. While completing flight training in Athens, Georgia, Del's class was informed that due to the surplus number of trained pilots already in the fleet, 50 percent of them would not win their wings, regardless of performance. Del was one of the unlucky ones.

At Cecil Field near Jacksonville, Florida, he was allowed to take the exam to become chief aviation ordnanceman. He passed it, and spent the next twenty years in a succession of Navy assignments that took him to Florida, Puerto Rico, Jacksonville, Brunswick, Maine, Newfoundland, and on two long cruises to the Mediterranean.

He retired from the Navy as a master chief, aviation ordnanceman, and became an agent of the New York Life Insurance Company. At the age of eighty-six, Del lives with Effie in Fairhope, Alabama. They have two daughters, five grandchildren, and nine great-grandchildren.

### ROBERT "ANDY" DIVINE

Along with Smiley Morgan, Andy Divine was assigned to Composite Air Squadron 35 (VC-35) out of Seattle, Washington. When Smiley became the commanding officer of the composite squadron, Andy was appointed his executive officer.

When the war ended, Divine retired from the Navy and became a crop-dusting pilot near Fresno, California. He and his wife, Sarah, had two children, Dennis and Denise. In November 1986, they were returning to their home in Fresno when a trailer truck ran a stop sign and hit their pickup truck broadside. Sarah was killed instantly. Andy passed away from burns and internal injuries a few days later.

### WILLARD HENRY DYE

Curly Bill Dye, the pilot with the most flying hours in Torpedo Eight and the lowest rank, was promoted to lieutenant in September 1943. His wartime assignments included service with Composite Air Squadrons 41 and 34. He retired from the Navy in 1946.

### WILLIAM ESDERS

Bill Esders, one of the handful of survivors of the three torpedo squadrons that fought at Midway, continued to fly torpedo planes through the rest of the war. After his active-duty service in the Navy, he retired to Pensacola, Florida, where he served as a volunteer guide at the naval history museum.

When Swede Larsen visited the museum in 1980, Bill Esders was surprised to see that his former commanding officer was in a wheelchair. Personally committed to remaining in good physical condition, Bill Esders ran every day regardless of the weather.

During a morning run in 1995, he collapsed and died of a heart attack.

### ROBERT EVARTS

Bob Evarts returned to the States long enough to serve as the best man at the wedding of Gene Hanson and his fiancée, Joy. Always the hard-luck pilot of Torpedo Eight, Evarts was shot down during the air battle over Saipan in 1944. He and his crew disappeared in the sea.

### HARRY FERRIER

Upon his return to the States, Harry went home to visit his mother in West Springfield, Massachusetts. Boarding a train in Los Angeles, he was assigned a seat next to an enlisted soldier whose sister had come to see him off. When she left, the soldier told Harry that she was an aspiring movie actress, and that her name was Ava Gardner. Harry had never heard of her.

Harry continued to fly in torpedo planes and dive-bombers for most of the war, serving aboard the carriers *Enterprise* and the second *Yorktown*. He was commissioned as an ensign at the age of nineteen in January 1945, and decided to make the Navy his career.

Married in August 1945, he and his wife, Chris, had two children, four granddaughters, and five great-grandchildren. In the 1950s, he participated in two atmospheric nuclear tests in Nevada. Kneeling in a trench not far from ground zero, he was told to keep his head down when the flash came. He remembers feeling the hot blast of the explosions sweep over him. To this day, he blames his poor blood-platelet count on those tests.

During the Vietnam War, Harry made three combat cruises aboard a helicopter carrier supporting Marine amphibious troops. He retired from the Navy in 1970 with the rank of commander.

Following his retirement, he served as a public school director, a planning commissioner, and the elected auditor of Whideby Island, Washington. In 1998, he accompanied Dr. Robert Ballard in his successful search to find the remains of the first USS *Yorktown* where it sank in the Central Pacific after the Battle of Midway in 1942.

His military awards include the Distinguished Flying Cross, the Purple Heart, and three Air Medals. Today, Harry Ferrier lives on Whideby Island. He still has the baseball cap he was wearing when he was wounded at Midway.

### GEORGE FLINN

At the conclusion of the war, the independently wealthy Yale graduate joined the naval reserve, eventually being promoted to the rank of captain. Always proud of his service as the personnel officer of Torpedo Eight, he lived in Greenwich, Connecticut.

On March 8, 1967, he met with the author Walter Lord, who was writing a book about the Midway battle to be called *Incredible Victory*. In the interview, Flinn expressed great admiration for John Waldron as an extraordinary combat leader who never resorted to patriotic harangues or locker-room speeches.

### George "Tex" Gay

Tex never asked for the celebrity he earned as the one man from Waldron's squadron to come back alive. The nationwide publicity he received as the sole survivor came with a high price.

A few of the widows and fiancées of the Torpedo Eight pilots killed in the battle concluded that he was only after personal glory. The fact that he hadn't sought any didn't keep them from resenting the massive publicity he received.

Admiral Chester Nimitz did not subscribe to this view. After meeting Gay at Pearl Harbor right after the battle, he took a genuine liking to his fellow Texan, and later in the war invited him to go on private fishing excursions in Hawaii and Florida.

Tex served his second tour in the Pacific as a member of Torpedo Squadron Eleven, which was based at Guadalcanal between April and July 1943. There, he won an Air Medal for flying numerous combat missions against Japanese naval and land-based targets.

Tex came back to serve as a flight instructor at the Naval Air Station in Jacksonville, Florida. Appreciating the value of Tex's celebrity to the nation's continuing war bond drives, the Navy periodically ordered him to travel across the country, visiting patriotic organizations, shipyards, aircraft plants, and high schools, and giving radio and newspaper interviews.

Tex met his future wife, Tess, at a going-away party arranged for him shortly before he was transferred from the Jacksonville Naval Air Station. For Tex, it was love at first sight, and they were married on May 14, 1946. Recruited to become a commercial airline pilot, he enjoyed an unblemished thirty-year career with Trans World Airlines.

Occasionally, he was invited to speak at historical forums commemorating the American victory at Midway. At one of them, Bert

Earnest and Harry Ferrier were also invited to attend. They were standing at the back of the auditorium when Tex was introduced as the sole survivor of Torpedo Eight. Someone asked them why they were there, and Bert replied, "We're the other sole survivors."

Tex Gay died on October 21, 1994. Prior to his death, he had requested that his cremated ashes be flown out to the grid coordinates in the Central Pacific where John Waldron and the rest of his squadron had gone down while attacking the Japanese fleet. There, they were scattered on the wind.

### Rete Gaynier

After Ozzie Gaynier went missing at Midway, Rete remained confident that he had somehow survived. The vivid dream in which he visited her bedside after the battle had convinced her that he was alive, perhaps on an island or as a captive of the Japanese.

Needing to support herself, she started work at the Naval Air Station in San Diego in the overhaul and repair shop. One of her jobs was to ride in a gas-powered scooter to meet each arriving aircraft and check its serial numbers to make sure they matched the manifest. She would always ask the men coming back from the Pacific if they had ever met Ozzie.

It was only after Swede Larsen came to visit her many months later that she finally changed her mind. In a surprisingly gentle way, Swede told her that Ozzie wasn't coming back. Later, she came to interpret his dream visit in a different way. When Ozzie had told her he was all right, it must have meant that he was in a better place.

Rete didn't fall in love again until she met Roy Janiec, a Navy flier who commanded an air squadron. She and Roy were married in 1949, and raised two sons, Chris and David. Both boys attended Annapolis and became Navy aviators.

Today, Rete and Roy live in Oregon.

### William R. Grady

The other "Tex" in Torpedo Eight recovered from the injuries he suffered falling out of the back of a truck on his second day at Guadalcanal. Considered by other squadron members to be an overly risk-taking pilot, he was killed in a training accident later in the war, purportedly while performing air acrobatics. Unable to pull up, his plane crashed and burned.

## JAMES C. HAMMOND

Chief Petty Officer Hammond received a Silver Star for his service at Guadalcanal, in large part for reconstructing three combat aircraft to fly missions against the Japanese during the most critical weeks of the campaign, and while under daily attack from enemy artillery and aircraft. As was the case with Bill Dye, the author was unable to learn more about this remarkable man.

## EUGENE HANSON

Gene returned from Guadalcanal having earned two Navy Crosses but with a lingering sense of unwarranted guilt over the death of Major Michael Mahoney on October 23, 1942.

In early 1943, Gene married his fiancée, Joy. Bob Evarts was his best man at the ceremony. It would be the last time Gene saw Evarts before he was shot down and killed off Saipan.

After joining a new composite squadron in Alameda, California, Gene headed back out to the Pacific aboard the carrier *Lexington* in early 1944. He and Joy had arranged a primitive code so he could send her clues about where he was, but the campaigns moved so quickly that she could rarely keep up with him. At the Battle of Leyte Gulf, the *Lexington* was hit by a kamikaze plane. It slammed into the carrier's island and exploded close to where Gene was standing on the flight deck. The man next to him was killed when a piece of shrapnel tore through his abdomen. Gene was miraculously uninjured.

When the war ended, Hanson became the operations officer for VS-27, an antisubmarine squadron that began monitoring the movement of Soviet submarines off the East Coast of the United States. Gene was promoted to its commanding officer, and the squadron earned the Navy "E" for excellence that year, marking it as the best naval air unit in the Atlantic Fleet.

Gene and Joy had two sons, David and Robin. After graduating from the Naval War College, Gene served in a succession of important posts. His last job was on the staff of Admiral John McCain, the father of the senator from Arizona.

Gene retired from the Navy in 1966 as a captain. After his retirement, he accepted a job with the City of New York, taking command of the small fleet of vessels that dumped the city's sewage sludge far out in the Atlantic. He jokingly told old friends that he had finally made admiral.

In 1980, he was planning to attend a reunion of Torpedo Eight and had already booked his reservations when he discovered that Swede Larsen was planning to attend. He canceled his plans.

Joy Hanson passed away after a long illness in 2007. Gene lives today with his son Robin in Pensacola, Florida. At ninety, he feels he has been blessed with living on borrowed time ever since 1942.

### Bruce Harwood

Admired by every man in the squadron for his quiet humility, Bruce returned from his service at Guadalcanal to join his wife, Sadie, in San Diego. Appointed to the staff of the commander of Fleet Air in Seattle, Washington, he was promoted to commander in March 1944. He left the staff to become the air officer on the USS *Princeton,* an Independence-class light carrier that was heading out to the Pacific as part of soon-to-be-legendary Task Force 58, commanded by Admiral Pete Mitscher. By all accounts, Mitscher had grown into a brilliant carrier tactician and combat leader in the years after Midway.

On October 24, 1944, during the Battle of Leyte Gulf, a Japanese dive-bomber scored a direct hit on the *Princeton,* setting off a series of violent explosions. With intense fires raging along the hangar deck and threatening to ignite the *Princeton*'s ammunition magazines, Bruce Harwood personally led the crews' firefighting efforts as they attempted to save the ship. Showing utter disregard for his own safety, he repeatedly went belowdecks to compartments in which men were trapped by fire and smoke, dragging a number of them to safety. In a final attempt to save another group of trapped men, he ordered the rest of his team to stay behind as he went forward alone. A few minutes later, a bomb exploded in the compartment, killing Harwood and everyone inside. The *Princeton* went down later that day.

Recommended by his commanding officer to receive the Medal

of Honor for his consummate valor, Bruce Harwood posthumously received a third Navy Cross, the first having been awarded for leading the attack against the carrier *Ryujo,* and the second for leading Torpedo Eight on six successful missions against the Tokyo Express during the Guadalcanal campaign. The destroyer USS *Harwood* was named in his honor.

### HERB JAY

Jay, the first Jewish pilot who served in Torpedo Eight, was flying cross-country on a training mission later in the war when his aircraft disappeared over the Great Lakes. No trace of him was reportedly ever found.

### AARON KATZ

After enjoying home leave with his parents and seven sisters in Cleveland, Aaron reported to VT-37, an air squadron assigned to the escort carrier USS *Sangamon.* Shortly before the carrier left for the Pacific, Katz received an invoice from a supply officer in Alameda, California, requesting reimbursement to the United States government of $25.69. The charges were for one scarf, one pair of goggles, and one flying suit that he had not turned in after the Guadalcanal campaign. He sent his check.

Promoted to executive officer of VT-37, he participated in combat actions at Tarawa, Palau, Hollandia, Saipan, and Leyte Gulf. In addition to the Navy Cross he won on August 24, 1942, for his part in the attack on the *Ryujo,* Katz went on to earn the Distinguished Flying Cross and five more Air Medals.

After the war, Aaron returned to Cleveland, where he joined his father, Sam, in the family scrap-metal business. In August 1945, he married the lovely Marjorie Osher, whom he had met while on leave after his second Pacific tour. They had three children, Roger, Rick, and Barbara.

Katz was a stoic man, and one of the few times his children ever saw him become emotional was when the family visited Hawaii. After riding out in the harbor to see the *Arizona* memorial, he remained in the launch, quietly weeping.

Aaron remained proud of his service with Torpedo Eight, and of the friendships he had made with many of its pilots and crewmen. When it came to his commanding officer, he only told his sons that Swede Larsen was a "tough guy."

Aaron Katz passed away on June 21, 1999.

### ZYGMOND "SKI" KOWALEWSKI

While on leave at his parents' home, Ski learned that he had been awarded the Silver Star for bravery for his missions as a radioman-gunner aboard the *Saratoga* in August 1942. It took a spot on his mother's mantelpiece alongside the medal he received from Admiral William Halsey for his missions as a turret gunner during the Guadalcanal campaign.

Like Frank Balsley, Ski wanted to become a Navy flier, and put in an application for flight training. There was no response. In 1944, he was serving in a ground-support role at Quonset, Rhode Island, when Swede Larsen happened to visit the airfield. It was the first time Ski had seen him since they had left Espiritu Santo on the *Kitty Hawk*.

Ski told Swede that he had applied for flight training, but hadn't heard anything for more than a year. Swede asked for a copy of his application. Two weeks later, Ski received orders to attend flight school. He won his wings in 1944, and went on to enjoy a wide range of flight assignments all over the world. After retiring from the Navy in 1960, he became a flight inspector for the Federal Aviation Administration.

At the age of eighty-nine, he lives in Anchorage, Alaska.

### HAROLD HENRY "SWEDE" LARSEN

Swede got his wish to go back to Guadalcanal, but he never succeeded in winning the Medal of Honor. Along with the two Distinguished Flight Crosses he earned during the early months of the Guadalcanal campaign, he was awarded two Navy Crosses, the first for his attack against the Japanese cruiser force on August 24, 1942, and the second for his leadership in the critical weeks of October 1942, when he often went up alone to deliver air strikes against Japanese ships and positions.

After family leave in Alabama with his wife, Sadie, and their young daughters, he returned to Guadalcanal as operations officer of the air command still operating there. Shot down on a night mission off the Japanese-held island of Kolumbangara, he survived in the sea until he was rescued. During his second tour, he earned a Bronze Star with combat "V" for meritorious service.

Released from combat duty, Swede served on the staff of the chief of naval operations before becoming an assistant naval attaché in England. After the war, he served as executive officer of the USS *Norton Sound,* a guided missile ship, before graduating from the Naval War College. Later he commanded the USS *Tripoli,* a transport carrier. His last operational assignment was as a Navy task group commander.

By most accounts, Swede mellowed as he got older. Lee Marona, who saw him several times through the 1980s, said that Swede spoke proudly of the record achieved by Torpedo Eight, and fondly remembered most of the men who served in it. He retired from the Navy as a captain in 1965, and settled in Birmingham, Alabama, where he became a real estate agent and was active in St. Mary's Episcopal Church. Happily married until Sadie's death in 1987, Swede and Sadie had four daughters: Sarah, Melissa, Maria, and Evelyn. Their son, Harold Jr., passed away in 1972.

In 1980, Swede attended a reunion in Pensacola of the pilots who served in Torpedo Eight. Although he was in declining physical health, he clearly enjoyed visiting the Naval Aviation Museum, and receiving a tour from former squadron pilot Bill Esders.

He died on February 6, 1994, and is buried in Elmwood Cemetery next to his wife and son.

### NANCY LEWIS

The younger sister of Vic Lewis was broken-hearted at his loss, as were Vic's parents, and Anna McGory, the young woman Vic had hoped to marry. Tragically, Anna died soon after Vic. In 1944, the Lewis family attended the launching of the USS *Victor Lewis,* the destroyer escort named in his honor. Vic's mother, Serena, christened the hull before it slid down the slipway.

After his son's death, Maurice Lewis continued his work as a traveling salesman for the American Safety Razor Company. His territory included the state of Maine. Later in the war he was returning home after a business trip when he saw a small group of enlisted sailors thumbing a ride from the side of the road. He stopped to pick them up, and one of them expressed his gratitude. Their leave had nearly expired, and they were required to report back aboard their ship within the next few hours. "What ship is that?" Maurice asked them.

The *Victor Lewis,* one of them responded.

### WILLIAM MAGEE

While enjoying home leave in New Castle, Pennsylvania, Bill decided to apply for flight training. His application was approved a few months later. After winning his wings, he was commissioned ensign and assigned to fly Curtiss Seahawk observation planes. For the next two years, he participated in air-sea rescue operations. He left the Navy in 1946.

Hired as the personal pilot to a wealthy banker, he found the job boring, and decided to go into business for himself, initially operating a feed store in San Diego and then starting a pet supply company, before eventually becoming a successful contractor and construction consultant, specializing in interiors for major department stores.

He married his first girlfriend, Ann, a professional singer whose books he used to carry to school in the third grade. They currently live in Phoenix, Arizona. Bill often wakes up remembering the night of October 13, 1942, when the Japanese battleships shelled Guadalcanal and he survived the wild ride down to the beach while bent over the front fender of the ammo delivery truck.

### GENERAL LEE MARONA

On June 5, 1942, the day after Torpedo Eight was virtually wiped out at Midway, Lee applied for flight training aboard the USS *Hornet.* His inspiration to become a Navy flier was Robert Miles, the young enlisted pilot who replaced Frenchy Fayle after his injury at Pearl Harbor, and was killed in his place at Midway. Miles had become a mentor to the young Marona, and Lee wanted to honor his sacrifice.

After the squadron was decommissioned in December 1942, Lee and his brother Jess were transferred to an engine overhaul unit, Acorn One, based in Espiritu Santo, a decision that made neither one of them happy. In mid-1943, Lee was standing in the rain near the runway at Espiritu Santo when he saw a jeep go by with a familiar figure in the back. It was Swede Larsen. Lee told Swede that although he had applied for flight school a year earlier, he hadn't heard anything since. A few weeks later, Lee's orders assigning him to flight training came through.

Assigned to the same flight class as Eddy Velazquez and Frank Balsley, he won his wings at Pensacola and became a commissioned officer. In 1948, his plane was forced down in Japan during a storm and he met his future wife, Mary Armstrong, the daughter of an Army major serving there in the occupation forces. He and Mary had three sons, Christopher, Jonathan, and Patrick, before Lee retired from the Navy as a lieutenant commander. His last active service was as the guided-missile officer on the USS *Midway* off Vietnam in 1964.

Lee started an insurance business in Phoenix, spending as much time as possible skiing, fishing, and hunting with his three boys. He and Mary still live there. His younger brother Jess lives in San Francisco, California.

### Frederick Mears III

Arriving back home in Seattle in the middle of a January blizzard, Fred basked in the company of several young women before deciding to write a reminiscence of his experiences as a Navy flier, beginning with the day he and several other Navy pilots learned that the Japanese had attacked Pearl Harbor.

He showed the first few chapters to his sister, Betty, an award-winning writer, and she pronounced it highly readable. She recommended submitting the pages to an editor she knew at Doubleday, Doran publishers. After reading the work, the editor expressed interest in publishing the finished manuscript. Drawing heavily on the daily journals he maintained through the first year of the war, Fred completed the manuscript in less than three months, the last part of it while training with his new air squadron, VC-18.

Upon receiving the completed draft, the editors at Doubleday agreed to publish it in early 1944, and expressed the hope that he would consider writing a follow-up book. By then, his new composite squadron, VC-18, was still training near San Diego. On June 26, 1943, Fred took off in his Avenger on a routine training flight, leading a formation that included two other planes.

Fred was leading the formation in a bombing exercise about one mile north of Otay Mesa, California, when he pushed over and dove his plane at an almost vertical angle. As he was attempting to pull out from his dive, part of the plane's tail surface peeled off, followed by the plane's left wing. Hopelessly out of control, the Avenger dove into the ground and blew up.

The investigative report on the accident concluded that Fred was flying too fast. Killed in the aircraft with him were his two crewmen, gunners Jack Booth and Joe Daniels.

Smiley Morgan was deeply moved by the news of Mears's death. One of his enduring memories of Guadalcanal was Fred wearing his striped pajamas and steel helmet as he streaked to his bomb shelter during the Japanese shelling attacks. Fred's death was particularly hard on his mother, Jessie, whose brother, four-star general Jonathan Wainwright, was still being held prisoner by the Japanese. Fred was her only son.

When his ashes arrived home, Betty asked Bob Ries, who was then stationed in Seattle with his new squadron, to fly them out over Puget Sound and scatter the ashes to the wind.

Fred's book, *Carrier Combat,* was published by Doubleday, Doran in 1944. It was met with critical acclaim, and hailed as one of the finest combat memoirs to come out of the early war years.

## DeWitt "Pete" Peterkin

Pete was the first member of the squadron to make it back to the States, managing to secure a coveted seat on a clipper leaving Pearl Harbor, and landing in Alameda, California, on November 22, 1942, exactly six months from the day Torpedo Eight had departed for the Pacific aboard the USS *Chaumont.*

After calling his wife, Jane, to say that he was all right, he arranged to visit the grieving family of Langdon Fieberling at their home on Wesley Avenue. Lang's fiancée was already there when he arrived. After six months of agonizing uncertainty, she was still clinging to the hope that he might be alive. Pete tried to sound encouraging.

Assigned to another carrier squadron, Pete remained on active duty in the Navy until the end of the war. After going into private life, he decided to stay in the naval reserve, eventually reaching the rank of captain. For his leadership in helping to keep Torpedo Eight's Avengers flying at Guadalcanal under appalling conditions, he was awarded the Distinguished Service Medal.

Pete spent the rest of his professional career working as an executive at J. P. Morgan & Co., eventually becoming vice chairman of the bank. Retiring in 1976, he undertook a range of philanthropic pursuits, serving as chairman of United Fund-NY, president of Roosevelt Hospital, chairman of the Yale University development campaign, and chairman of the board of trustees, Kent School.

Married to Katharine Urban after the passing of his first wife, Jane, Pete was father to five children: Clare, Kate, DeWitt III, George, and Patrick. He passed away on August 29, 1997.

### CARROLL "JACK" STARK

While home on leave in Terre Haute, Indiana, Jack met a girl from Bismarck, North Dakota, who was visiting a neighboring family. He and Adeline were married in 1943, shortly before he returned to the South Pacific for his second overseas tour.

Promoted to chief yeoman, he was honorably discharged from the Navy in October 1945, went to college on the GI bill, graduated from Indiana State in 1948, and then served as a high school guidance counselor until retiring in 1985. He and Adeline were married for fifty-nine years, and had a daughter, Kimberly Anne.

Sensing the importance of what Torpedo Eight had accomplished during its months in the Pacific, Jack saved copies of many of the records from his service with the unit, including the daily diary of the squadron, and individual records of the men who served in it.

He passed away from cancer in the summer of 2007.

### WILLIAM TUNSTALL

The machinist's mate whom Swede once accused of trying to kill him came back to the States and promptly fell in love with a young woman who was serving as a Navy WAVE. He and Dottie were married on August 21, 1943.

Assigned to the carrier *Kitkun Bay*, Bill went back out to the Pacific in 1944. In the climactic Battle of Leyte Gulf, the carrier received fire from the largest battleship in the world, the *Yamato*, before barely surviving a kamikaze attack. The Japanese plane came straight over the catwalk where Bill Tunstall was standing and exploded farther down the deck.

Later in the war, he was promoted to ensign for his distinguished service, and left the Navy as a lieutenant in 1946. With his and Dottie's first daughter on the way, he tried selling insulation door to door, and made one sale after three weeks of effort. It was time to try something else. He went to work for the Bell Telephone Company and has never looked back.

Thirty years later, he retired to focus on enjoying life with Dottie in Portland, Oregon. In 2007, he visited Midway Atoll with a small group of veterans to commemorate the sixty-fifth anniversary of the American victory there.

### EDWARD VELAZQUEZ

One of the handful of Torpedo Eight machine gunners who was credited with shooting down a Japanese fighter, Ed learned long after the war that the pilot of the Zero he shot down on August 24, 1942, had claimed credit for destroying several of the Torpedo Eight aircraft at Midway less than three months earlier.

Ed returned to the States with the same ambition as many of the enlisted men: to become a Navy flier. After earning his wings as a naval aviation pilot, he was assigned to fighter squadron VF-12A, based in San Diego.

He met his future wife, Charlotte, on a train heading from Omaha to Los Angeles. After marrying, they raised five children together. Ed left the service with the rank of lieutenant commander, and moved his family to California. After discovering his gifts as a printer and linotype operator, he went on to develop several successful entrepreneurial ventures.

Edward Velazquez lives today in Huntington Beach, California.

### Ervin "Judge" Wendt

Swede's favorite turret gunner, and the man whom Gene Hanson credited with teaching him many of the skills he needed to survive as a combat pilot, spent months recovering from the wound he received while flying air support missions on Guadalcanal. At Pearl Harbor, doctors removed the shrapnel still embedded in his arm and elbow.

After his arm healed, Judge was assigned as a senior instructor at the training school for bombardiers in San Diego. Eighteen months later, he was assigned to a patrol squadron based on Saipan that rescued B-29 flight crews forced to ditch in the Pacific after they attacked Japan.

When the war ended, Wendt was given a succession of important operational assignments, including a senior instructional position at the Fire Control School in Jacksonville, Florida. Later on, he served as the senior noncommissioned officer responsible for maintaining the seaplanes operating out of Adak in the Aleutian Islands. He remained in the Navy for thirty years.

On home leave in Audubon, Iowa, in 1943, he met Marie Smith. They enjoyed fifty-nine years together before her death in 2002. At the age of ninety-two, Judge Wendt now lives in San Diego. His home overlooks the naval base where he served for many years.

*The author urges readers to visit the Web site Adawnlikethunder .com, which is devoted to the memory of the men who served in Torpedo Eight, and includes material about each of them, including many of the letters, diaries, and photographs that could not be included in the book. Hopefully, the Web site can be updated to reflect information provided by other family members in the years ahead.*

# APPENDIX ONE

# The Undaunted Mr. Weisheit

In *A Dawn Like Thunder,* I set out to write a story about the men of a single torpedo squadron who gave their lives helping to buy the precious battle time that allowed another group of brave aviators to win an incredible victory in the battle that changed the course of the Pacific War.

It was not my intention to gather evidence that at least some of these men died that day because of the egregious mistakes of their commanding officers, and that these mistakes would later be suppressed in a cover-up of the truth.

Admiral Marc "Pete" Mitscher died in 1947. At his request, his personal papers from the Second World War were burned. In Theodore Taylor's subsequent biography, *The Magnificent Mitscher,* which was published in 1954, Admiral Mitscher was justifiably lionized for his exceptional performance as a carrier task force commander during the last years of the Pacific War.

By any measure, including his own, Admiral Mitscher was clearly not magnificent during the Battle of Midway, his first engagement against the Japanese navy. I did not come to this harsh judgment through any personal animus. My uncle flew an Avenger off the USS *Cowpens* as part of Admiral Mitscher's legendary Task Force 58, and he revered him.

Yet the conclusions are seemingly inescapable, even accepting that men's memories are imperfect, that confusion often reigns in the fog of battle, and that honest mistakes are inevitable for every commander in war. In this case, the harsh judgment is compounded by the fact that Admiral Mitscher attempted to evade responsibility for his decisions, and to veil the unpleasant truth of his failures in a long-standing lie. Given the emerging consensus among distinguished historians about what actually occurred on June 4, I felt it was important to tell this part of the story.

Few men were aware of what occurred on the bridge of the *Hornet* on the morning of June 4. Admiral Raymond Spruance, Mitscher's task force commander, surmised the truth, and he passed it along to his own superior, Admiral Nimitz, who chose not to address the issue publicly.

In June 1942, naval aviation was faced with a burgeoning rivalry with the Army Air Forces, which were actually claiming credit for winning the Battle of Midway. Admiral Nimitz was not about to air the Navy's dirty linen in public. The cover-up was allowed to stand, just as a few years later, Admiral Nimitz would give Admiral William Halsey similar dispensation in the wake of Halsey's disastrous decisions during a December 1944 typhoon, and his impetuous actions during the Battle of Leyte Gulf. Nimitz's only punishment of Mitscher for his actions on June 4 was to give him a dull shore assignment when he was desperately anxious for another combat command aboard fast carriers.

One can imagine the humiliation and embarrassment Mitscher felt at his failures during the Midway battle. If it had been lost, his actions might well have cost him his professional career, just as Admiral Husband Kimmel was publicly humiliated and cashiered after the Pearl Harbor disaster. But Midway had been a great victory, and, fortunately for Mitscher, no one in Washington wanted to see the Navy's first triumph of the war tarnished.

According to his biographer, Mitscher was melancholy and at times distraught on the passage back to Pearl Harbor because he felt he had "personally failed to deliver." Some of his actions on the trip were bizarre. For example, a young lieutenant apparently misplaced a pair of bridge binoculars while standing watch during the battle and Mitscher ordered that the ship be searched for them. The binoculars were not found, and Mitscher came to the conclusion they had been stolen. After the ship arrived at Pearl Harbor and his crew was given leave, Mitscher had naval intelligence agents scour the pawnshops in Honolulu looking for the binoculars. Later, they were found behind a couch in the *Hornet*'s chart room.

The falsehood about where the *Hornet* air group was sent on the morning of June 4 withstood public scrutiny for more than thirty years. In their superb historical works on Midway, historians Samuel Eliot Morison, Walter Lord, and Gordon Prange never probed beneath the surface of Mitscher's "official" account of the *Hornet*'s actions on the morning of June 4.

The lie remained embedded in the public consciousness until Bowen P. Weisheit, a trial lawyer from Bel Air, Maryland, embarked on a personal quest to discover the truth. The reasons he did so are worth noting.

One of the pilots in the *Hornet* fighter squadron who was forced to ditch in the Pacific on June 4 was Ensign Markland Kelly Jr. Along with Ensign G. R. Hill, he was never seen again. Kelly's death was a great blow to his father, a wealthy Marylander who owned the Buick automobile dealership in Baltimore, Maryland. Mr. Kelly died shortly after the war, leaving his estate to a foundation created in honor of his son.

Bowen Weisheit, who was a fraternity brother of Ensign Kelly's, was eventually appointed one of the trustees of this foundation. While attending a board meeting, he noticed a ten-dollar bill framed in a glass case, and was told that it was the "short snorter" bill that had been presented to Mark Kelly's father by a PBY rescue pilot who had rescued four of the fighter pilots after they ditched in the Pacific near Mr. Kelly's son. It was a Navy tradition that after a man was rescued from the sea he would give his rescuer the largest bill he had with him at the time. These were called "short snorter" bills.

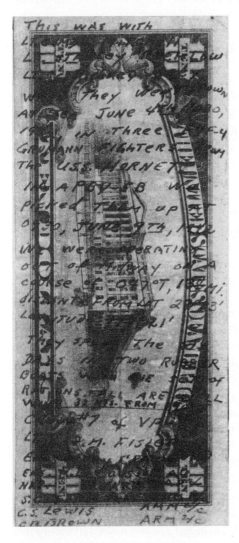

When Bowen Weisheit removed the ten-dollar bill from its frame and turned it over, he saw that the rescue pilot, Jerry Crawford, had recorded on it the navigational course the plane had been flying when it had picked up the survivors, along with the longitude and latitude of the spot where the PBY had landed in the sea.

Bowen P. Weisheit was not just any Maryland lawyer. As a student at St. John's College in Annapolis, he had not only learned the classics, but had studied celestial aerial navigation under the legendary Annapolis professor of navigation, Commander P. V. H. Weems. After finishing law school at the University of Virginia, Weisheit was recruited to teach navigation at the newly created Weems School of Navigation.

In 1942, Weisheit joined the Marine Corps, becoming a navigation instructor, and eventually flying hundreds of hours as a navigator, many of them across the Pacific. As Weisheit pointed out to me when we first met, he had plotted long-range ocean aircraft flights to a point where they were part of his fabric.

After making a copy of the short snorter bill, Mr. Weisheit went home to examine his old navigational charts of the Pacific, carefully plotting the coordinates of the location where the pilots had been rescued. After comparing the location to the accounts described by Samuel Eliot Morison and Walter Lord, he was astonished to find that Crawford's coordinates pointed to a spot that was nearly two hundred miles east of the place where the ditching had supposedly taken place.

So began Weisheit's mission to solve the mystery.

Eventually, his relentless intellectual curiosity took him all over the country to conduct personal interviews with every living *Hornet* fighter pilot he could locate who had flown the June 4 mission. He also interviewed several of the dive-bomber pilots, including Walter Rodee, as well as Admiral John Foster, Mitscher's air operations officer during the Midway battle. Later, he was able to track down Jerry Crawford, the PBY pilot who had presented Mark Kelly's father with the short snorter bill. The detailed account of Weisheit's three-year journey can be found in his self-published book, *The Last Flight of Ensign C. Markland Kelly, Junior, USNR.*

After sifting through his fifty hours of interview transcripts, Weisheit began to reconstruct the flight of the *Hornet* air group from the moment it left the carrier until the mission came to its tragic end, eventually building a body of evidence that permitted him to come to one inescapable conclusion. The course reflected in the official map that was part of Admiral Mitscher's After Action Report was irreconcilable with the course the air group had actually followed that morning.

The handwritten coordinates scrawled by Ensign Jerry Crawford on the short snorter bill on June 9, 1942, augmented by the testimony of the pilots and staff officers he interviewed, were the keys to learning the truth. Weisheit was finally able to draw a new map that reflected what happened to the *Hornet* air group on the morning of June 4, 1942. I am proud to have his permission to reprint it as part of this appendix.

The noted Pacific War historians John Lundstrom, Robert Cressman, Jon Parshall, Anthony Tully, Mark Horan, Alvin Kernan, and James Sawruk have all endorsed Weisheit's findings.

Perhaps the strongest endorsement came from Admiral Thomas H. Moorer. Upon reading Mr. Weisheit's book, Admiral Moorer, who had served as a young naval aviator aboard the USS *Lexington* and was eventually promoted to Admiral Nimitz's job as the commander-in-chief of the Pacific Fleet (CINCPAC) before becoming chairman of the joint chiefs of staff under President Nixon, requested a personal meeting with Weisheit.

After spending two hours probing Weisheit's case with a barrage of tough questions, Admiral Moorer's conclusion was that the Navy "hadn't gotten it

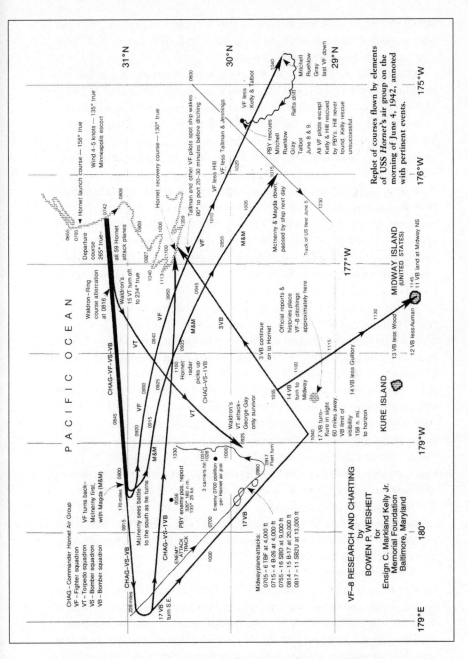

ACTUAL FLIGHT OF THE *HORNET* AIR GROUP,
JUNE 4, 1942

right." He then made a bulk order of Weisheit's work, making sure the book went to every American naval library in the world, starting with the Naval War College in Newport, Rhode Island.

Why was Bowen Weisheit's quest so important? It was significant because the Midway battle might well have turned out differently if Pete Mitscher hadn't sent his air group in the wrong direction. If Stanhope Ring had chosen to follow John Waldron to the Japanese fleet, the *Hornet*'s thirty-four dive-bombers, ten fighters, and fifteen torpedo planes would have made a simultaneous attack. Conceivably, the death toll in Torpedo Eight might not have been so high.

Admiral Spruance believed that all four Japanese carriers would have been sunk on the morning of June 4 if the *Hornet* air group's dive-bombers had participated in the battle, and that the American carrier *Yorktown* would have survived to continue the fight in the Central and South Pacific.

In April 2006, I met Bowen Weisheit, then eighty-seven, in his unimposing street-front law office in Bel Air, Maryland. My first impression was of a tall, craggy-faced man with bright and youthful blue eyes. He was wearing a tweed sports jacket with a red scarf around his neck and looked more like a retired college professor than the legal lion he was once reputed to be.

His large desk and the tables behind it were cluttered with piles of maps and navigation charts, and he was quick to tell me that he was in the middle of another quest, this one trying to help the family of a missing Army Air Force general who disappeared in a B-17 over the Japanese-held island of Rabaul. An hour later, we hadn't even begun to touch on the subject I had come a long way to see him about. In our ensuing talk, and in many hours of conversation thereafter, we went over all of the raw material of his investigation into the death of his fraternity brother Mark Kelly, including the interview transcripts and the notes from his conversations with many of the men who were part of the *Hornet* air group on the morning of June 4.

Ultimately, the only aspect of the Midway controversy that Weisheit did not have a strongly held view on was why Pete Mitscher would send the *Hornet* air group so far north of the last reported location of the Japanese striking force, losing almost half of his planes in the process.

In a later interview, John Lundstrom, the leading historian on American naval aviation in the Pacific during the 1942 battles, stated his firm belief that the air group's course was unquestionably chosen by Mitscher, who by temperament and personality would never have delegated responsibility to a subordinate on such an important decision. By all accounts, Pete Mitscher was incredibly strong-willed. Other historians have used words like "headstrong" and "obstinate."

Mitscher had won his wings at Pensacola in 1916, one of the first thirteen men to go through the program, and in early 1942, he was convinced that he knew far more about carrier aviation than just about anyone else in the Navy, including his superiors at Midway, Fletcher and Spruance, neither of whom had any aviation training.

Lundstrom's reasoning for why Pete Mitscher sent his air group west is that Mitscher had a strong hunch that the last two Japanese carriers in the striking force were lagging far behind the first two when they were initially spotted by American search planes.

American naval doctrine in early 1942 called for separating its own carrier forces so they would be less vulnerable to a single attack. In the wake of the Pearl Harbor attack, American naval planners believed that the Japanese carriers had been separated by as much as five hundred miles.

If Pete Mitscher thought that the four Japanese carriers in the Midway striking force were operating in separate groups, it could explain why he sent his air group west instead of southwest.

Regardless of the reasoning, Admiral Mitscher never accepted responsibility for his decision, instead allowing Stanhope Ring to bear the weight of denigration and scorn from the *Hornet* pilots for the rest of his life. Ring never publicly confirmed the course he flew on the morning of June 4, although he was well aware that many of the men who flew with him at Midway thought he was a bungler and a coward.

If a Faustian bargain to remain silent was indeed struck, Stanhope Ring benefited by receiving the Navy Cross for his leadership at Midway, the same medal bestowed on John Waldron and the pilots who died with him. Before his retirement, Ring eventually reached the rank of vice admiral. He died of a cerebral hemorrhage at the age of sixty in May 1963. The headline of his obituary in the *Washington Post* read ADM. STANHOPE RING, HERO OF MIDWAY BATTLE.

Bowen Weisheit wrote another book about his own wartime experiences in the South Pacific, entitled *How Nature's Deadly Foresight Fashioned Weisheit Hindsight*. It consists of his many adventures, some deadly, some whimsical, including a harrowing flight from Bougainville to Leyte in which his flight crew fought to survive the December 1944 typhoon that sank three American destroyers in Admiral Halsey's task force.

Bowen Weisheit says he has several more books to write before he finally puts down his pen.

# APPENDIX TWO

## "They're Still Out There"

The following list of the dead from Torpedo Squadron Eight is taken from a list of dead and missing dated November 26, 1942, and is reproduced exactly as written in the muster compiled by Yeoman Carroll "Jack" Stark. The list is part of the official squadron records.

| DEAD OR MISSING | NEXT OF KIN |
|---|---|
| William W. ABERCROMBIE<br>Ensign A-V(N), USNR | Mr. G. W. ABERCROMBIE (father)<br>5811 Mastin Road<br>Merriam, Kansas |
| Charles E. BRANNON<br>Ensign A-V(N), USNR | Mr. W. T. BRANNON (father)<br>808 Mulberry Street<br>Montgomery, Ala. |
| Charles E. BRANNON | Mrs. C. E. BRANNON (wife) |
| George M. CAMPBELL<br>Lt. (jg), USN | Mrs. Genevive CAMPBELL (wife)<br>3160 Suncrest Drive<br>San Diego, California |
| James H. COOK<br>Ensign, A-V(N), USNR | Mrs. Marjorie Stevenson COOK<br>(wife)<br>4002 Curtis Lane<br>Shreveport, La. |
| William W. CREAMER<br>Ensign, A-V(N), USNR | Mrs. Dora E. CREAMER (mother)<br>Route #2, Box 545<br>Riverside, California |

Harold J. ELLISON
Ensign, A-V(N), USNR

Mrs. Audrey Faye ELLISON (wife)
707 7th Street
Coronado, California

William R. EVANS, Jr.
Ensign, A-V(N), USNR

Mr. William R. EVANS (father)
5019 N. Meridian Street
Indianapolis, Indiana

Langdon K. FIEBERLING
Lieut., USN

Mr. Charles A. FIEBERLING
(father)
623 Wesley Avenue
Oakland, California

Oswald J. GAYNIER
Ensign, A-V(N), USNR

Mrs. Ireta GAYNIER (wife)
563 Maple Street
Plymouth, Michigan

John P. GRAY
Ensign, A-V(N), USNR

Mrs. Roy C. GRAY (mother)
713 Missouri Avenue
Columbia, Missouri

Henry R. KENYON, Jr.
Ensign, A-V(N), USNR

Mrs. Verna M. Kenyon (wife)
122 J. Avenue
Coronado, California

Victor A. LEWIS
Ensign, A-V(N) USNR

Mrs. S. V. LEWIS (mother)
245 Allen Street
Randolph, Massachusetts

Raymond A. MOORE
Lieutenant, USN

Mrs. June Anita MOORE (wife)
155 Halifax Avenue
Petersburg, Virginia

Ulvert M. MOORE
Ensign, A-V(N), USNR

Mr. L. E. MOORE (father)
440 Union St.
Bluefield, West Virginia

James C. OWENS, Jr.
Lieutenant, USN

Mrs. Helen Marie OWENS (wife)
1446 Belfast Drive
Los Angeles, California

John (n) TAURMAN
Ensign, A-V(N), USNR

Mr. Chastian TAURMAN (father)
2115 Gilbert Avenue
Cincinnati, Ohio

Grant W. TEATS
Ensign, A-V(N), USNR

Mr. Bert A. TEATS (father)
Sheridan
Oregon

John C. WALDRON
Lieutenant Commander, USNR

Mrs. Adelaide W. WALDRON
(wife)
932 Brandon Avenue
Norfolk, Virginia

Jeff D. WOODSON
Lieutenant (jg), USN

Mrs. J. D. WOODSON (wife)
30 Hermosa
Vallejo, California

R. R. BIBB, Jr. (Ross E.)
ARM2c, USNR

Mr. Ross R. BIBB, Sr. (father)
Warrior, Alabama

Max Arthur CALKINS
ARM3c, USN

Mr. W. S. CALKINS (father)
417 So. 11th Street
Wymore, Alabama

Nelson Leo CARR
AM3c, USNR

Mr. Leo J. CARR (father)
263 Kenwood Court
Grosse Point Farms, Michigan

Nicholas Thomas CHORAK
Sealc, USNR

Mrs. Mary SHILEY (sister)
1430 Shermer Avenue
Northbrook, Ill.

Darwin L. CLARK
ARM2c, USN

Mr. Lawrence CLARK (father)
Rodney, Iowa

Otway David CREASY, Jr.
ARM2c, USNR

Mr. O. D. CREASY, Sr. (father)
327 Sowman Street
Vinton, Virginia

Horace F. DOBBS
ACRM(PA), USN

Mrs. Velma Margaret DOBBS
(wife)
PO Box 1266
San Diego, California

Benjamin Monroe DOGGETT
CAP(AS), USN

Mrs. Nana B. DOGGETT (wife)
4101 Colonial Avenue
Norfolk, Virginia

Bert "O" EDMONDS
AOM1c, USN

Mrs. Kathe EDMONDS (mother)
1009 Alta Street
Longmont, Colorado

Charles Edison FAIR
AOM3c, USN

Mrs. Laura FAIR (mother)
East South Street
Whitesboro, Texas

George A. FIELD
ARM3c, USN

Mrs. Franklin E. SMITH (mother)
1935 Second Avenue
St. Petersburg, Florida

Ronald Joseph FISHER
ARM2c, USN

Mr. and Mrs. Joseph H. FISHER
117 West 3rd Avenue
Denver, Colorado

James Cleveland HAWKINS
Ptr3c, USN

Mr. J. F. HAWKINS (father)
Cove City
North Carolina

John Duane HAYES
ARM3c, USN

Mr. & Mrs. George E. HAYES
(parents)
Nashua
Iowa

Robert K. HUNTINGTON
ARM3c, USN

Mrs. E. C. WELSH (mother)
1118 Donaldo Court
South Pasadena, California

William Clare LAWE
AM3c, USN

Mrs. Nancy Lee LAWE (wife)
2403 Devries St.
San Diego, California

Conrad Hugh LAWRENCE
AM1c, USN

Mrs. Magnolia PHELPS (mother)
P.O. Box 414
Vivian, Louisiana

Amelio MAFFEI
ARM1c, USN

Mr. U. MAFFEI (father)
2207 Olivet Rd.
Santa Rosa, California

Jay Darrell MANNING
AMM3c, USN

Mr. Jay MANNING (father)
Port Orchard, Washington

Hollis MARTIN
ARM2c, USNR

Mrs. Josephine MARTIN (mother)
1525 Sixth Avenue West
Seattle, Washington

Stephen Joseph McGOWAN, Jr.
Sea1c, USNR

Mr. S. J. McGOWAN, Sr. (father)
323 Leah Street
Utica, NY

John William MEHLTRETTER
EM3c, USN

Mr. John MEHLTRETTER
(father)
Dousman, Wisconsin

Arnold Theodore MEARS
Ptr2c, USN

Mr. John MEARS (father)
Ramel, Minnesota

Robert Bruce MILES
AP1c, USN

Mrs. Doris Pauline MILES (wife)
3449 Myrtle Avenue
San Diego, California

Arthur Raymond OSBORN
ARM2c, USN

Mrs. Beulah May OSBORN
(mother)
3736 Tejon Avenue
Pine Bluffs, Wyoming

Tom Hartsell PETTRY
ARM1c, USN

Mrs. T. H. PETTRY (wife)
Beaver, West Virginia

Bernard P. PHELPS
ARM2c

Mr. Ernest PHELPS (father)
Arthur, Illinois

Aswell Lovelace PICOU
Sea2c, USNR

Mr. Lovelace PICOU (father)
Houms, LA., L.C. Route

Howard William PITT, Jr.
Sea1c, USN

Mr. Howard William PITT, Sr.
(father)
Berlin, Illinois

Francis Samuel POLSTON
Sea2c, USN

Mr. Coy F. POLSTON (father)
Orange, Missouri

John ROBAK, Jr.
Sea1c, USN

Mr. & Mrs. John ROBAK, Sr.
(parents)
5898 Broadway
Lancaster, N.Y.

William Franklin SAWHILL
ARM3c, USN

Mr. Earl SAWHILL (father)
409 West 4th St.
Mansfield, Ohio

Charles Earnest THOMPSON
Sea1c, USN

Mr. Maynard Allen Thompson
(brother)
841 N.W. 69th Street
Miami, Florida

Darrel "D" WOODSIDE
AMM1c(NAP), USN

Mrs. Beulah WOODSIDE
(mother)
Clearfield, Iowa

# Acknowledgments

My first awareness of the story of Torpedo Squadron Eight came from the pen of novelist Herman Wouk, author of the masterpiece *The Caine Mutiny*. While working in my previous profession, I remember the jolt of pleasure I felt when informed by my staff that Mr. Wouk had given the maximum personal contribution to my first successful campaign for Congress in 1982.

That pleasure paled in comparison to the thrill I received reading his novels *Winds of War* and *War and Remembrance*. It was Mr. Wouk's account of the sacrifice of the torpedo squadrons at Midway that first brought their story alive for me. My initial tentative thoughts of researching the lives of these men took root after reading the following words in *War and Remembrance*, which punctuated his riveting account of their action that day.

> *What was not luck, but the soul of the United States of America in action, was this willingness of the torpedo plane squadrons to go in against hopeless odds. This was the extra ounce of martial weight that in a few decisive minutes tipped the balance of history. So long as men choose to decide the turns of history with the slaughter of youths — and even in a better day, when this form of human sacrifice has been abolished like the ancient, superstitious, but no more horrible form — the memory of these three torpedo squadrons should not die.*

Those lines have echoed within me ever since.

The second inspiration for writing this book was my uncle, Lieutenant Commander Robert Slezak, who was a Grumman Avenger combat pilot aboard the carrier USS *Cowpens*. A career naval officer, he was killed flying a jet fighter off Point Mugu, California, in 1955. We loved him very much.

A final source of inspiration was my longtime friend, the noted documentary filmmaker, Martin "Andy" Andrews. His laconic and self-deprecating accounts of being among the first American B-17 pilots to fly daylight bombing raids far into Germany in 1943 had a profound impact on me. Shot down in a mission over Stuttgart in September 1943, he later told me many stories of the bravery of these young American pilots that instilled a sense of awe in me.

I began to seriously investigate the story of Torpedo Eight in 2001, largely because I could not put the story out of my mind. My initial research was limited to John Waldron and the pilots who flew with him from the *Hornet* on June 4. It was only later that I came to focus on the relatively untold story of the pilots and crews from Langdon Fieberling's detachment of Torpedo Eight at Midway Atoll.

I am grateful to my old friend and mentor Julian Muller for encouraging me to pursue the story. As a young naval officer at the Battle of Salerno in 1943, Julian was awarded the Navy Cross for saving the lives of trapped shipmates in his shattered gun turret aboard the USS *Savannah*.

In 2005, I had finished my fourth novel, and decided to fully commit my time and energy to the Torpedo Eight story in order to see where the trail might lead. At that time, I wondered whether I had waited too long to attempt to resurrect the stories of young men killed more than sixty years ago.

My gifted agent at the Robbins Office, David Halpern, strongly urged me to start the journey, giving me sagacious advice at each step of the process as I gathered and organized the material that I hoped would someday become a book. Over the years we have worked together, he has become a stalwart friend.

Thanks to another good friend, the renowned Civil War historian Bob Krick, I received contact information for Torpedo Eight pilot Bert Earnest. After I called him in Virginia, Captain Earnest agreed to my coming down to see him for an interview, and I subsequently spent three days with him and his wife, Millie, at their home in Virginia Beach.

At the end of each day, I would go back to my room at the Dam Neck Bachelor Officers' Quarters with a tape full of his stirring and powerful recollections. After I reluctantly said good-bye to Bert and Millie, my chase was on for the rest of the stories. It hasn't stopped since.

This journey has been the most satisfying experience in my professional life. In time, it became an almost sacred trust. In the two years after meeting Bert Earnest, I was able to locate numerous other survivors of the squadron, many of whom I visited at their homes across the country. I was also able to contact or visit many of the lost pilots' families, friends, and schoolmates, which led to the discovery of hundreds of letters and photographs that helped to illuminate their lives.

The men of Torpedo Squadron Eight were not unique. John Lundstrom once told me that I could have researched any number of naval or Marine air

squadrons in early 1942, and found similarly compelling stories. He is probably right. Nevertheless, I feel privileged to have gotten to know these men.

My principal regret is that after the passage of sixty-five years, the trail to
reconstructing the abbreviated lives of many of the men in the squadron had
simply gone cold. I apologize to the families of those whose stories do not appear in these pages.

I wish to express my deep appreciation to the many individuals who as-
sisted me in writing this book. First, I would like to thank the survivors of the
squadron whom I was able to meet or interview over the course of my research, including Frank Balsley, Wiley Bartlett, George Bernstein, Del Delchamps, Bert Earnest, Harry Ferrier, Gene Hanson, Ski Kowalewski, Ridgeway
Liccioni, Bill Magee, Lee Marona, Smiley Morgan, Jack Stark, Bill Tunstall,
and Judge Wendt. It was a privilege to talk to them all.

I am also grateful for the opportunity to have met so many of the family
members, loved ones, and friends of those who never came back from the Pacific. They have kept the memories of the fallen aviators alive in their hearts.

In particular, I want to thank the sagacious Roy Gee, Rich Morgan, Nancy
and Al Willis, Rete Gaynier Janiec, Nancy Mahi, John Peterkin, Russellyn
Kenyon Edwards, Thomas E. Evans, Charles Gillispie, Sherry Moore Cullaty,
Roger Katz, Richard Katz, Heber Stafford, Lois Fieberling Castor, Marilyn
Richards, Jane Eagle, Don Velazquez, Eric Fieberling, Elizabeth Gaynier Wallin, Billy Herring, Gail Gaynier Grimm, Marcella Whitlock, Mary and Catherine Corrigan, Bill Archer, Kelley Gaynier, Dennis Divine, Grover Connell,
Helen Lyddon, Ted Scarritt, Jessie Thompson, Gerald Harwood, Lonnie
Smith, Patrick Peterkin, Lodwrick Cook, Catherine Dunn, Christopher Morgan, Millie Earnest, and Jack Tobein, for helping to bring the stories of these
men to life in my mind. I am also grateful to the family of George Gay, and in
particular to his grandson Eric Staalesen, for providing access to Ensign Gay's
private diary. I owe the same debt of gratitude to Pete Peterkin's family.

The profound impact of the deaths of the Torpedo Eight fliers on their
families and friends cannot be overstated. In an interview with Lodwrick
Cook, who idolized his older cousin James Hill Cook when they were growing
up together in tiny Grand Cane, Louisiana, Mr. Cook told me that much of
what he had accomplished in his own life was an attempt to live up to the expectations that James Hill would have had for him. Lodwrick Cook eventually
became the chairman and CEO of the Atlantic Richfield Company, and also
serves as a director of the Ronald Reagan Presidential Library, among many
other accomplishments.

Professor Charles Colston Gillispie, who was Bill Evans's roommate at
Wesleyan and went on to become the distinguished professor of the history of

science at Princeton, still has a photograph of Evans on his desk more than sixty-five years after his death. Professor Gillispie believed him to be a visionary and said Evans was one of the three most extraordinary men he met in his life.

As I've described in Appendix One, I am indebted to Bowen Weisheit, whose devotion to the memory of Mark Kelly led him to travel all over the country in a quest to delve into the mystery of Mr. Kelly's death. Due to the unique combination of Mr. Weisheit's gifts as a navigator, a lawyer, and an independent thinker, he was able to solve the puzzle of the "Flight to Nowhere," and actually rewrite a small but important piece of American history.

My sincere appreciation also goes to John Lundstrom, the foremost living authority on the Pacific air war in 1942, whose pursuit of history led him in the early 1970s to undertake hundreds of interviews with the pilots who served aboard the Pacific carriers. A number of these interviews helped to shed light on this story. I was also fortunate to be able to draw on the exhaustive research conducted in recent years by Jon Parshall, Anthony Tully, Richard Frank, Alvin Kernan, James Sawruk, and Mark Horan, for which I am deeply grateful.

I also want to express my thanks to Harold Towne, the grandson of Lieutenant George M. Campbell, who dedicated many years of his life to learning the truth of Torpedo Eight's role at the Battle of Midway, and who generously shared with me the product of his research into the decisions made on June 4, 1942.

In the course of writing this book, I received wise counsel from naval historian and author Paul Stillwell, whose generosity of time and insight provided invaluable leads to important material, as well as smoothing the passage for its retrieval. At the Nimitz Library in Annapolis, the late Gary Lavalley of the special collections division helped me track down copies of academic records and other pertinent information on the "blue school" officers in the squadron.

At the Naval Historical Center in Washington, D.C., I am especially thankful to Robert Cressman, head of the ships history branch of the naval warfare division, for helping me locate many important biographical documents, as well as photographs of the men in the squadron. Thanks also to Kathy Lloyd at the operational archives division, who prepared the cataloging of the new Walter Lord collection of his multitudinous notes from *Incredible Victory,* to Ed Finney of the photographic division, and to Roy Grossnick at the naval aviation history branch. Mr. Clark Peckham, a wonderful restorer of old and washed-out photographs in Homer, New York, was responsible for rejuvenating several of the faded images of the men of Torpedo Eight.

At the Naval Aviation Museum at Pensacola, Florida, I thank Hill Goodspeed, whose assistance was critical in securing flight records for some of the

Torpedo Eight pilots. In addition, he shared with me his collection of personal letters written by several Marine pilots serving at Midway on June 4, 1942.

I am also grateful for the enthusiastic support of Paul Brockman at the Indiana Historical Society, and Douglas Clanin, the remarkable Indiana historian who personally interviewed three hundred WWII veterans over the course of twenty years, and whose accounts are now part of the Douglas Clanin collection at the society.

For helping me find other important source material, I am grateful to Nathaniel Patch at the National Archives and Records Administration; Bob Aquilina at the Historical Division of Marine Corps University; Colonel Joe Alexander; Mike Musick; Jessica Lacher-Feldman at the University of Alabama; Maria Davis at the Eastern Michigan University Archives; the EMU Athletic Hall of Fame; Timothy Woodbury and Mrs. Nell Horn at the U.S. Naval Academy Alumni Association; Keith Gibson, Director of the VMI Museum; Donald Goldstein, Gordon Prange's collaborator on *Miracle at Midway*, at the University of Pittsburgh; and Ellen Fearday, supervisor of alumni records at the University of Illinois.

To achieve a better understanding of what it was like for the men of Torpedo Eight to fight alongside the Marines defending Henderson Field during the Japanese ground campaign, I relied on the memories of Edson's Raiders James "Horse" Smith and Frank Guidone. Their recollections of the battle brought alive for me the fighting at Edson's Ridge on September 13, 1942, the night Torpedo Eight arrived at Guadalcanal to become part of the Cactus Air Force.

I wish to express my appreciation to Julie Krick, a superb mapmaker whose work in this book helped to bring alive the complex confrontations at both Midway and Guadalcanal, and to Dan Farnham, whose haunting and evocative photograph of the submerged plane wreck for the chapter, "When the Sea Shall Give Up Its Dead," is only one of many he has taken in the waters off Kwajalein.

I would also like to thank Professor Lamont Lindstrom, chairman of the anthropology department at the University of Tulsa, for his assistance in helping to illuminate for me the enduring impact of Swede Larsen's air strike on the island of Malaita on August 7, 1942.

Another important source of information was the Battle of Midway Roundtable (www.midway42.org), a forum for students of history to learn more about the battle from the men who fought in it. Ron Russell, its current editor and webmaster, remains dedicated to strengthening the understanding of this pivotal conflict. Mr. Russell has written his own book on Midway, *No Right to Win*, utilizing the personal accounts of the men who were there. Fred Branyan and Bill Roy were two members of the roundtable who were helpful in providing me with important bits of information to help complete the complex historical mosaic of Torpedo Eight's role at Midway.

I owe a tremendous debt of gratitude to my wife, Carolyn, who transcribed many hundreds of pages of my interviews and read my initial drafts of each chapter with a fine sense of how to distill a long narrative to its essentials.

Researching the story of these men was only the first step in a long process. For helping me to shape and structure this book, I am deeply indebted to my editor at Little, Brown, Asya Muchnick. It is remarkable that a woman so young could also be so wise. Her unerringly fine judgment and editorial prowess are felt in every chapter, and *A Dawn Like Thunder* is immeasurably stronger as a result of her guidance.

# Photograph Captions and Credits

Page 159    A Mitchell PBJ-1H bomber from squadron VMB-613 at the bottom of the Pacific. (Photographed in 2007 by Dan Farmham. Used with permission)

Page 187    The official Navy Cross citation endorsed by Admiral Chester Nimitz after Bert Earnest's epic flight on June 4, 1942. (U.S. Navy Official Document. Courtesy of the Earnest family)

Page 190    USS *Saratoga* (CV-3). (U.S. Navy)

Page 216    U.S. Marines shortly after landing at Guadalcanal on Dog Day, August 1942. (U.S. Marine Corps)

Page 239    Japanese carrier aircraft attacking Guadalcanal, August 1942. (U.S. Navy)

Page 273    A group of sailors relax in the waters off Espiritu Santo, 1942. (U.S. Navy)

Page 291    Colonel Ichiki's dead warriors, half buried in tidal sand, Guadalcanal, August 1942. (National Archives and Records Administration)

Page 310    Corwin Morgan on a mission over Guadalcanal, September 1942. (U.S. Navy. Courtesy of Corwin Morgan)

Page 341    Night explosion, Pacific. (U.S. Navy)

Page 353    Dauntless dive-bomber after Japanese attack at Guadalcanal. (National Archives and Records Administration)

Page 381    U.S. Marines contending with daily life at Guadalcanal, August 1942. (U.S. Marine Corps)

Page 403    Injured man aboard USS *Minneapolis* (CA-36), 1942. (National Archives and Records Administration)

Page 418    Bert and Millie Earnest on their honeymoon, 1943. (Courtesy of the Earnest family)

Page 447    The ten-dollar "short snorter" bill given to PBY pilot Jerry Crawford after his crew picked up three pilots from the *Hornet* fighter squadron, June 8, 1942. (Presented by Jerry Crawford to the C. Markland Kelly Jr. Foundation. Courtesy of Bowen Weisheit)

# Sources

## The Sentinels

### Smiley

The principal source for the account of the arrival of Swede Larsen's Torpedo Eight detachment at Pearl Harbor on May 29, 1942, was Corwin "Smiley" Morgan. The author spent four days with Morgan at his home in Tampa, Florida, during two separate visits in March 2006 and February 2007. Morgan's further recollections of his service with Torpedo Eight were recorded in more than twenty telephone interviews between February 2006 and February 2007. Morgan also permitted the author to review hundreds of pages of his contemporaneous notes, journal entries, flight logs, newspaper articles, and the letters he wrote and received during his service with the squadron.

In addition to Morgan's reflections on John Waldron, James Hill Cook, Victor Lewis, John Taurman, and Langdon Fieberling, the author also relied on the unpublished diary and war memoir, *Carrier Squadron Torpedo 8*, by DeWitt "Pete" Peterkin, as well as personal interviews with numerous squadron members who arrived with Morgan at Pearl Harbor on May 29, 1942. They included William Tunstall, Albert K. Earnest, Eugene Hanson, and William Magee.

### The Skipper

The primary sources for this chapter include the unpublished private diary of George Gay; the Torpedo Squadron Eight War Diary (official source); the USS *Hornet* Deck Log (official source); John Lundstrom's *The First Team: Pacific Naval Air Combat from Pearl Harbor to Midway*; Frederick Mears's *Carrier Combat*; Walter Lord's *Incredible Victory*; Gordon Prange's *Miracle at Midway*; Lloyd Wendt's "The True Story of Heroic Squadron 8"; Clark G. Reynolds's *The Saga of Smokey Stover*; Bowen P. Weisheit's *The Last Flight of Ensign C. Markland Kelly, Junior, USNR*; and George Gay's *Sole Survivor*. The author is indebted to Bowen Weisheit for providing him with the transcripts and notes of interviews he conducted with Samuel G. Mitchell and John G.

Foster. The author also found valuable information in the interview notes and completed author questionnaires compiled by Walter Lord after meetings and/or correspondence with Edward Creehan, George Flinn, Robert "Ruff" Johnson, and Stan Ruehlow.

References to John Waldron's early life and his experiences at Annapolis were drawn from his academic records at Annapolis, from the 1924 Annapolis yearbook, *Lucky Bag,* and interviews and questionnaires with classmates of Waldron amassed in 1966 and 1967 by the author Walter Lord for *Incredible Victory.* The author also utilized material from a six-page handwritten letter describing Waldron's early life by his daughter, Nancy Waldron LeDew, which is on file in the Waldron collection at the South Dakota Hall of Fame, and from Alvin Kernan's *The Unknown Battle of Midway* (pp. 64–71).

Details of Lieutenant Commander Waldron's training methods were drawn from author interviews with Torpedo Eight squadron members Ervin Wendt, Bert Earnest, Corwin Morgan, Eugene Hanson, Carroll "Jack" Stark, and William Magee. They are also documented in Gay's *Sole Survivor* as well as in Gay's private diary. The author also relied on personal letters written by squadron members Grant Teats, Rusty Kenyon, "Whitey" Moore, and Oswald Gaynier in which they reflected on the squadron's training period in Norfolk, Virginia, from the summer of 1941 to its departure for the Pacific in early 1942.

Lieutenant Commander Waldron's interactions aboard the *Hornet* with Edward Creehan, the carrier's engineer officer, were drawn from Creehan's correspondence with Walter Lord in 1966, which is on file in the *Incredible Victory* archive at the Naval Historical Center in Washington, D.C.

The account of Stanhope Cotton Ring's Annapolis years as well as his early career in the Navy was drawn from his academic records, from the 1923 Annapolis yearbook, *Lucky Bag,* from Kernan's *The Unknown Battle of Midway* (pp. 72–75), and from portions of his military service record (Advisory Board Proceedings, official source).

Admiral Ring's capabilities as a pilot and combat leader were seriously questioned prior to the battle by many of the officers who flew under his command. Specific references to Ring's qualifications as the *Hornet* air group commander, including his getting lost leading the group in a training flight over the Gulf of Mexico, were drawn from author interviews with *Hornet* dive-bomber pilot Roy Gee, an interview taped by Bowen Weisheit with pilot John McInerny, a personal reminiscence by fighter pilot Tom Cheek in a June 2002 interview with www.internetmodeler.com, and Kernan's *The Unknown Battle of Midway* (pp. 73–74). In a letter to the historian and author John Lundstrom on April 23, 1981, *Hornet* fighter pilot Henry A. Carey referred to

Admiral Ring as "a pompous ass and a coward." In Ron Russell's *No Right to Win* (pp. 128, 130), *Hornet* dive-bomber pilot Clayton Fisher, who flew as Ring's wingman during the Midway strike on June 4, 1942, expressed polite misgivings about him, summing up Ring as "a decent officer in general terms, but he did not exhibit the qualities of a skilled pilot and navigator."

An author interview with historian James Sawruk was the source of the account in which several *Hornet* pilots seriously discussed a plan to kill Stanhope Ring. In a written communication to the author on August 17, 2007, Sawruk recounted details of his interview with the group's "ringleader," Lieutenant George Ellenberg, a senior Dauntless pilot on the *Hornet.*

The reference to a "near mutiny" against Ring by the pilots of the *Hornet* air group during the same time period appears in the diary of fighter pilot Elisha Stover via Reynolds's *The Saga of Smokey Stover* (pp. 28–29), and in a 1981 letter from *Hornet* pilot Henry A. Carey to John Lundstrom.

The Advisory Board Proceedings referenced above include a forty-two-page summary of Ring's performance in flight school at Pensacola Naval Air Station in 1926–27. The report culminates in the recommendation by Lieutenant T. L. Sprague, the officer in command of the flight school, that he be dropped from flying status. On July 14, 1926, then-Ensign Ring formally requested that instead of being dropped, he be allowed to return to flight school, stating that he believed he had "gone stale, temporarily." He was given another opportunity, and earned his wings.

The substance of Lieutenant Stephen Jurika's briefing to the senior commanders of the *Hornet* air group on May 31, 1942, and his subsequent briefings to all its pilots prior to the battle, are included in the oral history he provided to the U.S. Naval Institute in Annapolis, Maryland, during twenty-seven taped interviews (pp. 495–498). George Gay offered an independent account of the briefing to the pilots in his private diary.

Details of the May 31, 1942, meeting in which Captain "Pete" Mitscher, Stanhope Ring, and the *Hornet*'s four air squadron commanders planned the attack on the Japanese striking force were drawn from John Lundstrom's *The First Team* (pp. 407–408), and Gay's private diary, in which he cites Lieutenant Commander Waldron's concerns about the plan.

The sources for the internal debate that took place aboard the *Hornet* over how fighter protection was to be divided between Waldron's torpedo squadron and the carrier's two dive-bomber squadrons include Lundstrom's *The First Team* (p. 407); Walter Lord's 1966 lengthy interview with Stan Ruehlow; Bowen Weisheit's 1981 interview with Pat Mitchell; and *Sole Survivor*, in which Gay recounted Waldron's increasingly desperate attempts to secure fighter protection, if even only one plane, for his squadron (p. 115).

## SWEDE

The domineering leadership style of Harold H. "Swede" Larsen after he was placed in command of the receiving detachment by John Waldron was well documented within Torpedo Eight. Of the thirteen surviving members of the squadron whom the author interviewed at length, or who wrote about their experiences with Swede, all but two commented on his dictatorial nature. Three went so far as to say they still hated him sixty-five years later. One enlisted man told me that he seriously fantasized about shooting Larsen while the squadron was training in Norfolk.

At the same time, no one questioned Larsen's personal courage and almost reckless bravery. At least one officer, Smiley Morgan, heard Swede say that he would come back from the Pacific with the Medal of Honor.

The account in which Swede accused Tunstall of attempting to kill him came from the author's 2006 interview with Tunstall at his home in Portland, Oregon.

At least two of the pilots who volunteered for the dangerous mission to Midway, Bert Earnest and Gene Hanson, stated in author interviews that one of the reasons they volunteered was to get away from Swede.

The account of Swede's being denied the opportunity to lead the mission to Midway by Admiral Noyes is documented in Ira Wolfert's *Torpedo 8: The Story of Swede Larsen's Bomber Squadron* (pp. 9–11, 14), and in author interviews with Earnest, Hanson, and Morgan.

Preparing the six planes and flight crews for the more than 1,200-mile flight to Midway was an experience that left an indelible memory on every man who was there at Luke Field. William Magee and Smiley Morgan had particularly vivid recollections, which in Morgan's case were supplemented with an account he wrote shortly afterward.

## THE SQUIRE

The content of Lieutenant Stephen Jurika's second briefing to all of the pilots in the *Hornet* air group was chronicled by George Gay in his unpublished diary posting on that date. The briefing was remarkably detailed, and included the names of many of the ships in the Japanese striking force. It was also the first time that the pilots of Torpedo Eight learned that Avengers in Swede Larsen's receiving detachment would be joining the air garrison at Midway Atoll.

The information about Bill Evans's life before the war was drawn from interviews with Tom Evans, Bill's younger brother; a three-hour author interview with Charles Gillispie, Bill's roommate at Wesleyan University; several remembrances written by his classmates from Shortridge High School and

Wesleyan; an article written for the *Aircraft Journal* by Wesleyan classmate Douglas Holmes; and Evans's own evocative writings and letters. The remembrances and article were shared with the author by Tom Evans.

For the accounts of Bill's involvement in the life of the squadron, both during its months of training in Norfolk, and then aboard the *Hornet,* the author drew from Bill Evans's own writings, as well as those of squadron members Fred Mears, George Gay, and Grant Teats. The author also received insightful reflections about Evans's personality from squadron member Gene Hanson.

## OLD LANGDON

The most important source of information for this chapter was DeWitt "Pete" Peterkin, Langdon Fieberling's closest friend in the squadron. Peterkin maintained a lively and insightful diary that was edited after the war into an eighty-two-page memoir for his family and fellow VT-8 veterans entitled *Carrier Squadron Torpedo 8.* In this personal account of his experiences with Torpedo Eight, Peterkin wrote at length about Fieberling and his star-crossed romantic relationship with his fiancée, whose name has been altered by the author due to family considerations.

Additional material about Langdon Fieberling's early life was sent to the author by his first cousin Lois Fieberling Castor and his nephew Eric Fieberling. Information about his college career at the University of California, Berkeley, was provided by the university's alumni association.

Reflections on Fieberling's leadership style, his personal characteristics, and his interaction with other squadron members, both officers and enlisted men, were related to the author in interviews with William Tunstall, Ervin Wendt, Gene Hanson, and Bert Earnest.

The substance of the meeting in which Lieutenant Fieberling met with the pilots who were about to undertake the mission to Midway was provided in an author interview with Corwin Morgan, the squadron's navigation officer at the time.

The departure of the six crews of Torpedo Eight who flew to Midway on the morning of June 1, 1942, was witnessed by nearly every pilot and enlisted man in the squadron, many of whom had vivid memories of this last leave-taking. The account here was drawn from author interviews with William Magee and Carroll "Jack" Stark. Bert Earnest is the source for the last anecdote in the chapter, in which he and Charlie Brannon exchanged their own version of Swede Larsen's "Attack" hand salute.

## TEX

Most of the material in this chapter was drawn from George Gay's writings, both from his private diary and his book, *Sole Survivor*. Gay wrote candidly about his fears of how he would perform in combat, and whether he would live up to his own expectations.

His recollections about the specific talks to the squadron made by Lieutenant Commander Waldron in this time period are supported by the recollections of Fred Mears in his book, *Carrier Combat*.

The description of the incident in which squadron pilot Eddie Fayle received a serious leg wound on the day before the *Hornet* left for Midway is drawn from Gay's unpublished diary and the Torpedo Squadron Eight war diary.

The material about Gay's life prior to the war was drawn from the book *Sole Survivor* and from author interviews with Gay's grandson, Eric Staalesen. Descriptions of his personality as the squadron underwent training in Norfolk, Virginia, came from author interviews with Bert Earnest, Gene Hanson, and Rete Gaynier Janiec.

## BERT AND HARRY

The account of Bert Earnest's flight from Pearl Harbor to Midway Atoll on June 1, 1942, and his subsequent mission on June 4, was drawn from the more than fourteen hours of taped personal interviews conducted with Captain Earnest by the author, the first series during a three-day visit to Earnest's home in Virginia Beach, Virginia, February 9–12, 2006, and in nineteen telephone interviews over the course of the following year.

The details of his early life in Richmond, his college days at the Virginia Military Institute, his relationship with Jerry Jenkins, and his experiences training with Torpedo Squadron Eight were also the product of author interviews, supplemented by copies of letters and academic records provided to the author by Earnest.

Harry Ferrier shared his recollections of the flight to Midway with the author in a 2006 visit to his home in Oak Harbor, Washington, and in subsequent telephone interviews. These interviews are also the source for the details about his early life, the unusual circumstances surrounding his enlistment in the Navy, and his training experiences.

The six Avengers' arrival at Midway on the afternoon of June 1, 1942, was chronicled in author interviews with Earnest and Ferrier. Specific material about the B-26 Marauders and their flight crews came from notes compiled by Walter Lord based on questionnaires completed by James P. Muri and Pren Leonard Moore.

## GRANT AND WHITEY

A copy of the *Hornet* Plan of the Day, including the typed message from Commander G. R. Henderson about the expected arrival of the Japanese striking force, was reproduced in its entirety in George Gay's *Sole Survivor.*

Grant Teats's niece, Nancy Mahi, provided the author with copies of Diana's letters, which were returned to the Teats family after the Battle of Midway along with Grant's own letters and personal effects. The author chose not to use Diana's real name out of family considerations. Nancy Mahi also provided important information about Grant's early life, family history, and his accomplishments in high school and college. The author also received useful insights from two of Grant's high school classmates.

Sherry Moore Cullaty provided the author with several dozen of Whitey Moore's 1942 letters, as well as a cross-section of correspondence from Betty Watkins, Diana's best friend at Norfolk Naval Hospital. Whitey wrote his parents that he expected at some point to ask Betty to marry him. The two different sets of letters helped to illuminate the background to both romantic relationships.

Pertinent information about Grant's interaction with his fellow fliers, as well as other aspects of his life in Torpedo Eight, can be found in the more than one hundred letters he wrote home to his parents and his sister, Charlotte, Nancy Mahi's mother.

Sketches of Grant's physical prowess and gentle personality can be found in commentaries by Fred Mears in *Carrier Combat,* by George Gay in *Sole Survivor,* and in an author interview with *Hornet* pilot Roy Gee, Grant's roommate during training in Norfolk, who was sitting with him at a Washington Redskins football game in Washington, D.C., when they learned that the Japanese had attacked Pearl Harbor on December 7, 1941.

The unique personality of Ulvert Matthew "Whitey" Moore was characterized in detail in *Sole Survivor* and *Carrier Combat,* as well as in Lloyd Wendt's multipart series "The True Story of Heroic Squadron 8." Whitey's sleep proclivities were described by Gay, Mears, and Bill Evans. Evans spent most of a leave with Grant Teats and Whitey Moore in Florida.

Details about Whitey Moore's early life in Bluefield, West Virginia, are drawn from several lengthy author interviews with Whitey's high school classmate, Heber Stafford, as well as separate author interviews with Howard Hale and Marcella Whitlock.

The account of Moore's romantic relationship with Catherine Dunn was drawn from multiple author interviews with Catherine Dunn Hall, who recently gave his Kappa Alpha fraternity pin to the Mercer County World War II Museum.

## OZZIE AND RETE

According to fellow pilots Smiley Morgan and Gene Hanson, Ozzie Gaynier was one of the most naturally gifted leaders they had met during the early months of the war. Smart and unflappable, he approached problems with a combination of logic and thorough planning that set him apart from other junior officers.

In one of his last letters home, Ozzie summed up the challenges the nation faced in defeating a fiercely dedicated opponent like Japan, and the need to confront the enemy with the resources available to them until the nation built up an effective arsenal.

A full copy of Colonel H. D. Shannon's general orders for the defense of Midway, dated May 23, 1942, can be found on the Battle of Midway Roundtable Web site: www.midway42.org.

The sources for the squadron's official activity, including the briefings of Langdon Fieberling by Colonel Ira Kimes, the Marine air group commander, and Fieberling's subsequent briefings of his squadron pilots and crews include Walter Lord's *Incredible Victory* (pp. 55–56), Gordon Prange's *Miracle at Midway* (pp. 207–209), and the personal recollections of Bert Earnest and Harry Ferrier in multiple author interviews.

The most valuable resource for recounting Gaynier's early life was his sister, Elizabeth "Dudie" Gaynier Wallin, who provided the author with many details of his childhood in Monroe, Michigan, and recounted family Christmas memories and Ozzie's adventures riding freight trains across the Far West. The author also had an opportunity to review much of Ozzie's correspondence to his family while he was undergoing training with Torpedo Eight, including letters to his younger brother Jim, who was committed to following in his footsteps as a Navy flier.

Details of Ozzie's athletic ability in high school and college were provided by the Eastern Michigan University Athletic Hall of Fame, which enshrined him in 1993 for his track and field and boxing accomplishments.

The story of how Ozzie and Rete met was provided by Rete Gaynier Janiec in an interview with the author at her home in Oregon. Further details were drawn from letters he wrote during his first months at flight school, and from Reynolds's *The Saga of Smokey Stover*, in which Stover wrote about his friendship with Ozzie and Rete while he was renting a room in their apartment in Norfolk. *The Saga of Smokey Stover* also includes a number of photographs of both Ozzie and Rete during the early days of their marriage.

## FREDDY

Details of Fred Mears's early life were found in the wonderful book *Get Mears!* by Katharine Carson Crittenden. It is the story of how Fred's father built the Alaska Railroad across hundreds of miles of wilderness and subsequently created the railroad town that became Anchorage, Alaska. Other family memories, news articles, and photographs were generously provided to the author by Fred Mears's nieces Marilyn Richards and Jane Eagle. The author was also given important details about the Mears family life by Jack Tobien, a family friend.

Information about Fred's military service, including all of his unit postings and subsequent military awards, was found in his service record, as well as in the biographical material he submitted to the Bureau of Navigation in 1941, a copy of which is on file at the Naval Historical Center in Washington, D.C. The author also reviewed a copy of the official accident report of his death near El Centro, California, on June 26, 1943.

The principal source for describing Fred's life at Yale College, his subsequent romantic pursuits, and his approach to flying was his book, *Carrier Combat*. He maintained an intimate diary for several years prior to the war, and continued this practice after joining the Navy. In 1943, Fred used this diary as the basis for his book.

The author is indebted to Smiley Morgan for sharing copies of his correspondence with Fred Mears's sister Betty, which began after Morgan was stationed in Seattle in early 1943. Her letters provided an interesting and provocative assessment of Fred's weaknesses and strengths.

## EVENTIDE

Chronicling the last period of activity for the men of Torpedo Squadron Eight aboard the *Hornet* on the night of June 3–4, 1942, required synthesizing a number of accounts. The principal sources were the private diary of George Gay and his book, *Sole Survivor* (pp. 108–115); Mears's *Carrier Combat* (pp. 39–54); Wendt's "The True Story of Heroic Squadron 8"; the letters of John Waldron, Rusty Kenyon, and Grant Teats; and the writings of Bill Evans.

The continuing campaign by Lieutenant Commander Waldron to secure fighter protection for his torpedo squadron was highlighted in both George Gay's diary and his subsequent book. His account is supported by the taped interviews conducted by Bowen Weisheit with Pat Mitchell, as well as in the notes compiled by Walter Lord from his interview with Pat Mitchell's flight officer, Stan Ruehlow.

The final night on Midway Atoll was primarily reconstructed from author interviews with Bert Earnest and Harry Ferrier, who was at the final briefing given by Langdon Fieberling on the night before the battle.

Due to security concerns, no one on Midway Atoll was aware that three American carriers were steaming northeast of Midway in a planned attempt to ambush the Japanese striking force. As far as Langdon Fieberling knew, the air garrison on Midway was the sole means to defend the islands by air against the enemy forces. His subsequent decisions were made accordingly.

The life of Vic Lewis was reconstructed largely from author interviews with his younger sister Nancy and her husband, Al Willis, from Lewis's service record, and from his last letters home, which were shared with the author by his family. Bill Tunstall provided the author with the account of the near-fatal flight accident at Norfolk that changed Vic's attitude about risk-taking.

In author interviews, Bert Earnest shared his memories of purchasing "chits" for beer from the young Marine, and of his subsequent discovery of the two-dollar bill next to the runway on his way to bed.

## HE THAT SHALL LIVE THIS DAY AND SEE OLD AGE

The primary sources for the important decisions and events that took place aboard the *Hornet* on June 4, 1942, as well as what occurred on its air group's mission that morning, include War Diary, Commander, Carriers, Pacific Fleet (Task Force 16, official source); USS *Hornet* Deck Log (official source); *The Battle of Midway, Strategical and Tactical Analysis* (official source); John Lundstrom's *The First Team;* Robert E. Barde's *The Battle of Midway: A Study in Command;* Jonathan Parshall and Anthony Tully's *Shattered Sword;* Frederick Mears's *Carrier Combat;* Walter Lord's *Incredible Victory;* Gordon Prange's *Miracle at Midway;* Ron Russell's *No Right to Win;* Bowen P. Weisheit's *The Last Flight of Ensign C. Markland Kelly, Junior;* and George Gay's *Sole Survivor.*

The author had an opportunity to closely examine the transcripts of more than fifty hours of taped interviews conducted by Bowen Weisheit with *Hornet* pilots Ben Tappan, Samuel G. Mitchell, Richard Gray, Johnny Talbot, Humphrey Tallman, John McInerny, Walter F. Rodee, and Troy Guillory. Weisheit also allowed the author to read the notes of his interviews with the *Hornet*'s air operations officer, Lieutenant Commander John G. Foster.

At the Naval Historical Center in Washington, D.C., the author carefully reviewed the handwritten notes compiled by Walter Lord after meetings and/ or correspondence with Edward Creehan, George Flinn, Robert "Ruff" Johnson, and Stan Ruehlow, all of which are part of the center's newly cataloged collection. Also included in the Lord collection is a copy of a September 8, 1948, letter from Rear Admiral Apollo Soucek, Mitscher's air officer on the

*Hornet,* to Lieutenant Commander Joseph Bryan III, detailing Soucek's recollections of the events of June 4.

The author also solicited the most recent scholarship devoted to understanding these events, including conducting interviews with noted historians John Lundstrom, Robert Cressman, James Sawruk, and Mark Horan. Lundstrom generously provided the author with numerous letters written to him about these events from *Hornet* pilots Henry A. Carey, J. F. Sutherland, Stan Ruehlow, and John Adams. He also sent the author a thirty-two-page transcript of an official interview conducted less than two weeks after the Midway battle with Lieutenant Commander Edward O'Neill, a senior pilot aboard the *Hornet,* in which O'Neill provided his recollections of what he saw and heard during the battle.

For the last few hours of Torpedo Eight's existence aboard the *Hornet,* the author relied on Fred Mears's *Carrier Combat* and George Gay's *Sole Survivor* as they waited in the ready room for orders to launch, and their accounts of Lieutenant Commander Waldron's periodically giving the squadron what little information he had received. These accounts were supplemented by the personal recollections of *Hornet* fighter pilot Henry A. Carey, who was not scheduled to fly the first mission on the morning of June 4, and who was in and out of the ready room visiting friends in Torpedo Eight. His recollections were incorporated in three lengthy letters to author John Lundstrom. A final source for John Waldron's words to his pilots was George Flinn, who outlined his recollections in a letter to Walter Lord in 1966.

At Midway Atoll, these same predawn hours were largely used by the pilots and crews of Torpedo Eight to make their final preparations for the mission. For their recollections of this period of time, the author relied principally on author interviews with Bert Earnest and Harry Ferrier.

Material about Darrel Woodside's early life was contributed by school classmates Helen Lyddon and Mary Lou Swartwood. The source for Woodside's short-lived relationship with the singer Peggy Lee was an author interview with William Magee, who accompanied Woodside to the propeller school at Providence, Rhode Island, when Woodside and the singer met for the last time.

Additional insight into the reasoning that led to Langdon Fieberling's decision to attack the Japanese fleet alone was provided in Robert Cressman's *A Glorious Page in Our History* (p. 47), in which General Hale expressed his increasing concern about Kimes's mental stability under the stress of the impending invasion.

The description of the dramatic events leading up to the takeoff from Midway Atoll of Langdon Fieberling's Torpedo Eight detachment was drawn from author interviews with Bert Earnest.

Back aboard the *Hornet,* the attempts to lighten the mood in the Torpedo Eight ready room prior to the order to launch, including the description of Rusty Kenyon's limericks, were highlighted in Fred Mears's *Carrier Combat.*

The actions of Admiral Raymond Spruance aboard the USS *Enterprise,* including the scene in which he used his small chart board to determine the time to launch his attack, were drawn from Thomas Buell's *The Quiet Warrior.*

The author's sketch of the final minutes in Ready Room Four prior to Torpedo Eight's being ordered to man its planes was drawn from Mears's *Carrier Combat,* Gay's *Sole Survivor,* and the letters from Ensign Henry "Hank" Carey to John Lundstrom. In one of his letters to John Lundstrom, Ensign Carey also expressed how deeply moved he was by John Waldron's last words to his squadron pilots.

What happened during the final conference between Pete Mitscher and his squadron commanders on the *Hornet'*s bridge before its fifty-nine-plane air group took off to attack the Japanese striking force will never be known in its entirety. The author reconstructed these events based on the direct testimony of the following:

Harold Towne, the grandson of Lieutenant George M. Campbell, who flew to his death with Torpedo Eight on June 4, 1942, dedicated many years to learning the truth about his grandfather's last mission. In the course of his research, he conducted three interviews with Ensign Fred Mamer, who was a watch officer on the bridge of the USS *Hornet* that morning. In author interviews, Towne related the detailed contents of his conversations with Mamer.

Mamer witnessed the argument over what navigational course the air group would follow to intercept the Japanese carriers. According to Towne, Mamer confirmed that he had witnessed a "heated disagreement" on the bridge over the course the air group would follow, as well as over the separate issue of whether Waldron's torpedo squadron would be given a share of fighter protection. Waldron was on one side of the argument, Mamer stated, and he was supported by at least one of the other air squadron commanders. Commander Ring and Captain Mitscher were on the other side of the argument.

In the Towne interviews, Mamer did not recall the specific course the group was ultimately ordered to take, but had a clear recollection that Captain Mitscher ordered the fighter squadron to remain up with the dive-bombers. Mamer's account is supported by George Gay, who spoke to Waldron immediately after the conference. The verbal dispute on the bridge was also chronicled in Cressman's *A Glorious Page in Our History* (p. 84), Lundstrom's *The First Team* (pp. 418–19), and in author interviews with *Hornet* dive-bomber pilot Roy Gee.

Pat Mitchell participated in this bridge conference, and later spoke about what occurred that morning. In his interview with Bowen Weisheit in 1981, Mitchell, who commanded the fighter squadron, stated that he formally requested of Mitscher that his entire squadron be assigned to protect the torpedo planes, and that Mitscher ordered him and his squadron to remain with Commander Ring and the dive-bombers. In an interview with Walter Lord on April 11, 1966, Mitchell's flight officer, Lieutenant Stan Ruehlow, asserted that Mitscher made the decision "against the recs of both Mitchell and Ruehlow."

The quest by amateur historian and retired Marine Corps navigator Bowen Weisheit to learn the truth about the course that *Hornet* air group actually flew on June 4, 1942, is explored in depth in Appendix One of this book. This appendix also seeks to answer the possible reasons for Pete Mitscher's order to send his air group west on a course of 265 degrees, instead of 240 degrees southwest, which was the last reported position of the Japanese carriers. It was a decision that would eventually culminate in an official cover-up of the truth.

Mitscher's air staff certainly knew the group's planned flight course, and at least one of these officers later confirmed this information after the war. In an interview with Bowen Weisheit in 1982, Lieutenant Commander John G. Foster, the *Hornet*'s air operations officer, stated that he tracked the air group formation on radar until it disappeared approximately sixty miles out from the carrier. According to Foster, the course it was following at that time was almost due west.

In a 1982 taped interview with Weisheit, Walter Rodee, who commanded one of the *Hornet*'s two dive-bomber squadrons that morning, also weighed in on the question. The transcript reflects that at one point, Weisheit specifically asked Rodee what course the group had flown, even first prompting him with the falsified course of 240 degrees. "No," Admiral Rodee answered. "It was about 265. . . . It was almost due west."

Rodee gave the identical answer in a separate telephone interview with historian James Sawruk after being asked the same question. He told Sawruk that the group had flown out on a course of 265 degrees west and that he had written down the course in his log book.

A number of eyewitnesses stated they saw the *Hornet* air group fly west that morning, including pilots who were in the air that day. In an interview questionnaire collected by Walter Lord in preparation for his book, *Incredible Victory*, Lawrence French, a fighter pilot who was flying cover that morning directly above the *Hornet*, stated that he watched the group, including both the high and low squadrons, move off to the "west northwest" until it disappeared from view.

Another piece of direct evidence confirming the course of the *Hornet* air group can be found in the USS *Hornet* Deck Log (official source). It is an entry made by watch officer Lieutenant A. H. Hunker, recorded as the first group of Rodee's dive-bombers were returning to the ship after their morning mission. At 1300 (local ship's time), Lieutenant Hunker wrote in the log that radar operators reported to the bridge "a large group of planes bearing 260 true, distant 56 miles." These were Walt Rodee's dive-bombers returning to the *Hornet* on the reciprocal course of the one the group had flown out on three hours earlier. If Rodee had been coming up from the south, as later claimed in the USS *Hornet* After Action Report (official source), he would have been flying a course closer to 180 degrees.

Author interviews with Bert Earnest and Harry Ferrier were the primary sources for what occurred on the early-morning mission led by Langdon Fieberling from Midway Atoll on the morning of June 4. The author also relied on the written account by Captain Mitsuo Fuchida in *Midway: The Battle That Doomed Japan*, when he witnessed the arrival and subsequent destruction of the remaining Avengers from the bridge of the *Akagi*.

Brief glimpses of what happened during the final minutes of the Avengers' attack were later recalled by two B-26 pilots, James Collins and James Muri. Both of them provided this information in written questionnaires submitted to Walter Lord for *Incredible Victory*. In addition, Pete Peterkin happened to meet Major Collins on his way back to the States after Peterkin's time on Guadalcanal, and Peterkin confided in his diary what Collins had observed.

For the factors that went into Admiral Nagumo's decision to rearm his planes for a second strike on Midway, including his reaction to the attack by Fieberling's Avengers, the author relied on the narratives in Lord's *Incredible Victory*, Fuchida's *Midway: The Battle That Doomed Japan*, and Prange's *Miracle at Midway*.

Anecdotal material about the last few minutes on the *Hornet*'s flight deck, including the conversations between crew members of Torpedo Eight, was provided in an author interview with William Tunstall, and also drawn from Lloyd Wendt's "The True Story of Heroic Squadron 8."

The events that occurred on the controversial "Flight to Nowhere" by the *Hornet* air group will undoubtedly continue to be the subject of speculation and further analysis in the years ahead. What cannot be disputed is the fact that the *Hornet* air group was sent in a direction significantly divergent from the course that would have led them to the Japanese carriers, and that there were profound consequences to this failure.

The breaking of radio silence by Lieutenant Commander Waldron and the content of his verbal confrontation with Commander Ring was confirmed in the transcripts of Bowen Weisheit's taped interviews (each sixty-two pages) with Ensign Troy Guillory and Ensign Ben Tappan, who both flew Dauntless dive-bombers on June 4 in close proximity to Commander Ring. Fifteen years prior to his Weisheit interview, Guillory went on the record in a February 21, 1967, letter to author Walter Lord, stating his recollection of the verbal confrontation between Waldron and Ring shortly before Waldron pulled away from the rest of the group. Lord chose not to include the information in his book, *Incredible Victory*. Although there is no official record of the actual words spoken by Waldron and Ring, the account in this book is consistent with Guillory's and Tappan's independent recollections after the war.

Additional confirmation of the radio exchange between Waldron and Ring can be found in the classified report prepared by Lieutenant Commander John G. Foster, the *Hornet*'s air operations officer, entitled "Defects Observed During the Action off Midway on June 4, 1942" (official source). Foster reported that at exactly 0816 (local adjusted time), radio silence had been broken on the "combat patrol frequency." Due to the garbled nature of the transmission, and his belief that none of the *Hornet* pilots would disobey the orders on maintaining radio silence, Foster concluded it was coming from pilots flying from the *Enterprise*.

Troy Guillory also stated in his interview with Weisheit that he had been one of the censors who had reviewed John Waldron's last letters to his wife and daughters on the night before the squadron's last mission. In a letter to John Lundstrom dated June 1, 1981, Ensign Henry Carey confirmed that he had also reviewed the letters.

After Lieutenant Commander Waldron radioed Commander Ring that he was breaking away from the rest of the group, Radioman Richard Woodson watched them leave the formation, and then reported the news to his pilot. Woodson provided his account to the Battle of Midway Roundtable Web site (www.midway42.org) on March 4, 2004. His account is also included in Russell's *No Right to Win*.

In 1982, Bowen Weisheit interviewed *Hornet* fighter pilot Humphrey Tallman about what Tallman saw that day from his Wildcat fighter and the story of his subsequent ditching in the Pacific along with the rest of his squadron. In his taped recollections, Tallman told of watching Waldron's squadron pull away to the south. "I can see them now," he said to Weisheit.

The harrowing passage of Bert Earnest's return flight to Midway, culminating in the crash landing of his battered Avenger on one wheel, was drawn from the many hours of author interviews with both Earnest and Ferrier.

The account of Torpedo Eight's flight after John Waldron broke away from the rest of the *Hornet* air group, the pilots' first sighting of the Japanese striking force at 0917, and the squadron's subsequent destruction in the minutes that followed was provided by George Gay in *Sole Survivor*, Lloyd Wendt's

"The True Story of Heroic Squadron 8," and in Gay's After Action Report (June 7, 1942). His recollection of seeing the moon centered in the middle of his windshield provided former navigator Bowen Weisheit with another piece of information he needed to extrapolate their actual course based on the moon's azimuth at that time.

Further confirmation that Waldron's squadron was heading in a southerly rather than northerly course as it approached the enemy fleet can be found in Japanese official records, which were incorporated into Parshall and Tully's *Shattered Sword*. The records state that at 0917, one minute before Waldron's squadron was sighted by Japanese lookouts, Admiral Nagumo had turned onto a course of 070 degrees, or a northeast heading. These reports also state that Waldron's attack came from "almost dead ahead," which could only have been the case if Torpedo Eight was coming from the north rather than the south.

The actions of Ensign John McInerny in leading the *Hornet*'s fighter squadron away from Commander Ring's air group were well chronicled in the forty-six-page transcript of his interview with Bowen Weisheit in 1982. The most riveting account of his actions can be found in Lundstrom's *The First Team* (pp. 435–37). Personal details about McInerny's life and exploits in the Navy were drawn from author interviews with Smiley Morgan. According to Weisheit's *The Last Flight* (p. 18), McInerny also contended that he saw the Japanese fleet far to the south when he was leading the rest of the fighters away from the group.

The brief narrative describing the laborious process undertaken by the Japanese carrier crews to rearm their planes with torpedoes following Admiral Nagumo's discovery that American carriers were within attacking range was drawn from a number of sources, including Parshall and Tully's *Shattered Sword*, Lord's *Incredible Victory*, Prange's *Miracle at Midway*, Lundstrom's *The First Team*, and Fuchida's *Midway: The Battle That Doomed Japan*.

Further insights into what occurred during the squadron's subsequent attack on the Japanese carriers were gleaned from the radio transmissions made by John Waldron, most if not all of which were received by Gay, among others. On June 5, one day after the battle, Radioman Leroy Quillen, who had been monitoring radio transmissions while flying in a dive-bomber directly behind Commander Ring in the *Hornet* air group, filed an official report of everything he heard Lieutenant Commander Waldron say before he was killed. In a lengthy oral interview provided to a naval historian on October 12, 1943, George Gay asserted that he heard Waldron calling Ring on the radio, and that there was no answer. In *Incredible Victory* (p. 144), Walter Lord stated that Waldron repeatedly called "Stanhope from Johnny One," with no apparent success.

A description from the Japanese point of view of the squadron's final attack on the striking force was provided by Commander Minoru Genda, Admiral Nagumo's operations officer aboard the *Akagi*. This part of the story appeared in a detailed statement Genda submitted to author Gordon Prange prior to the publication of his *Miracle at Midway*.

In their monumental Midway battle study, *Shattered Sword*, Jon Parshall and Anthony Tully deliver a compelling narrative of the moment when Lieutenant Commander "Ruff" Johnson, who was leading the dive-bomber squadron on the left wing of Ring's formation, received word of John Waldron's radio transmission that Waldron was under attack by enemy fighters. Realizing that the Japanese carriers were well to the south of them, Johnson quickly turned his seventeen-plane squadron southeast to find the enemy (p. 272). In an interview with the author, *Hornet* dive-bomber pilot Roy Gee confirmed that until Ruff Johnson led their Dauntless squadron off to the southeast, the carrier's air group had never deviated from its original course.

The final minutes of George Gay's penetration of the Japanese escort screen in the last surviving Devastator, and the launching of his torpedo at the Japanese carrier *Soryu*, were drawn from Gay's account in *Sole Survivor*, as well as his first detailed After Action Report (June 7, 1942; official source). In the Japanese battle reports, officers on the carrier *Soryu* confirmed the specifics of Gay's attack, including the launching of his torpedo from approximately eight hundred yards, his flight down the length of the ship's deck, and the destruction of his plane by Japanese Zeroes, according to *Shattered Sword* (p. 207).

The description of Bert Earnest's remarkable flight back to Midway in his battered Avenger was provided to the author by Earnest and Harry Ferrier. Additional details were drawn from Earnest's After Action Report (June 23, 1942; official source), which was submitted to CINCPAC after the battle.

The actions of Admiral Nagumo, and the frantic activity aboard his flagship *Akagi* from the moment of the destruction of Torpedo Squadron Eight at approximately 0945, to the arrival of the American dive-bombers at 1020, were distilled from Lord's *Incredible Victory*, Parshall and Tully's *Shattered Sword*, Prange's *Miracle at Midway*, and Fuchida's *Midway: The Battle That Doomed Japan*.

Gay's account of the arrival and attack of the *Yorktown* and *Enterprise* dive-bombers after his plane was shot down, and his subsequent survival in the ocean for nearly thirty hours, came from the first statements he made to debriefing officers at Midway after his rescue on June 5 (Action dispatches, June 4–5, 1942; official source), and the in-depth After Action Report (June 7, 1942; official source).

The fruitless search by John McInerny and the rest of his fighter squadron to find the *Hornet* before their Wildcats ran out of gas was drawn from the taped interviews Bowen Weisheit conducted with John McInerny, Pat Mitchell, Richard Gray, Johnny Talbot, and Humphrey Tallman, along with the detailed interview notes Walter Lord transcribed after his lengthy interview with Stan Ruehlow. Additional details were supplied by Ruehlow in two letters to John Lundstrom in 1974.

The brief sketch of Commander Ring's return alone to the *Hornet* at 1118, and his refusal to go to the bridge, was provided to the author by historian Mark Horan in a taped telephone interview in September 2006, and by Harold Towne in a separate interview. These sources were complemented by a November 2007 e-mail to the author from historian James Sawruk, in which he confirmed that he received a similar account from Ring's wingman, Ensign Clayton Fisher, who landed aboard the *Hornet* shortly afterward. Bowen Weisheit confirmed to the author that in a 1982 interview, *Hornet* officer Clark Barrett told him that Commander Ring's unwillingness to go to the bridge made it necessary for Walter Rodee to report the results of the air group's mission to Captain Mitscher.

The only published comment Commander Ring ever made on this subject came from an unpublished letter he wrote on March 28, 1946, excerpts of which were released by his family, and which formed the basis for a sympathetic article by retired Navy captain Bruce Linder in the U.S. Naval Institute *Proceedings* (August 1999). In his letter, Admiral Ring wrote that after returning to the *Hornet* from his morning mission on June 4, "I was shaken at the realization of such losses and will admit that I was in poor condition to take the air in a renewed attack on the Japanese carriers which had, by then, been located. About one hour after my landing the remaining aircraft of the group were ordered launched for the next attack."

It is unclear how Commander Ring could have possibly known the extent of the losses within his air group at that particular time unless it was from Waldron's radio transmissions. There are a number of other inconsistencies in the letter.

The background information on Pete Mitscher's academic record at Annapolis, including his struggle to graduate, was drawn from Theodore Taylor's *The Magnificent Mitscher* (pp. 20–27).

The description of the flight of Lieutenant Commander Ruff Johnson and his seventeen-plane dive-bomber squadron after he led it south away from the rest of the air group was culled from a variety of sources, including author interviews with pilot Roy Gee, Bowen Weisheit's interview with pilot Troy Guillory, a completed questionnaire submitted by Ruff Johnson to Walter Lord in 1966, the account of Johnson's mission in *Shattered Sword,* and the narrative of these events in *Miracle at Midway.*

The account from a Japanese perspective of the first dive-bombing attack by the Dauntless pilots from the *Enterprise* and the *Yorktown*, followed by Admiral Nagumo's last hours aboard his doomed flagship *Akagi*, the escape to the *Nagara*, and the subsequent destruction of the four Japanese carriers, was drawn from Fuchida's *Midway: The Battle That Doomed Japan* (pp. 153–177).

## WHEN THE SEA SHALL GIVE UP ITS DEAD

The aftermath of Bert Earnest's and Harry Ferrier's flight back to Midway, including Bert's subsequent meeting on the runway with pilots from Ruff Johnson's dive-bomber squadron, was drawn from author interviews with Earnest and Ferrier.

The narrative scenes of Gay's thirty hours floating in the Pacific were re-created from his personal recollections in *Sole Survivor*. The details of his rescue, as well as the initial statements he gave to intelligence officers at Midway of what he saw during the battle, were drawn from classified Action Dispatches (official source) sent to CINCPAC on June 5. His appearance and demeanor at his first meeting with Admiral Nimitz in Pearl Harbor were described by Commander Ernest Eller in the oral history he provided to the U.S. Naval Institute, at Annapolis, Maryland.

The sketch chronicling the reaction of the Japanese Imperial Navy to the defeat it suffered at Midway, including the cover-up of the catastrophe to the Japanese people, and the subsequent quarantining of Midway survivors after their return to the home islands, was documented in Parshall and Tully's *Shattered Sword*, Lord's *Incredible Victory*, Prange's *Miracle at Midway*, and Fuchida's *Midway: The Battle That Doomed Japan*.

The cover-up by newly promoted Admiral Pete Mitscher and his staff of his disastrous decisions on the first day of the Midway battle cannot be found in any written records or oral histories. Eminent historians of the Pacific War, including Samuel Eliot Morison, Walter Lord, and Gordon Prange, relied on Mitscher's "official" version of what took place during the *Hornet* air group's morning mission on June 4.

However, Admiral Mitscher's mistakes were not limited to the first mission on June 4. The account of the failure of the *Hornet*'s second strike mission against the fourth Japanese carrier, *Hiryu*, including the botched launching of the *Hornet* air group, was drawn principally from the recollections of men who fought in the battle, including an author interview with pilot Roy Gee, and Henry A. Carey's letters to John Lundstrom. Additional confirmation is provided in John B. Lundstrom's *Black Shoe Carrier Admiral* (p. 273), in which he describes the "marooning" of the "entire leadership" of the air group due to Mitscher's egregious error.

The account of the *Hornet*'s failed mission on June 5, in which many of the

*Hornet*'s dive-bombers were armed with heavy ordnance in contravention of Admiral Spruance's direct order, was drawn from John Lundstrom's *The First Team*, as well as from author interviews with Roy Gee, who told the story of Commander Ring's return from the mission on June 5, when he complained to the other pilots that he had been unable to launch his bomb because the launch mechanism was inoperative. According to Gee, Ring had absolutely no idea how to drop a bomb from the Dauntless.

This stunning fact was further confirmed in a 1987 interview given to historian James Sawruk by dive-bomber pilot Clay Fisher, who told Sawruk of being summoned to Commander Ring's stateroom on the evening of June 5. Worrying that he might be in trouble, Ensign Fisher was amazed when the group commander asked Fisher to instruct him in the specific procedures needed to launch a bomb.

The anger of Admiral Spruance after learning that Mitscher had failed to comply with his order about the size of the ordnance to be carried by the dive-bombers on June 5 was then compounded by the *Hornet* air staff's attempt to lie about it. Admiral Spruance's heated reaction is documented in Thomas Buell's *The Quiet Warrior*. Buell further amplified his thoughts on Admiral Spruance's lack of trust in Mitscher in an oral history interview conducted by historian Paul Stillwell on May 9, 1982, which is on file at the U.S. Naval Institute in Annapolis, Maryland.

The most solid evidence of Mitscher's cover-up of the June 4 fiasco is the false USS *Hornet* After Action Report (official source) he submitted to Admiral Nimitz shortly after the battle. It is unlikely that anyone will ever know who actually drafted the report, along with its accompanying map purporting to show the many convoluted directions its air squadrons supposedly flew on June 4, 1942. It is also noteworthy to point out that the "official" map contains no specific navigational headings for the course followed by the air group after leaving the *Hornet*. Certainly, no one ever took credit for these documents after they were declassified on November 23, 1964, more than twenty years after the battle took place.

The captains of all three American carriers in the battle were required not only to submit an After Action Report on behalf of their ship and its crew, but under Navy regulations, they were also required to forward the After Action Reports submitted by the air group commanders and the air squadron commanders. In the case of the *Yorktown* and the *Enterprise*, not only were the ships' After Action Reports submitted to CINCPAC, but individual reports were forwarded from each air group commander and all eight air squadron commanders.

Admiral Mitscher alone failed to submit the additional reports.

Certainly, Admiral Raymond Spruance was aware of the falsehoods in the

*Hornet* After Action Report. He was required to endorse it before the report was submitted to Admiral Nimitz. In his endorsement, Spruance wrote Nimitz that the *Hornet* report "contains a number of inaccuracies." In a separate communication to CINCPAC, he stated, "Hornet dive-bombers failed to locate the target and did not participate in this attack (June 4). Had they done so, the fourth carrier could have been attacked and later attack made on *Yorktown* prevented."

Spruance held Mitscher indirectly responsible for this costly failure. Like Mitscher, Spruance was part of the Annapolis elite, "blue school Navy," and he was almost unfailingly magnanimous when it came to an Annapolis peer. His uncharacteristically blunt language was an indication of the anger he felt at Mitscher's conduct during the battle, and Mitscher's subsequent attempt to cover up his mistakes. Further amplification of Spruance's views, including his ongoing distrust of Mitscher later in the war, can be found in Buell's *The Quiet Warrior* (p. 149), and in Prange's *Miracle at Midway* (p. 244).

Based on the 265-degree course the *Hornet* air group actually followed on June 4, and the fact that some of the group's pilots had seen the fighter squadron turn back, it was theoretically possible for the *Hornet* air staff to extrapolate that one of the sectors where Mitchell's squadron might have ditched was to the northeast of Midway Atoll instead of to the northwest, as suggested in their subsequent After Action Report and its accompanying map. The spurious map shows the fighter squadron heading in a direction to the northwest of Midway Atoll, which is where the Midway rescue planes focused their search for them from June 4–8.

The author was unable to find any dispatches indicating that the *Hornet* staff provided clues to the rescue pilots as to where their lost squadron went down. The air staff may have thought the squadron had headed for Midway, and had actually gone down northwest of it. Ultimately, the eight survivors were found through sheer chance nearly two hundred miles to the east.

The ordeal of the ditched fighter pilots as they floated in the Pacific was documented through interviews conducted by Bowen Weisheit with Pat Mitchell, Richard Gray, Johnny Talbot, Humphrey Tallman, John McInerny, and PBY rescue pilot Jerry Crawford, as well as the interview conducted by Walter Lord with Stanley Ruehlow.

The sketch of Fred Mears as he went through the personal effects of each one of the lost pilots and crewmen from Torpedo Eight was sourced from his own description in *Carrier Combat*.

The final letters written by Russell "Rusty" Kenyon to his wife, Brownie, before Torpedo Eight's last mission were provided to the author by Kenyon's daughter, "Rusty" Edwards.

The account of Rete Gaynier's personal torment in waiting to hear word of the fate of her husband was provided to the author by Rete Gaynier Janiec. It was representative of what so many of the wives and loved ones endured as they waited for news of the missing combatants.

The letter written by Jennie Teats on June 11 to her already dead son Grant was provided to the author by Grant Teats's niece, Nancy Mahi.

The discovery by George Gay that he had become famous as the lone survivor of John Waldron's attack, and the resulting emotional roller-coaster ride it led to upon his return to the States, was recounted by Gay himself in *Sole Survivor*. Rete Gaynier Janiec provided additional details about the resulting fractured relationship with two of the wives of lost pilots. Other pertinent information on this subject was provided in letters to Brownie Kenyon from Hal Ellison's widow, Audrey Faye, which were provided to the author by Rusty Kenyon Edwards.

Copies of the letters to Bert Earnest's parents from the bereaved father of Charlie Brannon, as well as the letters sent to Brannon's family from James Earnest were given to the author by Bert Earnest, along with copies of both Navy Cross citations Bert received for his actions at Midway.

The account of Earnest's and Ferrier's final days at Midway after the battle was provided by them to the author in separate interviews. The story of the Marines falling asleep under the blood-soaked Avenger when it was being shipped back to Pearl Harbor came from an interview with Ferrier, who met one of the Marines who had taken shelter under the plane.

## SISTER SARA

The reaction of Swede Larsen's detachment at Pearl Harbor to the news that forty-five out of forty-eight of their squadron mates had been killed at Midway was drawn from interviews by the author with William Magee, Ervin "Judge" Wendt, Smiley Morgan, and Jack Stark.

The story of Swede Larsen's assumption of command of Torpedo Eight on the hangar deck of the *Hornet* on June 12, 1942, including his disparagement of George Flinn in front of the men, was recounted to the author by Smiley Morgan. The excerpts of Swede's speech came from Ira Wolfert's *Torpedo 8* (pp. 25–27).

The anecdote in which Commander Stanhope Cotton Ring offered to stand a round of drinks for every pilot at the Ewa Field Officers' Club in Hawaii, and the subsequent refusal of the *Hornet* pilots in the bar to drink with him, was described in detail in a letter to John Lundstrom from *Yorktown* fighter pilot Johnny Adams, who was an eyewitness.

The description of the post-Midway celebration that took place on Waikiki Beach, including the fistfights and drunken brawls between Army and Navy aviators, is documented in Lord's *Incredible Victory,* Mears's *Carrier Combat,* and the author's interviews with Smiley Morgan.

The narrative describing Torpedo Eight's reorganization under Swede Larsen, and its training period from June 15 to July 6, 1942, was drawn from the Torpedo Squadron Eight War Diary, Wolfert's *Torpedo 8,* and author interviews with Gene Hanson, Smiley Morgan, and Bert Earnest.

The impressions of Bruce Harwood after he arrived to become Torpedo Eight's executive officer were distilled from author interviews with eight survivors of the squadron. All of them remembered him as one of the finest men they served with in the war. The assessments of the other pilots in the squadron by the enlisted men who served under them were provided to the author in interviews with William Magee, Ski Kowalewski, Frank Balsely, Del Delchamps, Harry Ferrier, Bill Tunstall, Judge Wendt, and Wiley Bartlett.

The scene in which Fred Mears and Harry Ferrier learned they had become new crewmates aboard the *Enterprise* was drawn from Mears's *Carrier Combat* and an author interview with Ferrier.

The narrative chronicling the squadron's first two weeks aboard the carrier *Saratoga* was re-created from the private diary of Pete Peterkin, along with author interviews with Gene Hanson, Jack Stark, and Bill Tunstall. The makeup of the carrier task force and the course it followed toward Guadalcanal were drawn largely from Lundstrom's *Black Shoe Carrier Admiral* and *The First Team and the Guadalcanal Campaign,* as well as from the USS *Saratoga* Deck Log (official source).

The description of the *Saratoga*'s crossing of the equator, the subsequent appearance of King Neptune, and the initiation of Torpedo Eight's "pollywogs" into "shellbacks" was re-created from the diary of Pete Peterkin.

The first briefing of the *Saratoga* air group by Harry Don Felt about Guadalcanal and the following discussion and questions from the pilots were drawn from Lundstrom's *The First Team and the Guadalcanal Campaign* (p. 23), and an interview with Gene Hanson.

The account of Aaron Katz's arrival aboard the *Saratoga,* including his introduction to Swede Larsen in the Torpedo Eight squadron office, was provided to the author in interviews with Jack Stark and Smiley Morgan. Swede's prejudices were never cloaked behind polite verbiage. He was very direct about them. His animosity toward Jews and minorities was described to the author in interviews with Gene Hanson, Jack Stark, Smiley Morgan, Bert Earnest, and Ski Kowalewski. The exchange between Larsen and Katz in their first meeting was something that remained indelibly in Morgan's memory.

The information related to Katz's formative years in Cleveland prior to becoming a Navy pilot was given to the author by Katz's two sons, Rick and

Roger. Their help was invaluable in reconstructing his life before and after the war.

The substance of the controversial planning session for the Guadalcanal invasion that took place aboard the *Saratoga* between its senior commanders on July 27, 1942, came from a variety of sources, including Lundstrom's *Black Shoe Carrier Admiral*, Richard B. Frank's *Guadalcanal*, and Alexander Vandegrift's *Once a Marine*.

The description of the preinvasion exercise at Koro Island was drawn from Mears's *Carrier Combat*, Vandegrift's *Once a Marine*, the Torpedo Squadron Eight War Diary, and author interviews with Ski Kowalewski, who flew that day with the unlucky Bob Evarts.

## Dog Day

The primary sources utilized by the author in describing the panorama of the August 7 invasion of Guadalcanal and Tulagi were Richard Frank's authoritative masterpiece, *Guadalcanal*, Vandegrift's *Once a Marine*, Lundstrom's *The First Team and the Guadalcanal Campaign*, Clark Lee's *They Call It Pacific*, Richard Tregaskis's *Guadalcanal Diary*, Jon Hoffman's *Once a Legend*, Thomas Miller's *The Cactus Air Force*, Clark Reynolds's *The Saga of Smokey Stover*, and Colonel Joseph H. Alexander's superb *Edson's Raiders*.

The account of Torpedo Squadron Eight's participation in the invasion on August 7 was drawn from author interviews with Gene Hanson, Bert Earnest, Jack Stark, and Smiley Morgan. Other sources include the Torpedo Squadron Eight War Diary, the Torpedo Squadron Eight After Combat Action Reports (official source) submitted by Swede Larsen after each mission, Wolfert's *Torpedo 8* (pp. 28–38), and the private diary of Pete Peterkin, in which he describes many of the invasion day preparations aboard the *Saratoga*, including the successful launch of every plane in the squadron.

The morning attack by Swede's element of Torpedo Eight on the coastal native village on Malaita was described in detail in author interviews with Hanson and Earnest, both of whom participated in the attack. They also described the subsequent confrontation aboard the *Saratoga* between Swede Larsen and several of the pilots, including Taurman and Earnest. For many years after the war, attorneys representing the victims of the bombing and strafing attack sought legal redress against the United States government for what they viewed as an atrocity.

The descriptions of the August 7 missions led by Bruce Harwood in Torpedo Eight's attacks on Guadalcanal were re-created from AP correspondent Clark Lee's *They Call It Pacific* (pp. 328–333), and from author interviews with Smiley Morgan, who participated in those attacks.

The description of the controversial decision made by Admiral Frank Jack Fletcher to withdraw the American carriers from Guadalcanal on August 8, and the events culminating in the annihilation of the Allied screening force in the Battle of Savo Island, was drawn from Lundstrom's *Black Shoe Carrier Admiral* and *The First Team and the Guadalcanal Campaign,* and Vandegrift's *Once a Marine.*

The portrayal of the aftermath of the Savo Island battle on August 9, in which General Vandegrift gave his inspirational talk to his officers in the rain, was drawn from *Once a Marine* (pp. 131–134). The reaction of Admiral Yamamoto after receiving news of the invasion, and the outlining of the steps he immediately undertook to retake Guadalcanal, was drawn from Lundstrom's *The First Team and the Guadalcanal Campaign* (pp. 91–94) and Frank's *Guadalcanal* (pp. 142–146).

The reactions of the Torpedo Eight pilots to their part in the invasion as the *Saratoga* headed away from Guadalcanal were drawn from author interviews with Hanson, Morgan, and Earnest.

## THE GALLOPING DRAGON

The seemingly wayward cruising of the American carriers August 8–19, 1942, as Admiral Fletcher waited for the opportunity to re-engage the Japanese navy, was chronicled in Reynolds's *The Saga of Smokey Stover* and Lundstrom's *The First Team and the Guadalcanal Campaign.*

The description of the 1st Marine Division's hellish first two weeks on Guadalcanal and Tulagi was distilled from Vandegrift's *Once a Marine,* Frank's *Guadalcanal,* and Martin Clemens's *Alone on Guadalcanal: A Coastwatcher's Story.*

For the narrative of the August 21 attack by Japanese shock troops led by Colonel Kiyonao Ichiki against the Marine positions along Alligator Creek, the author relied on material in Frank's *Guadalcanal,* Vandegrift's *Once a Marine,* Tregaskis's *Guadalcanal Diary,* Roger Butterfield's *Al Schmid — Marine,* and Meirion and Susie Harries's *Soldiers of the Sun: The Rise and Fall of the Imperial Japanese Army.*

The account of the death of Torpedo Eight pilot James Hill Cook was recounted to the author by Cook's friend and roommate Smiley Morgan. Additional details were found in the private diary of Pete Peterkin, and in the author's interview with William Magee, who also witnessed the fatal crash.

The narrative of the August 23 mission from the *Saratoga* to Guadalcanal, in which Butch Schindler, Admiral Fletcher's gunnery officer, delivered baked goods to General Vandegrift, was drawn from author interviews with Newton "Del" Delchamps.

The description of the flight led by Commander Harry Don Felt on August 23, in which the *Saratoga* air group attempted unsuccessfully to find and destroy a Japanese naval force in the middle of a brutal storm, was re-created from the narrative that appears in Lee's *They Call It Pacific* (pp. 339–347). Lee also provided details of his interaction with Butch Schindler after reaching Guadalcanal, and his eventual accommodations in Swede Larsen's plane. Bill Dye's attempted flight back to the *Saratoga* with Del Delchamps in the tail compartment, and its subsequent return to Guadalcanal after encountering the same storm, the account of Swede dressing down Delchamps over the bomb hoist, as well as Delchamps's account of his tussle with the Japanese souvenirs, were provided in an author interview with Delchamps.

The dramatic combat missions by two separate elements of Torpedo Eight on August 24, 1942, the first led by Bruce Harwood and the second by Swede Larsen, were drawn from a number of sources, including firsthand recollections of Harwood's mission and its aftermath and author interviews with Bert Earnest, Gene Hanson, Smiley Morgan, Ervin Wendt, Frank Balsley, Del Delchamps, and Ski Kowalewski, all of whom participated in the attack on the *Ryujo*. Gene Hanson's handwritten account of this mission was particularly helpful.

In an author interview, Jack Stark provided the description of Swede Larsen's preparations and takeoff for the August 24 mission. The diary of Pete Peterkin also provided important details. The events that took place during and after the Larsen mission are also described in significant detail in Wolfert's *Torpedo 8* (pp. 50–71). The discovery that Jack Barnum failed to launch his torpedo appeared in Swede's After Combat Action Report (official source). His angry outburst against Barnum was witnessed by Jack Stark.

Important aspects of both these missions came from the Torpedo Squadron Eight After Combat Action Reports (official source), the Torpedo Squadron Eight War Diary (official source), Hammel's *Guadalcanal: The Carrier Battles*, Miller's *The Cactus Air Force*, Lee's *They Call It Pacific*, and Lundstrom's *The First Team and the Guadalcanal Campaign*. Other sources reviewed by the author include the CO USS *Saratoga* to CINCPAC, Report of Action against Enemy Forces in Solomon Islands Area on August 24, 1942, including group and squadron reports, and Tactical Situation and Chronological History of Events (official source), and the newspaper story by Jack Singer, "Jack Singer's Last Despatch Is Thrilling Account of Bomber-Torpedo Plane Attack on Japanese Ships," which appeared in the *Honolulu Advertiser*. Singer, a reporter who was killed when the *Wasp* was later sunk, rode with Harwood's plane on the August 24 mission.

For the account of the final moments before the *Ryujo* sank, including the cause of its sinking, the author relied on Lundstrom's *The First Team and the*

*Guadalcanal Campaign* (pp. 122, 155), Frank's *Guadalcanal* (p. 179), and the official Japanese war history, *Senshi Sosho* (vol. 49, p. 566). According to the Japanese Imperial Navy report, the sole cause of the sinking was the torpedo launched into its starboard side by either Harwood, Earnest, or Grady. Interestingly, every pilot who made the attack on the *Ryujo* was awarded the Navy Cross except Earnest, who may well have launched the torpedo that sunk her. One possible reason was that he had already won two Navy Crosses in the first five months of the war.

Swede's words to Bruce Harwood after the August 24 mission appear in Wolfert's *Torpedo 8* (p. 71).

### RESURRECTION BLUES

The description of the aftermath of the August 24 battle, including the opposing assessments of its results by the senior American and Japanese commanders, was distilled from Lundstrom's *Black Shoe Carrier Admiral,* the USS *Saratoga* War Diary (official source), and the report by Fletcher, CTF–61 (ComCruPac) to ComSoPac, Preliminary Report of Actions, August 23–24, 1942 (September 6, 1942; official source).

The depiction of the mission flown on August 24 by Fred Mears was principally drawn from *Carrier Combat* and author interviews with Harry Ferrier. Mears's description of the dead sailors in the gun gallery aboard the *Enterprise* can be found in *Carrier Combat* (pp. 115–116).

The author is grateful to Gene Hanson for providing him with a copy of the humorous "Gedunk Investigative Report," which was created by John Taurman aboard the *Saratoga* shortly before his first disappearance.

The story of Taurman's ditching in the Pacific and his survival along with his crew on San Cristobal Island was re-created from several different accounts of his adventures, including an extract in Pete Peterkin's diary, and full narratives in Mears's *Carrier Combat* and Wolfert's *Torpedo 8.* Gene Hanson told the author of Taurman's being offered survivor's leave back in the States, and his turning the opportunity down to stay with the squadron.

An account of Frenchy Fayle's mission appeared in Wolfert's *Torpedo 8.* Other important details were provided in an author interview with Don Velazquez, the son of Edward Velazquez. The author is deeply grateful to historian James Sawruk, who discovered the fact that the Zero shot down by Velazquez during Fayle's mission was piloted by Yoshio Iwaki, who had eight "kills" to his credit, including three of the six Avengers in the Torpedo Eight detachment led by Langdon Fieberling on June 4.

The story of the rescue of Frenchy Fayle and his crew was provided in author interviews with Jack Stark and Don Velazquez. This tale also merited inclusion in Fred Mears's journal, *Carrier Combat,* and in Wolfert's *Torpedo 8.* All of the surviving pilots of Torpedo Eight remembered Fayle's decision to accept survivor's leave rather than stay with the squadron.

The torpedoing of the *Saratoga* was a seminal event in the lives of the men who were aboard her at that time. The author drew on his interviews with Bert Earnest, Bill Magee, Del Delchamps, Bill Tunstall, Jack Stark, and Smiley Morgan to tell the story of how the attack affected each man. AP correspondent Clark Lee wrote about his own experiences in *They Call It Pacific.* Pete Peterkin also described the torpedoing in his diary.

The story of Bill Dye's hair-raising flight from the *Saratoga* to Espiritu Santo in the overburdened Avenger was told to the author by Del Delchamps. The sketch of the transfer of Yeoman Jack Stark's filing cabinet from the *Saratoga* to the *Grayson* was related to the author by Stark.

Life for Torpedo Eight on the island of Espiritu Santo after the squadron flew off the *Saratoga* was described at length by Pete Peterkin in his diary. The author also drew upon interviews with Bert Earnest, Frank Balsley, and Jack Stark. In *Carrier Combat,* Fred Mears recorded his own pungent observations about conditions on Espiritu Santo after flying there with Harry Ferrier.

## The Canal

For the description of the plans developed by General Kiyotake Kawaguchi to retake Henderson Field, and their subsequent execution, the author relied on Frank's *Guadalcanal.* The account of the Tasimboko raid was drawn from Alexander's *Edson's Raiders.* The verbal description of General Vandegrift's reaction to Admiral Robert Ghormley's message of September 11 came from Vandegrift's own *Once a Marine.*

The author's interpretation of the attack by General Kawaguchi on September 12 was refined from the authoritative descriptions in Alexander's *Edson's Raiders,* Hoffman's *Once a Legend,* Tregaskis's *Guadalcanal Diary,* Vandegrift's *Once a Marine,* and Herbert Merrilat's *Guadalcanal Remembered.* Further detail was provided in an author interview with Marine Raider James "Horse" Smith.

The description of Swede Larsen's talk to the squadron on September 13 at Espiritu Santo, when he told them what was at stake in the battle for Guadalcanal, was drawn from author interviews with Jack Stark. For this account, the author also benefited from reading the Torpedo Squadron Eight War Diary (official source).

The events of September 13, including the moment that Torpedo Eight arrived at Henderson Field shortly before the most intensive Japanese ground attack up to that point in the campaign, was drawn from author interviews with Gene Hanson, Bert Earnest, and Frank Balsley. The sketch of the battle on Edson's Ridge was derived from Tregaskis's *Guadalcanal Diary*, Vandegrift's *Once a Marine*, Alexander's *Edson's Raiders*, and author interviews with raiders James "Horse" Smith and Frank Guidone.

Torpedo Eight's first few days and nights on Guadalcanal were re-created through author interviews with Gene Hanson, Frank Balsley, Wiley Bartlett, and Bert Earnest, and supplemented with the Torpedo Squadron Eight War Diary (official source).

For the Japanese reaction to the defeat of General Kawaguchi's force when it failed to retake Henderson Field, September 12–14, including the steps taken by Admiral Yamamoto to regain the initiative in the Solomons, the author utilized Frank's *Guadalcanal* and John Toland's *The Rising Sun: The Decline and Fall of the Japanese Empire*.

The account of the sinking of the *Wasp* and the torpedoing of the *North Carolina* was drawn from Frank's *Guadalcanal* and Mears's *Carrier Combat*.

## THE GROOVE

The loss of the American carrier *Wasp* and its emotional impact on the men of the Cactus Air Force was drawn from Lundstrom's *The First Team and the Guadalcanal Campaign*, Mears's *Carrier Combat*, and author interviews with Gene Hanson.

Torpedo Eight's first combat mission as part of the Cactus Air Force on September 16, 1942, including the squadron's claim of having torpedoed a Japanese cruiser, was drawn from the After Combat Action Report submitted by Swede Larsen, and author interviews with Gene Hanson, Ervin "Judge" Wendt, and Frank Balsley. The account of the September 17 mission in which Swede Larsen attacked two Japanese warships alone came from his After Combat Action Report and an author interview with Judge Wendt, who flew with him that day.

The descriptions of the squadron's living conditions on Guadalcanal, including the impact of the first shelling attack after the arrival of Bruce Harwood's detachment, the experiences of Smiley Morgan while bathing in the Lunga River, the quality of the food the men ate, the breakout of dysentery among the pilots, and the thriving black market in Japanese war souvenirs, were drawn from author interviews with Smiley Morgan, Bert Earnest, Frank Balsley, William Magee, and Harry Ferrier, as well as an excerpt from Mears's *Carrier Combat*. The source for the story of the theft of a case of bourbon from General Geiger was Vandegrift's *Once a Marine*.

The passage describing Swede's September 22 air attacks on the Japanese landing beaches came from the Torpedo Squadron Eight War Diary and an author interview with Morgan, who flew with him on the mission. For the account of Gene Hanson's mission in which he led a September 24 attack on a

Japanese cruiser, followed by his debriefing with General Roy Geiger, the author utilized a contemporaneous written account of the mission by Hanson, supplemented by an author interview with Hanson, along with the mission's After Action Report.

The narrative of the September 25 combat mission led by Swede Larsen was drawn from an author interview with Hanson along with the After Action Report. The subsequent confrontation between Swede Larsen and gunner J. D. Hayes was witnessed by squadron mate William Magee. In a 2006 author interview, Magee recalled that his first thought after seeing it happen was that Hayes had just been saved from spending the rest of his life in a penitentiary.

The account of the savage three-day engagement between General Vandegrift's Marines and the remnants of General Kawaguchi's force along the Matanikau River from September 25–28, 1942, was drawn from Vandegrift's *Once a Marine,* and author interviews with raiders James "Horse" Smith and Frank Guidone, who fought in the battle.

The story of the combat mission led by Bruce Harwood on October 1, 1942, after which three of the Avengers on the mission went missing, was recreated from the After Action Report and from an author interview with Del Delchamps, who was flying in Bill Dye's Avenger. The aerial search for the three lost Avengers by Evarts, Mears, and Katz was recounted in the Torpedo Squadron Eight War Diary (official source), as well as Mears's *Carrier Combat.* The personal story of the rescue of one of the lost crews was provided to the author by Del Delchamps.

Pete Peterkin's anecdote about knocking himself unconscious in a newly repaired bomb crater while under a Japanese shelling attack came from his diary. The story of Smiley Morgan's foot injury, which led to his encounter with General Geiger, was provided by Morgan in an author interview.

The account of Fred Mears's first mission at Guadalcanal, including the critical wounding of his tail gunner, can be found in *Carrier Combat* (pp. 125–128). The sources for the narrative of his second mission to Rekata Bay on October 5 include the Torpedo Squadron Eight War Diary, the After Combat Action Report of the flight, *Carrier Combat,* and an author interview with Ski Kowalewski, who flew with pilot Bob Evarts that day.

The tragic mission of October 6, which cost the lives of squadron members Red Doggett, John Taurman, J. D. Hayes, Charlie Lawrence, and John Robak, was chronicled in detail by Pete Peterkin in his private diary. Additional material was drawn from *Carrier Combat,* Wolfert's *Torpedo 8,* the Torpedo Squadron Eight War Diary, the After Combat Action Report for the mission, and author interviews with Gene Hanson.

The sources for the first mission Swede Larsen flew with Aaron Katz on October 8, in which Bert Earnest scored a torpedo hit on a Japanese warship, came from author interviews with gunner Frank Balsley, who flew with Katz, and with Bert Earnest. The author also drew from *Carrier Combat* and the After Action Report. The account of the confrontation between Swede Larsen and Aaron Katz's crew after the mission was provided to the author by Frank Balsley in a 2006 interview. The anecdote of Bert Earnest being awarded a samurai sword by General Vandegrift at his command post came from author interviews with Earnest.

The account of the October 10 mission was drawn from Lundstrom's *The First Team and the Guadalcanal Campaign* (p. 291), the After Action Report filed by Swede Larsen, and an author interview with pilot Gene Hanson.

For the description of the increasingly depleted physical and mental state of the men of Torpedo Eight, the author utilized the diary of Pete Peterkin. The tactical situation on land and sea was culled from Vandegrift's *Once a Marine,* and Lundstrom's *The First Team and the Guadalcanal Campaign.*

The story of the October 12 combat mission of Torpedo Eight in which either Aaron Katz or Gene Hanson delivered a direct hit on a Japanese warship was drawn from the Torpedo Squadron Eight War Diary, Mears's *Carrier Combat,* Wolfert's *Torpedo 8,* the After Action Report of the mission, and author interviews with Bert Earnest, Gene Hanson, Ski Kowalewski, and Frank Balsley.

Swede Larsen's decision to go back and attempt to sink the crippled Japanese warship was drawn from author interviews with Bert Earnest and Gene Hanson, the After Action Report filed by Larsen, and the account that appears in Wolfert's *Torpedo 8* (pp. 101–102).

## DIVINE FIRE

The horrific shelling by two Japanese battleships on October 13 was etched in the memory of every man who lived through that night at Henderson Field. The author was able to record the personal stories of a number of the men who were there, including Pete Peterkin, who wrote about it at length in his diary, and through author interviews with Bert Earnest, Judge Wendt, Frank Balsley, Bill Magee, Wiley Bartlett, Ski Kowalewski, and Gene Hanson. Further details of the attack were supplied in Fred Mears's *Carrier Combat,* Vandegrift's *Once a Marine,* and Frank's *Guadalcanal* (pp. 313–319). For the devastating impact of the October 13 shelling attack, including the complete destruction of Torpedo Eight's camp in the coconut grove, the author relied on interviews with the men who lived through it and who are named above.

The subsequent evacuation of their camp, and their encounter later on October 14 with Major Michael Mahoney, was richly portrayed by Pete Peterkin in his diary. Details of these events appear in *Carrier Combat,* Wolfert's *Torpedo 8,* and the Torpedo Squadron Eight War Diary. For the descriptions of Major Mahoney's iconoclastic and fascinating personality, the author relied on the written observations of Peterkin and Fred Mears, as well as the valuable information about his military career provided by the U.S. Marine Corps History Division in Quantico, Virginia (official source).

The announcement by Swede Larsen of his decision to remain on Guadalcanal after learning that all six of the squadron's Avengers were apparently unsalvageable was recalled in author interviews with Bert Earnest and Gene Hanson.

## Out of the Ashes

For the overall situation on Guadalcanal as of October 15, 1942, including the continued Japanese air attacks and the later discovery of the hidden cache of aviation fuel, the author is indebted to Frank's *Guadalcanal* and Lundstrom's *The First Team and the Guadalcanal Campaign.*

The story of Torpedo Eight's first days inside the Marine defense perimeter with Major Mahoney's company, including the account of Swede Larsen ordering Chief Hammond to build him a serviceable combat plane from the six written-off Avengers, was drawn from Peterkin's diary. The description of the sniper patrol undertaken by Judge Wendt and Bert Edmonds came from author interviews with Wendt.

The details of Chief Hammond's extraordinary undertaking to build his first "Frankenstein" Avenger by cannibalizing five other wrecked aircraft were provided in Peterkin's diary. The account of the Japanese attack on the destroyer *McFarland* on October 16 was also drawn from Peterkin's diary, as well as author interviews with Bill Magee and Ski Kowalewski, both of whom were aboard the *McFarland* during the attack. Further details came from *The Saturday Evening Post* article "The McFarland Comes Home," Lundstrom's *The First Team and the Guadalcanal Campaign,* and Miller's *The Cactus Air Force.*

The description of Swede's first test flight in Chief Hammond's aerial creation was drawn from Wolfert's *Torpedo 8* (pp. 113–114), the Torpedo Squadron Eight War Diary, and author interviews with Gene Hanson. The sketch of the squadron's enlisted men digging foxholes near Bloody Knoll was drawn from Pete Peterkin's diary, the Torpedo Squadron Eight War Diary, and author interviews with Wiley Bartlett.

For the scenes depicting the preparations by Japanese general Masao Maruyama to launch the ground attack by his Sendai Division against the southern Marine defense perimeter, including the history of the Sendai Division and the details and execution of his plan, the author relied on Frank's *Guadalcanal,* Toland's *The Rising Sun,* and Samuel Griffith's *The Battle for Guadalcanal.*

The account of Swede Larsen's first two bombing missions on the morning of October 23 came from the diary of Pete Peterkin, the Torpedo Squadron

Eight War Diary, the After Action Reports, and author interviews with Judge Wendt.

The account of Gene Hanson's first mission on October 23 was drawn from the Torpedo Squadron Eight War Diary, the After Action Report, and author interviews with Hanson. The description of Hanson's second mission, during which Major Mahoney was killed when their plane was shot down in Sealark Channel, was also provided by Hanson. Additional details were found in Wolfert's *Torpedo 8* (pp. 114–115), Mears's *Carrier Combat* (p. 147), Pete Peterkin's diary, the After Action Report, and the Torpedo Squadron Eight War Diary. The source for the final anecdote of that night, in which Fred Mears and Aaron Katz pointed their pistols at one another while attempting to defend themselves against a Japanese sniper, was *Carrier Combat*.

The major source for the portrayal of Torpedo Squadron Eight's preparations for defending their section of the Marine defense perimeter on October 24 was Pete Peterkin's diary, with additional details provided in author interviews with Wiley Bartlett, Frank Balsley, Bert Earnest, and Gene Hanson.

The account of the October 24 night battle in which Torpedo Eight fought from their foxholes along the southern perimeter was drawn from the Torpedo Eight War Diary, Pete Peterkin's diary, Burke Davis's *Marine! The Life of Chesty Puller*, Mears's *Carrier Combat*, Vandegrift's *Once a Marine*, and the author's interviews with Hanson, Bartlett, Balsley, and Earnest.

The actions of the men of Torpedo Eight on October 25, including the killing by R. T. Williams of a Japanese sniper, the continued work of Chief Hammond's crew to construct a second "Frankenstein" Avenger, Fred Mears and Peterkin's witnessing of the aerial battle over Henderson Field, and the resumption of their foxhole positions in the defense line for that night's continued assaults by the Sendai Division, were pooled from Pete Peterkin's diary, the Torpedo Squadron Eight War Diary, *Carrier Combat*, and author interviews with Balsley, Earnest, Bartlett, and Hanson.

The deterioration in the mental and physical condition of the men of Torpedo Squadron Eight after nearly six weeks of combat on Guadalcanal was highlighted by Mears in *Carrier Combat* (p. 149), the recollections of Earnest and Hanson in author interviews, and Peterkin in his diary.

For the portrayal of the Battle of Santa Cruz between Japanese and American carrier forces on October 26, the author relied on the excellent accounts in Toland's *The Rising Sun*, Lundstrom's *The First Team and the Guadalcanal Campaign* and *Black Shoe Carrier Admiral*, Miller's *The Cactus Air Force*, and Hammel's *Guadalcanal: The Carrier Battles*.

The reactions of the men of Torpedo Eight to the sinking of the *Hornet* were drawn from author interviews with Bert Earnest and Gene Hanson, who were on Guadalcanal at the time, and with Smiley Morgan, Bill Tunstall, Jack

Stark, and Bill Magee, who were at Espiritu Santo. The decision of Fred Mears, Bert Earnest, Gene Hanson, and Aaron Katz to return to Espiritu Santo was recalled in an author interview with Gene Hanson, and chronicled in the Torpedo Squadron Eight War Diary and Mears's *Carrier Combat*.

## Swede's Refrain

The "lull" in activities of the squadron members who remained on Guadalcanal while Chief Hammond attempted to resurrect another flyable Avenger was emphasized in both Pete Peterkin's diary and the Torpedo Squadron Eight War Diary.

The description of Swede's successful flight in Chief Hammond's second creation and of the move of the squadron's camp to a new location was drawn from Peterkin's diary. The results of the six routine solo missions Larsen flew in the new plane November 1–3, 1942, were collected from the After Action Reports filed by Larsen and the Torpedo Squadron Eight War Diary. The source for the account of Larsen intercepting the letter sent by Earnest to Peterkin was an author interview with Earnest.

The improving condition of the men of the squadron at Espiritu Santo was drawn from author interviews with Jack Stark, Del Delchamps, and Smiley Morgan, along with Mears's *Carrier Combat*.

For the overall assessment of the strategic situation from the Japanese point of view on November 6, 1942, the author drew on Toland's *The Rising Sun*, Frank's *Guadalcanal*, and Lundstrom's *The First Team and the Guadalcanal Campaign*.

The account of the November 7 mission led by Swede Larsen against the eleven-ship enemy task force was drawn from his After Action Report, the Torpedo Squadron Eight War Diary, Wolfert's *Torpedo 8*, Lundstrom's *The First Team and the Guadalcanal Campaign*, and the award citation for the Distinguished Flying Cross that Larsen later received for leading the attack.

The refusal of Swede Larsen to leave Guadalcanal until he was "properly relieved" was recorded by Fred Mears in *Carrier Combat* (p. 151). The concern about whether the squadron had pushed its luck too far was expressed by Peterkin in his diary. Details of letters of the squadron's enlisted men on Guadalcanal to squadron mates on Espiritu Santo about their desire to be relieved were provided to the author by Jack Stark.

The account of the arrival on November 12 of the first six Avengers from the Marine air group relieving Torpedo Eight, including the fact that two of them were damaged by American naval gunfire, was chronicled in Peterkin's diary.

The author's re-creation of the opening round of the naval battle of Guadalcanal on the night of November 12–13, 1942, was drawn from Lundstrom's

*The First Team and the Guadalcanal Campaign,* Eric Hammel's *Guadalcanal: Decision at Sea,* Miller's *The Cactus Air Force,* and Toland's *The Rising Sun.*

For the description of the aerial assault on the crippled Japanese battleship *Kiei* on November 13, the author relied on Miller's *The Cactus Air Force* and Hammel's *Guadalcanal: Decision at Sea.* For Swede Larsen's participation in the attack, including his attempt to indoctrinate the new Marine replacement pilots of Marine Group 131, the author drew on the Torpedo Squadron Eight War Diary, Peterkin's private diary, and Wolfert's *Torpedo 8* (p. 124). The background material on Captain George Dooley came from Miller's *The Cactus Air Force* and an author interview with John Lundstrom.

The sources for the account of the ceremony in which Swede officially accepted relief by Marine Air Group 131 on November 14, followed by the turning over to the Marine group of all of Torpedo Eight's remaining planes and equipment by Chief Hammond, included the Torpedo Squadron Eight War Diary and Peterkin's diary.

The description of the destruction of six of the eleven Japanese troop barges as they headed toward Guadalcanal on November 14 was drawn from Lundstrom's *The First Team and the Guadalcanal Campaign,* Frank's *Guadalcanal,* Miller's *The Cactus Air Force,* and Hammel's *Guadalcanal: Decision at Sea.* Similarly, the account of the naval battle on the night of November 14–15, which culminated in the sinking of the Japanese battleship *Kirishima,* was derived from the same sources.

The account of the last air attack of Torpedo Squadron Eight at Guadalcanal on November 15, flown by Swede Larsen and Larry Engel, was drawn from Mears's *Carrier Combat* (pp. 152–53), Miller's *The Cactus Air Force* (p. 206), the Torpedo Squadron Eight War Diary, the After Action Report for this mission, Wolfert's *Torpedo 8* (pp. 125–127), and Peterkin's diary.

For the sketches of Torpedo Eight's last morning on Guadalcanal on November 16, their flight to Espiritu Santo, the brief reunion of the squadron members prior to their departure back to the States, and the discussion of how each one of the pilots was going to make his way back home, the author relied on Peterkin's diary, Mears's *Carrier Combat,* and author interviews with Bert Earnest, Gene Hanson, and Smiley Morgan.

The departures of Peterkin and Morgan by air from Espiritu Santo on November 17 were re-created from Peterkin's diary and an author interview with Morgan.

The portrayal of the unofficial ceremony on November 17 in which Swede Larsen gathered the men of the squadron together and began to make "on the spot" assessments of each man's performance came from author interviews with Jack Stark, Harry Ferrier, Bill Tunstall, and Wiley Bartlett. In particular, Stark and Ferrier vividly remembered the moment when Delchamps cocked the forty-five pistol and threatened to kill Larsen. Delchamps was particularly helpful in describing the incident to the author from his perspective and in recounting his November 18 conversation with Lieutenant Harwood.

The scenes of the squadron's trip home aboard the *Kitty Hawk,* including the copy of the letter Swede wrote to Chastian Taurman and the completion of the Torpedo Squadron Eight War Diary, were drawn from author interviews and letters supplied by Jack Stark.

Morgan's experiences returning home, including the detour to Pearl Harbor where he received the Navy Cross from Admiral Nimitz, were provided to the author by Morgan. The author also referred to excerpts of Morgan's award citation.

## Squadron Members' Private Diaries/ Personal Letters (Unpublished)

This material provided the most important written sources of information about the personal stories of the men who served in Torpedo Eight from its formation in 1941 until its decommissioning in 1942.

**William R. Evans Jr.** Collected writings, including sketches of life aboard the *Hornet,* his joy of flying, journal entries, letters to family and friends, his final poems (36 pages).

**George Gay Jr.** Private diary, written from February to June 1942, describing his months of training in Norfolk, his candid views of squadron mates, the Doolittle Raid, events and important developments aboard the *Hornet* from May 29 to the night before the Battle of Midway (95 pages).

**Gene Hanson.** Detailed accounts of missions from the *Saratoga* and from Guadalcanal, June to October, 1942, along with letters to wife, Joy, and other notes and letters recording his impressions of squadron activities and the men who served with him (31 pages).

**Aaron Katz.** Letters to family, including commentaries on squadron life aboard the *Saratoga* and at Guadalcanal, poetry, mission notes (19 pages).

**Henry Russell "Rusty" Kenyon Jr.** Letters to wife and family from his training in Florida through assignment to VT-8 in Norfolk, at sea aboard the *Hornet,* including his final letters to Verna Kenyon. Also a biography describing his early years, college life, his marriage to Verna, his time with Torpedo Eight, and the anticipated birth of his daughter, Russellyn (86 pages).

**Corwin F. Morgan.** Private diary excerpts, descriptions of Ford Island, life aboard the *Hornet,* the *Saratoga,* and at Guadalcanal, letters to and from family and friends, letters to Walter Lord, and numerous mission accounts (76 pages).

ULVERT MATTHEW "WHITEY" MOORE. Letters to family from his time at West Virginia University through his service with VT-8, his views of other squadron members, the Douglas Devastator, and his last letters from the *Hornet*. Also more than a dozen letters from his fiancée, Betty Watkins, discussing their relationship and that of her friend Diana with Grant Teats (96 pages).

DEWITT PETERKIN. Private diary/family memoir, entitled *Carrier Squadron Torpedo 8: Aboard* Hornet-Saratoga *and Henderson Field, Guadalcanal 1942,* describing his arrival at Pearl Harbor with Swede Larsen's detachment, his close friendship with Langdon Fieberling, the torpedoing of the *Saratoga,* life at Espiritu Santo and Guadalcanal, the October 13 shelling by Japanese battleships, the construction of Chief Hammond's "Frankenstein" planes, fighting alongside the Marines during the October 23–24 ground battles, and the death of Major Michael Mahoney (82 pages).

GRANT TEATS. Letters to family from March 1941 to June 1942, including his impressions of squadron members, his chafing at senior officers and Navy regulations, his problems with gaining weight, his life aboard the *Hornet* until June 4, 1942. Also letters from his fiancée, Diana, vowing her love and dealing with the frustration of his being away from her (122 pages).

## AUTHOR INTERVIEWS

Frank Balsley (VT-8 survivor): Two interviews in 2006 (11/29, 11/30).

Wiley Bartlett (VT-8 survivor): Three interviews in 2007 (7/19, 10/26, 10/27).

Lois Fieberling Castor: Two interviews in 2006 (3/16, 3/18).

Lodwrick Cook: One interview in 2006 (9/6).

Mary and Catherine Corrigan. One interview in 2006 (3/17).

Robert J. Cressman: One interview and five e-mail correspondences between September 2006 and October 2007 (Interview 9/24/06).

Sherry Moore Cullaty: Three interviews in 2007 (7/23, 8/10, 8/11).

Newton Delchamps (VT-8 survivor): Five interviews in 2007 (7/8, 7/9, 7/19, 8/16, 9/18).

Jane Eagle: Three e-mails between April and August, 2007.

Albert K. Earnest (VT-8 survivor): Twenty-eight interviews between February 2006 and August 2007 (2006: 2/9, 2/10, 2/11, 2/12, 2/20, 3/13, 3/18, 3/26, 4/1, 4/2, 4/4, 4/23, 6/11, 7/10, 7/31, 8/25, 11/17, 11/18, 12/30. 2007: 1/25, 1/29, 2/8, 2/27, 4/16, 5/27, 6/10, 6/17, 8/20).

Russellyn "Rusty" Kenyon Edwards: One interview in August 2006 (8/22).

Thomas E. Evans: Seven interviews in 2006 (4/26, 5/1, 5/3, 5/8, 5/31, 9/19, 11/13).

Eric Fieberling: Four interviews in 2006 (3/20, 3/27, 4/3, 5/9).

Harry Ferrier (VT-8 survivor): Five interviews in 2006 (3/27, 4/10, 4/11, 4/27, 4/29).

Roy Gee (*Hornet* Dauntless pilot): Seven interviews in 2006 (5/1, 5/30, 8/18, 8/22, 8/23, 8/26, 10/26).

Charles Gillispie: Two interviews and seven e-mails in 2006 (Interviews: 4/30, 10/18).

Gail Gaynier Grimm: Four interviews in 2007 (1/1, 1/3, 1/7, 1/10).

Frank Guidone: One interview in 2007 (9/16).

Nellie Haenny: One interview in 2006 (4/12).

Howard Hale: One interview in 2006 (3/18).

Catherine Dunn Hall: Two interviews in 2006 (4/3, 4/4).

Gene Hanson (VT-8 survivor): Eleven interviews in 2006 and 2007 (2006: 7/18, 7/31, 8/1, 8/7, 8/9, 8/30, 12/20. 2007: 4/25, 6/19, 8/23, 10/11).

Mark Horan: Two interviews in 2006 (9/27, 9/28).

Rete Gaynier Janiec: Eight interviews in 2006 and 2007 (2006: 2/24, 3/6, 4/11, 5/15, 10/15, 12/13. 2007: 3/4, 10/27).

Rick and Roger Katz: One interview in 2006 (9/22).

Alvin Kernan: One interview and four e-mails in 2006 (Interview: 7/25).

Zygmund "Ski" Kowalewski (VT-8 survivor): Three interviews in 2007 (4/13, 5/2, 7/7).

Ridgeway Liccioni (VT-8 survivor): One interview in 2008 (2/9).

John Lundstrom: Eight interviews in 2007 (4/11, 4/12, 4/19, 4/26, 5/27, 8/16, 10/5, 10/14).

Helen Lyddon: Three interviews in 2006 (2/23, 2/24, 3/13).

William Magee (VT-8 survivor): Eight interviews in 2006 and 2007 (2006: 11/28, 11/29, 12/7, 12/13, 12/17, 12/18. 2007: 2/27, 4/22).

Nancy Mahi: Four interviews and eight e-mails in 2006 (Interviews: 3/27, 3/31, 4/12, 5/19).

General Lee Marona (VT-8 survivor): Five interviews in 2008 (1/28, 1/29, 1/30, 2/4, 2/6).

Corwin F. Morgan (VT-8 survivor): Twenty-five interviews in 2006 and 2007 (2006: 2/21, 3/3, 3/10, 3/13, 3/29, 3/30, 4/5, 4/6, 4/21, 4/25, 5/2, 5/8, 5/9, 7/8, 7/16, 7/18, 7/25, 8/13, 9/7, 9/23, 10/4, 12/20. 2007: 1/1, 1/19, 2/27).

Dorothy Agee Olson: One interview in 2006 (4/12).

John Peterkin: Five interviews in 2006 and 2007 (2006: 3/30, 4/2, 9/27. 2007: 1/12, 4/8).

Marilyn Richards: One interview in 2007 (4/19).

James Sawruk: One interview and ten e-mails in 2007 (Interview: 2/21).

James "Horse" Smith: One interview in 2007 (9/16).

Eric Staalesen: Four interviews in 2006 and 2007 (2006: 11/9, 11/20. 2007: 1/28, 2/16).

Heber Stafford: Three interviews in 2006 (3/16, 3/17, 3/18).

Carroll "Jack" Stark (VT-8 survivor): Five interviews in 2006 and 2007 (2006: 8/12, 12/8. 2007: 4/25, 6/9, 6/10).

Jack Tobein: One interview in 2007 (1/13).

Harold Towne: Four interviews and sixteen e-mails in 2006 (Interviews: 9/27, 9/28, 11/30, 12/17).

William Tunstall (VT-8 survivor): Five interviews in 2006 and 2007 (2006: 2/21, 4/13, 9/27. 2007: 1/6, 1/16).

Don Velazquez (son of VT-8 survivor): Seven interviews in 2007 and 2008 (2007: 5/2, 10/29, 12/18, 12/22. 2008: 2/4, 2/8, 2/9).

Elizabeth Gaynier Wallin: Two interviews in 2006 (3/14, 3/15).

Bowen P. Weisheit: Six interviews in 2006 and 2007 (2006: 3/6, 3/8, 3/12, 7/27. 2007: 2/8, 2/9).

Ervin "Judge" Wendt (VT-8 survivor): Three interviews in 2006 and 2007 (2006: 8/12, 11/30. 2007: 4/30).

Marcella Whitlock: One interview in 2006 (3/17).

Nancy Lewis Willis and Al Willis: Two interviews in 2006 (2/25, 2/26).

## OTHER IMPORTANT INTERVIEWS

In writing his book about Midway, *Incredible Victory,* Walter Lord interviewed or corresponded with many of the officers who served aboard the *Hornet* during the Midway battle. The author had the opportunity to review these newly available letters, interview notes, and/or completed author questionnaires at the Naval Historical Center in Washington, D.C.

The officers included: Rear Admiral **Edward P. Creehan,** USN-retired, Captain **Arthur A. Cumberledge,** USN-retired, Lieutenant Commander **Stephen Dewey,** USN-retired, Rear Admiral **Allan F. Fleming,** USN-retired, Captain **George H. Flinn,** USNR-retired, Rear Admiral **John G. Foster,** USN-retired, Captain **Lawrence C. French,** USN-retired, Lieutenant Commander **Edgar Gold,** USN-retired, Captain **Troy T. Guillory,** USN-retired, Commander **Ralph B. Hovind,** USN-retired, Commander **Richard Hughes,** USN-retired, Rear Admiral **Robert Ruffin Johnson,** USN-retired, Vice Admiral **Charles P. Mason,** USN-retired, Commander **Robert S. Merritt,** USN-retired, Captain **Stanley E. Ruehlow,** USN-retired.

Several pilots who flew against the Japanese striking force from Midway Atoll on June 4, 1942, were also interviewed by Walter Lord, including Lieutenant Colonel **James P. Muri,** USAF-retired, Captain **Albert K. Earnest,** USN-retired, and Lieutenant Colonel **Pren Leonard Moore,** USAF-retired. In addition, the author reviewed a letter in the Lord collection written by Rear Admiral Apollo Soucek to LCDR Joseph Bryan III, on his recollections of the June 4 battle while serving as the *Hornet*'s air officer.

In writing *The Last Flight of Ensign C. Markland Kelly, Junior, USNR,* Bowen P. Weisheit conducted taped interviews with eight *Hornet* pilots who flew the June 4 morning flight. He provided copies of all the interview transcripts to the author. In addition, Mr. Weisheit conducted numerous follow-up telephone interviews with the same pilots, seeking to confirm specific elements of their stories, including the Ring-Waldron exchange on the radio and the course followed by the group. On March 8, 2006, Mr. Weisheit went over the substance of these interviews with the author.

The eight pilots, including their rank at the time of the flight, were: Lieutenant **Richard Gray,** 1981 (fifty-two pages), Ensign **Troy T. Guillory,** 1983 (sixty-two pages), Ensign **John E. McInerny,** 1982 (forty-six pages), Lieutenant Commander **Samuel G. Mitchell,** 1981 (fifty pages), Lieutenant Commander **Walter F. Rodee,** 1982 (six pages), Ensign **Johnny A. Talbot,** 1982 (sixty-eight pages), Ensign **Humphrey L. Tallman,** 1982 (sixty-six pages), and Ensign **Ben Tappan,** 1981 (sixty-two pages).

On August 28, 1984, Mr. Weisheit also interviewed Ensign **Jerry Crawford,** one of the pilots of the PBY plane that rescued four survivors of the *Hornet* fighter squadron after they ditched in the Pacific. Ensign Crawford accepted the ten-dollar "short snorter" bill given to him by Richard Gray, and then wrote down the longitude and latitude of the location where the PBY picked him up. Mr. Weisheit also interviewed Lieutenant Commander **John G. Foster,** the air operations officer aboard the *Hornet* during the Battle of Midway, and reviewed his notes of those conversations with the author.

# Bibliography

## BOOKS, ARTICLES, AND WEB SITES

### BOOKS

Alexander, Col. Joseph H. *Edson's Raiders*. Asheville, NC: Edson's Raiders Association, 1999.

Archer, William R. *Bluefield*. Charleston, SC: Arcadia, 2000.

Barde, Robert E. *The Battle of Midway: A Study in Command*. PhD dissertation, College Park, University of Maryland, 1971.

Buell, Thomas B. *The Quiet Warrior*. Boston: Little, Brown and Company, 1974.

Butterfield, Roger. *Al Schmid — Marine*. New York: Farrar & Rinehart, 1944.

Clemens, Martin. *Alone on Guadalcanal: A Coastwatcher's Story*. Annapolis, MD: Naval Institute Press, 1998.

Cressman, Robert, et al. *A Glorious Page in Our History*. Missoula, MT: Pictorial Histories Publishing, 1990.

Crittenden, Katharine Carson. *Get Mears!* Portland, OR: Binford & Mort, 2002.

Davis, Burke. *Marine! The Life of Chesty Puller*. New York: Bantam, 1964.

Ferrier, Harry H. "Torpedo Squadron Eight, The Other Chapter." U.S. Naval Institute Proceedings, October 1964.

Frank, Richard B. *Guadalcanal*. New York: Penguin Books, 1990.

Fuchida, Mitsuo, and Masatake Okumiya. *Midway: The Battle That Doomed Japan*. New York: Ballantine Books, 1958.

Gay, George, Jr. *Sole Survivor*. Naples, FL: privately printed, 1980.

Griffin, Alexander R. *A Ship to Remember: The Saga of the* Hornet. New York: Howell, Soskin, 1943.

Griffith, Samuel B., II. *The Battle for Guadalcanal*. Philadelphia: J. P. Lippincott, 1963.

Hammel, Eric. *Guadalcanal: The Carrier Battles*. New York: Crown Books, 1987.

———. *Guadalcanal: Decision at Sea*. Pacifica, CA: Pacifica Press, 1988.

Harries, Meirion, and Susie Harries. *Soldiers of the Sun: The Rise and Fall of the Imperial Japanese Army*. New York: Random House, 1994.

Hoffman, Jon T. *Once a Legend: "Red Mike" Edson of the Marine Raiders*. Novato, CA: Presidio Press, 2000.

Hoyt, Edwin P. *Blue Skies and Blood: The Battle of the Coral Sea*. New York: Jove, 1986.

Kernan, Alvin. *The Unknown Battle of Midway*. New Haven, CT: Yale University Press, 2005.

Larrabee, Eric. *Commander in Chief: Franklin Delano Roosevelt, His Lieutenants, and Their War*. New York: Simon & Schuster, 1987.

Layton, Edwin T., with Roger Pineau and John Costello. *And I Was There: Pearl Harbor and Midway — Breaking the Secrets*. New York: William Morrow and Co., 1985.

Lee, Clark. *They Call It Pacific: An Eyewitness Story of Our War Against Japan from Bataan to the Solomons*. New York: Viking Press, 1943.

Linder, Bruce R. "The Lost Letter of Midway." U.S. Naval Institute Proceedings, August 1999.

Lord, Walter. *Incredible Victory*. New York: Harper & Row, 1967.

Lundstrom, John B. *Black Shoe Carrier Admiral: Frank Jack Fletcher at Coral Sea, Midway, and Guadalcanal*. Annapolis, MD: Naval Institute Press, 2006.

———. *The First Team and the Guadalcanal Campaign*. Annapolis, MD: Naval Institute Press, 1994.

———. *The First Team: Pacific Naval Air Combat from Pearl Harbor to Midway*. Annapolis, MD: Naval Institute Press, 1984.

Mears, Frederick, Jr. *Carrier Combat*. Garden City, NJ: Doubleday, Doran, 1943.

Merrilat, Herbert. *Guadalcanal Remembered*. New York: Dodd, Mead & Co., 1982.

Miller, Thomas G., Jr. *The Cactus Air Force*. Toronto: Bantam Books, 1987.

Parshall, Jonathan, and Anthony Tully. *Shattered Sword: The Untold Story of the Battle of Midway*. Washington D.C.: Potomac Books, 2005.

Potter, E. B. *Nimitz*. Annapolis, MD: Naval Institute Press, 1976.

Prange, Gordon, with Donald Goldstein and Katherine Dillon. *Miracle at Midway*. New York: Penguin Books, 1983.

Reynolds, Clark G. *The Saga of Smokey Stover: From His Diary*. Charleston, SC: Tradd Street Press, 1978.

Russell, Ron. *No Right to Win: A Continuing Dialogue with Veterans of the Battle of Midway*. New York: iUniverse Inc., 2006.

Scrivner, Charles L. *TBM/TBF Avenger in Action*. Carrollton, TX: Squadron/Signal Publications, 1987.

Taylor, Theodore. *The Magnificent Mitscher.* Annapolis, MD: Naval Institute Press, 1991.

Toland, John. *The Rising Sun: The Decline and Fall of the Japanese Empire.* Toronto: Bantam, 1971.

Tregaskis, Richard. *Guadalcanal Diary.* New York: Random House, 1943.

Vandegrift, Alexander, as told to Robert B. Asprey. *Once a Marine.* New York: Norton, 1964.

Weisheit, Bowen P. *The Last Flight of Ensign C. Markland Kelly, Junior USNR.* Baltimore, MD: privately printed, 1993.

Wolfert, Ira. *Torpedo 8: The Story of Swede Larsen's Bomber Squadron.* Boston: Houghton Mifflin Co., 1943.

### ARTICLES AND INTERVIEWS

Earnest, Bert. Interview by Frederick Hodge. *Reading Between the Lines.* WREN, December 19, 1942.

Larsen, Swede, and George Gay. Interview. *We, the People.* Columbia Network, January 16, 1944.

Lee, Clark. "Navy Pilot Tells How Jap Carrier Was Knocked Out." *Tampa Tribune,* September 14, 1942.

McDonald, William H., Ens. "Charlie Brannon Lives On in Spirit." *Montgomery Advertiser-Journal,* February 28, 1965.

Rawlings, Charles. "The McFarland Comes Home." *Saturday Evening Post,* January 1943.

Singer, Jack. "Jack Singer's Last Dispatch Is Thrilling Account of Bomber-Torpedo Plane Attack on Japanese Ships." *Honolulu Advertiser,* September 23, 1942.

Smith, M. LeFevre. "The Avengers Strike." *Skyways,* July 1944.

Unknown Author. "Ensign Wm. R. Evans Is Reported Missing After Midway Fight." *Shortridge Summer Echo,* July 10, 1942. (High school newspaper.)

Unknown Author. "Role of Local Flier's Lost Squadron Told." *Bluefield Daily Telegraph,* July 15, 1942.

Wendt, Lloyd. "The True Story of Heroic Squadron 8." *Chicago Sunday Tribune,* May 20–July 25 (multipart series), 1948.

### WEB SITES

Battle of Midway Roundtable Web site: *www.midway42.org*
Tom Cheek memoir: *www.internetmodeler.com/2002/june/aviation/Cheek.htm.*

## MILITARY SOURCES

Action dispatches, classified, sent to CINCPAC from Midway Atoll on June 4–5, including the first dispatch sent after the rescue of George Gay, describing what he saw after being shot down. Courtesy of John Lundstrom.

Advisory Board Proceedings in the case of Lieutenant (jg) S. C. Ring, US Naval Air Station, Pensacola, Florida, July 14, 1926. National Archives and Records Administration.

After Action Report and debriefing of George Gay at Pearl Harbor by Commander R. A. Ostie, June 7, 1942, including Ostie's conclusions of what Gay saw on June 4. Courtesy of Robert Cressman.

After Action Report of June 4 mission by VT-8 Detachment (Midway) submitted to CINCPAC by Ensign A. K. Earnest as the only surviving pilot of Fieberling's VT-8 detachment, June 23, 1942. Courtesy of Bert Earnest.

Battalion Instructions Memorandum: Impending Attack by Japanese Forces, delivered to 6th Defense Battalion, Fleet Marine Force by H. D. Shannon, Colonel, U.S. Marine Corps, Commanding, May 30, 1942. USMC.

*The Battle of Midway, Strategical and Tactical Analysis;* U.S. Navy, Office of Naval Intelligence, 1942. Courtesy of John Lundstrom.

CO USS *Saratoga* to CINCPAC, Report of Action against Enemy Forces in Solomon Islands Area on August 24, 1942, including group and squadron reports, and Tactical Situation and Chronological History of Events. Courtesy of John Lundstrom.

CTF-61 (ComCruPac) to ComSoPac, Preliminary Report of Actions, August 23–24, 1942 (6 September 1942). Courtesy of John Lundstrom.

"Defects Observed During the Action off Midway on June 4, 1942," Lieutenant Commander John G. Foster, Air Operations Officer, USS *Hornet,* 1942. Courtesy of Bowen Weisheit.

Interview of Lieutenant George Gay USNR, on October 12, 1943, Operational Archives Branch, U.S. Naval Historical Center.

Interview of Lieutenant Commander H. H. Larsen by Bureau of Aeronautics Air Information Branch about his experiences as commander, Torpedo Squadron Eight at Guadalcanal, January 18, 1943. Courtesy of James Sawruk.

Interview of *Hornet* fighter pilot Lieutenant Commander Edward J. O'Neill by Bureau of Aeronautics Air Information Branch about his experiences at the Battle of Midway, June 18, 1942. Courtesy of John Lundstrom.

Investigation of Gunfire Damage, Earnest TBF-1 Airplane, J. F. Engforth, July 31, 1942. Courtesy of Bert Earnest.

Mahoney, Michael, official biographical material. Excerpts from service record, circumstances of death, burial records, provided by the U.S. Marine

Corps History Division in Quantico, Virginia. Courtesy of Joe Alexander.

Mears, Frederick, official biographical material. Excerpt from service record; Bureau of Navigation biographical record; official accident report, June 26, 1943. U.S. Naval Historical Center, Courtesy of Robert Cressman.

Report of Operations — Tulagi, Guadalcanal and Malaita Area, on 7 and 8 August, 1942, from H. H. Larsen to Commanding Officer, USS *Saratoga,* August 12, 1942. Courtesy of John Lundstrom.

Report of Operations at Guadalcanal, 13 September to 16 November, 1942, from H. H. Larsen to Commander Air Force, Pacific Fleet, December 1, 1942. Courtesy of U.S. Naval War College.

*Senshi Sosho,* Volume 49. Southeast Area Naval Operations, 1, To the Beginning of Operations to Recapture Guadalcanal. Japanese archives.

Statement by Quillen, Leroy, ARM3c, U.S. Navy, Bombing Squadron Eight, on first flight, June 4, 1942, Search in Plane S-B-2 (Ensign K. B. White, Pilot). Cover sheet endorsed by Lieutenant George H. Flinn Jr., Lieutenant, USNR.

Torpedo Squadron Eight War Diary, May 22, 1942, to November 17, 1942. Courtesy of Jack Stark.

Torpedo Squadron Eight After Combat Action Reports for missions flown, August 7, 1942, to November 15, 1942. Courtesy of U.S. Naval War College.

USS *Hornet* After Action Report, serial 0018, submitted to CINCPAC by Captain M. A. Mitscher, Commanding Officer, June 13, 1942, officially declassified on November 23, 1964. Courtesy of Robert Cressman.

USS *Hornet* deck log, May–June 1942. Courtesy of U.S. Naval Historical Center.

USS *Hornet* Plan of the Day, June 2, 1942. Courtesy of George Gay.

USS *Saratoga* deck log, July–August, 1942. Courtesy of U.S. Naval Historical Center.

USS *Saratoga* War Diary, Commander, Carriers, Pacific Fleet (Task Force 16), Midway, June 1942. Courtesy of John Lundstrom.

## Oral Histories

The following oral histories were reviewed by the author at the U.S. Naval Institute in Annapolis, Maryland. Rear Admiral **Ernest M. Eller** (Volume 2, 1974–78), Captain **Stephen Jurika** (Volume 1, 1975–76), Captain **James R. Ogden** (1982), Commander **Thomas B. Buell** (2002), Commander **Albert K. Murray** (1980), and Admiral **Harry Don Felt** (Volume 1, 1972).

## CORRESPONDENCE

Congressman Karl Stefan to Superintendent, U.S. Naval Academy, re: H. H. Larsen, March 19, 1935. Courtesy of Nimitz Library.

DeWitt Peterkin to Corwin F. Morgan, June 1944–September 1946. Courtesy of Corwin Morgan.

H. H. Larsen to Chastian Taurman after death of John Taurman, December 1, 1942. Courtesy of Robert Cressman.

*Hornet* fighter pilot Henry A. Carey to John Lundstrom, April 23, 1981, June 1, 1981, March 11, 1986, on his recollections of John Waldron, Stanhope Ring, the men of Torpedo Eight, and the June 4 mission. Courtesy of John Lundstrom.

*Hornet* fighter pilot J. F. Sutherland to John Lundstrom, August 14, 1974, October 24, 1974, describing Waldron's final words to his squadron pilots before takeoff on June 4, 1942. Courtesy of John Lundstrom.

*Hornet* fighter pilot Stanley Ruehlow to John Lundstrom, July 8, 1974 and July 25, 1974, asserting that he and Mitchell advocated providing fighter support for Torpedo Eight to Captain Mitscher. Courtesy of John Lundstrom.

Letters from Dauntless pilot Thomas J. Gratzek, 2nd Lieutenant, USMCR to his family from Midway Atoll, April–May 1942. Courtesy of Hill Goodspeed.

Letter and completed author's questionnaire sent from Minoru Genda to Gordon Prange in preparation for his work, *Miracle at Midway*, detailing his recollections of the Midway battle. Courtesy of University of Pittsburgh.

Letter from Rear Admiral Raymond A. Spruance to Admiral Chester W. Nimitz, with enclosure, June 8, 1942. Courtesy of John Lundstrom.

Letter from *Yorktown* pilot John P. Adams to John Lundstrom, August 22, 1974, relating in detail the story of Commander Ring offering to stand a round of drinks at the Ewa Field Officers' Club and meeting "deadly silence" from the *Hornet* pilots in the room. Courtesy of John Lundstrom.

Letter from Nancy Waldron LeDew (Waldron's daughter), undated c. 1976, on file in the Waldron collection at the South Dakota Hall of Fame (six handwritten pages).

# Index

# ABOUT THE AUTHOR

ROBERT J. MRAZEK is a former five-term congressman who authored laws to preserve the Tongass National Forest in Alaska and the Manassas Civil War battlefield in Virginia. He also wrote the Amerasian Homecoming Act, which brought home the children of American military personnel from Vietnam, and the National Film Preservation Act, which established the Federal Film Registry in the Library of Congress. Since his retirement from Congress, he has served on the boards of numerous charitable organizations, including ten years as the cofounder and chairman of the Alaska Wilderness League.

In 1999, his first book, *Stonewall's Gold,* won the Michael Shaara Prize for the best Civil War novel of the year. In 2007, his third novel, *The Deadly Embrace,* earned him the W. Y. Boyd Prize for excellence in military fiction. His books have been published in fourteen countries around the world.

## Flyboys
### A True Story of Courage
by James Bradley

"A gripping story. . . . Bradley tackles head-on the thorny issues of Japan's wartime villainy and America's problematic response."
—Mark Lewis, *Los Angeles Times*

"An unforgettable story about eight forgotten World War II flyers and a ninth who became the 41st president of the United States. . . . Like his previous work, *Flags of Our Fathers*, *Flyboys* will be a part of the historical record for years to come."
—*Pages*

## A Terrible Glory
### Custer and the Little Bighorn—The Last Great Battle of the American West
by James Donovan

"The Custer battle has never been as vividly and comprehensively told as in *A Terrible Glory*."
—Dale L. Walker, *Dallas Morning News*

"A great pleasure to read. . . . Donovan has given us the new benchmark of literary scholarship on the Little Big Horn, this most controversial engagement at the core of our national identity."
—Hampton Sides, author of *Blood and Thunder*

## The General's War
### The Inside Story of the Conflict in the Gulf
by Michael R. Gordon and General Bernard E. Trainor

"A superb account and analysis of what went right and what went wrong in the Gulf War. All of the inside stories of the people and the policies, the triumphs and the blunders are here. This book will be read by would-be generals and commanders-in-chief for generations to come."
—Jim Lehrer, *The MacNeil/Lehrer NewsHour*

Back Bay Books • Available wherever paperbacks are sold

## Lone Survivor

*The Eyewitness Account of Operation Redwing and*
*the Lost Heroes of Seal Team 10*
by Marcus Luttrell with Patrick Robinson

"One of the most gripping and heartbreaking descriptions of heroism in combat to come out of the wars in Afghanistan and Iraq. . . . An astonishing survival tale."　　　　　　　　—Fritz Lanham, *Houston Chronicle*

## Tiger Force

*A True Story of Men and War*
by Michael Sallah and Mitch Weiss

"*Tiger Force* adds a graphic, frightening dimension to our knowledge of the Vietnam tragedy as well as our knowledge of ourselves."
　　　　　　　　—Stanley Karnow, *Washington Post Book World*

"Both sobering and relevant. . . . The authors vividly convey the demanding environment in which the soldiers had to survive. *Tiger Force* makes for timely reading."　　　　　　　　—Jack Kelly, *American Heritage*

## Endgame, 1945

*The Missing Final Chapter of World War II*
by David Stafford

"The last century's great drama yields another great book. . . . Stafford's epic narrative is illuminated with telling detail."
　　　　　　　　—Christopher Hirst, *Independent*

"Fascinating. . . . The purpose of this book is to put a human face on the bewildering scale of death and devastation. David Stafford does it most compellingly."　　　　　　　　—Allan Mallinson, *Times* (London)

Back Bay Books • Available wherever paperbacks are sold